LODOVICO DOLCE, RENAISSANCE MAN OF LETTERS

RONNIE H. TERPENING

Lodovico Dolce, Renaissance Man of Letters

UNIVERSITY OF TORONTO PRESS
Toronto Buffalo London

ISBN 0-8020-4159-0

Printed on acid-free paper

Toronto Italian Studies

Canadian Cataloguing in Publication Data

Terpening, Ronnie H., 1946–
  Lodovico Dolce, Renaissance Man of Letters

Includes bibliographical references and index.
ISBN 0-8020-4159-0

1. Dolce, Lodovico, 1508–1568 – Criticism and interpretation.

PQ4621.D3Z82 1997   858'.409   C97-930954-9

University of Toronto Press acknowledges the financial assistance to its publishing
program of the Canada Council and the Ontario Arts Council.

This book was published with the help of grants from the Office of the Provost at
the University of Arizona and the University of Arizona Foundation.

Contents

Acknowledgments

I would like to thank the following institutions for their support at various stages of this book's development: for a Research Fellowship for Recent PhD Recipients, the American Council of Learned Societies; for a research grant and a paid leave of absence, Loyola University of Chicago; and for grants and a fellowship to attend two institutes in the archival sciences, the National Endowment for the Humanities, the Center for Renaissance Studies at the Newberry Library, Loyola University of Chicago, and the University of Arizona.

For help in translating an occasional troublesome word, I thank Lise Leibacher (French), Cynthia White (Latin), and Richard P. Kinkade (Spanish). My copy-editor, Beverley Beetham Endersby, helped in the pursuit of consistency.

The staffs of various interlibrary-loan offices have also been of aid – in particular, Cindy Austin and Snowden Wyatt at the University of Arizona, Ceres B. Birkhead at the University of Utah, and Bruce W. Swann of the Rare Book and Special Collections Library at the University of Illinois at Urbana-Champaign.

I am indebted to all my former professors of Italian, to whom this book is dedicated: at what was then Portland State College (now University), Michele Ricciardelli; at the University of Oregon, the late Emmanuel S. Hatzantonis, Walter Nobile, Gino Casagrande, Antonio Illiano, and Chandler Beall; at the University of California, Berkeley, the late Arnolfo B. Ferruolo, Louise George Clubb, Cecil Grayson, Nicholas J. Perella, Gustavo Costa, Ruggero Stefanini, and Gavriel Moses.

RONNIE H. TERPENING

LODOVICO DOLCE, RENAISSANCE MAN OF LETTERS

1

'Miserabile Insieme, e Glorioso': Introduction to the Life, Works, and Milieu of Lodovico Dolce

Fame: That Was Then, This Is Now

Were Lodovico Dolce to have penned a line similar to that used by Carlo Goldoni in the 'Préface' to his *Mémoires* ('Ma vie n'est pas intéressante'), his contemporaries would have laughed at such a blatant example of feigned humility.[1] Though a similar statement from Dolce would have been only too apt for this century, in his own day it would have seemed an egregious use of what E.R. Curtius was to call the topos of 'affected modesty.'[2] After all, Dolce was a man who had produced more than a hundred volumes bearing his name, whether as author, editor, translator, or critic – a writer who had gained, in his own century, universal renown, standing out as an exemplar of the ideal *poligrafo*, in the best sense of the word – a well-rounded man in the field of humane letters.[3]

But it would be a mistake, looking at the paucity of laudatory studies of Dolce in this century, to think that his fame died with him. On the contrary, it lasted, in varied form, for at least three hundred years. His immediate renown is attested to by the posthumous publication of not only six previously unpublished volumes, but also seventy-three Venetian reprints of his works. Near the end of the sixteenth century, Tommaso Porcacchi was to write of him that 'he can sooner be admired than equalled.'[4] And in the middle of the seventeenth century, the abbot Gerolamo Ghilini, noting that Dolce appeared to his compatriots to be an example of human misadventure, both *miserabile* and *glorioso* to the end of his unlucky days, claimed that our author 'deserves to be numbered among the famous men of letters, since he showed himself to be of a most lofty genius in every manner of delightful disciplines; ... he was particularly successful in his translations, in which more surely than in anything else, having turned out marvellous, he gained immortal praise for himself and performed a very great service to the professors of Tuscan speech.'[5] Over 50 years later (that is, 130 years after Dolce's death), critics such as Gio. Maria Crescimbeni could still write that 'his many labours took him to the height of universal esteem, and placed him among the brightest literati of the century, with that famous accolade that there was no deed that could resist the felicity of his pen.'[6]

This is not to say that others did not sound more discordant notes in this chorus of praise. Ludovico Antonio Muratori may suffice as one example of somewhat greater restraint: 'If in Dolce there was evident a fecundity of wit and an extraordinary indefatigability in writing, for which he has a place among historians, orators, grammarians, rhetoricians, philosophers, physicists, ethicists, writers of tragedies, comedies, epics, lyrics, and among editors, translators, collectors, and commentators, on the other hand he succeeded in nothing with excellence.'[7] Nevertheless, as late as the nineteenth century, the Venetian humanist continued to be held in high esteem. Girolamo Rosasco, writing in the context of the polemic regarding the *Questione della lingua*, notes that, 'even though Dolce was not a correct writer in everything, he was nevertheless a lover of the Tuscan language, in which he wrote various praiseworthy things. He was a man without presumption and self-conceit, who wrote only to help others, not out of a desire to seem a master, like Ruscelli and Muzio, who, though they knew many things about language, had no skill whatsoever at many other things ...'[8] And Marco Foscarini, writing in 1854, expressed his judgment that 'the ability of that man stands out, even if he did not always reach the mark of perfection in all the manners of composing. Yet, he did so well in each manner that one can infer that it was within his ability to become great, in whatever area he might have chosen to focus his own activity.'[9]

Why then, one might ask, has Dolce's fame been eclipsed in this century? Perhaps the answer, in part, lies with the modern reluctance to read the works of an author who has slipped from the canon of the *maggiori*. The descent, in Dolce's case, however, has been too extreme; over time, he has fallen not only from the second rank of notables, but also from that of the *minori*, until today, for the most part, he has to be considered one of the *minimi*, invisible except for a text or two.

A rereading of various works written by Dolce may help explain why his contemporaries could praise him so highly, writing such things as:

... The *Sacripante*, no less lovely than in love, helped me to get through a bit of heat this summer without annoyance. (Veronica Gambara)

Certainly God has given you such outstanding natural qualities that no one can resemble you ... Quick, fertile, and generous is the lively spirit of intellect that dictates to you what you say, note, and think. (Pietro Aretino in a letter to Dolce, where he also calls him 'divino')

... Dolce was truly a noble poet, in that he was soft and delicate in his style, at ease with conceits, both purified in language and quick in verse. (Francesco Sansovino)[10]

The gap between Dolce's reception in his own time and in our own is startling. But, as Paul Oskar Kristeller points out, 'it has been shown in more than one instance that a direct reading of an author's works will quickly dispose of certain conventional labels and judgments that have been repeated for centuries.'[11]

The Current State of Dolce Studies

In a study of selected vernacular works of Lodovico Dolce, it is by no means an unpleasant task to begin with a general introduction to his life and works, for it is difficult to write about the Venetian *poligrafo* without mentioning his tremendous versatility. In fact, the traditional epithet which seems to have been most often affixed to his name is 'l'infaticabile.' One does not have to be interested in too many literary fields to find an area in which Dolce's name figures, if not prominently, at least not insignificantly. Among the genres and forms in which Dolce laboured are dialogues (on wives, husbands, women, a maritime militia, painting, memory, and colours), treatises (on gems, love, and Aristotelian philosophy), emblem books, fortune-telling by cards, history and biography (writing on Dante, Boccaccio, Charles V, Ferdinand I, Giammatteo Bembo, and world history), literary criticism (dealing with grammar, the *Questione della lingua*, rhetoric, and style), narrative poems, epics, sacred poems, mythological fables, lyric poetry, burlesque *capitoli*, comedy, tragedy, letters, translations, and editions of others' works.[12]

Yet, despite the fact that Dolce's bibliography, as mentioned, runs to well over a hundred volumes, including original works, translations, and editions of other writers' works, there is to my knowledge, apart from Emmanuel Antonio Cicogna's bio-bibliographical study, no major work, not even a monograph, dealing analytically with Dolce's vast production. Surprisingly, he is even lacking in the Marzorati series devoted to *I minori;* and, in the reference works where he is mentioned, erroneous, scant, or derivative information is often provided, indicative of a general failure to approach the man directly for any but a few of his works. To cite just one example dealing with material to be treated in chapter 2, Azelia Arici, following the opinion of many others, claims that the *Sacripante* 'derives from the *Orlando furioso*' – but only, one must add, as Ariosto 'derives' (i.e., continues) from Boiardo – and that the *Prime imprese del conte Orlando* derives from the last book of the *Reali di Francia* (when the reality is that only the first four cantos of twenty-five are based loosely on this source).[13] As a result of statements similar to that made by Arici, repeated over the generations, this century's major literary historians of the sixtenth century in Italy usually devote to Dolce at most a few scattered paragraphs, often depreciative, and only in conjunction with other *poligrafi*.[14]

The situation is not much better among those who study the *poligrafi* in greater detail. Paul Grendler, for example, in his fine work on Anton Francesco Doni, Nicolò Franco, and Ortensio Lando, dismisses Dolce, in part on the grounds that he produced fewer original works than the seventeen of Doni, the fourteen of Lando, and the eight of Franco. Of the Venetian *poligrafo*, Grendler writes: 'Ludovico Dolce produced forty-five translations, twenty-eight editions and commentaries on the works of others, and five original prose works exclusive of drama. He also wrote a number of comedies and tragedies in prose and verse but, as Toffanin exclaims, 'Where does the original author begin and the translator end? Not even he [Dolce] knew!'[15] But, in counting Dolce's original works, why does Grendler automatically exclude the comedies and tragedies? While many are translations or loose *rifacimenti* of the classics, others, such as the tragedy *Marianna* or the comedy *Il ragazzo*, meet the standards of originality applied to any other work of the Renaissance.[16] To discount Dolce's efforts on the grounds that he borrowed his argument from Latin and Greek sources is to denigrate the very foundations of much of Renaissance drama, if not of the Renaissance itself. While Dolce translated the works of Euripides and Seneca, he also wrote original comedies and tragedies, some (and this is why the issue is so confusing) with the same titles as his translations. Quite often, however, Dolce attempts to note the distinction between a *rifacimento* and a translation on the title page itself, where he distinguishes between a work 'tratta da' (usually a free adaptation) and 'tradotta da' (a translation).

And what about Dolce's other works in verse? A count of them shows that Dolce has more than the eight original works claimed by Grendler for Doni. As we will see in chapter 2 of this study, two of Dolce's chivalric romances, the *Sacripante* and the *Prime imprese del conte Orlando*, are as original in intent and in execution as any other retelling of traditional material along the lines of Pulci's *Morgante* (of which the first twenty-three cantos are drawn from the anonymous *Orlando*, and the last five from the *Spagna in rima* and the *Rotta di Roncisvalle*.)

A comparison of Dolce's *Prime imprese* with the sources pointed out by Francesco Fòffano – the *Reali di Francia*, the *Aspramonte* in prose, the *Aspramonte* in verse of Andrea da Barberino, and the French *geste Girard de Viane* (*Il poema cavalleresco*, p. 129) – reveals that Dolce impressed his own personality upon the traditional material and developed his sources (within the context of Renaissance *imitatio*) with originality. Moreover, when the works are *rifacimenti*, as in the *Palmerino* (1561) and the *Primaleone, figliuolo di Palmerino* (1562), both based on Spanish romances,[17] they are at least as noteworthy as Dolce's model Bernardo Tasso, whose *Amadigi* (1560), first edited by Dolce, was itself based on the Spanish *Amadís de Gaula*.[18]

With this in mind (I will have more to say about Dolce's work as a writer, editor, commentator, and translator in chapter 2), it is not difficult to justify a re-examination of some of Dolce's original productions. Even were one to consider him justly a minor or secondary author, most scholars, one hopes, tire of always walking *per cacumina montium*. True, the mountain peaks are always illuminated, allowing one to bask in the sunlight, while the valleys, regrettably, lie in shadow. Still, that is where the bulk of society dwells, from the commoner to the more learned. An author like Dolce, active in nearly every field available to the humanist of the day, is perhaps a better (i.e., more typical) example of a Renaissance humanist than is a *maggiore*. This, of course, is a gentle polemic – an attempt to bring more light to a writer whose truly creative works either too often are disparaged or have already slipped into unmerited oblivion. Which is not to say that no one is studying Dolce. Many of his works do figure in studies devoted to general topics, particularly literary criticism, and are sometimes discussed in surveys of a particular genre (such as comedy, tragedy, the chivalric romance, and dialogues), or appear in their own right, receiving individual attention, in more specialized efforts. Still, a comprehensive overview of Dolce's vast production is lacking. The present study aims to fill in part of that picture by concentrating on several of the more interesting and more original of Dolce's creative efforts, while at the same time suggesting other areas for further investigation. Despite the fact that space and time do not permit an examination of all of Dolce's accomplishments, this survey concentrates on a number of significant works, sufficient in themselves to attest that Dolce deserves to be elevated above other *poligrafi* in the history of Italian literature. This monograph, then, is not an attempt to provide the definitive modern biography of Dolce (and readers looking only for that will be necessarily disappointed), but rather a series of critical essays that concentrate on his more interesting works in several significant genres, all analysed with the overriding goal of clarifying Dolce's role in the diffusion and expansion of culture in the cinquecento.

My approach is similar to that of social historians who use the term 'micro-' as opposed to 'macro-'history. Carlo Ginzburg, in an article published under the title 'Spie' in 1979 and translated a year later as 'Morelli, Freud and Sherlock Holmes: Clues and Scientific Method,' makes the point that micro-history is an inductive approach that takes as its first principle the claim that small traces are often better indicators of the features of an age than are large events.[19] A minor figure is sometimes a better mirror of his or her age than a major one, since the latter is often unique. Dolce, it is safe to say, was not unique, other than perhaps for his singular productivity. He is, just as clearly and for the same reason, a good mirror of the varied activities and fields of interest of Renaissance individuals – a compendium, as it were, of the age. If he does not stand on the same level as Bembo, Ariosto, or Tasso, to cite just three of the century's major authors, he is not as far below them as is sometimes thought and, were his personal situation less constrictive, he might have produced works of similar quality.

The Author's Life and Milieu

Before turning to an examination of specific works in the chapters to follow, let me say a word or two about Dolce the man. What little is known of his life derives on the whole from three major sources – the memoir of Emmanuel Antonio Cicogna, who published a hundred-page, bio-bibliographical study of Dolce's life and works in 1863–4; the social-cultural history of Claudia Di Filippo Bareggi, a statistical analysis of the editorial production of fourteen Venetian intellectuals, including Dolce; and G. Romei's entry in the *Dizionario biografico degli Italiani*. The details that follow are based primarily on these sources, although, when possible, other archival discoveries have been integrated into the literary portrait.

The son of Fantino, Lodovico was born in Venice either in 1508 or more likely in 1510 into a family that had seen better days.[20] An ancient branch of the family had been part of the Maggior Consiglio (the Great Council), but this particular line died out in 1248 with a man named Filippo. Another branch, one that was excluded from the council by the doge

Pietro Gradenigo, gave rise to the Dolces, who, as citizens (rather than patricians), served the state primarily as secretaries.[21] In later times, that is, following 1648, the descendants of Lodovico's brother Daniele were accepted again into the patrician class.[22] But, unlike other members of his family, before and after, Lodovico chose not to involve himself in the duties of a state secretary, dedicating himself instead, as befitted his talents and inclination, to the study of literature.[23]

As a child, Dolce (along with his brothers Daniele, Angelo, and Agostino) led a difficult life. His father, a former *castaldo delle procuratorie* (steward to the public attorneys) for the Republic of Venice, died when the boy was only two, necessitating the receipt of support from other families. Poverty, in fact, was a condition with which Lodovico had to contend all his life, and one that forced him to work assiduously to support himself. Perhaps his later productivity as a young man and an adult derives in part from the hard necessities of these early years and from the continuing pressure to provide for his family. The abbot Gerolamo Ghilini saw in this the reason for Dolce's failure to produce a masterpiece that would have elevated him to the ranks of the greatest authors of the century.[24]

At any rate, for his early studies, Lodovico depended on the protection of two patrician families, one being that of the doge Leonardo Loredano, who had already aided Lodovico's father and grandfather (as attested to by Dolce in the dedication of his *Dialogo della pittura*),[25] the other the Cornaro family, who financed Dolce's studies at Padua.[26] Bareggi questions whether Dolce might have worked as a *procuratore* or a *notaio* (p. 39), but we know nothing for sure about his scholastic program, other than that he received an excellent education in the classics and published his first work, *Il sogno di Parnasso con alcune altre rime d'amore* in 1532, at the age of twenty-two, perhaps an indication that he studied letters from the start, unlike so many of the other ambitious scholars in his circle who started out as lawyers.

Having completed his studies, Dolce returned to Venice, where he found work as a teacher of children and an aid to the press of Gabriel Giolito, 'drawing from both jobs his sustenance,' as Cicogna notes, 'since he lacked family wealth' (p. 93).[27] Cicogna concludes that the poet's life was 'one of continual study, directly mainly towards cultivating Italian studies and to transporting into Italian the works of classical Greek and Latin authors, in addition to furnishing notes and commentaries for the works of other Italians, writing his own poems, comedies, tragedies, rhymes of every sort, and learned prose, such that he takes a deserved seat among the *benemeriti* of Italian literature who lived during the sixteenth century' (pp. 93-4).[28] Despite this Herculean effort, Dolce failed to accumulate any wealth. The singular lack of documents relating to Dolce's life, pointed out by Bareggi (p. 257), is an indication of his poverty. He apparently never owned any property in Venice, and no will is extant; during thirty-six years of assiduous work for the Venetian presses, in fact, he never once had to present a declaration of property to the Savi alle Decime (Tax Magistrates).[29]

Despite the differences between Dolce's existence and that of other adventurers of the pen who were often at the same time both rebels and sycophants (Doni, Franco, Lando) and sometimes courtier-poets who employed flagrant self-promotion (Aretino), the Venetian *poligrafi*, whatever their social status, lived and worked in the same milieu. That is, none was immune from the desire for both public acclaim and financial gain. Like other working authors, Dolce wrote at all times for the press, with an attentive eye on public demand. In his case, however, one senses this difference: the works that flowed from his pen seem not only to have responded to the needs of the time, but to have captured, and then directed, the interests of the reading public. Writers like Aretino and his cohorts rode the vernacular into literary prominence, but they did so without the humanistic and classical overtones so ingrained in Dolce. Like Bembo before him, he was an educator of the masses as well as a purveyor of pleasure. Many of his works, while written for a broad segment of the public and populist in tone, were scholarly in nature. He rarely descended to hack work simply in order to please. Unlike others, he was not a columnist, a social commentator, or a gossip-monger, to use terminology applied by Grendler to Lando, Franco, and Doni (p. 14).

The importance of Dolce as a man of letters can be seen from two perspectives – his own publications, on one hand, and the press for which he did most of his work, on the other. In her statistical analysis of the editorial work and the cultural and social significance of fourteen intellectuals active in Venice,[30] Claudia Di Filippo Bareggi notes that Dolce's numbers, compiled during thirty-six years of uninterrupted work, are truly impressive. Of the 358 books that passed through his hands, she counts a total of 96 editions of original works, 202 editions of works by others, 54 translations, and 6 translations/editions (p. 58).[31] Grouping the editions of classical, medieval, and contemporary works, Bareggi arrives at 263 editions, which represents 73.4 per cent of Dolce's total production (p. 58). Though Dolce's interests were largely literary, he was nevertheless, she says, a true *poligrafo*, in the sense that almost all the currents discovered in the global examination appear in his production: he has 29 historical texts, 25 works of linguistic interest, 24 treatises, 11 esoteric works, 5 that can be considered philosophical, and 1 religious (p. 59).

As regards the literary forms employed by Dolce and the genres he favoured, one finds again a situation of leadership. Speaking in general terms of Venice, Bareggi notes that, as regards literature (713 editions), the public preferred works based on the ancient *romans de geste* (84 editions of Ariosto, plus 13 *rifacimenti*), collected lyrics (73 editions of *rime*, 14 of *stanze*, and 2 of *madrigali*), epistolaries (82 editions), and, above all, theater (77 editions of comedies and 31 of tragedies, for a total of 108 editions), which supersedes all other genres. In fact, counting editions of ancient comedies, the total comes to 120 (p. 89). In contrast, only 8 editions of *novelle* were published, and the preferred form for short prose appears to be *facezie* (23 editions) and *imprese* (12 editions). Dolce, as we will see in the course of this study, was quite active in all these areas, with the exception of short stories and joke-books. The obvious question of whether he led or followed public demand is perhaps a problem of the chicken and the egg, although, judging from today's marketplace, leaders create demand, after which others follow along to satisfy the public's appetite. In Dolce's case, he appears to have been both – now a leader, now a follower. In the area of literature, he appears often to have created demand; as regards other genres, such as history, he appears, instead, to have satisfied the marketplace.[32]

Second in importance to literature, in fact, came history, with (again as regards Venice) 214 editions appearing in the cinquecento, two-thirds of which were contemporary (Bareggi, p. 146). Forty-nine editions show an interest in Muslims, attested by Dolce's 2 editions of the *Lettere del gran Mahumeto imperadore de' turchi* (p. 89). The most popular modern historical figure was Charles V, the subject of 11 editions. Ferdinand I was next in importance, with 4 editions (p. 91). Dolce, of course, wrote lives of both.

The third great sector was *trattatistica*, consisting of 151 editions. This was a production aimed, not at the schools, but 'alle esigenze di un pubblico adulto e mediamente acculturato' (at the exigencies of an adult and moderately acculturated public; p. 93). Dolce's work in this area is discussed in chapter 6 of this study. The linguistic sector, in Bareggi's count, includes 92 texts (p. 95), another area that engaged Dolce's attention.

Dolce is weakest in the section devoted to religion; of the 64 Venetian editions, only one was his. While not evident from Bareggi's computation, Dolce's moralism will be evident in the chapters to follow. As regards published titles, he more clearly demonstrates an interest in the area of philosophy, where of the 45 texts published in Venice he contributed ones on Aristotle and Pliny (p. 96). Finally, of the 31 editions Bareggi calls 'magico-ermetiche,' Dolce produced 9, all being editions of his translation of Ovid's *Metamorphoses*, a work, however, that seems to ill fit this category. Other more appropriate works, such as Dolce's *Trattato delle gemme*, in fact, were not counted by Bareggi – justly so in this case since the treatise is an unacknowledged translation and thus outside Bareggi's criterion for inclusion. Still, the translation itself is an indication of Dolce's encyclopedic interests.

All the favourites passed through his hands as an editor, including Dante, Boccaccio, Petrarch, Sannazzaro, Berni, Castiglione, Bembo, Ariosto, and Tasso. Dolce's edition of the *Furioso*, his best-seller, went through at least 62 Venetian editions (plus at least 4 elsewhere) in the cinquecento alone; his Petrarch, 13 editions; his *Decameron*, 8; his *Amorosa Fiammetta*, 13 Venetian and 1 Florentine; the *Courtier*, at least 6 Venetian editions; Sannazzaro's *Rime*, 4 editions and the *Arcadia* 5; Bembo's *Prose*, 5; Dante's *Commedia*, 3; and so forth.[33]

No other *poligrafo* comes remotely close to Dolce. A comparative table, not provided by Bareggi but based on her totals, shows the following levels of productivity:

Dolce	358	Parabosco	77
Sansovino	176	Toscanella	53
Domenichi	172	Doni	48
Ruscelli	125	Betussi	32
Porcacchi	111	Lando	28
Ulloa	81	Baldelli	26
Brucioli	78	Franco	18

As a whole, then, the numbers by themselves are quite revealing. Of the 1,330 editions examined by Bareggi (works that passed through the hands of these fourteen individuals), Dolce was responsible for 26.9 per cent.

Approaching Dolce's work from the point of view of the publisher for whom he worked most frequently, Gabriel Giolito, one notes that Giolito released one-fourteenth of the 14,000 books published in Venice in the sixteenth century. The rest of the books were divided among five hundred other publishers, with an average, then, apart from the three or four other major publishers, of 20 to 30 titles each. Only twenty-three presses produced more than 10 works (Bareggi, p. 283). The importance of Giolito's press for the intellectual life of the time cannot be over-emphasized.

From 1542, when Dolce first went to work for Giolito, until the *poligrafo*'s death in 1568, he edited 184 texts out of just over 700 titles published by Giolito, making Dolce responsible for 26 per cent of the total.[34] But during Dolce's busiest decade, from 1550 to 1560, he was responsible for 40 per cent of the total (124 volumes out of 316 published), and during some years over 50 per cent. As the most active writer and editor for the largest and most productive Venetian press, Dolce played a decisive role in the dissemination of culture in the cinquecento.

Since the writing trade (and, early on, teaching) provided Dolce's only visible means of support, his activity, like that of the other *poligrafi*, centred, as we have seen, on the printing press. It bears repeating that this means that, when not writing or supervising the publication of his own works, Dolce was actively involved in editing and translating those of others, both ancient and modern. In this area, he can be accused of being sometimes sloppy, sometimes little concerned with plagiarism.[35] The freedom he feels in dealing with other authors is perhaps, however, simply a reflection of the times (a period when printing was expanding, initially with a minimum of regulation, and when an author's works circulated freely, often without the benefit of copyright) or the exigencies of the book trade, where prolificacy was as important as quality. Whatever his imperfections, Dolce played an important role in promulgating vernacular literature, whether by publishing corrected editions of such classics as Petrarch's *Canzoniere* (for which he used the autograph manuscript in the library of Pietro Bembo, now Vaticano Lat. 3195, which includes the *Trionfi*), Castiglione's *Book of the Courtier*, and Ariosto's *Orlando furioso*; by translating Homer, Euripides, Cicero, Virgil, Horace, Ovid, Seneca, and other minor authors; or by publishing original works in the literary genres of widest appeal.[36]

As a popularizer, Dolce attempted to present information to non-specialists who were too busy to learn Greek or Latin. His work in the area of history is one example of many.[37] Both his *Vita di Carlo Quinto* (1561) and his *Vita di Ferdinando Primo* (1566) were very successful in the cinquecento. Pietro Aretino, in fact, in a letter to Benedetto Varchi, referred to Dolce as a 'great trumpet of fame.'[38] In the earlier history, a fluidly written work that presented Charles as a Christian champion (despite the Sack of Rome), and in the latter, a work that covered Ferdinand's life *sotto brevità* from 1503 to 1564, Dolce made no claim to originality, availing himself of the work of other well-known historians such as Giovio.[39] As customary with him, however, Dolce did not simply passively receive and transmit the thoughts of others, but was actively involved in reformulating ideas, often through condensation and simplification, sometimes through amplification to render material more germane to the intended audience. Aware that his readers expected information that was organized to save time and presented with clarity, he used his own critical insight to transform a complex historical moment into a lesson that was clear and simple.[40]

Dolce was also aware that other learned men of the time lamented the debasing of culture represented by summaries of knowledge. In his summation of Aristotle's philosophy (*Somma della filosofia d'Aristotele, e prima della dialettica*), he noted that 'molti letterati mostreranno di prender dispiacere che un filosofo di tanta stima si faccia famigliare al volgo' (many literary men will show their displeasure that a philosopher of so much esteem is being made familiar to the common people), but, more important, he continues, these men should not envy the benefits that derive thereby for those desirous of knowledge ('ma questi tali non dovrebbero invidiare il beneficio, che ne possono conseguire i belli intelletti'; 'Prefazione'). The goal was to help others, society in general, as much as one could, while earning a living at the same time.

In addition to what Mark Roskill calls his 'huge workload of writing and literary research' (p. 5), Dolce travelled back and forth between various Italian cities, as attested by his letters to other scholars. We know, for example, that Dolce was in Padua in 1538, 1542, 1543, and 1544; in Mantua in 1543, in Tivoli in December 1544, and in Pieve di Sacco (near Padova) for an extended visit in 1545.[41] Cicogna also cites a letter of 1544 from Fortunato Martinengo, in which the author's son-in-law refers to Dolce's many travels undertaken for pleasure.[42] In the same letter, Martinengo invites Dolce to visit Milan, Genoa, and the Benaco (Lake Garda). And others wrote to Dolce, describing their travels and thus indirectly attesting to his curiosity regarding Italian cities and states.[43] Still, the range attests more to a sedentary existence than to that of an adventurer. In fact, Dolce's love for his native city, a 'nido d'ogni virtù dolce et sereno' (nest of every virtue sweet and serene), shines through all his works.[44]

During these years, Dolce continued to work for Giolito, correcting the texts of others, providing tables, indices, commentaries, notes, and so forth in various editions, each one claimed to be better than the previous. Ugo Foscolo's complaint in this regard is cited by Cicogna: 'Il Dolce ridusse quel libro alla vera lezione tre volte, e per allettare compratori alla seconda edizione, censurò la sua prima, e nella terza e l'una e l'altra; e il Ruscelli vituperandole tutte e tre, propose la sua lezione come l'unica vera, e riuscì la più infame delle altre' ('Dolce brought that book [Boccaccio's *Decameron*] back to its true reading three times, and in order to attract buyers to the second edition, he censured his first, and in the third, both of the earlier editions; and Ruscelli, criticizing all three, proposed his own reading as the only true one, which turned out to be worse than the others'; p. 96). The only thing one can say in Dolce's favour is that each of his succeeding editions usually was an improvement, as opposed to that of Ruscelli. The claim of a better reading, then, was not empty, but at times does attest to the haste with which Dolce was forced to work as an editor.

The same haste sometimes characterized his translations. A telling case is provided by Dolce's letter of 1 January 1550, to Antonfrancesco Corso, appended to his translation of Philostrato's *Life of Apollonio Tianeo*. There, Dolce states that the printers began to send sections to the press before he had even finished the first book, requiring him to hand over his work day by day, thus not allowing him the chance to correct the pages, which were also filled with printing errors. And all this time, he adds, he was afflicted by a high fever. He does take advantage of the moment to correct another error – namely, that the translation of Sabellico's *Historie vinitiane* was not his (as the edition claims), since all he did was write the preface and translate a few pages at the beginning.[45]

In addition to the supplementary editorial features mentioned above, Dolce's work as a literary critic extends, as well, to the many prefaces he wrote for these editions and for his translations, some of which are discussed in the chapters to follow.[46] Significant also in this respect are his collections of contemporary poems and letters, though some of the beneficiaries of his goodwill were later to complain about his treatment of their works.[47]

From Dolce's own letters and poems one gains a general idea of the variety of his contacts and his many friends. These range from writers such as Annibale Caro, Benedetto Varchi, Pietro Bembo, Lodovico Domenichi, Francesco Maria Molza, Anton Francesco Doni, Luigi Groto (il Cieco d'Adria), Giovanni Donato, Alessandro Piccolomini, Bernardo and Torquato Tasso, Sebastiano Erizzo, Trifon Gabriele, and Pietro Aretino to women poets such as Veronica Gambara, Vittoria Colonna, Laura Terracina, and Chiara Matraini; from political figures such as the doges Andrea Gritti and Pietro Gradenigo, the Procuratore di San Marco (and thus senator for life) Alessandro Contarini, the patricians Girolamo Loredano, Federico Badoer, and Domenico Venier (the last-named admitted to the Great Council in 1537), Guidobaldo II della Rovere (the Duke of Urbino), Gian Giacomo Leonardi (the Count of Montelabbate and the Duke of Urbino's ambassador to the Signoria of Venice), Girolamo Faleti (ambassador of Alfonso d'Este, Duke of Ferrara), and churchmen such as the cardinals Gasparo Contarini and Marc'Antonio da Mula to men of culture such as Battista Pittoni, Virginio Ariosto (son of Lodovico), and Francesco Sansovino; from printers such as Paolo Manuzio, Gabriel Giolito, and Francesco Marcolini to makers of type such as Francesco Alunno (a calligrapher from Ferrara), and painters such as Titian.[48]

In this, Dolce stands apart from most of the other *letterati* of Venice, who appear to have lacked his contacts with figures of similar importance.[49] Though many of the relationships must have started over matters of editorial business, they demonstrate a noteworthy insertion on the part of Dolce into both the middle and upper levels of cultured society, and this is the more notable in that Dolce does not appear to have gained his access to the great through the usual servile flattery of some of his contemporaries (although dedications to the famous are by no means lacking in his literary works).[50] On the contrary, quite often the illustrious approached Dolce for his help in inserting themselves and their works into the world of the Venetian printers. Good examples of this are the letters addressed to Dolce by Pietro Bembo, Vittoria Colonna, Veronica Gambara, Annibale Caro, Benedetto Varchi, and Alessandro Piccolomini, with the last-named requesting a ticket so he can see one of his own comedies performed in the city during carnival.[51] The request, though startling, is not the most unusual one Dolce received. At the request of a 'sier Battista Darduin,' he himself wrote a letter to Pietro Aretino, asking him to intercede with the emperor's ambassador so that one of the emperor's governors might provide a licence for Darduin and his companions to fish in the valley of Cervignan ('una licenza di quattro o sei giorni ... di poter pescare in detta valle').[52]

Among his closest friends one has to count Pietro Aretino. Though Dolce's relationship with Aretino was sometimes rocky, the two friends not only exchanged many letters and poems, but also chose each other as interlocutors in dialogues.[53] A community of interests between the two can be attested to as early as 1533, when Dolce was in his mid-twenties, with very likely a collaboration in the preparation of translations, where Dolce, along with others, would have helped Aretino make up for his lack of Latin.[54] Dolce also performed a crucial role in helping Aretino prepare works for publication. He not only may have edited Aretino's second book of letters (Aretino sent the manuscript to him with full authority to revise it as needed), but provided material as well for his other literary works, including very likely the *Marescalco*.[55] In addition, some would see Dolce as an important figure behind Aretino's apparent Erasmian convictions, at least prior to the early 1540s, at which time a Nicodemite reticence falls over both men.[56]

Certain aspects of Dolce's existence can be gleaned from the letters written to Aretino, including Dolce's love of the countryside as an ideal refuge. In a letter dated 18 June 1537, he describes the idyllic environment of Pieve di Sacco, a castle ten miles from Padua, where he used to spend time, as he put it, 'per alleggiar in qualche parte, se io ciò poteva, l'animo dalle gravi infirmità e passioni, che la crudeltà di troppo cara et amata cosa mi induce a portar di continuo' (to relieve my mind in part, if possible, from the grave infirmities and passions that the too dear and beloved thing leads me to bear continuously).[57] That he was referring to a woman becomes clear soon after, when he refers to the 'imagine di quel volto, chi io sopra tutte le cose amo' (image of that face that I love above all things) and adds that, in contemplating in his mind her angry and disdainful eyes he no longer hears the singing of the birds or sees the pleasant greenery (p. 270). Love, he says later, has got him but good ('amor m'ha concio male'; p. 271). The only remedy turns out to be, not Ovid, who, though he teaches one how to break the bonds of love, has no effect on Dolce, but the power of the pen and ink of Aretino himself (p. 271). In effect, the letter is an elegant request for a brief reply that will serve as a cure for Dolce's illness.[58]

Among the more famous enemies of Dolce one can list Nicolò Franco and Girolamo Ruscelli.[59] Franco, a guest in Aretino's house on the Canal Grande in Venice, made the mistake of speaking ill of Dolce, who, in turn, complained to Aretino, referring to Franco's 'arroganzia e bestialità' and mentioning the 'penuria che egli [Franco] ha delle lettere latine, e delle volgari (delle quali esso, secondo lui, è molto dotto)' (the dearth that he [Franco] has of both Latin and vernacular letters [in which he, according to himself, is very learned]).[60] The comment illustrates the source of the problem. Apparently, Franco had come to Dolce with a request for publication, and Dolce, who refers to his having composed 'cento epigrammi di sorte, che fanciulli ne compongono ogni giorno de migliori nelle scole' (one hundred epigrams of the sort that children daily compose better in schools), had judged his work as inferior. Franco responded by calling into question Dolce's knowledge of Latin ('dice, me non aver giudicio, né intendimento di lingua latina').[61]

Dolce's opinion of Franco was later seconded by Aretino, who had his own reasons to hate the man who in time became an arch-enemy. Three years later, Aretino wrote a long letter (dated 7 October 1539) in which he referred to Franco as a filthy beast who 'simiglia un cane da ogniuno scacciato e a tutti odioso' (seems a dog driven away by everyone and hateful to all; *Lettere*, ed. Procaccioli, Book II, Letter 4; vol. 1, p. 393). Aretino excoriates Franco at great length, calling him, among other things, a pig, ass, hangman, plebeian, sheep, sodomite, buffalo, ox, scoundrel, thief, Jew, madman, and worm. The violent tone of the letter attests both to Aretino's hatred of his former guest and to his love for Dolce. In effect, as Bareggi notes, Dolce succeeded in creating around Franco 'un ambiente ostile, rendendo assai tesi i suoi rapporti con tutto l'*entourage* dell'Aretino' (a hostile environment, rendering very tense his relations with all of Aretino's entourage; p. 168).

The literary quarrel between Dolce and Ruscelli, instead, was initiated by the competition between the two men and highlighted by the latter's publication of his *Tre discorsi a M. Lodovico Dolce*, a work attacking Dolce's edition of the *Decameron*, his *Osservationi della lingua volgar*, and his translation of Ovid's *Metamorphoses* (*Le trasformationi*).[62] Dolce's anger erupted in a letter to Benedetto Varchi, dated 15 May 1555, in which he wrote, in part:

Il Ruscelli è un gaglioffo, baro, truffatore, ignorante e repieno di tanti vitii, che uno solo basta a fare tenere un huomo tristissimo; in modo che, non gli essendo riuscita punto l'alchimia; la pedantesca professione d'insegnare tutte le dottrine a qualunque asino; la bravura di voler tradurre Plutarco dalla lingua greca, della quale non vi è più dotto d'una gazza; la Bibbia dall'hebrea, di cui similmente ne sa quanto il mio cane, e dopo mille ricette ridicole da ciarlatano, delle quali non ho tempo di scrivere a V.S. alcuna; finalmente s'è ridotto all'arte del ruffianesmo, et ha empiuto la casa, dove egli habita, di diverse cortigiane di bella mano, accattando per questa via agramente il pane, che non sono atte a fargli havere le sue virtù! Ma dico virtù in un mariuolo? Anzi pure le sue poltronerie. (Cited in Salvatore Bongi, *Annali di Gabriel Giolito de' Ferrari*, vol. 1, pp. 398–9)

[Ruscelli is a knave, a cheat, a swindler, ignorant, and stuffed with so many vices that one alone would be enough to hold a man as most wicked; in such a way that, not having succeeded at all in alchemy, in the pedantic profession of teaching all doctrines to any ass whatever, [having] the daring to want to translate Plutarch from the Greek, of which he is no more learned than a magpie, the Bible from Hebrew, of which he likewise knows about as much as my dog, and after a thousand ridiculous remedies typical of a charlatan, about which I don't have time to write to you, he's finally been reduced to the art of pimping, and he's filled the house where he lives with several beautiful courtesans, in this way begging bitterly for his bread, since his virtues are not sufficient to earn it! But am I saying virtues in a scoundrel? Indeed, not even his vices.

By the 1560s, however, the two men, by all indications, were reconciled. In the sixth edition of the *Trasformationi* (1561), Dolce honoured Ruscelli by including him once again in the list of learned men at the beginning of canto 4. And Ruscelli, for his part, wrote to King Philip on 3 April 1561, telling him that the King's father, Charles V, ill in Flanders and certain of his death, had failed to remunerate Dolce, who had formally dedicated the first edition of the *Trasformationi* to him, and that it was up to the son to make up for the father's forgetfulness (Bongi, pp. 399–400).[63]

About Dolce's wife, Polonia, almost nothing is known. He appears to have met her in the context of the theatre. Bareggi, in fact, refers to her as 'una comparsa di scena' (a bit player).[64] He had at least two children by her, a daughter who married Fortunato Martinengo (who praises her beauty, gracefulness, and speaking abilities in a letter to Dolce), and a son, Marcello, praised by Dolce in a letter to Jacopo Marmitta.[65]

In addition to his familial and occupational responsibilities, Dolce belonged to at least two academies, the Accademia Frattegiana and that of the Pellegrini (Cicogna, p. 108), and possibly to the Infiammati.[66] The academies, in general, served as gathering-places for the purposes of learned conversation, although some had more specific cultural goals. The Pellegrini, for example, focused on honouring Petrarch, one of the authors edited by Dolce, while the Infiammati had a wider range of goals, including to read Homer and Theocritus, Virgil and Horace, with lessons on theology, philosophy, medicine, law, and the liberal arts.[67] In addition to the social and cultural benefits membership in the academies provided, it also represented a sign of professional and official recognition as a *letterato*. As Bareggi notes, they enabled their members to demonstrate to the Venetian printers their professional status as men of culture (p. 145), and, for Dolce, one might add, culture was recognized as a benefit that was both useful to society and significant in a modern sense.

Surprisingly, given his contacts with the Venetian patriciate and his apparently pacific nature, Dolce was imprisoned once. On 22 March 1537, the Consiglio dei dieci (Council of Ten), preoccupied by brawls and quarrels and the fact that most people went around armed, ordered that anyone bearing arms in the city, by day or by night, should be arrested immediately.[68] Dolce wound up in jail, having been arrested, as he recounts it in his *supplica*, while he was about to set out for Padua 'in habito di forestier con la spada, come a tal cammino si costuma di far' (in travel clothes with a sword, as is customary for such a trip).[69] This sort of arrest must have been common, for Dolce once wrote an undated letter to Pietro Aretino, appealing for help in getting a servant out of prison for having committed the same offence.[70]

Given the world in which he worked, that of the Venetian presses, Dolce, like other intellects of the time, apparently came into contact with heterodox or heretical ideas, particularly around 1545, the year in which the Council of Trent first met. His contacts with reformational ideas and evangelical thought came in part through Andrea Arrivabene, a printer originally from Mantua, whose bookstore and press could be found 'al segno del Pozzo.'[71] The significant connection, however, appears to have been Orazio Brunetto, a heterodox doctor from Friuli, who was very close to Arrivabene. Dolce ended up editing Brunetto's *epistolario*, published in Venice in 1548 by Arrivabene. Brunetto himself had been introduced to Dolce by Paolo Crivelli, a young man of culture who, like Dolce, was a native Venetian and in touch with the city's cultural circles.[72]

Dolce and Crivelli exchanged several letters in the winter of 1545, six of which have survived: five from Dolce, one from Crivelli. In these they discuss topics such as the art of oratory and problems of metrics. In effect, Crivelli functioned as an intermediary between Giolito and Dolce when the latter was outside Venice. Dolce, for example, asked Crivelli to arrange for his *Capitano* to be published (although Dolce later wrote to ask Crivelli to hold off the 'impressione' so he himself could correct the proofs).[73]

The indications that Dolce might have belonged to an evangelical group in Venice are provided by the letters exchanged between these men. At one point in the correspondence between Dolce and Brunetto regarding the latter's *Lettere*, the language becomes ambiguous. Dolce wrote: 'Havrei caro di parlarvi con vostro commodo et solo' (I would very much like to speak to you alone and at your convenience; Brunetto, *Lettere*, p. 155^v). Brunetto's responses were: 'A bocca le dirò poi la mia bisogna' (I'll tell you then by mouth what I need; ibid, p. 158^v) and 'Dimane verrò a casa Vostra Signoria; dove ho da ragionarvi cose, che m'hanno spaventato fuor di modo, in certa materia mia particolare: intenderete a bocca il tutto' (Tomorrow I'll come to the house of your lordship; where I need to discuss with you some things that have frightened me more than normal, regarding certain material of mine in particular: you'll hear it all by mouth; ibid, p. 160^r).

During the same period of time in 1545, specifically 19 February, Dolce wrote to Paolo Manuzio from Padua, announcing his return to Venice in

April and concluding with a reference to a spiritual sonnet he had written as a sign of his conversion: 'Vi mando un sonetto spirituale per segno della mia conversione' (*Della nuova scielta di lettere* [1582], II, pp. 418–20).

Dolce and Brunetto were also involved in a dispute with Fra Sisto de' Medici, a Jewish convert who became a minor friar of the Franciscans and a man who was very close to reform ideas, at least for a time. Notice of the dispute, which comes to us from letters of Brunetto, concerned whether 'la eloquenza sia necessaria al predicatore del Vangelo' (Brunetto, *Lettere*, p. 39[v]). Brunetto and Dolce held the contrary – namely, the necessity of a return to the customs of the Church of the apostles, which 'operò col fuoco de le parole, o con la semplicità de lo spirito, che le inspirava i concetti et le formava le parole d'una in una, et con la fede, la quale li univa a quello sapientissimo vivo fonte di saluberrima eloquenza, Dio benedetto' (carried out its work with the fire of the words, or with the simplicity of the spirit, which inspired the concepts and formed the words one by one, and with faith, which united them to that most wise and living fount of redemptive eloquence, blessed God; ibid, pp. 40[r–v], for which see Bareggi, p. 204).

Perhaps the conclusion that one should draw from these sources, despite the fact that they demonstrate an acquaintance with individuals and ideas that were of suspect orthodoxy, is not that Dolce was part of an evangelical group in Venice, but rather, as Bareggi notes, that reformation ideas circulated widely among those in the city's editorial circles. None of Dolce's literary works displays heterodox attitudes. In fact, Dolce appears to have distanced himself from any connection with unacceptable doctrines, a distancing that becomes clear when one examines a more precarious moment in his life – the two trials he underwent at the hands of the Holy Office regarding published material. In this case, the individual responsible for Dolce's involvement in questionable matters was Alfonso di Ulloa.[74]

Ulloa and Dolce were tried together twice in 1558, when they were accused by the Sant'Uffizio of having contributed to the publication of a book held to be suspect: the *Secreti* of Pompeo dalla Barba di Pescia, a work published by Giolito but subsequently burned.[75] When Ulloa was brought before the Auditore on 3 March and questioned about permission to publish his translations, he at first thought he was being investigated for the *Institutione de un re christiano*, a work written by Felipe de la Torre, published in the original by Giolito in 1557 and in a translation of Ulloa by Valvassore in the same year.[76] The *Institutione*, however, was subsequently freed from suspicion. Attention then turned to the two dialogues of Pompeo dalla Barba. On 22 March, the members of the tribunal went to Dolce's home, where they found him on a mezzanine near the stairs ('in quodam mezato prope scalam') in black work clothes of the sort usually worn by domestics in the home ('vestitus habitu nigro qui domestice in domo gestari solet'). Dolce expressed surprise at the intrusion and was then asked if he had ever certified ('fatto fede') any works for publication. He said that he had received requests to do so from 'Giulito libraro' and 'un spagnol nomine Alfonso Ugliova' (who had asked 'ad instantia de altri') and had responded affirmatively, based on his qualifications as one whose profession was 'lettere de humanità.' He was then asked if he had certified the work having seen it first or merely having read the title. His response was that his judgment was based 'su la fede di un theologo' (on the witness of a theologian). In fact, two months earlier, he said, he had undersigned a certification of a Carmelite father, at the request of Alfonso, at which point he saw only the title of the work, which was *Dialoghi di secreti de la natura*. He added: 'et vedendo io la fede di un maestro di theologia mi persuasi ch'el libro fosse catholico' (and seeing the attestation of a master of theology I was convinced that the book was Catholic).

The questioning was rather rigorous, and at the end Dolce summed up his statement by saying: 'Certo io ho fatta inconsideramente tal fede, ma son excusabile perché l'ho facta vedendo la fede de un theologo et regente per la qual mi ho reportato a lui' (Certainly I approved the work without due consideration, but I am excused because I did it having seen the approval of a theologian and regent, on which I based my decision). Having heard all sides, the Venetian Holy Office prohibited the Carmelite friar from preaching during Lent in 1559, deprived Dolce of the right to approve all copies of the *Dialoghi*, which were then publically burned because they contained 'hereticam dottrinam.'[77]

The second trial was a more important one, involving Gabriel Giolito.[78] It is also interesting for what it tells us about Dolce's methods of research and scholarship. The case began, probably as a matter of personal vendetta, in Giolito's branch office in Naples, where his director, a man from Brescia named Pietro Ludrini, had been fired for being a poor administrator. Aware of several dangerous secrets of Giolito and possessing the *lista librorum* of his successor, Battista Cappello, which contained around seven hundred volumes, many of them prohibited, Ludrini denounced Giolito to the Neapolitan inquisition. When an unspecified number of books listed on the index were found in Cappello's home, he absolved himself of any responsibility, saying that he had not kept the books 'per mal fare o per venderli; ma come factore de altri per ne possere rendere conto' (to do ill or in order to sell them; but as an agent for others, in order to be able to render an accounting).

The trial then moved to Venice, where, in May 1565, three years before Dolce's death, Giolito was interrogated about the matter. Giolito, in turn, tried to blame other unidentified agents, responsible for storing the books. These individuals, he said, could easily have stored books without realizing there were some prohibited titles among them. The inquisitors then probed Giolito's personal beliefs and his circle of friends, trying to see if he was affiliated with any pro-Calvinist group in Venice. After questioning him about Francesco Spinola, a 'correttore di stampa' (printer's proofreader) and tutor he had hired for his son (but fortunately let go), the inquisitors wondered if Giolito had ever asked Spinola for a 'Historia o commentarij di Giovanni Slejdano,' a work placed on the index in 1554, apparently prior to publication.[79] Giolito responded in the affirmative: 'Signor sì che l'ho ricercato, et l'hebbi' (Yes, sir, I looked for it and I found it).

When interrogated as to what purpose, he answered that 'il signor Ludovico Dolce componendo la vita di Ferdinando imperatore, come l'ha composta, mi ricercò che li dovesse far havere alcuni historici, et fra gli altri questo Sleidano per cavar da loro delli particolari pertinenti alla sua *Historia* [the reference is to the *Vita di Ferdinando, primo imperadore di questo nome, discritta da M. Lodovico Dolce, nella quale sotto brevità sono comprese l'historie dall'anno M.D. III al M.D. LXIIII* (Venice: Appresso Gabriel Giolito, 1566)], et così io ne trovai, et ricercando di questo, lo Spinola me lo fece havere, non sapendo io che libro el si fosse, et servito che ne fu il Dolce, il libro fu restituito ad esso Spinola' (Signor Lodovico Dolce, in composing the life of the emperor Ferdinand as he composed it, sought me out to say that he needed me to get him some histories, and among these this Sleidanus, in order to extract from them some particulars pertinent to his *History*, and thus I found some, and in looking for this book, Spinola let me have it, without me being aware what book it was, and once Dolce had availed himself of it, the book was returned to this Spinola). With this, the Holy Office was apparently satisfied. Despite the lapse in judgment displayed by Giolito and Dolce, neither seems to have suffered any consequences from the trial.

One of the conclusions to be drawn from the episode, apart from any question of heterodoxy (it seems clear that Dolce's contacts with suspect works and individuals was a matter not of religion but of scholarship), is the extent to which Dolce sought to be thorough in his research. Not content to rely on one source, in this case Alfonso di Ulloa, who also published a *Vita dell'imperatore Ferdinando I* (Venice: Per i tipi di C. e F. Franceschini, 1565), Dolce cast his net more widely, utilizing a work originally published in Strasbourg in 1555 and then made available a year later in a clandestine edition in Florence. The dangers attendant on such an activity were not sufficient to dissuade him from the endeavour. And dangers there were. Other intellectuals of the time who were tried by the Holy Office found their careers effectively over. A case in point is offered by Antonio Brucioli, who, after his second Venetian trial in 1555, disappeared from the publishing scene; in fact, nothing appeared under his name for almost twenty years, from 1559 to 1576 (although Brucioli died in 1566; see Bareggi, pp. 249, 255–6).

After various periods of illness, including a severe one around 1549–50, Dolce died in January 1568 from a 'catarro salso che da molto tempo il travagliava, e che avealo privato di gran parte della vista' (a salty catarrh that had bothered him for a long time and which had deprived him of a large part of his sight).[80] He is buried in the Church of San Luca in Venice, along with other *poligrafi* of the time (Pietro Aretino, Alfonso di Ulloa, Gerolamo Ruscelli, Dionigi Atanagi, and Orazio Toscanella), although in which pavement tomb is unknown.

One record of his appearance exists, an anonymous woodcut of 1561, in profile, published in the 1572 edition of Dolce's *Le prime imprese del conte Orlando* and his *L'Achille et l'Enea*, and on the jacket of this volume.

2

Between Ariosto and Tasso: The *Sacripante* and the *Prime imprese del conte Orlando*

At one point in Lodovico Dolce's tragedy *Marianna* (1565), the tyrant Herod interrupts a faltering counsellor with the accusation 'Tu pigli da lontan la tua risposta' (You take from afar your response). His reproach applies as well to this chapter, since I, too, will begin from afar. My purpose is twofold: to describe Dolce's work as a critic, editor, and translator of classical epics and chivalric romances, and, more important, to discuss his own poetic contributions to these two related genres. Of Dolce's four chivalric romances, I concentrate on the two most original works, the youthful *Sacripante* (1535–6), a continuation of the action of Ariosto's *Orlando furioso*, and the later, more lengthy *Prime imprese del conte Orlando* (posthumous, 1572), a poem whose material fills in the *antefatto* for both Boiardo's *Orlando innamorato* and the *Furioso*.

Dolce as Critic

As suggested in chapter 1, Dolce merits more intensive study, for he delved into all the major literary genres, including epic and chivalric romance, and he took part in several of the literary polemics that rocked the sixteenth century. To speak only of those events which relate Dolce to the literary currents of immediate concern: he authored a linguistic and grammatical treatise (*Libri delle osservationi*, 1550, 1562), drawing examples from and commenting on Dante, Boccaccio, Poliziano, Boiardo, Pulci, Francesco Bello (il Cieco da Ferrara), and Ariosto, among others;[1] entered into a polemic with Giovan Battista Gelli regarding the antidantismo of Bembo (1564);[2] and, in 1555, employing, he claims, 'un esemplare frascritto dal proprio scritto di mano del figliuolo di Dante' (an exemplar transcribed from the handwriting of the son of Dante), published an edition of the *Commedia* (the first, incidentally, to bear the adjective *divina*) 'alla sua vera lettione ridotta.'[3] Other authors of epic and chivalric romances edited by Dolce include Poliziano, Ariosto, and Bernardo Tasso. In addition, Dolce also left renditions of Homer's *Iliad* and *Odyssey* and Virgil's *Aeneid*.[4]

As well as being the first to translate Horace's *Ars poetica* into the vernacular, Dolce contributed to the developing genre of literary criticism with a variety of prefaces, *espositioni*, and *annotazioni* of significance.[5] In his 'Discorso sopra la poetica' accompanying his translation of Horace, for example, he speaks of the necessity of avoiding discordant notes, such as the mixture of lofty and lowly, and cites Ariosto as a praiseworthy example.[6] His critical comments are often incisive. In his preface to the *Amadigi* (1560), to cite an example at somewhat greater length, Dolce underscores the modern quality of the work, and in doing so tells us much about his own poetics, based on an awareness of the publishing writer's public rather than on academic standards. In this instance, he criticizes those who, in opposition to the 'giudizio comune,' are 'dati del tutto allo studio delle Greche e delle Latine lettere' (given over completely to the study of Greek and Latin letters) and who 'non pur non comendano, ma riprendono questa nuova, vaghissima, e dilettevolissima maniera di Poesia, ed ogn'altra, che non sia disposta secondo l'arte d'Aristotele, e ad imitazione di Virgilio, e d'Omero' (not only do not commend but reprove this new, most graceful manner of poetry, and every other sort, that is not laid out according to the art of Aristotle and in imitation of Virgil and Homer).[7]

Thus, while addressed to the 'lovers of this new poetry,' Dolce's introduction is directed against those academic critics who do not consider 'la qualità de' tempi presenti, e le diversità delle lingue' (the nature of the present time and the diversity of languages) or the poet's duty to entertain according to the custom of his own time, but would have the poet write for the dead (pp. iv–v). Bernardo Tasso, Dolce tells us, had written a good part of the *Amadigi* imitating the ancients and following the precepts of Aristotle; the single action, for example, was to have been Amadigi's despair (p. vi). But, when he saw that the work, like Alamanni's *Giron cortese*, did not delight, unlike the *Furioso*, which did, Bernardo changed his mind, embracing multiple actions and approaching 'quella piacevole varietà, che nell'Ariosto è stata dall'universale giudizio degli uomini lodata, ed approvata' (that pleasing variety which in Ariosto has been praised and approved by the universal judgment of men; p. vi). In all of Dolce's works, even those written well after the diffusion of Aristotle's *Poetics*, he embraces the same principle of varied action.

Dolce goes on to affirm that the fundamental aim of poets (especially those wishing to be read) is to delight. If they are good poets as well, they conjoin the *dilettevole* with the *utile*, concealing under the pleasing veil of their inventions the precepts of Moral Philosophy (p. vii). Stressing Bernardo Tasso's freedom, Dolce analyses the poet's innovations, both when he chooses *not* to follow Ariosto (as in varying the introductions to each canto rather than always beginning with 'la moralità') and when he elects to imitate the ancients, enriching his work with *epiteti*, *traslati*, *iperboli*, and other *figure* which embellish a poem and render it magnificent. Bernardo Tasso's own genius is evident in his style, which is florid, graceful, and more ornate than that of those who have written up to now (p. viii). His language is 'sceltissimo ed accurato' (very well chosen and accurate; p. ix), although not limited to the vocabulary of Petrarch, who was a lyric rather than a heroic poet. Bernardo Tasso's verse is pure, lofty, and elegant, and always sufficiently grave. The *Amadigi*'s 'facilità' is accompanied by 'maestà'; the poet's 'sentenze' are abundant, his comparisons appropriate. He depicts the marvellous with propriety and holds the reader in suspense ('tenendo sempre in una dolce e grata aspettazione il lettore'; pp. ix–x).

As Dolce had once praised Ariosto's visual technique, he now refers to Bernardo's ability to paint his scenes with ocular clarity, 'che non più potrebbe far dipingendo il pennello di Apelle, o di Tiziano' (which neither the brush of Apelles nor that of Titian could paint better; p. x). Bernardo is equally adept at engaging the emotions: 'Muove gli affetti in guisa, che sembra tiranno degli animi' (He moves our feelings in such a way that he seems a tyrant of the mind; p. x). The poet is further praised, not only for his masterful depiction of the sweetness, bitterness, and passions of love, but for his descriptions of battles, the latter of which, incidentally, were to antagonize Benedetto Croce in another age (for which see chapter 1, note 18). The significance of these features as a whole is that they are those of a poet who desires that his work be read. It is not the academicians who determine fame but the 'giudizio comune,' the people who buy books to read for pleasure, not for study.[8]

Dolce was also one of the earliest interpreters and defenders of the *Furioso*, of which, as Nino Borsellino writes, Dolce 'colse l'effetto ottico rilevando come il *Furioso*, piuttosto che leggerlo sembra di vederlo' (caught the optical effect, emphasizing how rather than reading the poem one seems to see it).[9] In his *Apologia contra ai detrattori dell'Ariosto* (1539), Dolce anticipates several of the 'conquests' of modern criticism, in particular Croce's ideas on organic unity and harmony. After praising Ariosto's variety –

Egli giova e diletta parimente: quando muove a tristezza, quando a riso l'animo dell'ascoltante: hora col suono dell'arme lo spaventa ed innaspera; ed hora con la descrittione di qualche piacevole amore lo indolcisse ricreandolo; e l'una estremità con l'altra non senza il suo mezzo temperando, ed il soggetto variando, con sì mirabile arteficio; che ogni cosa va per sè, e tutte insieme ci invaghiscono al leggere, ne ci apportano satietà

[He aids and delights equally, both when he moves the mind of the listener to sadness and when to laughter; now with the sound of arms he frightens and hardens the mind, now with the description of some pleasing love he sweetens and refreshes it; and the one extreme with the other not without tempering the middle and varying the subject, with such marvellous artifice that every element functions on its own, and all together they enthral us to read, and do not cause satiety] –

Dolce emphasizes that everything which Ariosto has 'raccolto' and 'abbracciato' in his volume is gathered and embraced in such a way that 'niente in se stesso [è] discordante, niente mostruoso ma ogni cosa risulta in un corpo solo, ed in tutte parti corrispondente' (nothing in itself is discordant, nothing monstrous, but each thing results in a single body with all its parts corresponding).[10]

In his comments on Ariosto's language, Dolce also reveals himself as decisively on the side of the moderns. He justifies the use of words such as 'matto,' for which Ariosto had been censured, by pointing out that Dante employed it also (even though he, too, is criticized by some) and by asserting furthermore that poets are permitted to introduce new words if they are appropriate to the context.[11] Ariosto's verse, criticized as swollen and harsh by those who fault Ariosto for the very thing for which he merits greater praise, is, in his words,

alto e grave, e quale apunto si conviene all'Heroica Maestà: ne meno in un luogo è elevato, in un'altro depresso ed humile (come si può dire de' versi d'alcuno, che ha qualche grido:) ma sempre procede con una medesima grandezza, e dignità, serbando di continuo uno stile uguale, nel che si chiude la bontà e nitidezza d'un verso. (II, p. iiii[r])

[lofty and grave, and just as it should be for Heroic Majesty: nor is it elevated in one place and lowly and humble in another (as can be said of the verses of someone who has a certain renown), but always procedes with the same grandeur and dignity, continually maintaining the same style, in which consists the goodness and clarity of a verse.]

Dolce's comments on imitation, finally, are significant in the light of his own chivalric romances, which are often a reworking of traditional sources. With lively vexation, he accuses those who criticize Ariosto of having 'poco ingegno' and of robbing from others as having themselves 'poca intelligentia: perciò che niuno è così poco tinto di lettere, che non sappia l'imitatione (sicome ancho nella pittura, e nell'altre cose; dove occorra l'arte e l'ingegno) esser la prima e principalissima parte, che si richieggia a un Poeta' (little intelligence, because no one is so little tinged with letters as not to know that imitation [just as in painting, and in other things where skill and wit are needed] is the first and foremost thing required of a poet; II, p. iiii[v]). To imitate well is difficult:

... è di bisogno che quello, che tu d'imitar tenti, paia più tosto illustrato, che imitato: e quel soggetto o sententia, che tu rubi ad alcuno, fa di mestieri che lo sappia cangiar e tramutar in tal guisa, che paia proprio tuo e non tolto d'altrui: non altrimente, che faccia il ladro in un drappo da lui involato: alquale egli astutamente rimoverà qualche parte, ed andrà variandonela con tanta sottilità, che 'l drappo non si dimostrerà più esser quello, anchora che egli vi ritenesse alcuna similitudine: facendo ultimamente, come fanno le Api; le quali vanno dipredando diversi fiori, e di quelli ne partoriscono il mele. (II, p. v[r])

[... it is necessary that that which you try to imitate seem rather to be illustrated than imitated; and that subject or maxim that you steal from another, you must know how to change and transform it in such a manner that it seems your own and not taken from another: not otherwise than does the thief with a piece of cloth he has stolen, from which he astutely removes a piece and goes about varying it with such keenness that the cloth no longer seems what it was, even though he might have retained there a certain similarity: doing lastly as do the bees, who go around plundering different flowers and from them bring forth honey.]

Ariosto, who imitated not only the Latins, but the Spanish ('i quali nelle inventioni ed in esprimer un lor concetto sono mirabilissimi' [who are most marvellous in inventing and expressing their concepts]), was excellent, he says, in this respect.

Dolce's attentive study of and dedication to Ariosto can be seen in the many supplementary features he provided for the *Furioso*. Numerous sixteenth-century editions of the poem (and in that century alone Dolce's edition went through at least sixty-two Venetian reprintings) contain either his *Apologia*, his sonnet in praise of Ariosto, his allegories for each canto, or his 'Espositione di tutti i vocaboli et luoghi difficili, che nel libro si trovano' (1542). Some of these studies were translated into other languages in conjunction with Ariosto's poem.[12] Equally famous was Dolce's *Modi affigurati e voci scelte et eleganti della volgar lingua, con un discorso sopra a' mutamenti e diversi ornamenti dell'Ariosto,* a work examining Ariosto's use of metaphors and praising his language and artistry.[13] As evidence of Dolce's thoroughness, even the symbols used by Ariosto in the second edition of the *Furioso* came in for comment. In the critic's *Dialogo dei colori,* he thought it worthy of particular attention that the symbol chosen was that of two snakes, one whose tongue is cut out and the other about to suffer the same fate. The emblem, which was changed in the third edition, was one that 'l'Ariosto pose contra l'invidia' (Ariosto placed against envy).[14]

Mention must also be made of Dolce's translations and *rifacimenti,* several of which belong to the genres of epic or chivalric romance. While his *L'Achille et l'Enea* has been mistakenly or unjustly labelled a failed attempt to renew the classical form of epic in Trissinian fashion, the work is in large part simply a translation in octaves of the *Iliad* and the *Aeneid.*[15] Dolce completed the Homeric cycle with his translation in octaves of the *Odyssey,* published posthumously in 1573 as *L'Ulisse* (which contains, as well, Dolce's version of the *Batracomiomachia*). Other forms of classical epic, such as Ovid's *Metamorphoses,* translated in octaves as *Le trasformationi* (1st book, 1539; complete ed., 1553) and of Greek romance, such as Achilles Tatius's *Amorosi ragionamenti* (1546), flowed from his fertile pen. And finally, like Folengo and Aretino, Dolce, encouraged by others, thought of redoing Boiardo's *Orlando innamorato* but left the task to Francesco Berni (posth. 1541) and Lodovico Domenichi (1545).[16] On the whole, however, his opinion of Boiardo appears to have been high. In discussing the history of the 'ottava rima' in his *Osservationi,* for example, Dolce observes that Luigi Pulci 'fu poscia lasciato a dietro dal Boiardo sì di stilo, come d'inventione' (was afterward left behind by Boiardo as regards both style and invention; p. 236).

Dolce as Poet

Dolce, then, did not approach the chivalric romance as a dilettante. Both the *Sacripante* (1536), one of his earliest published works, and the *Prime imprese del conte Orlando,* published posthumously in 1572, attest to his lifelong devotion to the genre. And Dolce's *Palmerino* and *Primaleone,* as well as his *Stanze* on the African victory of Charles V, must also not be forgotten. The *Stanze,* for example, are said to have possibly influenced

Tasso. Vincenzo Vivaldi, in discussing the classical sources of the *Gerusalemme*'s first octave, notes that 'il primo verso della *Liberata* risente moltissimo del primo verso di un poemetto del Dolce, scritto per la vittoria di Carlo V sui Musulmani: "Io canto l'arme, e l'onorate insegne / Mosse in favor di Cristo e de la fede"' (the first verse of the *Liberata* very much shows the effect of the first verse of a poem of Dolce, written for the victory of Charles V over the Moslems: 'I sing of arms and the honoured banners / Moved in favour of Christ and of the faith').[17] The same scholar mentions, among many possible sources of Tasso's Argante, Dolce's *Prime imprese* (see Vivaldi, p. 59) and finds the first canto of the *Primaleone* of significance for the duel of Tancredi and Clorinda (ibid, pp. 96–7). He adds that Tasso was a reader and admirer of Dolce's works and that, while the *Primaleone* was first published in 1562 and Tasso's first efforts on the *Gerusalemme* date to around 1559–60, Tasso says nothing of Tancredi and Clorinda until after 1566.

While the many poems written in Italy between the times of Ariosto and Tasso, as Roberto Battaglia notes, derive some of their significance from the fact that they develop schemes of a conventional epic world which will be those of the *Liberata*, they also often reflect the critical thought of the Counter-Reformation and possess noteworthy religious or moral aims.[18] The heroes after Ariosto are not *spensierati* but conscious of honour: 'Si ricerca una maggiore se non assoluta fedeltà alla donna, una nuova e approfondita arte della guerra, una coscienza più profonda della propria dignità' (One seeks a greater, if not absolute, faithfulness to the woman, a new and more learned art of war, a more profound awareness of one's own dignity; p. 174). These traits, indeed, are all typical of Dolce, and they appear not only in the late *Prime imprese*, but also in the early *Sacripante*. In this, I would disagree with Ulrich Leo, who denies a Counter-Reformation spirit to Dolce, labelling his *Sacripante* 'pre-controriformista' and contrasting the innocuous pleasure of the old material (i.e., as used by Dolce) with the 'moralismo' of Brusantini (*Angelica innamorata*, 1550).[19] Dolce is most likely writing in the early 1530s, by which time Italian religious unrest, as Grendler notes, had become more widespread following the penetration of new ideas from the north, the disasters of war, and the shock of the Sack of Rome in 1527 (*Critics of the Italian World*, p. 105 and ch. 4 *passim*). As will be seen, Dolce's concern for individual moral reform is a constant motif in his literary works. He is clearly attuned to the spirit and attitudes of the time, including Italian evangelism as influenced by Erasmus. In this he reflects, and perhaps even anticipates, reformist desires that came to the forefront in the 1540s.

The *Sacripante*

The moral depth of the Sacripante is apparent in the motifs developed with greatest insistency by Dolce. The motives of honest love (where passion is restrained by reason), of honour and of fidelity are evident from the very first lines of, and throughout, the *Sacripante*. Both major and minor characters struggle, on the one hand, with the conflict among duty, honour, and utility, and, on the other, with appetite, which leads to folly. Dolce is careful to point out that the fault for human woe lies not with others and not with fortune, but with oneself and one's desires. The thematic interplay of passion and reason forms the basis of many of the poem's episodes.

Given that the *Sacripante* is not as well known as other chivalric romances of the cinquecento, perhaps a summary of the poem's action would be beneficial in providing a fuller context for an analysis of the work as a whole. The risk for confusion is great, however, since the poem is one with many threads, and its technique of entwinement is similar to that employed by Ariosto.

The poet's subject-matter, as the introductory octave puts it, is 'l'arme, li sdegni, e gli amorosi ardori / Gli animi accesi di virtute e gloria, / Le chiare imprese d'e [de'] tempi migliori / Degni di eterna et immortal memoria' (the arms, the disdain, and the amorous passions, the minds inflamed with virtue and glory, the illustrious deeds of better times, worthy of eternal and immortal memory), all presented 'per infiammar (s'io posso) mille cori' (to inflame [if I can] a thousand hearts).[20] More specifically, his focus is on the sufferings and labours of Sacripante, who left on earth and in hell an eternal example of rare and true faith (oct. 2). The valorous Sacripante, King of Circassia and a Saracen, is yet another of those heroes tormented by his love for Angelica.

The poem begins with the death of Rodomonte at the hands of Ruggiero, who rejoices with his sister Marphisa. Orlando's wits have been returned to him by Astolfo, and Rinaldo, having drunk again of Merlin's fountain, is no longer in love with Angelica, now married to Medoro. But others are not so fortunate. Both Ferraù and Sacripante have been wounded by the rumour of Angelica's marriage; Ferraù vows to kill her husband, Medoro, while Sacripante sets out on a trail of lamentation. The two meet each other at an inn and, as competitors, exchange harsh words. Meanwhile, Agrismonte, the bastard son of Gradasso, wants to avenge his father's death on the Paladins (canto I).

While Agrismonte's fleet is assailed by a storm, back in the inn Ferraù wakes up to find Sacripante already gone. The innkeeper detains Ferraù with a story of his disastrous love for a married woman, a love that eventually turned to hate and that resulted in the murder of the woman and her husband. Ferraù departs and is about to leave Europe for Asia when he comes across a knight and a woman he believes to be Angelica. At this point, the author returns to the court of Charlemagne, where the knights are preparing for a joust. Orlando, however, seeking to regain his honour and his helmet, leaves for the East, with Astolfo following behind. In the joust, one knight from Spain, a sixteen-year-old pagan named Selannio, does so well that Marphisa falls in love with him (c. II).

Sacripante, meanwhile, after his early-morning departure from the inn, has arrived at the sea, where he encounters an old woman in tears who tells him about a monster. The lord Oronte has promised gold and his daughter Ericina to anyone who can kill the beast, which he keeps in a lake in his garden. Sacripante, desiring neither the gold nor the girl, but only to save others from death, kills the monster, spurns Ericina's advances, and continues on his pilgrimage to the East. Before long, he comes across a woman fleeing a band of armed men. After he rescues her, she tells her story. Returning from France one day with her lover, she stopped to rest in a castle, only to discover in the morning that her host, because of his love for her, had killed her beloved. The host explains that he killed the boy unwillingly but of necessity. He then narrates his story to explain why (a story within a story) – namely, because of a law he established after his daughter-in-law killed her husband. All men who stay at the castle are now sacrificed to the memory of his son. The woman, who now returns to *her* story, says she was set free by the man who killed her lover, so that she could be chased by other men for sport. When Sacripante vows to avenge her, she reveals herself to be Melissa, the enchantress who freed Ruggiero from Alcina (as narrated in Ariosto's poem). Since Sacripante is unarmed, Melissa tells him that a sorceress named Erina has the weapons of Aeneas, made for him by Vulcan. Melissa promises to help Sacripante against Erina's magic. Meanwhile, a messenger tells Sacripante that his kingdom of Circassia is under attack from a woman named Orestilla.

Following her success, Orestilla has set out to challenge the best of Charlemagne's men. On her way, she comes across a magnificent riderless horse, chased by a knight. To explain who this is, the author says he will return to his 'historia' (c. III).

In canto IV, we return to the joust in Paris, where other amorous adventures and misfortunes are taking place. Ricciardetto, for example, would like to marry Oliviero's sister, Cynthia, but others desire her hand as well. Charlemagne promises her to the winner of the joust, but when this turns out to be Ricciardetto, we learn that Cynthia herself is in love with Gherardo. Gherardo, though defeated on the field, flees with Cynthia, who drops from a balcony by rope to join him, after which he is forced to kill some fellow Christians in order to escape. Pursued by the Paladins, the two lovers are separated when surprised by a lion while they are drinking at a fountain. Cynthia, who flees into the forest with the lion on her heels, is rescued by armed men.

In canto V, the author takes up the thread of Orlando and Astolfo. Orlando has come across Angelica, who fails to recognize him and whom he barely remembers. While he listens and asks for details, she narrates all the problems caused by her beauty, including the fact that she has been pursued by Orlando, Rinaldo, Sacripante, and Ferraù, and then married a common soldier, Medoro, who has now chased her out of her own realm, after trying to shoot her with arrows during a hunt. While Angelica talks, Ferraù, the rival of Sacripante, arrives on the scene and challenges Orlando, not knowing who he is. Orlando is happy to duel him, since Ferraù is wearing his helmet. The duel is broken off when a giant arrives, stuns the observer Astolfo with a blow to the head, and abducts Angelica.

After Orlando and Ferraù leave in pursuit of the giant, Astolfo awakens, goes looking for Angelica, and comes upon a beautiful woman, who invites him to a life of pleasure on an island. The woman, we learn, is the sorceress Erina, whose island contains an enchanted palace and garden. The two fall in love and consummate their passion in an idyllic wonderland.

Orlando, meanwhile, in pagan terrain, decides to help King Bardano in his fight against Artabia, a woman who has spurned him for an unknown knight. Gherardo, in turn, is still searching for his beloved Cynthia, who is now a captive along with other women. The three knights pursuing Gherardo and Cynthia (Rinaldo, Oliviero, and Ricciardetto) find her, but she escapes again. One of the other captives, a woman named Hersilia, narrates her sad story, which contains an episode with pirates and is reminiscent of Boccaccio's tale of Alatiel (*Decameron* II, 7).

Canto VII returns to Charlemagne's court and to Bradamante and Ruggiero. In search of Rinaldo and accompanied by Marphisa, the three come across a shepherd, who invites them to a rustic meal of cheese, milk, and fruit. Violence breaks in on this world of pastoral tranquillity when Gano and his men arrive to kill Ruggiero. Soon after, the trio of Rinaldo, Oliviero, and Ricciardetto arrive, and in the ensuing slaughter many villains, as the author puts it, are sent to find Charon ('gli altri a trovar Charon furon mandati'; oct. 34).

After the battle, the victorious Paladins decide to spend the night with the shepherds. When Ruggiero's horse, Frontino, runs off, Rinaldo chases him on Baiardo. Before long, he encounters Orestilla, the pagan woman looking for Paladins to fight after her victory in Circassia. The author informs us that he (as narrator) told us she met a knight charging through the forest after a riderless horse; now here he is, Rinaldo himself. The two duel, stopping when night falls, after which Orestilla reveals she is a woman. Struck with her beauty, Rinaldo speaks sweetly with her as the two ride through the night. At dawn they decide to join up as companions.

At the end of canto VII, we return to Sacripante on the coast, with Melissa almost dead in his arms. Erina invites him to her island (just as she had done with Astolfo), and he manages to kill the giant guarding the weapons made by Vulcan for Aeneas. In canto VIII, Sacripante gains the arms with the aid of Melissa's magic arts. The castle and garden of Erina disappear while she flees, and the enthralled knights, including Astolfo, regain their wits.

Sacripante, on foot, finds Ruggiero's Frontino – a horse that was originally Sacripante's, under the name Frontalatte. Accompanied by Melissa, he travels to the castle and kills the father who murders all men as a sacrifice to the memory of his son. A gruesome description of the dead bodies found in the castle follows.

We then return to Angelica, whom we last saw in the arms of the giant who bore her away during the duel between Orlando and Ferraù. Selannio comes upon the two and chases the giant into water, where he is attacked by monstrous serpents. Marphisa, in love with him, arrives on the scene, wants to help, but is afraid of offending Selannio. Instead, before she realizes what is happening, she is knocked unconscious by the giant, and Selannio suffers the same fate. The two are tied together and carried into the water by the giant. When they awaken, they find themselves in front of a king called 'Tempio' (Time), along with another woman awaiting judgment. This turns out to be Angelica, who is sentenced to be punished for having disdained love. Part of her punishment, she is told, will be to have people write about her in the future, and the one to rescue her from her imprisonment and daily whippings will be Sacripante (octs. 59–63).[21]

The evil Agrismonte, caught in a storm at sea for three days (this was back at the start of canto II), lands on an island belonging once to King Gradasso, now dead. His son Marbotto, also a giant (one with eyes of fire, just as the devils in hell are painted), has succeeded him.[22] This Marbotto has another giant in his service named Macatruffo, a vile creature reminiscent of Pulci's Margutte. The two help Agrismonte cross Spain.

In canto IX, the poet announces a new style and a new theme – the laments of the defenders of Christ. King Marsiglio of Spain joins forces with Agrismonte to attack Charlemagne. Battle scenes are described at some length, including the damage caused by the giant Macatruffo. In canto X, finally, following a Golden Age motif, discussed below, Dolce returns to his story, depicting battles in which monsters from hell join the fray. Christians are slaughtered, women killed and raped, God's temples profaned. (One has to remember that, even though Dolce was lavish in his praise of Charles V barely fifty octaves earlier, the Sack of Rome was still fresh in the memory of Italians.)

Shortly before the end of the incomplete poem, the author returns to more pleasant motifs – namely, Ericina's efforts to win Sacripante by disguising herself as Angelica. Instead of being discovered by Sacripante, however, she falls into the hands of Ferraù, who thinks she is Angelica, and at this the poem breaks off, with the author promising to continue her lament in the next canto.

As stated earlier, the motives of honest love (where passion is restrained by reason), of honour, and of fidelity are evident from the very first lines and throughout the first canto of the *Sacripante*. Dolce's beginning, while imitative of Ariosto's, reverses the chiastic structure – (rather than women–knights–arms–love we find arms–disdain–love–glory) – and introduces the thematic opposition between love and ingratitude. The conflict between passion (or appetite) and reason is presented in our first vision of Sacripante, who is a knight, as in Ariosto, in love with Angelica. The change in tone, however, is immediately evident. Sacripante, aware that his kingdom is under attack, tells himself he should ignore Angelica, a 'vil meretrice,' and not be a prisoner of his appetites (I, 32). Love, at this point however, easily surmounts these thoughts and dispoils him of his 'intelletto' to the extent that he ignores the news of his realm, forgetting 'l'utile e l'honore' (I, 34).

That night, in an inn, Sacripante gives vent to his sorrow. In Ariosto (I, 39–44), Sacripante laments that another has enjoyed Angelica before him ('che debbo far, poi ch'io son giunto tardi, / e ch'altri a corre il frutto è andato prima?' [what should I do, since I've arrived late and another has gone first to pluck the fruit?]).[23] In Dolce, these thoughts are behind the knight; they belong to the past, to what he was before. In fact, before retiring to his room, Sacripante had mocked Ferraù (who wanted to duel because they both love Angelica) by telling him that another already enjoys her (*Sacr.* I, 39). Now, instead of a *carpe diem* lament, Sacripante protests his fidelity, speaking of the great deeds he has accomplished because of his love (I, 49–50). When misogynistic thoughts overwhelm him ('Ahi sesso femminile infame e vile' [ah, the female sex, infamous and vile]), he convinces himself that rather than hating Angelica he should excuse her (I, 52–3). His conquest is confirmed the next morning when the innkeeper informs him no payment is necessary provided he swear to hate all women. Sacripante refuses because of his love for one (I, 57).

The *questione della donna* returns to centre stage in canto II, when Ferraù is faced with the same question. Dolce's procedure reminds one of the polemics so common to the *trattati d'amore* from the *Asolani* onward.[24] It is the innkeeper who speaks at length of women's evil deeds:

> Di quante crudeltà, di quante pene,
> Ruine, et opre misere e funeste
> Sien le femine a l'huomo; i' potrei dire,
> E mille esempi un dopo l'altro, unire. (II, 11)

> Tutto quel, che tra noi si prova e sente
> Di misero, d'amaro, e d'infelice,
> Tutto quel che ci strugge, e parimente
> È d'ogni human riposo involatrice;
> Da le femine vien, non altrimente
> Ch'arboro o pianta vien da sua radice;
> Create qui nel nostro viver bello
> Sol per esser de gli huomini flagello. (II, 13)

[I could tell how many cruel acts, how many sorrows, disasters, and wretched, fatal deeds women have done to men, and add a thousand examples, one after the other.

Everything we feel and experience that is wretched, bitter, and unhappy, everything that consumes us, and similarly is a thief of all human repose, comes from women, no differently than a tree or a plant comes from its root, women created here in our beautiful life only to be a scourge of men.]

To prove his point, he narrates a lengthy Boccaccian intrigue story (one of the first of several narrated episodes in the poem) depicting his sufferings at the hands of an evil woman. Before he can finish, however, Ferraù breaks in, claiming he sees no reason to hate all women, because of the evil deeds of one (II, 44):

> Empia fu quella, e tu sciocca e leggiero:
> Ma per una fra mille, infame e vile
> Non dei biasmar il sesso almo e gentile.
>   Quanto è di bello e di gentile in terra,
> Vien da le donne, e dal suo foco scende
> Virtute in noi, ch'ogni vil voglia atterra;
> E d'alti e bei pensier l'anima accende.
> Dove è la fiamma lor fugge ogni guerra,
> Et ogni noia, che la vita offende:
> E senza queste a noi felici scorte
> Saria il viver human peggio che morte. (II, 44–5)

[That one was evil, and you foolish and weak, but because of one among thousands, infamous and vile, you ought not to blame the life-giving, noble sex. Whatever is beautiful and noble on earth comes from women; and from her fire, a virtue descends to us that overcomes all evil desire and inflames the soul with lofty and beautiful thoughts. Where their flame is, all war flees, and every trouble that vexes life, and without these happy guides for us human life would be worse than death.]

The fault for man's woes, he adds, is man's desire itself, which leads him to do things he should not. The moral, clearly expressed, is that he who allows himself to be carried 'fuor di ragion' loses first 'honor,' and then 'la vita' (II, 46).

When the action switches to Carlo's court, we find Orlando thinking of Angelica, 'l'antico errore' (II, 49). Wherever he looks, he seems to see himself, wandering 'folle et ignudo' without 'intelletto' (II, 50). His new goal is to regain his honour, and it is this which now propels him on his quest. The importance of the theme of honour is confirmed at the beginning of canto III, when Dolce, as author, comments on the subject, and in doing so reverses the patriotic language of Petrarch's Canzone 128 ('ché l'antico valore / ne l'italici cor non è ancor morto' [because the ancient valour in Italian hearts is not yet dead], verses with which Machiavelli so stirringly closes the *Principe*), writing instead:

> Alta vaghezza d'immortal honore
> Fu tra gli antichi duchi e cavalieri;
> Ch'apprezzar l'arme assai più per ardore
> Di gloria, che di regni, oro, et imperi.
> Al secol nostro è così spinto fuore

Questo sì bel desio d'altri pensieri,
Che quel valor (e 'l ciel s'accusa a torto)
Ne gli Italici cor è in tutto morto. (III, 1)

[A lofty desire of immortal honour existed among the ancient dukes and knights, who valued arms much more out of ardour for glory than for realms, gold, or empires. In our century this so beautiful desire is thrust aside by other thoughts, because that valour (and heaven is mistakenly accused) is completely dead in Italian hearts.]

The lament and the refusal to blame fortune rather than man reappear in Dolce's tragedy *Marianna* (1565), where the chorus, having traced the decline of man, concludes: 'e non il Fato, o la crudel Fortuna / Ma sol malvagità ci sferza e preme' (and not fate or cruel fortune, but evil alone whips and prods us).[25] The moral depth of the later tragedy, I would like to emphasize, is not a passing fancy, but finds its preparation in the earliest works of Dolce's vast production, as seen in the *Sacripante*.

Adding to the poem's moral depth, Dolce reinstates Orlando's wife, Alda, present in Pulci and Boiardo, but lacking in Ariosto. Dolce's reasons for calling attention to Alda are not frivolous. Women, including wives, play an integral part in the life of the court. One of the nice descriptions of courtly activity – 'Comedie, Farse, Canti, e vari suoni / De la notte [tengon] la maggior parte'; 'Sol de Venere bella è ogni lor detto / Dolce, festoso, e pieno di diletto' (Comedies, farces, songs and various sounds occupy most of the night; each of their comments, sweet, festive and full of delight, derives only from Venus; IV, 8–9; cf. *Orl. fur.* IV, 32) – is prefaced by a description of women, including Aldabella (IV, 6), and ends with a reference to the married couple Ruggiero and Bradamante, who enjoy each other in bed at night (IV, 10).[26] Many of the knights, we soon learn, would like to marry also. All, however, is not syrupy moralism: When Gherardo is hindered in his plans to marry Cynthia, sister of Oliviero, who has promised herself to him in return, the thwarted knight absconds with the maiden, committing murder to escape, and makes love to his beloved in an 'ameno loco' near a fountain and flowers (IV, 11–55).

The pastoral topoi, used later so successfully by Tasso in both the *Aminta* and the *Liberata*, continue when a lion arrives at the fountain and then pursues Cynthia, who flees into the woods, where she is lost to Gherardo. The story breaks off at this point in canto IV, takes up again briefly in canto VI to show us Cynthia's desperate situation, underlined by her fear that her brother will kill her (VI, 79ff.), and is not concluded in the incomplete work. Passion, however, has overcome reason (canto IV), resulting in punishment (cantos IV and VI), which can be atoned for only by fidelity. The latter resolution, of course, is hypothetical – although Gherardo is seen incessantly searching for his beloved (VI, 75) – but follows the pattern employed by Dolce for others in the book.

The thematic interplay of passion and reason forms the basis of many of the poem's episodes. Dolce, like Ariosto, and later Tasso, embellishes his poem with a magic realm. His enchantress, Erina, is a *maga*, born of Circe, whose power is expressed through a typical use of *adynata*: 'Fa notte giorno, e quando è notte oscura; / Rende l'aere seren di doppio Sole' (She makes day of night, and when it is dark night renders the air serene with a double sun) (III, 119).[27] Like Lucan's Haemonian witch, she calls bodies from graves and, like the Sirens, has a beautiful voice. Compared with her, the poet tells us, Bibli and Myrrha would seem chaste (III, 121). Dolce contrasts her transformations of discarded lovers (obedient guardians of her castle) to those changes effected by Ariosto's Alcina (rivers, rocks, and plants) and by Homer's Circe (fierce beasts; III, 121–2).

Erina's paradise is described at greater length in canto V, with many features reminiscent of Boccaccio and Poliziano.[28] Her palace, constructed by demons (V, 73), also brings to mind Carandina's in Francesco Bello's *Mambriano* (1509).[29] The reminiscence is appropriate, because, like Bello, Dolce has entitled his poem after a pagan hero. In both works, the magic kingdom lures an enemy of Carlo Magno – Mambriano and Sacripante.[30] In Dolce's poem, however, it is Astolfo who is first attracted into the prison-paradise. The episode is one which antedates the action of the *Furioso*, for, in Ariosto's work, Astolfo is a former lover of Alcina (here Erina). Dolce's ironic authorial comment is that he is afraid Orlando will have to bring back Astolfo's brains from the moon (VI, 3).

Following Astolfo's arrival in Erina's realm, Dolce describes the *maga*, imitating Ariosto's description of Alcina (*Orl. fur.* VII, 11–15) and his technique by beginning with and concentrating on her head (*capelli, ciglio, occhi negri, bocca, labbra, denti*; *Sacr.* VI, 15). Ariosto's 'Bianca nieve è il bel collo, e 'l petto latte' (Her beautiful neck is white snow, and her breast milk) is lightly and prosaically transformed to 'Bianca neve è il bel collo: e a le mamelle / Conforme è il latte' (Her beautiful neck is white snow, and milk conforms to her breasts; VI, 16). Having paid his homage, Dolce stops short at this point, unlike Ariosto, who finishes with the feet.

Sacripante, upon his arrival in Erina's realm, fares better than Astolfo, in large part because he is aided by Melissa's magic arts (VIII, 8). The moral, as Dolce has informed us in his introduction to canto VIII, is that *ingegno* is better than force of hand (oct. 1). His example there, a premonitory intrusion of present-day reality (cf. the end of the poem), is Venice, who has repelled France, Spain, and even Italy herself! (oct. 3). Thus, while love is the predominant motif of the first eight cantos, the theme of arms is not entirely lacking. The deeds of war, to which the poet now turns in cantos IX and X, however, call for a new style: 'Odo i danni, i lamenti, e 'l pianto tristo, / che s'apparechia ai difensor di Christo' (I hear the harm, the laments, and the sad plaint prepared for the defenders of Christ; IX, 1). Still, though the theme is new, the underlying moral code remains the same. Honour and virtue, praised in canto X, motivate Dolce's heroes. The poet avails himself of this motivation to reverse his earlier lament at Italy's loss of valour and to praise Charles V (X, 2) and other famous men and women of his time (X, 3–21). The topos, a catalogue of the illustrious, is familiar from Ariosto and was imitated by others following Dolce, including Trissino (*L'Italia liberata dai goti*, Book 24), who refers disdainfully to Ariosto 'col *Furioso* suo, che piace al vulgo' (with his *Furioso*, pleasing to the crowd).[31]

In praising Carlo, Dolce employs the customary metaphors of rebirth. The present age has reflowered, in many respects similar to that under Augustus: 'Le muse, che sepolte e poste al fondo / Eran; veggio per lui tornate al mondo' (The muses, which were buried and placed in the deep, I see through him returned to the world; X, 2). After praising Erasmus and Melanchthon ('Tra li Thedeschi Erasmo e Melantone / Sento fiorir, e mille e mille ingegni' [Among the Germans, Erasmus and Melancthon I hear flourish, and thousands and thousands of geniuses]),[32] Dolce passes to the Italians:

In Italia d'antichi a paragone
Pontano, il Sannazaro, et altri degni:
L'unico Pietro Bembo, il Castiglione;
E quel, che i dotti et alti suoi disegni
Mostra con maraviglia: e chi con vero
Nomar si puote il Ferrarese Homero.
  L'Ariosto io vuo dir; cui deve tanto
Ferrara nel gentil nostro Idioma. (X, 3–4)

[In Italy, comparable to the ancients, Pontano, Sannazzaro, and other worthies: the unique Pietro Bembo, Castiglione, and he who shows with marvel his lofty and learned schemes, and he who truly can be named the Homer of Ferrara. Ariosto I mean, to whom Ferrara owes so much in our noble language.]

In the *Furioso*, it was Bembo 'che 'l puro e dolce idioma nostro, / levato fuor del volgare uso tetro, / quale esser dee, ci ha col suo esempio mostro' (who showed us with his example how our pure and sweet language ought to be raised above the gloomy vulgar use; XLVI, 15).

Pietro Aretino, Dolce's close friend, is described in terms which have become traditional (cf. *Orl. fur.* XLVI, 14), just as has the epithet for Ariosto:

> Vegio il sublime e sopra humano ingegno
> De' principi flagel Pietro Aretino.
> Questo è l'huom, che pogiando oltre ogni segno
> Merta anchor vivo il titol di divino. (X, 5)

> [I see the sublime and superhuman wit of the scourge of princes, Pietro Aretino. This is the man who moving beyond every mark deserves, yet alive, the title of divine.]

Brusantini, as Ulrich Leo notes, comes close to repeating Dolce's words (but less poetically, one might add) in the *Angelica innamorata* (1550): 'otterrà d'esser, per grazia del cielo, / il flagello dei principi tremendo' (through the grace of heaven he will become the tremendous scourge of princes; XXXII, 109).

Referring to 'la navicella del mio basso ingegno' (the little boat of my low wit; cf. *Purg.* I, 2), Dolce returns to his story, but the battle scenes are of short duration, in contrast to the later *Prime imprese*, where they predominate (given modern tastes perhaps to excess). Here, at least, Dolce prefers the material of romance:

> Io lasso Carlo, et Agrismonte ingiusto,
> E 'l ragionar di morte, e di dolore:
> E tenterò, se 'l cielo mi seconda,
> D'ordir cosa più vaga e più gioconda. (X, 55)

> [I leave Charles and unjust Agrismonte and talk of death and grief, and will try, if heaven helps me, to weave something more graceful and gay.]

The final episode of the incompleted poem is thus the attempt of Ericina, a woman who had saved Sacripante's life, to gain him as a lover. Her solution is to disguise herself as Angelica and to lie in a meadow while a spirit goes for Sacripante (X, 61–5). Falling asleep, she dreams that Sacripante finds her sleeping, that he thinks she is Angelica and kisses her a thousand times (X, 67). Instead, Ferraù arrives, also looking for Angelica, sees Ericina asleep, cannot believe his luck, and decides to gather the fruit he deserves before she awakens (X, 68–71). The references to Ericina's beauty are openly pictorial, bringing to mind Botticelli's painting of Venus and Mars: Ericina is a 'Nympha dipinta' with 'pargoletti' playing around her (X, 74). In fact, she is a beauty, Dolce tells us, illustrating his love of art, perhaps as not even Titian, Michelangelo, Raphael, or Pordenone would paint (X, 76).

Dolce promises to save her lament for the next canto, and then concludes his work abruptly, much as Boiardo does the *Innamorato*.[33] Dolce writes,

> Ben seguirei: ma sento il fiero Marte;
> C'hor sanguinoso va per la campagna.
> Veggio nel bel terreno aparte aparte;
> Che l'alpe serra, e 'l mar circonda e bagna
> Col ferro e 'l fuoco in man le genti sparte
> Quinci Francia superba, e quindi Spagna
> E minacciano pianti, offese, e morti;
> Se Dio che può, la pace non apporti. (X, 78)

[Rather would I continue, but I hear fierce Mars, going now bloody through the countryside. I see all around, in the beautiful land that the Alps enclose and the sea surrounds and bathes, people spread out with iron and fire in their hands, on one side proud France, on the other Spain, and they threaten tears, offences, and death, if God, who can, does not bring peace.]

The reference is one which should help date the composition of the poem. While Ulrich Leo's 1520 is assuredly too early (as proven by the reference to the Marchese di Pescara's death in 1525 and the fact that Dolce would have been as young as ten at the time), the poem might have been written in the late 1520s, perhaps around the time of the Battle of Pavia itself (1525), when Dolce was fifteen, or the Sack of Rome (1527), when he was seventeen, but more likely in the years immediately following that disastrous event. Though the poem was not published until 1535 (five cantos against his wishes) and 1536 (ten cantos), a date in the early 1530s is perhaps less likely for, following Charles V's imperial coronation in 1530, the wars between the French and the Spanish, while they continued (the Ducato di Milano ceases to exist, for example, in 1535), took place mostly outside of Italy.

The *Sacripante* as a whole is a highly readable and enjoyable poem.[34] Dolce wisely chose as a title character someone thoroughly recognizable from Ariosto's poem, but a figure who appears there only in fascinating glimpses, the most notable, perhaps, being his lament in the first canto of the *Furioso* (39ff.).[35] In Ariosto, we first meet Sacripante as a knight in love (cantos I and II); we see him again searching for Angelica in the Palazzo d'Atlante (canto XII); he is listed in a catalogue of pagan warriors (canto XIV), fights both with the pagans against Carlo Magno's forces and with Rodomonte for a horse (canto XXVII), and then disappears from the poem (XXXV, 56), still pursuing Angelica.

For Dolce, Sacripante is a figure primarily in love, and the poem is of the romantic or Breton type, characterized by digressions and disconnected episodes; by knights and duels, heroes and heroines, as well as victims of both sexes; by evil enchantresses; giants, including a Macatruffo, reminiscent of Pulci's Margutte (*Sacr.* VIII, 77); monsters; and, only in passing, by the more typically Carolingian battle scenes. Traditional elements are employed with originality, such as the dreams, including one reminiscent of Homer, referred to in a simile: Pandragone, unable to fight a monster from hell, feels immobile: 'Né puote alzar il braccio; ond'ei si duole / A guisa d'huom, che di se in dubbio resti / Così spesso nel sonno avenir suole; / Che mentre esser si brama al corso presti / Mancano i piedi al gran desio che vuole; / E si rimane al fin languidi e mesti' (Nor can he lift his arm, whence he grieves like a man who doubts himself, as happens often in a dream, where, when one desires to be quick to run, the feet are lacking to the great desire which wants to, and one remains finally languid and sad; X, 37).[36]

Numerous other traditional motifs are employed with artistry. Of particular note are Dolce's depiction of adulatory advisers (I, 66–7); his praise of the life of poverty, which equals freedom (I, 79–81); the chilling death of a soothsayer who reads the future but is mocked for not foretelling his own death (I, 82); moments of descriptive beauty, as that of Spring –

> Era gia la stagion, che veste 'l mondo
> Di verdi spoglie e violette e fiori;
> Quando col tempo lieto almo e giocondo
> Torna Cupido a saettar i cori;
> E col poter a null'altro secondo
> Fa l'alme accese di novelli ardori.
> Ride la terra, riden gli elementi;
> Et a Zephiro ceden tutti i venti (II, 55)

[It was already the season that dresses the world in green clothes, in violets and flowers; when, with the happy time, life-giving, and gay, Cupid returns to shoot arrows at hearts; and with power second to no one else ignites the souls with new ardours. The earth smiles, the elements laugh; and all the winds give way to the Zephyr] –

and a description of the preparations for a joust, reminiscent of Poliziano's hunting scene in the *Stanze* (I, 29–30), where 'chi' and 'già' are rhythmically repeated:

Già s'ode il suon dei bellicosi corni,
Di trombe e di diversi altri instrumenti,
E già si veggion i guerrieri adorni
D'arme fregiate d'oro e rilucenti.
V'è chi va, chi si ferma, e chi ritorni
Per la gran piazza a passi hor presti hor lenti
Questo sprona il caval, quel lo ritira,
Questo lo volge, lo percuote e gira.
  Nembo di fior da palchi e da balconi;
Che bella man di bella Donna move;
Sopra gli armati Principi e Baroni
Diversamente hor quinci, hor quindi piove. (*Sacr.* II, 65–6)

[Already one hears the sound of bellicose horns, of trumpets and other diverse instruments, and already one sees the warriors adorned with arms, shining and embellished with gold. There are some who go, some who stop, and others who return through the great square with steps now quick, now slow, this one spurs his horse, that one holds his back, this one turns it, strikes it and wheels. A cloud of flowers from platforms and balconies, tossed by the beautiful hands of beautiful women, rains in diverse fashion now from here, now from there, on the armed princes and barons.]

Reminiscences of Virgil, Dante, Petrarch, Boccaccio, Lorenzo de' Medici, Poliziano, Boiardo, and Ariosto abound, demonstrating Dolce's wide-ranging interests, with emphasis on the vernacular poets. His concept of imitation is clearly that espoused in the quattrocento by Angelo Poliziano (selecting the best from many authors rather than employing only one great model) in his polemic with Paolo Cortese's Ciceronianism. Virgil's *Aeneid* will later be both translated by Dolce (*L'Achille et l'Enea*, posthumous 1570) and rewritten by him (*L'Enea*, 1568), while most of the vernacular authors of influence on his works (the only exception in the above-mentioned list is Lorenzo) will fall under his care as editor. Here, the description of the sixteen-year-old Selannio, with whom Marphisa (Ariosto's spirited warrior maiden) falls in love, is that of a Laura *al maschile*, earmarked by the Petrarchan 'un non so che':

> Era Selannio ben formato e bello,
> Che trasse l'elmo, et a nessun s'ascose:
> Simile a l'oro è 'l biondo suo capello.
> S'aggualiano le guance a latte e a rose.
> Lunghetto è 'l viso e pien di gratia: e in quello
> Di dolce un non so che natura pose;
> Ch'a qual si voglia duro et insensato;
> Render lo potea sempre amico e grato. (III, 17)

[Selannio was well formed and handsome; he took off his helmet and hid himself from no one. His blond hair is similar to gold. His cheeks are equal to milk and roses. His face is nicely long and full of grace: and in it nature put I know not what of sweet; which could make him, to anyone hard and senseless, a welcome friend.]

To this one might compare Tasso's more virile hero, also blond, in *Rinaldo* IX, 16–17.

The geography of the *Sacripante* is that of the *Innamorato* and *Furioso*, with seas (and sea storms), forests, castles, gardens, islands, magic realms, cities, and battlefields. Some of the narrated tales bring to mind Boccaccio.[37] Others recall techniques of Boiardo and Ariosto. The old woman in canto III, who tells a story of an evil man and a monster (and calls the place 'il varco de la morte' [the passageway of death; oct. 26]), describes a garden with a treasure of gold guarded by a serpent. The literary nature of this episode is startling evident: 'Più brutto Mostro alcun non *lesse*, o vide / Occhio mortal giamai' (An uglier monster one never *read*, or human eye never saw; III, 29; emphasis mine). The Hydra killed by Alcide (Hercules) was not as terrible, we are told. The moral of the story concerns the sin of avarice: After Sacripante (set nude in the garden but aided by the evil man's daughter Ericina, who knows the arts of Zoroaster) kills the multiheaded monster, he entombs it in a ditch, 'Dicendo: costà giù restati ogn'hora, / E teco sia sepolto ogni fellone; / Ogni crudel, in cui avaritia giace, / Nemico natural sempre di pace' (saying: stay down there forever, and let be buried with you every felon, every cruel person in whom avarice lies, the natural enemy of peace; III, 67). One thinks of Boiardo's tale of avarice, where Prasildo enters nude into the Orto di Medusa to gain a branch of gold for Tisbina (*Orl. inn.* I, xii, 11–45), and of Ariosto's two tales of jealousy (*Orl. fur.* XLIII).

Melissa, who helps Sacripante against Erina, speaks in the language of Virgil's priestess, who 'speaks with Acheron in lowest Avernus,' and of Juno ('Acheronta movebo'; *Aen.* VII, 91 and 312): 'So scongiurar gli spiriti de l'inferno, / E mover tutto a le mie voglie Averno' (I know how to conjure up the spirits from hell, and move all of Avernus to my desires; *Sacr.* III, 134). The Amazonian warrior Orestilla is compared with Camilla (III, 140). Angelica, following the plot lines of Ariosto, retells her story (including Orlando's deeds), speaking to an Orlando she does not recognize (V, 12)! Other open references to Ariosto's poem abound, on the nature of 'We all know the story of how Almonte's helmet was found near a fountain by Ferraù' (see *Orl. fur.* XII), and so forth.

Dolce's poem contains other intriguing events, some possibly of influence on Tasso, such as that of the 'sconosciuto cavaliero' who is shut outside the city gates and is challenged by Orlando (VI, 53ff.). In another scene, in which Dolce praises pastoral life at length and then shows it disrupted by war (VII, 17–34), one is reminded of similar motives in Ruzzante and Tasso. Again, one duel, between Rinaldo and Orestilla (a woman disguised as a knight), breaks off when darkness falls. When Orestilla learns with whom she is duelling, she reveals her identity, lifts her helmet, and stuns Rinaldo with her great beauty (much as Clorinda stuns Tancredi). Dolce's two figures ride all night, talking sweetly, after which they decide not to renew the battle at dawn (VII, 43–59). In addition, one scene of horror, apart from the customary battle deaths, also stands out. I refer to the dungeons of an evil Castellano, in which body parts are scattered and dead bodies are found tied to living (VIII, 34–6).

The theme of war, of course, brings to the page the ravages of battle, sieges of castles, and famines (IX, 29), as well as lengthy councils (IX, 7–19). The councils, in which pros and cons are seriously argued, is a motif lacking in Ariosto, as Ulrich Leo notes (p. 20), but is found in Boiardo earlier (*Orl. inn.* II, i, 32ff. and vi, 16ff.) and later in Brusantini (*Ang. inn.* XXV, 51ff.) and Tasso (*Ger. lib.* X, 35ff.). In this respect, Dolce once again functions as an intermediary, whether specifically imitated or not.

To conclude with brevity, one might merely point out yet again the richness of the plot and characterization, the multitude of sources employed, the creative variation in imitation, the introduction of the polemic on women, and the moral depth of the poem's leitmotives as a whole. All make the *Sacripante* worthy of attention.

The *Prime imprese del conte Orlando*

As Dolce's *Sacripante* reflects the tastes of the generations contemporary with and immediately following Ariosto, his *Prime imprese del conte Orlando*, published posthumously in 1572, reflects those of post-Tridentine Italy. The emphasis is no longer on romance, but on fighting for the faith; morality is of prime importance. Giovanni Giolito's dedicatory letter of 1 April 1572 to Francesco Maria della Rovere reinforces the new tone: Philosophy, he writes, the 'vera maestra dei costumi,' is a guide through this 'oscura selva del mondo.' Her wisdom is communicated by writers in varied manner:

Onde alcuni con Enigmi, alcune con favole, altri con parlar breve, e oscuro; altri in diversi modi, hanno voluto far partecipi gli huomini di così eccellente dono. Ma i Poeti con una nuova maniera, volendo dimostrare qual debba essere un'huomo forte, e quel che se gli convenga; quale un'huomo temperato; come un Principe pietoso, e pieno di virtù, che conditioni si ricerchino a uno nato di grandi Heroi, e di stirpe Reale e (come essi dicono) de gli Dei; pigliando dall'Historie qualche huomo segnalato; e tessendo i lor Poemi nel modo, che poi ad essi pare; vengono in un medesimo tempo non solo ad insegnare (come ho detto) la qualità dell'huomo nobile, et del Principe Illustre; ma ancora a far immortali, e felici i nomi di coloro, de' quali essi scrivono.[38]

[Whence some with enigmas, some with fables, others with brief, obscure speech, and others in different ways, have wanted to make men participate in such an excellent gift. But poets, with a new manner, wanting to demonstrate how a strong man should be and what is proper to him, how a temperate man, how a merciful prince, full of virtue, what conditions one looks for in someone born of great heroes and of royal stock and (as they say) of the gods; taking from history some remarkable man, and weaving their poems in the way that then seems best to them, at the same time come not only to teach (as I said) the quality of the noble man and of the illustrious prince, but even to make immortal and happy the names of those of whom they are writing.]

Such was Dolce's aim, he adds, even though the crowd, which does not penetrate any further than the skin, cannot know it (p. iij^r). The formation of an ideal prince, then, a motif familiar (though less obviously emphasized) in Ariosto's depiction of Ruggiero, becomes the focus and the editorial justification of the work.

Dolce chose the same Orlando, as did so many others, for his chivalric romance, but he selected the hero's youth and early deeds as his subject-matter. The last book of the *Reali di Francia* provides the material for the first four cantos of Dolce's twenty-five: the love affair between Orlando's father Milone and Berta, the sister of Charlemagne, and its outcome. A summary of the poem's action might be useful at this point, given the work's obscurity.

Disguised as a woman, the beardless, twenty-year-old Milone enjoys Berta, with the result that both are captured. Condemned by the court to exile or imprisonment, they learn instead that Carlo wants them bound together to a stake and burned to death (a scene that prefigures Torquato Tasso's episode of Sofronia and Olindo). Carlo is convinced by his counsellor Namo to exercise clemency and to exile the two (canto I).

Fleeing to Italy, Milone and Berta, after many adventures and deeds of daring, take refuge in a cave, eight leagues south of Rome, in Sutri, where Berta gives birth to Orlando. Baptized as a child, Orlando, at the age of five, is left behind to take care of his mother while Milone goes to seek his fortune, joining forces in Africa in the fight against the Moors (c. II).

While Milone is acquiring fame in Africa, the young Orlando provides early indications of his spirit, seeming, at the age of ten, to be a Samson in strength; once, for example, he fights and kills a bear with his hands alone (c. III). When Charlemagne visits Sutri, Orlando, driven by hunger, steals some food from a courtier who had taken too much from the emperor's table. Recognized by Charlemagne, the emperor and his sister are reconciled, after which Berta and Orlando are accepted into the court (c. IV).

In the following cantos, Dolce masterfully interweaves the stories of Milone's adventures with those of his son Orlando. Guarnieri, the brother of Agolante, king of Africa, whose father was killed by Charlemagne in one of the wars in Spain, invades Italy. Against him, Charlemagne sends Milone, recalled from his exile. Guarnieri is conquered and killed. Agolante, at this, puts together a formidable army in an attempt to avenge both his father and his brother, first sending a spy, Sobrino, to Italy (c. V). Against the advice of Sobrino, who has been impressed by the Christian warrior Ruggero in Rome and the strength of the Christians in Paris, Agolante attacks, sending his sister Galaciella and his brother Almonte ahead of him. Galaciella challenges Ruggero to a duel. Having already unhorsed Almonte three times, Ruggero defeats Galaciella and, following her baptism, marries her (c. VI–VIII).

Ruggero's evil brother Beltramo manages to kill Ruggero, but not before the hero impregnates Galaciella with twins – the Ruggero and Marfisa of

Ariosto's poem. Galaciella sees that Beltramo is condemned to death, then dies herself in childbirth. Carlo, meanwhile, marshals his troops for battle, reviewing the Paladins, who appear before him with their troops. Christians and pagans compete with each other in various cities of the realm, with miracles attesting the power of Christ (c. IX–XI). Battles continue, with the pagan Almonte demonstrating his prowess in Italy. Hearing of his successes, thirteen-year-old Orlando and Astolfo both ask to join the fight, but Carlo tricks them and has them locked in a castle for their own protection (c. XII).

Meanwhile, Orlando's father, Milone, challenges Almonte, while other knights undergo various adventures. Namo and his horse, for example, are carried off by a griffin as big as four oxen. In the battle between Christians and pagans, Almonte defeats and kills Milone (c. XIII–XIV). Almonte, in turn, meets his death at the hands of the young Orlando, who, along with Astolfo, has escaped from the tower where the two were imprisoned for their own protection (c. XV). Having saved Carlo's life, Orlando is knighted. He then turns his attention to Astolfo, who, after various fantastic adventures, has become enamoured of a sorceress, Voluttate (Voluptuousness; c. XVI–XVII). Orlando finds Astolfo, breaks the enchantment, and is cursed by the woman, who prophesizes that his love for a pagan will drive him mad (c. XVIII).

The battles between Christians and pagans continue, with various individual duels, including one between Orlando and Troiano, in which the pagan is defeated. With this, the Moors return to Africa. An unknown knight then challenges Orlando to a duel and, after fighting at length, reveals he is Orlando's cousin, Rinaldo. At a banquet honouring the two heroes, Orlando falls in love with the beautiful Alda, who reciprocates his affection but wants only what honest love should bring – matrimony (c. XIX–XX).

The following cantos present more duels and battles, each with interesting details such as the faithful dog that will not leave the grave of his master, Buoso, until forced to do so out of hunger. The dog travels to Paris, where it wags its tail before Orlando and then leads the hero back to the grave, after which the dog dies of grief (c. XXI). Bradamante also appears in these concluding cantos, looking for her brother Rinaldo and unhorsing those in her way. She explains why she is dressed in armour (she likes arms and the hunt, then one day had to protect herself from a man who tried to violate her). When she removes her helmet, out cascades her blonde hair (another scene prefiguring Tasso's more cinematographic presentation of Clorinda's golden hair streaming in the breeze after her helmet is dislodged in a duel; c. XXII).

In the poem's final three cantos, Orlando kills Donchiaro and Fieramonte, Gerardo flees to Africa, Aldabella admires Orlando in action, and, finally, the two chaste lovers are married in Paris, at which point the poem concludes (c. XXIII–XXV).

Earlier works in Italy had dealt with the events before the beginning of Boiardo's *Innamorato*, as, for example, the *Innamoramento di Meilone d'Anglante, et di Berta sorella del re Carlomagno. Ancora il nascimento d'Orlando, et le descese [genealogies] de' paladini di Franza* (published without date in Milan by Jo. Antonio da Borgo), but none with the same intent (Ferrario, vol. 2, p. 258). Each canto in Dolce's poem is preceded by an octave dedicated to the 'argomento' and by a prose 'allegoria.' The veiled meaning, on the whole, is revealed to be simplistic personification allegory and moral typology, as seen in the following two examples:

Canto I: Per *Milone*, che s'innamora di Berta; e per ottenere il fine dell'amoroso desiderio, pone da parte il rispetto del suo Signore, si comprende la forza d'Amore. Per *l'Imperatore*, che lui e la sorella condanna a morte, si dimostra un subito sdegno. Per *Namo* si appresenta un consigliere saggio e fedele.

Canto IV: Per la incoronatione di Carlo si dimostra l'ufficio di buon Pontefice, che da se medesimo si move a premiare i meriti di giusto e virtuoso Prencipe. Per la fierezza d'Orlando l'ardire e la generosità di nobilissimo Spirito.

[Canto I: For *Milone*, who falls in love with Berta, and to obtain the goal of his amourous desire puts aside the respect of his lord, one understands the strength of Love. For *the emperor*, who condemns him and his sister to death, one shows a quick disdain. For *Namo*, one presents a wise and faithful counsellor.

Canto IV: For the coronation of Charles, one shows the duty of a good pontiff, who of his own accord moves to reward the merits of a just and virtuous prince. For the fierceness of Roland, the daring and generosity of a most noble spirit.]

In canto VI, the pagan Sobrino is a 'buon vassallo,' whereas Agolante represents 'la temerità,' and his son Almonte 'il soverchio ardire' (excessive daring). In the following canto, Almonte incarnates 'l'alterezza e l'ostinatione' (haughtiness and obstination). Finally, in canto XIII, as if tired of the moralizing, Dolce writes: 'Per l'abattimento di Balante con

Carbone, si dimostra, che la ragione molte volte è male da gli avenimenti giudicata. *Il resto serve per adornamento'* (For the beating down of Balante with Carbone, one shows that reason many times is badly judged by events. *The rest serves for decoration*; my emphasis).

Unfortunately the embellishments of the *Prime imprese*'s twenty-five cantos are less intriguing, the action more monotonous, than in the *Sacripante*.[39] The element of love, however, is not entirely lacking. In fact, many of the *Sacripante*'s themes reappear in the *Prime imprese*, in particular those of appetite versus reason, and of error versus duty and honour. The thematic contrasts of order and disorder and of *virtù* and *furor* acquire greater significance in the later work, as does the design of Divine Providence seen in contrast with the fickleness of fortune.

Like Ariosto, Dolce begins most cantos with authorial insights, ranging from commonsense advice to the reader, and proverbial wisdom, to philosophical moralizations, personal judgments, and perplexed questions concerning existential events. In canto II, Dolce comments on love's inestimable bitterness, which far surpasses its sweetness, adding:

> Et una breve e inutile bellezza
> Cotanto vince in noi l'alma ragione,
> Che per seguir un vano e folle errore
> Poniam da canto il debito e l'honore. (II, 1)

> [And a brief and useless beauty so much conquers in us life-giving reason that in order to follow an empty and foolish error we put aside duty and honour.]

Milone, though a prudent and wise cavalier, falls into error: 'Ma 'l cieco senso adombrò il chiaro raggio, / Che metter suole a van desiri il freno: / Il raggio, onde s'alluma l'intelletto' (But blind sensation darkened the clear ray that usually puts a restraint on empty desires: the ray whence the intellect enlightens itself; II, 2). The inscrutability of Divine Providence and mankind's failure to change heaven's plans are emphasized in the introductions to cantos V and XIV, whereas VI descends to the practical level of mundane advice: 'Bisogna molto ben pensarvi sopra / Prima, che l'huomo alcuna impresa prenda' (Before any man undertakes a deed, he should think a lot about it; VI, 1).

In canto VII, Dolce tells us that 'virtù' conquers 'furor,' because the former employs wit and shrewdness, and then in canto IX he asks the rhetorical question of how a good and a bad son can be born of the same parents – his example 'Beltramo crudele, e Rugger pio' (IX, 1). Elsewhere, he criticizes treason (X) and notes that greatness cannot be restrained (XV), that pride causes much evil (XVI), that temerity leads to grief (XVII), and that the truth offends princes, therefore (as Guicciardini realized), forcing one to lie (XIX). The theme of fortune, always unstable but especially so in war, as developed in canto XIII, recalls the first octave of Book I, canto xvi, of the *Orlando innamorato*, one of Boiardo's few examples of a moral beginning.[40] In all, though often simplistic, these introductions do reveal a greater moral seriousness, which will be typical also of Tasso.[41]

One of the perplexing features of the *Prime imprese* concerns its composition. While to my knowledge none of the readers of the poem has commented on this feature, this reader was struck by the changes in tone, style, and themes to be found between cantos I–IV, V–XXI, and XXII–XXV, seemingly not all attributable to the change in sources.[42] Cantos I–IV and XXII–XXV seem the later written, containing themes and verbal structures which also appear in Dolce's tragedy *Marianna*, staged in Venice in 1565.[43]

Cantos I–IV also contain numerous references to God's Providence, typical of the Counter-Reformation climate, whereas the middle cantos refer often to Fortune. In canto VII, for example, when Almonte tries to convince Ruggero to leave Christ for Mohammed, the Christian hero refuses to yield: 'Ma sappi, che più volte il fin riesce / Diverso assai da quel, ch'era il pensiero: / E la fortuna anco sovente mesce / Con il dolce l'amar, co 'l bianco il nero' (But know that many times the end turns out very different from what one thought, and fortune, too, often mixes bitter with sweet, black with white; VII, 25).[44] The first four cantos have a more fluid style and are more elegant than the middle group. No attempt is made to correct reduplicated material which shows up in cantos V–XXI, sometimes resulting in open contradictions with what is said in cantos I–IV, just as canto XXII summarizes the action of earlier cantos (oct. 8–11).[45] The first four cantos contain a straight narrative flow (such as Tasso will use for the *Liberata*), in effect not a trait of immaturity, but a stylistic conquest, following the awkward breaks and temporal juxtapositions of the *Sacripante* and the middle part of the *Prime imprese*, both of which attempt to imitate Ariosto's inimitable technique. Canto V, after quickly concluding the Milone–Berta–Orlando story (octs. 2–4), begins with an octave reminiscent of Ariosto's opening stanza, and was thus perhaps originally the first book of a youthful work to which the poet later added four cantos of prefatory material and four of conclusion.[46]

The final group, cantos XXII–XXV, contains material not found in the *Aspramonte* and presents us for the first time with Bradamante, just as Rinaldo was only introduced in canto XX. Again, some of the speeches in the concluding section recall similar sections of the *Marianna*, in particular Donchiaro's speech to Gerardo, in which he warns him, much as Soemo warns Herod, that anger causes blindness and may lead to death (*Prime imprese* XXII, 43).

Whatever the case, the *Prime imprese* is a rich work, containing too much to comment on at length. Several elements, however, might be noted, among which the fact that the moral conflicts are more complicated when compared with those of the *Sacripante*. The external conflict between pagans and Christians is a conflict between *virtù* and *furor*. The internal conflict in the hearts and minds of the Christians is one between *ragione* and *volere*. Knights, like Ruggero, are just as concerned with conquering themselves as they are with defeating the enemy (see, for example, VIII, 50).

The theme of avarice, lamented in the *Sacripante*, returns as obloquy directed against the rich and as sympathy for the poor. In canto II, Dolce comments that

> Cosa non è più riputata vile
> Dal mondo rio, che l'humil povertate:
> Sia pur l'huomo di sangue alto e gentile,
> E di virtute adorno e di bontate;
> Il privato e 'l signor con pari stile
> Chiudon le porte a lei di caritate:
> Così 'l povero ogn'un discaccia e fugge,
> E men si move, quando ei più si strugge. (II, 14)

[Nothing is reputed more vile by the evil world than humble poverty: even though the man be of lofty and noble blood, and adorned with virtue and goodness; the commoner and the lord, in similar style, close the doors of charity to her: thus everyone chases off and flees from the poor man, and one does less, when he pines away more.]

He seems to manifest a greater awareness of the lower classes, including the *Romei*, with whom Milone and Berta are compared in their wanderings (II, 43).

As is true of certain elements of the *Sacripante*, the *Prime imprese* contain much that prefigures the world of Tasso's *Gerusalemme liberata*. By way of example, allow me to refer to the representation of duels and battles. Tasso, in the first discourse of his *Discorsi dell'arte poetica* (written *ca* 1564, but published in 1587) speaks of the material of a heroic poem, which must be developed so as to fulfil five criteria, among them 'la qualità dei tempi accomodati,' that is, that one must strive to transfer aspects of the present to the past. The duels, for example, such as that of Argante and Tancredi (*Lib.* VI, 42) or of Rinaldo and Mambriano in Tasso's youthful *Rinaldo* (XII, 48–68), are conducted according to the laws of fencing and the chivalric code, while the battles, such as the assault on Jerusalem (*Lib.* XI, 31), are modelled, with strategic precision, on military treatises.

In the *Prime imprese*, when Milone sees the disorganized formation not only of the enemy, but also of the troops of Balante (for whom he is serving as a mercenary), he reproves his lord for it, explaining that order is the first attribute of every *virtù* and that without it all valour in war is wasted:

> L'ordine, Signor mio, dice; che suole
> Esser d'ogni virtù primo ornamento,
> Come quel, che le tenebre dal Sole
> Divise, e diede luogo a ogni elemento:
> La guerra così in lei ricerca e vuole,
> Che senza quello ogni valore è spento.
> Questo ne la medesima regione
> Serbò Annibal contro il Gran Scipione. (III, 5)

[They say, my lord, that order is accustomed to be the first ornament of every virtue, like that which divided the darkness from the sun and gave a place to every element: war is thus sought and desired in order, since without that every valour is extinguished. Hannibal, in the same region, preserved this [order] against the great Scipio.]

Balante, embarrassed, recognizes the good advice and organizes his men using *ragione* (III, 7), whence they prevail over the *furor* of the enemy. Likewise, in canto V, when Guarnieri, inflamed by 'giovenil furore,' wishes to attack Carlo's forces immediately, his advisers restrain him: 'Però, che con ingegno e valore / Da lui poteva la vittoria haversi, / ... / Onde Guarnieri con ragione affrena / La furia' (Since he could have the victory with wit and valour ... whence Guarnieri restrained his fury with reason; V, 19), dividing his troops into four groups, while Milone apportions his into three.

Later, when the pagan hero Troiano and the Christian Donchiaro duel, the technique is emphasized. Troiano believes he is fighting Orlando:

> Onde tutto ripien di sdegno e d'ira
> Con lui si acconcia a la battaglia horrenda,
> E quando tagli, e quando punte tira.
> E mostra, quanto di militia intenda.
> Donchiaro hor ne va innanzi, hor si ritira,
> Accio c'hor si schermisca, hor si difenda. (XIX, 38)

[Whence full of disdain and anger, he prepares himself for the horrendous battle, both when he cuts and when he thrusts. And he shows how much he understands of military things. Donchiaro now goes towards him, now withdraws, so that now he evades, now defends himself.]

Tasso, in similar fashion, will write, 'or gira intorno, or cresce inanzi, or cede, / or qui ferire accenna e poscia altrove' (now he turns around, now moves forward, now gives way, or feigns to wound here and then elsewhere; *Lib*. VI, 42).[47]

Dolce's pagan heroine Galaciella is a progenitor of Tasso's Clorinda, without the tragic fate.[48] In the *Prime imprese*, Galaciella wishes to challenge Ruggero (the father of Ariosto's hero; VI, 30), but he falls in love with her when he sees her without her helmet on: 'E, perchè ancor tenea scoperto il viso, / Un'angiol lo stimò di Paradiso' (And, because she still kept her face uncovered, he considered her an angel of paradise; VII, 5). The expression and rhyme are traditional, and the vision is much less cinematographic, as mentioned above, than Tasso's.[49] Earlier, Dolce had employed the same expression and rhyme in presenting Carlo's sister Berta – 'E, dove ella volgeva il chiaro viso, / Parea, ch'ivi si aprisse il Paradiso' (And, where she turned her bright face, it seemed that a paradise was opening there; I, 17), bringing to mind not only Dante (*Par*. XV, 34–6), Petrarch ('le crespe chiome d'or puro lucente / e 'l lampeggiar de l'angelico riso / che solean fare in terra un paradiso' [the waving hair of pure, shining gold and the flash of the angelic smile that used to make a paradise on earth; *Canz*. CCXCII, 5–7]), and Chiaro Davanzati ('Di tanto son gioioso / c'ho visto lo suo viso, / la bocca e 'l dolze riso / e 'l parlare amoroso, / che d'altro paradiso / non saría mai voglioso' [I am so joyful of this, having seen her face, mouth, her sweet smile, and her amourous speech, that I would never be desirous of any other paradise; cited in Tommaso Casini, *La vita nuova di Dante Alighieri*, p. 91]), but also the writers of epic and chivalric romance preceding Dolce, among them Pulci (*Morgante* XVI, 12), Poliziano ('Lampeggiò d'un sì dolce e vago riso / ... /

che ben parve s'aprisse un paradiso,' [She flashed such a sweet and lovely smile that truly it seemed a paradise was opening; *Stanze* I, 50]), and Ariosto ('quel soave riso / ch'apre a sua posta in terra un paradiso,' [that soft smile that opens at will a paradise on earth; VII, 13]).[50] The rhyming of *viso*, *riso*, and *paradiso*, of course, was so common that Pulci had already mocked it in the *Morgante*, in his description of Antea, who has 'certi risi / ... / da far spalancar sei paradisi' (certain smiles that would burst open six paradises; XV, 102).[51]

Other features of interest in the *Prime imprese* include the use of angels in disguise, familiar in Trissino (where, however, they have pagan names).[52] In Dolce, a hermit who warns Orlando of Carlo's precarious state is revealed to be from heaven: 'E via disparve al fin di quella voce / Lieto tornando a la celeste chiostra. / Era angel questo' (And at the end of that speech he slipped away, returning happy to the celestial cloister. This was an angel; XV, 43). Tasso's Gabriele, while more fully and poetically detailed, also descends in disguise to Goffredo (*Lib.* I, 13). Dolce's description of Rome's effect on the pagan spy Sobrino (VI, 14), the statement of faith of Uggero il Danese (XI, 39), the prayer put in the mouth of a Parisian bishop (XI, 50–1), Carlo's speech on justice to Astolfo and Orlando as he dubs them knights (XVI, 24–5) are all effectively done.

Finally, the moralism that prevails throughout the poem does not prevent such exchanges as that between the young Astolfo (imprisoned with Orlando for their own protection) and one of his guards: 'Anche noi da la carne stimolati / Siam, come stimolato è ciascheduno. / Io per me amico mio, per dirlo schietto, / Bramo d'haver una fanciulla in letto' (We, too, are stimulated by the flesh, as each one is stimulated. I for myself, my friend, to speak frankly, long to have a maiden in bed; XV, 12). When the guard replies that lust offends and that it is more bitter than delightful (XV, 14–15), Astolfo protests that those are philosopher's reasons and notions proclaimed in church by devout people:

Talhor bisogna consolar la mente,
Né si trovan miglior consolationi
Cred'io qui in terra, u siam poco beati,
Che gustar quel piacer per cui siam nati. (XV, 16)

[Sometimes it is necessary to console the mind, nor are better consolations found here on earth, I believe, where we are little blessed, than tasting that pleasure for which we are born.]

His speech, we soon learn however, was feigned, a guise to aid the youths' escape. Neverthless, later in the poem, as mentioned in the summary above, Astolfo becomes the 'folle amante' of a *Fata* named Voluttate who undresses before him, telling him to do as he wishes (XVII, 42–3):

> Hor bene il giovenetto agghiaccia e suda,
> E si sente nel cor piaga mortale.
> E tutte alhor alhor si spoglia l'arme,
> Senza aspettar, ch'alcun ne lo disarme.
>   Ma torniamo a Rugger ... (XVII, 44–5)

[Now truly the youth freezes and sweats, and feels in his heart a mortal wound. And right then he strips off all his armour, without waiting for someone to disarm him. But let's return to Ruggero.]

Having left us in suspense, Dolce takes up the episode only at the moment of Orlando's arrival to save his cousin, who he finds embracing the *Fata* 'Tal che l'aere tra lor non saria entrato' (such that air couldn't get in between them; XVIII, 25). Orlando chastizes Astolfo, but his deed, Orlando is told, will not go unavenged. The *Fata*, in anger, prophesizes to Orlando that 'sì com'hora odi le Donne affatto, / Così ancor per amor d'una Pagana / Ne l'avenir diverrai folle e matto' (just as you now absolutely hate women, so in the future you will become foolish and mad for love of a pagan woman; XVIII, 31). But Dolce's work of course ends, as one might expect, not with an Orlando in pursuit of a 'bellezza rara' (Ariosto, *Orl. fur.* I, 8) but rather (in imitation of Orlando's uncle Carlo who marries Gallerana to begin the poem's action [I, 17]), with the marriage of the chaste hero to his beloved Aldabella (XXV, 25), just as Tasso's contemporary *Rinaldo* ends with his hero's marriage to Clarice (XII, 87ff.). For Dolce, social order (the legitimization of passion through marriage and restraint) is an ideal which fittingly crowns the youthful deeds of Orlando 'il saggio.'[53]

3

'I Costumi d'Hoggidì': Dolce and the *Commedia* of the Cinquecento

Dolce as *Commediografo*

Among the egregious writers of comedy cited by Tommaso Garzoni in his *Piazza universale di tutte le professioni del mondo* (1585), one finds, in the company of such writers as Ariosto, Ercole Bentivoglio, Alessandro Piccolomini, and Bernardino Pino, the name of our author (p. 547).[1] Though known today primarily for his earliest comedy, *Il ragazzo*, Dolce, in his own time, found his works acclaimed and performed with some success. And, as was true also for his tragedies, his fame as a writer of comedies was not limited to Italy. In France, to cite merely one example, Pierre de Larivey, the most important precursor of Molière, both translated him and cited him as a model for French comedians.[2]

Dolce's five comedies were written over the course of a decade from 1541, when *Il ragazzo* was first published,[3] to 1551, the date of *Il ruffiano*'s dedication. In addition to these two works, we have two plays in verse, *Il capitano* and *Il marito* of 1545, and one in prose, *La Fabritia* of 1549.[4]

Marvin Herrick notes, somewhat inaccurately, that 'all of these were "new" in the sense that they used old material in new ways.'[5] What Herrick ignores is that the newness is not necessarily attributable to Dolce. In fact, the prologue of *Il ruffiano* cited by Herrick, where Dolce attests the novelty of his play, is a direct translation of Dolce's source – the *Piovana* of Ruzzante.[6] Here is how Herrick presents the case:

In the prologue to *Il ruffiano* ('The Pimp'), the author called his work a new comedy 'made of old clothes,' and added, 'Old things are better than new if, however, they have not become stale from too much age.' Therefore, he said, 'You will see our comedy dressed in the ancient habit and redesigned in modern form.'

He assured his audience that it would never be offended by any outlandish terms, for he did not wish to depart from the 'lawful and common Italian speech.' (pp. 112–13)

In Ruzzante, only the final expression is different. For the Paduan artist, the defence is not of the Italian vernacular but of the 'lengua pavana grossa,' used 'per no strafare la snaturalitè' (rough Paduan tongue ... [used] in order not to exceed naturalness).[7] For this play, at least, Dolce's 'newness' is only that of having translated the play from Paduan dialect to Italian.

While Dolce almost always transforms his sources, in this case he has justifiably been accused of plagiarism. Unlike both *Il capitano*, a *rifacimento* of Plautus's *Miles gloriosus*, and *Il marito*, a *rifacimento* of the *Amphitruo*, which fall within the scope of what the Renaissance considered acceptable imitation (and thus originality), *Il ruffiano* is simply an unacknowledged translation of *La piovana*, which was published four years earlier, in 1548, but probably written before 1533, when Ruzzante first requested publication rights from the Doge and the Senate of Venice.[8]

Apart from *Il ruffiano*, then, we have two original plays and two *rifacimenti*. The latter works, even though based on Plautus, are not without original touches. Of *Il marito*, derived from the *Amphitryon*, Herrick says 'it is a free treatment of the ancient model' (p. 115). And *Il capitano*, based on the *Miles gloriosus*, 'is an excellent modernization of the ancient mercenary and therefore important in the development of the Renaissance braggart soldier,' though 'scarcely original' (p. 115). What Louise George Clubb says about erudite or regular comedy in general can also be said about Dolce in particular; that is, though the Italian playwrights thought they were continuing a classical tradition 'by doing to the Romans what they conceived the Romans to have done to the Greeks,' in reality, through their 'addition of *novelle* situations and vignettes of contemporary life ... [they] moved much further away from Terence and Plautus than even the latter had done from Attic New Comedy' (*Italian Plays*, p. xvi).

Dolce's ideas on imitation and originality can be found in the prologue to *La Fabritia*, where they are expressed by two youths in the context of the *querelle* between ancient and modern. Interestingly, Dolce presents both sides of the issue by means of the two interlocutors. Each youth speaks in turn, without interruption, presenting a different point of view and allowing the audience to select which they think more fitting. The technique is ingenious, although one can tell where Dolce's sympathies lie, since the second youth speaks twice as long as the first.

The first of the two *fanciulli* notes that the comedy is 'tutta nuova,' but goes on to add that this in itself is no cause for merit. While the author claims to have worked hard to make it new and pleasing, he recognizes that modern works cannot approach the perfection of the ancient. In fact, he seems to feel that everything has already been said ('niuna cosa si può dire, che da loro non sia stata detta prima' [p.3^v]. Thus, even the Latin writers of comedies did not dare to use their wits in writing new plays, but instead took them all from the Greeks.[9] While few comic poets have pleased all ages, given the difficulty of the task, one finds (he claims) an infinite number of modern writers who presume to have bettered the ancients the more dissimilar and far off their works are from the ancient ('tanto più le lor ciance stimano migliori, quanto più sono dissimili et lontane da quelle antiche'). This may please the crowd, but learned men know better.

Having set the stage by leaning towards the side of learned imitation rather than facile novelty, the author (according to the first youth) is constrained to admit that he expects no praise from men of judgment. Nevertheless, he promises his audience laughter and delight. After announcing the play's title, the youth is about to leave, when he sees that his companion wishes to speak in response: 'Listen to him,' he says, 'and judge which of the two of us has spoken better' ('Ascoltatelo e giudicare chi di noi due havrà detto meglio'; p. 3^r).

Dolce now turns the table by having the second youth protest that new times require new customs. As the boy notes, the ancient Romans dressed differently; they ate only once a day; their women drank no wine – customs very different from those of the present (p. 4^v). The same can be said of comedies, which have changed since antiquity:

Essi le recitavano cantando, et la musica era accompagnata da sonatori. Hora i recitanti ragionano; et canti nè suoni non adoperano: et forse con più ragione: perchè non è verisimile che chi favella di quello, che gli occorre; o che si sdegni, o che si allegri, o che si lamenti, ciò faccia cantando. (pp. 4^{v-r})

[They used to recite them singing, and the music was accompanied by players [of instruments]. Now the performers speak; they adopt neither singing nor sounds [of musical instruments]: and perhaps with more reason, since it is not verisimilar that someone who speaks about what happened to him or who gets angry or happy or laments should do so by singing.]

In the same fashion, he continues, moderns have decided that the ancient forms of footwear (the sandal and the cothurnus) are not necessary for the success of either comedy or tragedy. And while most ancient comedies were written in verse, most moderns use prose.

The Latins who imitated the Greeks, rather than inventing their own works, do not thereby merit a greater glory. Just as the intellect of moderns has surpassed the ancients in many things, so may the writer of comedies. The model to follow is that of the great contemporary explorers and circumnavigators of the world. The ancients believed one should not sail beyond the columns of Hercules, 'et pure si sono trovati nuovi paesi, et nuovi popoli: et tale vi fu, che ci navigò tanto avanti in verso la Tramontana di là, che poi ritornò dall'altra parte del mondo' (and yet new lands have been found and new peoples; and someone navigated so far out there that he later returned from the other side of the world) (p. 4^r). This voyage was possible only with a compass, a modern invention. Thus, he who invents his own comic material deserves greater praise than someone who takes his subject from others.

Not content to abandon the debate at this point, the speaker goes on to enumerate other parallels where the new is to be preferred to the old,[10] and concludes the argument by alleging that comedies should not be judged according to the scales of the severe and fastidious Aristotle. The criticism is directed specifically at those who are concerned only with details. As most creative writers would agree, it is easier to criticize something than to create it ('O quanto è più facile il riprendere una cosa, che il farla').

With this proviso then – namely, that Dolce's work varies from unacknowledged translation to modernization of ancient works to original stories imbued with traditional features – one can return to Herrick: 'Dolce believed in making use of the ancients but also in bringing ancient material up to date. He respected the classical dramaturgy and more often than not followed it, but he was a Modern.' Dolce did not follow the Aristotelian dictum 'that comedy should be a true story or a history. "Comedy," says the prologue to *Il marito*, "is a merry poem and not a history, invented by the first wise artificers solely as a pattern of life and order. Whence one can say that the stage is a clear mirror in which everyone can perceive what man should follow and what he should flee along this uncertain and wretched path"' (p. 113).

Herrick goes on to note that, while Dolce echoes the Ciceronian definition of comedy as transmitted by Donatus, 'he did not believe that its chief function was moralizing. In the prologue to *Fabritia*, he promised his audience that if it has come "to laugh and to delight the ears, no one will leave without delight and without laughter; and if he should have no other reason to laugh, he may at least laugh at the folly that has been introduced'' ' (p. 113). But one needs to add, in response to Herrick, that, while moralization is not the *chief* function of comedy, it is not entirely lacking from Dolce's comic poetics. The prologue to *Il marito* makes that quite clear when the author affirms that comedy was first written as an 'esempio de la vita e regola' (example and rule of life), so that in this uncertain and wretched path one would know what to follow and what to flee ('Quello, che in questa via incerta et misera / Per l'huom seguir si debba, e quel che fuggere'; p. 3^v). In fact, the author's conclusion is that, if the spectators will sit silently for two hours, they will receive from the play both delight *and* utility.

Aside from the source of the plots and the function of comedy, Dolce was also interested in the genre's correct form; that is, whether or not one should write in prose or in poetry. His own doubts and consequent experimentations mirror the period's uncertainty. After starting in prose with *Il ragazzo*, Dolce, influenced in part by the practice of Plautus and Terence, switched to verse for *Il capitano* and *Il marito*, where he used unrhymed *sdruccioli* under Ariosto's influence.[11] In the prologue to *Il marito*, Dolce notes that

> Poi, che'l mondo ha cangiato aspetto, et vedesi
> Ogni dì variar costumi, et huomini,
> E leggi, e Signorie, e linguaggi, et habiti;
> Maraviglia non è, se le Comedie
> Si fan diversamente al nostro secolo,
> Qual con voci legate, e qual con libere.[12]

> [Since the world has changed its appearance, and one sees customs, men, laws, lordships, languages, and habits change every day, it's no marvel if comedies are made differently in our century, some in verse and some in prose.]

He himself has used verse, he says, following both the author of *I suppositi* (Ariosto) and 'the most worthy, honoured, ancient comedians,' because comedy is a festive poem and not history.[13] Those who like verses should find the comic verse pleasing, since it is 'sweet and easy,' while those who like prose will find it so similar to prose that they will not be able to tell the difference ('Et chi vago è di prosa, a prosa simile / Lo troverà, di modo, che disciogliere / Non sapra, s'ella è prosa, o verso; i numeri / Udendo in lor, che ad ambedue si convengono'; p. 3^v). Despite his mastery of this difficult verse form, where he strove, above all, for naturalness, he returned to prose for *La Fabritia* and *Il ruffiano*.

Dolce's *Rifacimenti*: *Il capitano*, *Il marito*, and *Il ruffiano*

Dolce's comedies have undergone various readings, the most common focusing on the intertextual features – his sources, borrowings, and plagiarisms. As usual for Dolce, intertextuality is a given, since his works are often a rewriting of an earlier text or texts. Irrespective of the genre in which he is working, most of his plots, though not all, derive from what is already known and consist merely of a skilful reworking. In Dolce's case, a text is not only a product of an individual, at a given point in history, writing in a given form of discourse, but also a reworking of another author, writing quite often at an earlier time, in a similar form, but basing his work, in turn, on other antecedents. Each text, particularly the theatrical, has a long genealogy.

The technique was practised by most playwrights. To cite merely one example, that of Ruzzante's *La piovana*, since this is one of the plays Dolce is accused of robbing in turn, here is what the author has to say about his play, as recited by Garbinello in the prologue:

Oh men of merit, o all you good men, fear not and be silent, for you will hear a beautiful, new story. And I myself assure you that it's new, because not much time has passed since it was made, and after it was made, it was shut up in a desk, and has never come forth except for now. It's true that it was made of old wood, but you ought to be happier over that, since you'll be surer of its goodness ... And if it seems you've heard this rigamarole before, don't be surprised, because one can't be sure that it hasn't already been done. ... Nor has it happened that anyone has robbed anyone else, as someone might think – that this, too, was stolen. We wouldn't show it to so many if it was; we'd keep it hidden. If one were to find in an old chest one of those outfits they used to wear in ancient times, and the cloth was good but the style was out of date; if one were to make out of the cloth doublets, jackets, and corsets for the living, and leave the style to the dead, would this be robbing? I don't think so. It would be saving something for the living, without taking anything away from the dead, because the style would be for the dead and the cloth for the living, and in this way nothing would be lacking, and if nothing is lacking, nothing was stolen.[14]

Dolce, like most of his contemporaries, would have agreed. In translating the *Piovana*, he was, in effect, dressing it in new clothes. As the commonplace of the time would have it: Go and see if anything is lacking in ancient books, because of our theft.

The generic nature of Dolce's comedies can be seen in the titles – *Il ragazzo, Il capitano, Il marito, La Fabritia* (the only one named after a particular individual), and *Il ruffiano*. In his reliance on stock types, he falls in line with most playwrights of the time, who take Plautus and Terence as models. Probably the best of the three adaptations is the *Capitano*, completed by February 1545, when Dolce wrote to his friend Paolo Crivello announcing that he had already composed the work and was about to finish the *Marito* (Salza, p. 78).[15]

The novelty of Dolce's version of Plautus's *Miles gloriosus* must have struck the spectators, since Dolce refers not only to contemporary manners, but also to events and other figures of his time, as well as to literary works of medieval and earlier Renaissance writers. In addition, he sets the play in Ragusa (modern-day Dubrovnik) and changes the names of all the characters. The captain is called Torquato, the young lovers Fabio and Fulvia, both names common in the theatre of the time.[16] While the plot and scenes are translated literally from Plautus, Dolce occasionally enlarges on the dialogue and modernizes the captain's boasting, at times rendering in more mundane fashion Plautus's exaggerations, as when Dolce transforms the elephant (whose leg was fractured by Pyrgopolynices) into a horse, at times improving on the original, as in the same description, where Torquato's fist would have penetrated the horse, if his conscience had not held him back, and come out the far side harder and more solid than metal, rock, or anvil (I, 1; p. 3^r).[17] Having earlier claimed that his sword is more famous than Durindana, Torquato boasts that, when Roland's bones were discovered not long ago in France and were compared in height to him, the bones were like Margutte to Morgante (p. 4^r). His visage could be used by Michelangelo and Titian in their paintings (p. 5^v), and so forth.

One of the points to be made in discussing Dolce's reworkings of classical comedy is that, in the Renaissance, comedy, as Louise George Clubb has pointed out, is an original genre precisely because it is based on imitation.[18] Dolce and the other *commediografi* imitated the classics because to do so was to do something original. They saw themselves as not only the competitors of Plautus and Terence, but their heirs. Through *imitatio*, one arrives at universal principles, and does so in order to surpass the ancients. To attempt to find originality solely in regionalism – Dolce as a Venetian writer, Grazzini as Florentine, Della Porta as Neapolitan – or in the *contaminatio* of classical form with a novelistic or Boccaccian, and thus Italian, plot is to deny that Dolce, Grazzini, and Della Porta all wrote similar comedies (when we know they did) and to affirm that classicism entails something mechanical, sterile, and un-Italian (when we know, instead, that it is the essence of the Renaissance). None of which is meant to deny the significance of the regional features of an author like Dolce, nor the intriguing examples of simple and complex *contaminatio* found in cinquecento comedy. The aim, rather, is to attest the equal significance, especially in the period itself, of works that today are denigrated (and usually not read) simply because they are reworkings of the old.

Dolce's contemporaries would surely have recognized the significance and utility of his *rifacimenti*, especially for a non-erudite audience, for, as Giovanmaria Cecchi noted in the prologue of his *Incantesimi* (derived itself from the *Mostellaria*), Plautus 'oggidì (quantunque lacero, pur parlando latino) non può in pubblico uscire a viso scoperto, che intendere a mala pena lo saprè 'l quinto degli uomini; però va mascherato in questa favola e in quella, che per nuova oggi si recita' (nowadays, however lacerated, even speaking Latin, cannot go out in public with his face visible, since barely a fifth of men would be able to understand him; therefore he goes masked in this story or in that, which are recited today as new; cited in Salza, p. 21).[19] The achievement of the *rifacimenti*, then, was this: old plot elements and stock characters modernized with the customs of the time. These comedies, 'new from old cloth,' as Anton Francesco Grazzini expressed it in the prologue to *La gelosia*, correspond to the modern remake of an old movie, the retelling of an ancient story, which never fails to delight.

Salza notes that, while most of the *commedia* of the cinquecento is called *erudita* ('quasi volendo affermare che essa è un frutto non spontaneo ma riflesso, derivato dalla cultura classica' [almost as if to affirm that this is a non-spontaneous work of deliberation, derived from classical culture]), Hillebrand pointed out that these works, especially those of Ariosto and Aretino, were important for the study of the customs of the time (p. 15). The immorality of these comedies, which is not just incidental as in Aristophanes, but has become the main element, simply illustrates the life of the times. They are a reflection of a century that delighted in scandal, much like our own does. Dolce, attentive as always to his public, does not disappoint them.

There were authors, of course, who lamented this state of affairs, voicing criticisms of the sort against which Dolce was required to defend himself. In Benedetto Varchi's words:

Le più disoneste e le più inutili, anzi dannose composizioni che siano oggi nella lingua nostra sono le commedie: perciò che pochissime sono quelle ... le quali non facciano non solo vergonare le donne, ma arrossire gli uomini non del tutto immodesti. (Dedication of the *Suocera* to Cosimo de' Medici, cited in Salza, p. 16)

[The most immoral and useless, rather damaging, compositions that exist in our language today are comedies, since there are few of them that do not not only shame women, but make men who are not entirely immodest blush.]

Or as Sperone Speroni wrote:

La comedia è una scola di tutto il populo, ove se il padre della famiglia va a conoscere qual sia il male, il servo anch'egli, allo 'ncontro il parasito, et la meretrice impara a farlo eccellentemente, et il figliuolo assai volte, mentre egli guarda et ascolta, può imparare d'innamorarsi; et se io già dissi, che nelle risa della comedia riposa l'animo affaticato, et che gli è utile un tal riposo; torno anche a dirlo, et ridico, che altro è ridere in un teatro una, o due hore, et altro è scrivere per far ridere a bello studio; quello è ozio, et necessità; questo è fatica indecora, et incivile operatione. (*Apologia dei dialoghi nei dialoghi di Sperone Speroni* [Venice: Roberto Mejetti, 1596], p. 568)

Comedy is a school for all the people, where even though the father of a family goes to learn the nature of evil, and the servant, too, a parasite and a prostitute, on the contrary, learn to do their work excellently, and many times the son, while he watches and listens, can learn to fall in love; and even though I already said that in the laughter of comedy the tired mind finds relaxation and that such rest is useful, I come back to say and I repeat that it is one thing to laugh in a theatre for one or two hours and another thing to write in order to make people laugh intentionally. The former is ease and a necessity; the latter is an indecorous effort and an uncivil act.

As Salza notes, in the face of criticism by moralists like Speroni, Dolce excused his frequent use of salacious expressions by saying 'che a voler bene esprimer i costumi d'hoggidì, bisognerebbe, che le parole et gli atti interi fossero lascivia' (that if one wanted to express well the customs of today, one would have to use words and depict deeds that embodied lasciviousness; prologue of *Il ragazzo*). As a writer in need of a public, as an entertainer, Dolce did not hesitate throughout his comedies to show his public what they were and to give them what they wanted.

Il ragazzo

The most fortunate of Dolce's comedies is undoubtedly his first, *Il ragazzo*, published in 1541. This is a delightful play, truly worthy of its inclusion in the Scrittori d'Italia edition of the *Commedie del Cinquecento*, edited first by Ireneo Sanesi in 1912, and by Maria Luisa Doglio in a 1975 reprint. In addition to the various literary histories and studies of Italian theatre in which Dolce's works are briefly mentioned, *Il ragazzo* has been analysed at greater length, first by Abd-El-Kader Salza at the turn of the century, then more recently by Maria Luisa Doglio, Giorgio Padoan, and Luige Boni Ferrini.[20]

The comedy, set in Rome, has twelve speaking characters, ranging from Messer Cesare, the *senex amans*, to the two youths in love, Flamminio and the Spagnuolo. Flamminio and his father, Messer Cesare, both love Livia, who never appears on stage, while the Spaniard loves Cesare's daughter (and Flamminio's sister), Camilla, who does. The boy of the title, Giacchetto by name, in the service of the Spagnuolo, will be discovered to be Livia's twin, after first having been disguised as a girl to trick the old man. In addition to these characters and others, we have a pedant (who has little to do but provides for much comic relief), and a parasite named Ciacco. The parasite functions as the hero of the action, his role similar to that of Ligurio in Machiavelli's *La mandragola*, while the heroes of the romance, the Spaniard and Flamminio, take a back seat. Among the important plot points is the fact that Messer Cesare's daughter, Camilla, returns the Spaniard's love and will dress in Giacchetto's clothes to meet her lover (the excuse is that it will be safer on the streets at night if she comes as a boy), while Giacchetto, in girl's clothes, takes Livia's place.

Modern Critical Readings of Il Ragazzo

Salza finds the play to be filled with witty scenes and risqué ambiguities, with a plot that is quite comic, though not lacking entirely a certain moral intention. Still, the play, he says, is assuredly not one for polite society, since Dolce has a tendency to use indecent words and lingers with satisfaction and pleasure over the less honest scenes (p. 29). The playwright's excuse for this, I would respond, is presented in the prologue, where he blames the corruption of the times for what he depicts on stage. In Dolce's words: 'non pure in ogni città tuttodì si fa qualche comedia, ma anco in ogni casa. Oh! Ci sono di quelli che se le veggono fare nel proprio letto e non ne prendono alcun dispiacere' (not only is a comedy played in every city every day, but also in every house. Oh, there are those who see them done to them in their own bed and don't take any displeasure at it).[21]

In response to Dolce's assertion that the work is 'non rubata dagli antichi o trovata dall'ingegno de' moderni come le altre sono, ma, poco fa, avenuta in Roma' (not stolen from the ancients or found by the wit of moderns, as the others are, but having occurred recently in Rome; p. 207), Salza points out that, while we do not know how truthfully that claim struck the author's spectators, his play, in fact, derives without doubt, as least as far as its 'argomento principale,' from the *Casina* of Plautus. Salza tends to think Dolce might also have had in mind the *Clizia* of Machiavelli, since the two share the motif of the father/son rivalry and the ending, which favours the youth over the old man.

In discussing sources, one has to interject that the key word used by Salza here is 'derives,' which means no more (perhaps even less) in Dolce's case than it does in Machiavelli's. What these plays have in common is simply a similar plot feature, something that numerous playwrights have taken advantage of without thereby lessening the originality of their works. If Dolce knew the *Clizia* (and the plot twists in both plays are common enough to render the claim moot), he improved on the plot, at least as regards the details, as Salza himself admits (p. 36).[22] The improvement is in the direction of a more entwined plot, greater complexity, and a pleasing balance, while still maintaining a tight structure that flows naturally and with clarity from one complication to the next until the resolution is played out with its felicitous recognition scene and multiple marriages.

As regards one of the play's complications, Salza is less generous. He finds the scenes dealing with the Spaniard and Camilla somewhat distracting, since their relationship acquires as much importance as the trick played on Messer Cesare. But one might respond that, in addition to providing a much-needed balance, these scenes not only function to further characterize Messer Cesare, in particular as regards his failure to govern his own family, but also serve to enrich the thematic interplay of good and bad loves and the variations between them. In fact, rather than remaining exemplifications of abstract thematic motives, the relationships depicted in the play, including this one, touch on the subtleties of love in all its natural complexity. This feature, among others, then, might be cited to discount Salza's claim that, unlike Machiavelli, whose aim was to show a family that nearly succumbs to disorder because of the caprices of a father who once was a model of behaviour and to teach how to make a good family, Dolce wants only to divert the spectator with the diversity of action.[23] To believe this is to discount what Dolce himself says in the prologue – namely, that his play provides both delight and utility: 'mi rendo sicuro che a ciascuno sarà data materia, non pur di ridere, ma d'imparare' (p. 208).

Salza's negative judgment regarding what he perceives as Dolce's lack of a moral intention extends to the sexually ambiguous scene between Messer Cesare and Giacchetto, which Salza claims recalls the 'nozze maschie' (to use Sofronia's expression) of *Clizia*, Act V, scene 2, where Nicomaco gets in bed with Siro, disguised as a girl. But, according to Salza, the corruption is more refined in Dolce; he lingers over it to arouse the natural immorality of the public. Machiavelli is rougher, almost cruel, because he does not want his audience to enjoy the scene.[24] The differences between the two authors, however, should be sought, not on the grounds of morality or its lack, but on their ability as playwrights. And here, it must be admitted, Dolce surpasses Machiavelli. That Machiavelli intended his audience to laugh at the ridiculous scene is clear from Doria's speech in Act V, scene 1, where the verb *ridere* appears seven times in one form or the other.[25] But it is one thing to talk about laughing and another to make the audience laugh. After all, both the *Ragazzo* and *Clizia* are comedies. Dolce shows us the scene and makes us laugh; Machiavelli tells us about it, not once (Doria's speech), but twice (Nicomaco's narration of the event to Damone), both times failing to arouse much humour, although Damone at one point says 'egli è impossibile non ridere' (it is impossible not to laugh; p. 138).

After tracing the Plautine motif of the father/son rivalry in cinquecento theatre, Salza continues with his summary of the play, noting that the parasite's name (Ciacco) probably derives from Dante and Boccaccio (*Dec.* IX, 8) and that it was quite common in the comedy of the time for the parasite and the *ruffiano* (the go-between) to be combined, as they are in Dolce and his Latin model Curculione.[26] Again, the critic claims that Dolce, as opposed to Machiavelli, has no moral intent, and that Messer Cesare is simply 'a reduced messer Nicomaco' (p. 44). Messer Cesare's son, Flamminio, in turn, is colourless, speaking in exaggerated Petrarchan tones ('Flaminio è una figura parecchio scolorita, che all'amor suo dedica volentieri alcune esagerate e petrarcheggianti invocazioni'; pp. 45–6).

Citing a parallel between Flamminio's invocation of the night (III, 1) and that of Pietro Aretino's Neapolitan noble Parabolano (*Cortigiana* V, 13), Salza can only claim that the invocation is inappropriate for Dolce's young man, who is little more than an adolescent. That the invocation is false and out of place in the mouth of a young man, however, is simply not true. Dolce has taken a Petrarchan motif and exaggerated it for humorous effect; the fact that Flamminio may be younger than Aretino's nobleman is irrelevant. The reader can come to a judgment by comparing the two passages:

PARABOLANO: O beatissima notte a me più cara che tutti i felici giorni, di cui godono gli amici della cortese fortuna. Io non cangerei stato con l'anime, che suso in cielo gioiscono contemplando l'aspetto del mirabile Iddio. (*Cortigiana* V, 13)

[O most blessed night, dearer to me than all the happy days enjoyed by the friends of courteous fortune. I wouldn't change places with the souls up in heaven, who rejoice contemplating the appearance of wonderful God.]

FLAMMINIO: O notte da me disiata sì lungo tempo, o notte a me più che tutti i giorni lucente e chiara, notte dolce, notte beata, già sei pur finalmente venuta doppo tanti amari. Chi fia, notte, più aventuroso di me? poi che s'avicina l'ora che io debbo goder di colei la quale io sopra tutte le cose amo e senza la quale io non potrei vivere lungamente. (*Ragazzo* III, 1)

[O night desired by me for such a long time, o night brighter and clearer to me than all the days, sweet night, blessed night, you have finally arrived after so many bitter moments. Who, o night, is luckier than me? since the hour approaches when I shall enjoy her whom I love above all other things and without whom I couldn't live for long.]

The invocation as used by Dolce is actually quite appropriate to the character, a youth head over heels in love, someone from whom we would expect exaggerations of this sort. Simply because Dolce imitates another (whether Petrarch, or Petrarch through Aretino) is not, in itself, sufficient reason to criticize his characters. If nothing else, as we will see shortly, the *Ragazzo* stands as an exploitation of language in all its varied styles. Humour is found is distortions of what could only have been stale rhetoric.

Salza's discussion of the homosexual pedant is less negative in tone, since he finds the figure somewhat more involved with the plot than normal. As he notes, the pedant is usually a character whose speeches result in a pause in the action, a humorous digression after which the plot once again is set in motion. In Dolce's play, instead, the figure assumes some importance (pp. 48–9).

The rest of Salza's presentation focuses on the two main plot lines – Camilla's flight and the evil wedding of Messer Cesare – and is accompanied by a search for the characters' antecedents. Meriting discussion are the servants (pp. 50–2), the Spaniard (this one, however, raised in Italy and different from most, in that he is not mocked as a braggart captain and speaks excellent Italian), the boy (based in part on Plautus's *puer*, particularly Lucrio of the *Miles gloriosus*, but also on boys of the time;

pp. 56–68),[27] and other plot motifs, such as the resemblance between brother and sister, which derives from Plautus, possibly through Bibbiena's *Calandria* (p. 68). Among the more enjoyable scenes are those where the Spaniard and Camilla encounter each other (III, 8); where Giacchetto first appears dressed as a girl (III, 2), though here, Salza notes (with an excess of delicacy), the joke often derives from indecent speech ('dal più indecente parlare'; p. 65); and where Giacchetto describes his night with Messer Cesare (IV, 1; p. 67).

One of the more interesting possible sources pointed out by Salza for the trick played on Messer Cesare is a short story of Firenzuola (the second in the Le Monnier edition), where the youth Fulvio pretends to be a maid in order to gain entrance to the house of his beloved, married to Cecc'Antonio, an old man, who falls in love with the disguised maid and one day learns to his consternation that she is actually a he. Salza thinks this story might have influenced Della Porta's *Fantesca* (1592), which raises the possibility that Dolce's play, in turn, was of some influence on the Neapolitan.[28]

Finally, Salza's conclusion is that the play belongs to the genre of original sixteenth-century comedies. While the idea comes from Plautus, the development is Dolce's. The *Ragazzo*, in short, is 'una composizione dilettevole, vivace nel dialogo spigliato e ravvivato da motti e arguzie, sebben privo di quella comicità spontanea e briosa, che soli i comici fiorentini ebbero. E possiam dire che, se il *Ragazzo* non cede nella lubricità dell'argomento e nella licenza del linguaggio alle altre commedie del 500, nemmeno per i pregi di fattura è molto inferiore a quelle, che si stimano le migliori di quel secolo' (a delightful composition, vivacious in its free-and-easy dialogue, enlivened by quips and witticisms, although lacking that spontaneous and spirited humour that only the Florentine comics had. And we can say that, while the *Ragazzo* does not give way in the lewdness of its plot and the laxity of its language to the other comedies of the sixteenth century, neither as regards the fine qualities of its workmanship is it much inferior to those that are esteemed the best of that century; p. 69). This is high praise indeed, especially when one considers that most of Salza's objections deal with the play's more risqué moments, moments which today make of Dolce's play a very modern work.

Giorgio Padoan approaches Dolce as one of the central intellectual figures in the literary life of Renaissance Venice, important not only for his own works, but as an editor and translator.[29] For Padoan, the *Ragazzo*, in particular, is emblematic of the merits and limits of the theatrical production of the mid-sixteenth century, where one finds works based primarily on Plautus and Terence, yet open to the influence of Boccaccio and those modern authors of theatre who had by then become classics. As Padoan notes, imitation of the ancients served almost as a mark of guarantee, attesting to the nobility of the new product.

The *Ragazzo*, then, combines motives already widely used (the father/son rivalry, the resemblance between twins of both sexes, the exchanging of clothes and substitution of roles, the recognitions and concluding marriages), while also providing new complications and situations of greater richness. Still, though citing Sanesi's comment that Dolce's characters and types 'differiscono sensibilmente dai corrispondenti tipi e personaggi del teatro comico italiano del Cinquecento' (differ tangibly from the corresponding types and characters of sixteenth-century Italian comic theatre), Padoan is unwilling to concede that the work has original features ('non vi si avvertono momenti di vera originalità'), although unable to deny that the play has its own characteristic features ('benché non si possa negare al *Ragazzo* una sua propria fisionomia'; p. 190).

What the critic finds noteworthy is Dolce's unwillingness to employ (even at the level of linguistic indulgence) the Venetian tradition of caricature and buffoonery, and a pluralistic use of language. His point is that, considering the play in the abstract, one has no way of knowing that the work originated in Venice, as opposed to any other Italian city. Clearly, one could respond, such was Dolce's intention, and to say the work ignores a pluralistic use of language is to ignore the pedant's wonderful mixture of macaronic Latin. What is lacking (if one wishes to look through Padoan's narrow microscope) is the presence of Venetian dialect.

Maria Luisa Doglio, in her introduction to the Laterza reprint of Sanesi's edition of the *Ragazzo*, finds that the play signals a profound transformation of cinquecento comic theatre at mid-century. She points to Dolce's preoccupation with truth, or at least verisimilitude, as an exquisite example of artifice, not only because this desire for truth is tied to the didactic goal of the humanistic *exemplum* (i.e., to delight and to teach at the same time), but for two other reasons as well: first, Dolce dramatizes on the stage, the conventional place of *fictio*, an exemplary event presented as true; second, he leaves no room outside the discourse on stage for suspense, surprise, or other emotional response, because the action has already been defined, and thus limited by the oration in the prologue, where the author describes each of the play's three tricks (pp. xvii–xviii).[30] As such, in her words, 'non esiste spazio per l'azione: tutto è spiegato e acquisito in partenza' (there exists no space for action: all is explained and grasped at departure; p. xviii).

Doglio's observation is correct, though one might note, in addition, a possible reason for Dolce's explanation of what is about to unfold. Given the play's complications, the audience, knowing the plot twists in advance, is able to relax and enjoy the verbal action, rather than struggling to figure out what is going on and who is tricking whom. While there is delight in both activities – that is, both in trying to figure out plot complications and in following witty dialogue, Dolce clearly wishes his audience to enjoy the latter. What matters, perhaps, is less the action than the words. Suspense is not the goal, humour is – not delight in *what* happens, but delight in *how* it happens.

Doglio's conclusion is that the play's resolution establishes nothing, since everything is already established before the representation even begins (p. xix). As she justly notes, 'L'*actio*, nel senso primario e fondamentale di *drama*, si riduce a *oratio*, che si comunica sostanzialmente tramite la parola e tende a riassorbire in sé la forza d'attrazione dell'intrigo' (the *actio*, in the primary and fundamental sense of *drama*, is reduced to *oratio*, which is communicated essentially through the word and tends to reabsorb in itself the intrigue's power of attraction; ibid). Perhaps had Dolce been able to foresee modern objections, he should simply have warned his spectators 'if you don't want to hear the plot summary, plug your ears for a moment.' Aside from that brief moment in the prologue, the modern critic has nothing of which to lament.

A more extended rereading of the play has been offered recently by Luige Boni Ferrini, who seems to have been influenced by those critics of Dolce's *Dialogue on Painting* who see behind the work the thought of Pietro Aretino.[31] Following a brief summary of other critics' comments on the play, the most noteworthy being Mario Apollonio's assertion that Dolce adopted newly accepted rules that postulated comedy as a mirror of life and that his theatre can be seen as a forerunner of the *commedia dell'arte*, Ferrini emphasizes the play's analysis of the customs of the time, as seen through a disturbance of the social order caused by love (p. 473). The plot is enriched, as well, by traits derived from short stories, seen mainly in the secondary motif of the two lovers (Camilla and the Spaniard) who lose each other at night after running by chance into the police. Of interest is that Camilla represents the introduction into the theatre of the time of the ingenuous girl who comes from a good family and is willing to undergo a variety of subterfuges, without evincing, however, the shrewdness or the wickedness of the other characters.

For Ferrini, the fact that the boy Giacchetto is discovered to be of noble birth and is first presented to the spectators, not as a servant, but as the learned page of a gentleman makes the spectators accomplices – involved in the trick's perversion, since they come from the same courtly environment where tricks and broad-minded habits are common (p. 474). In this, he notes the parallels between Messer Cesare and Parabolano (in Aretino's *Cortigiana*), both not very believable in the moment when they come to their senses, and between the two plays' wise servants, both named Valerio. Interestingly (and the situation is parallel to that of the captain in Dolce's tragedy *La Marianna*, discussed in chapter 4), the servant, despite his commonsense approach and wise advice, fails to bring about the resolution of the play's plot lines, which results instead from a scene of recognition.

Following in Apollonio's footsteps, Ferrini sees in the *Ragazzo* a process of linguistic accumulation typical also of the *commedia dell'arte*. The only speech cited in this regard is Flamminio's apostrophe of night (referred to above), after which Ferrini passes to examples taken from some of Dolce's later comedies, where the use of repetition for humorous purposes (repetition sometimes to the point of exasperation) is more evident (pp. 474–5). In addition, says Ferrini, Dolce transforms Aretino's pedant (used for satirical intent in the *Marescalco*) into a buffoon, a character almost like those in a typical *commedia dell'arte* sketch. Ferrini sees this as a movement towards *la maschera*, a process that becomes more obvious in the figure of Doctor Pomponino in Dolce's *Fabritia*. But, having just claimed that Dolce's pedant is more a buffoon than a figure who satirizes others (as Aretino's does), Ferrini turns around and says the pedant, like *Fabritia*'s doctor, represents the satire of empty erudition, tied to the power of wealth and prestige, but without a definable social base. And having made this point, the critic reverses direction once again, claiming that both figures are essentially buffoons.[32] The conclusion one should make is that the two situations are not opposites (i.e., that one is either a buffoonesque character or a character used for satire), but the same. After all, how does one best satirize a pedant if not by making him a buffoon?

Another indication of Aretino's influence, according to Ferrini, is revealed in what the critic calls 'un'interessante distrazione dall'unità di luogo' (an interesting departure from the unity of place; p. 476). The so-called departure is simply the maid Belcolore's statement that she has looked in vain throughout the city of Rome (referred to with a variety of place names) for a priest Romano: 'Ho cerco tutto Borgo, la Pace, la Rotonda, il Culiseo, per insino alla Guglia' (IV, 4). The parallel in Aretino's *Cortigiana* (Messer Andrea, who says: 'Ah, ah, andiamo a vedere Campo Santo, la Guglia, San Pietro, la pina, Banchi, Torre di Nona' [II, 3]) is also called a 'Chiaro esempio di deroga dall'unità di luogo' (clear example of a deviation from the unity of place). The existence of the parallel is clear; the sophistries of the critic, who goes on to amplify the significance of the phrase, less so.[33]

Ferrini's ambivalence towards the play seems to arise from judging it against a background of thematics dear to Aretino. Ferrini finds in Dolce's theatre an 'original revival' of Aretino's polemic against certain aspects of power, but only in isolated exchanges which, though interesting as regards the satire, are often weakened and almost absorbed by the rapidity of the theatrical game.[34] Rather than praising the rapidity of the play's pace, a noteworthy comic achievement, or its quick, incisive wit and sharp (or subtle) satire, Ferrini apparently prefers to find in it a weakened rendition of Aretinian motifs that might not have been of concern to Dolce. Why judge him by what someone else did? Is his play successful for what it offers or not?

Here, for example, Ferrini concentrates on the play's final moment (when Caterina and Ciacco ponder keeping the stolen silver), claiming that their 'act of rebellion' sounds a discordant note in the midst of a happy ending and causes them to take on a hint of the arrogance of Aretino's servants, corrupt like their masters, who carry out their deeds in a Rome in full decline (p. 477). But rather than a discordant note, the final words of Caterina and Ciacco are joyful, if slightly naughty, a sign of ribaldry appropriate from a parasite and a servant girl who has run away and returned home. And, for the moralists who might be upset by their hint of disobedience, Dolce, whether intentionally or unintentionally, has provided an antidote in the prologue, where he tells us the silver *is* returned.

In concluding, the critic praises certain features and certain scenes of Dolce's play, though even here in noting the author's attentive care towards scenic time, the rapid pace with which the situations develop, and the plot full of movement, Ferrini feels constrained to label such care that of a 'operaio della letteratura' (literary workman), as if craft were something different from art (p. 478).[35] The same begrudging praise is paid to the monologues of the lovers, which are 'sintetici e tecnicamente ben riusciti' (synthetic and technically successful). Only near the end of his article does Ferrini's praise come without faint blame, and then only for a brief comment: The dialogues between Giacchetto and the pedant are swift and enjoyable (p. 479).

Ferrini's conclusion is that Dolce not only gave space to the plot's events, but did so with narrative facility, treating comedy as a successful mechanism open to new impressions, annotations, and solutions. Like other writers of the cinquecento, Dolce had 'the sensation and perhaps the awareness of creating scenes to be acted and recited with the irony of an external observer, who considers theater a world apart, reflected in the real world, just as reality can reflect the theater in an intellectual game.' As such, Dolce was 'active in a literary and historical situation that was becoming ever more static, after the first moments of crisis, and which would conclude with an involution from the social consequences of a progressive rigidity and an increasing isolation of the classes in power from the people.'[36]

Sources of Humour and Self-Reflexivity in Il ragazzo

In turning to two other features of interest – *Il ragazzo*'s sources of humour and the author's self-reflexivity, one must first note that the prologue's final words refer to language, more specifically to the fact that, if the author's intention were to express truly 'i costumi d'oggidí' (the customs of the day), he would need words that exemplified lust. With this apology for exceeding the boundaries of good taste, Dolce launches into a linguistic display, where one finds a vocabulary of sexual ambiguity, puns, malatropisms, metaphors, pedantic verbosity, macaronic Latin, creative insults, and visual imagery, all employed to humorous effect.

Before looking at representative examples of each, however, I would like first to note that the intellectual wordplay is not without its moral foundation. In fact, the first scene of Act I begins with a confrontation between Messer Cesare and his servant Valerio, pitting old against young, aristocrat against underling, madman against wise, and establishes Valerio as a faithful servant and good counsellor who speaks against flatterers and stands up for the family honour. That Messer Cesare at sixty has grown childlike is indirectly attested to by the old man himself when he calls Valerio a philosopher and 'il mio maestro!' (p. 210), after having earlier called him an 'asino temerario.' That Messer Cesare is morally blind is revealed when Valerio tells him to open his eyes and remember he is a father and at an age when he should be instructing others how to live.

In addition to the opening discussion of correct behaviour, Dolce also depicts a series of paired opposites at different social ranks – wise servants, like Valerio, and wicked ones, like Caterina; careless fathers, like Messer Cesare, and careful relatives, like the uncles who see to it that Flamminio marries Livia rather than enjoying her as his mistress. The same range is seen in the types of love, from the crazed lust of Messer Cesare to the noble love of Camilla and the Spaniard, with the bizarre sexuality of Giacchetto thrown in to leaven what otherwise might seem serious. If this is bitter medicine (an example, in one instance, of how *not* to act; in another, of the daring of true lovers), it is sweetened with enough honey that the spectator absorbs the message almost without realizing it.

As regards other themes of some seriousness (even if dealt with humorously), one might note that various characters comment on the *questione della donna*, from the behaviour of poor noblewomen to good and bad wives (Valerio, I, 6), on which sex has the most advantages in love-making (Ciacco, III, 2), on feminine wiles (Giacchetto, ibid), and on the risks of pregnancy, but the dangers of prostitutes (Valerio, III, 3). References to money or its lack also run throughout the play, from the greed of the parasite in Act I to the large dowry for Camilla in Act VI, with Messer Cesare ironically noting that people no longer care about virtue or nobility, but only about money (I, 3), and the parasite humorously wishing he could eat the golden words of the pedant (II, 4). Other humorous references to money include Ciacco's 'metallo di san Giovanni Boccadoro' and the Spaniard's 'il tesoro di messer San Marco' (metal of St John Goldenmouth ... the treasure of mister St Mark; III, 2; p. 249).

The honey mentioned above that sweetens the more serious moments is, of course, the play's humour, and the humour lies in the delightful distortions of language with which I began this discussion. Let me cite at least one example of each, with a prefatory comment on Dolce's ability to create comic tension through suspense. The author is very astute at drawing out the play's more dramatic moments, when the characters (and we through them) are desirous of information. To cite just one example, Messer Cesare at one point has to break in with 'Dillo tosto; non mi tener sospeso' (Tell it quickly; don't keep me hanging; IV, 3; p. 272, and see also p. 273). Thus, despite the fact that we were provided with a plot summary in the prologue, that information has very little to do with the play's comic vitality.

Sexual ambiguity is variously expressed, ranging from the use of vulgar epithets to the coaching of a transvestite. When the Spaniard calls Giacchetto a 'putanella,' the boy responds angrily: 'Non mi date nome di femina, se io son maschio' (Don't call me by a term for a female, if I'm a male; II, 1). The scene where Ciacco coaches Giacchetto on how to act like a girl (III, 2) is developed at much greater length, beginning as follows:

CIACCO: Esci fuora, sposa, ché non ci appar niuno.
GIACCHETTO: Io esco.
CIACCO: Questa voce è un poco aspretta. Di' in questa forma: 'io eesco.'
GIACCHETTO: Io eesco. (p. 246)

[CIACCO: Come on out, bride, since no one's around.
GIACCHETTO: I'm coming out.
CIACCO: Your voice is a little bit harsh. Say it this way: "I'm coming ow-ut."
GIACCHETTO: I'm coming ow-ut.]

In the subtle but effective doubling of the vowel *e*, Dolce has effectively captured the parasite's squeaky voice.

Giacchetto does such a good job that, for a moment, Ciacco pretends to wonder if a miracle might have occurred, and asks to touch the boy, at which Giacchetto exclaims, 'Orsú! Ritien le mani a te' (Come on! Keep your hands to yourself). This exchange brings to the page a discussion of whether the boy would rather be a girl in reality. His response is that he would like to be both, and when Ciacco asks why, Giacchetto says, to see which way is sweeter. A few exchanges later, Ciacco says that women have more advantages than men, and when asked why, his reponse is, because they can serve gallantly as both male and female (p. 246).

When the Spaniard protests twice that they are wasting time with jokes ('Il tempo fugge; e coteste son burle' and later 'Io dico che 'l tempo fugge'), Ciacco and Giacchetto ignore him for two more pages of exchanges, during which they act out what is going to happen between Giacchetto, disguised as Livia, and Messer Cesare. The humour lies in Giacchetto's skill at playing the coy *amorosa*. When Messer Cesare protests his love, s/he will keep her eyes fixed on the ground, and when he tries to caress her, s/he will give him a glance as if to say, do I look like I'm that type of girl? ('datogli allora una occhiatina, cosí, dirò: – Paiovi io, messere, femina di questa sorte? –'). The charade continues with Giacchetto's detailing the feminine responses he will provide in the face of the old man's advances, until Ciacco, marvelling, calls him 'uno imperadore' (p. 247), to which Giacchetto responds, 'Emperadrice.' The scene's risqué elements come to a climax with a demonstration on Ciacco of the sort of feminine kisses Giacchetto will give the old man. After one of the samples, Ciacco says, 'Quest'altro è bascio da cortigiana. Non voglio che tu ci metta la lingua' (This other kiss is too much like a courtesan. I don't want you to stick your tongue in; p. 248). The Spaniard's plaintive response to all this,

his first two references to time having been ignored, is a humorous 'Io penso che, oggimai, a mano a mano a mano, sia appresso la mezza notte' (I think that by now, little by little by little, midnight is approaching).

Adding to the humour throughout the play is a wide variety of puns and witticisms, some based on a technique of what might be called 'disappointed expectations,' others on rhyme, or misunderstandings of macaronic speech, or verbal joustings, for which see the excellent, colloquial exchanges in Act II, scene 3 – too long to cite in this text. Brief examples of the other methods, however, can be found throughout the work. To focus on just one scene, I, 3, after a discussion of love's ills, we find the following example of disappointed expectations:

MESSER CESARE: Dolce cosa sarebbe a trovarmi nelle braccia de ...
CIACCO: Della morte? (p. 213)

[MESSER CESARE: A sweet thing it would be to find myself in the arms of ...
CIACCO: Of death?]

To illustrate the use of rhyme for humour, Ciacco tells Messer Cesare to fear not for he will be able to bend to his will the columns, let alone the women: 'State, adunque, sicuro di piegare alle vostre voglie le colonne, non che le donne' (p. 214). The word 'colonne,' if not used literally, might be a veiled reference to the Colonna family in Rome, where the play is set. I am reminded, as well, not only of the Bible (Samson, who pulls down the columns on himself, reflecting metaphorically the disastrous conclusion of the old man's escapade), but also of an author who later will pun on a woman's legs as columns (G.B. Marino, 'Sovra basi d'argento in conca d'oro'). In this same scene, when Messer Cesare tells Ciacco that the glutton can be his doctor, even though he has never studied 'né Ipocrasso, né Avicenna né Galieno,' Ciacco creatively transforms the names, claiming 'Anzi, porco grasso, vino a cena e corpo pieno è stato sempre il mio studio' (On the contrary, fat pork, wine at dinner, and a full body have always been my field of study; p. 213).

Closely related to the use of puns and witticisms is what I have called the malatropisms, the misuse of similes and metaphors. An example can be found in the same scene (I, 3). When the parasite sees Messer Ciacco, he says he has grown younger like the elephant, at which Messer Cesare laughs and says, you mean like the phoenix (p. 212). The strangeness of some of the play's similes are such that they are even commented on by the characters themselves. Again in the same scene, we find this exchange:

CIACCO: Se la figliuola fosse l'Ancroia e la madre la fata Morgana, l'arete, avendo la borsa piena.
MESSER CESARE: Oh che nuova similitudine! (p. 214)

[CIACCO: If the daughter were the Ancroia and the mother the Fata Morgana, you would have her, if you have a full purse.
MESSER CESARE: Oh what a new simile!]

Ancroia, the protagonist of a popular poem called *La regina Ancroia*, had come to stand for a squalid, old woman, while the Fata Morgana, of course, was represented as a beautiful, virtuous woman. Whether Ciacco's speech is intentionally twisted by him to fool the old man or not, it provokes laughter.

An example of Dolce's use of extended comic metaphors can also be found in the same scene, where, after the synonymic iteration of Messer Cesare's amorous illnesses (vaguely recalling Jacopone da Todi's 'O Segnor per cortesia, manname la malsanìa') and Ciacco's initial fear that these represent an actual and horrifying disease, which makes him keep his distance, Messer Cesare says that, for him to get well, he will need the parasite to be his doctor. To heal the old man, Ciacco says they need four things – wit, great care, bravery, and luck, and above all the *conquibus*, which means, he says in response to Cesare's question, 'danari' (money; p. 215). As for luck, it is caught with 'le reti d'oro' (golden nets).

The extended medical metaphor will later be transformed to a military one (II, 4), with Ciacco presenting himself as the most fortunate man in the world guiding three in the field of battle. The son Flamminio will conquer the fortress and make it his, Messer Cesare will think he is conquering but will lose a castle, while another [Caterina] will prey on his own estate while he is away (II, 4).[37]

Perhaps most enjoyable among Dolce's many comic effects is his mocking of pedantic verbosity and macaronic Latin. The pedant punctiliously corrects the speech of the other characters, whether Italian or Latin, pointing out superfluous expressions; explicates Latin sayings word for word; translates part of his Latin into Italian in the middle of phrases or repeats the same thing three different ways ('Chi è lo sponso? chi è il consorte? chi è il marito' [IV, 5]); and quotes a verse of Petrarch with the insertion of a Latin word, while the parasite and the servants, in turn, both mock and misunderstand the pedant's language.[38] Among the more humorous mistakes are Ciacco's transformation of Latin 'codici' (codexes) into 'podici' (buttocks; II, 6; p. 240) and Valerio's interpretation of 'Paucis te volo' as 'Se i pesci volano, gli uccelli nuotano' (If fish fly, then birds swim; I, 5; p. 218). When the pedant laughs in Latin ('Ah! ah! Racca'), Valerio, after declaring that the word 'racca' must be Hebrew and hearing the pedant say, no, it is very Latin and 'Io rido alla antica' (I laugh in the ancient way), wants to know how one sneezes in Latin (I, 6; pp. 221–2). Truly, the various scenes with the pedant, including his monologue in Act II, scene 9, are delightful masterpieces of comic wordplay.

Also of note among the comic techniques employed by Dolce are the use of creative insults (see II, 3 and 6); neologisms, as when the pedant is called an 'assorda-cielo' (I, 5; p. 223); risqué jokes, such as the pedant's use of *iuvènculo* (youth) and Giacchetto's *vènculo*; and visual imagery, such as Ciacco's statement 'Volete voi ch'io vi cavi le parole di bocca con le tenaglie?' (Do you want me to pull the words out of your mouth with tongs?; I, 3; p. 214). Unlike other comic poets of the time, however, Dolce does not take advantage of one other language easily mocked – the Spaniard's Petrarchan vocabulary. If anything, the Spaniard's Petrarchisms (Camilla has a 'bella e bianca mano'; he hears 'un non so che'; thanks love and fortune with a 'Benedetti siano i dolori, le pene, i tormenti e i molti guai che io ho patito amando' [blessed be the sorrows, the pains, the torments and the many woes that I have suffered loving]) are used solely to characterize him as a noble lover (see II, 1, and III, 10). And, apart from one brief quote in Spanish, his Florentine is excellent, so good, in fact, that Giacchetto feels compelled to praise it (so that the author can inform us that the Spaniard was raised in Tuscany and Rome by his uncle, the Cardinal; II, 1). He is anything but a braggart captain.

Finally, a brief word about the author's self-reflexivity in *Il ragazzo*. This is a play filled with the names of other authors (or veiled references to their works), including Plato, Cicero, Cato, Virgil, Ovid, Terence, Boethius, Petrarch, Boccaccio, Calepino (actually a Latin dictionary for schools, compiled by Ambrogio dei conti di Calepio and published in Reggio Emilia in 1502), Sannazzaro, Ariosto (with a reference to his story of Bradamante and Riciardetto), Bembo, Molza, Pietro Aretino, and Erasmus. Ciacco sings a poem of his own composition, and then asks himself (and us) if he is not a good poet, to which his answer is yes (II, 2). In fact, it is the equal of Bembo, who is not only a poet, but a cardinal. Giacchetto says he enjoys reading and has memorized all of Boccaccio ('io mi diletto di leggere il Boccaccio e l'ho tutto a mente'; II, 1). Ciacco says Flamminio will have his quail – or, to say it right, he will put his nightingale in its cage (II, 8), a reference to *Decameron* V, 4. Messer Cesare, like Andreuccio da Perugia, goes from being the happiest to the most unlucky fellow in the world ('Ben sono io il più sventurato uomo del mondo, dove, pure ora, mi parea d'essere il più felice'; IV, 3).

The authorial awareness of the digressive nature of the pedant's speech at the end of Act I (where he notes that the play will take forever if the pace does not pick up) culminates in Act 4, first in scene 1, where Ciacco says 'la novella è bella'; then, in scene 2, where Valerio says someday they will be writing comedies about this; and, finally, again in scene 3, where Messer Cesare says that what happened to him is a comedy, since it turned out well: 'In fine, la mia sarà stata una comedia, poi ch'ella è fornita in bene.'

A literary exercise or a literary masterpiece? Or something in between? Whatever the reader's ultimate judgment (and I would tend to tip the balance towards the literary masterpiece, especially if one understands the word 'masterpiece' to mean a piece made by a craftsman aspiring to the rank of master), Dolce, as in so many of his works where his skill as a writer seems so natural, is simply a pleasure to read. Above all else, *Il ragazzo* is proof of his competence as a truly comic author.

La Fabritia

Dolce's second original comedy, *La Fabritia*, was first published by the sons of Aldus Manutius in 1549 and was probably composed shortly before. That Dolce took pride in his creation is evident from the *querelle* of ancient and modern embodied by the two boys in the double prologue cited at length in the first section of this chapter. Despite Dolce's protestations of novelty, later critics have tended to find parallels to his plot in various works of classical theatre, most notably those of Terence. The same, of course, can be said of nearly every comedy written in the sixteenth century and does not detract from the play's merits.

Dolce's modernity, in addition to the original features with which the plot is developed, lies in part in his complication of events. As Louise George Clubb notes in her study *Italian Drama in Shakespeare's Time*, the principle of *contaminatio*, defended by Terence, who had merged two Plautine plots in his *Andria*, and boasted of by Ariosto in the prologue of the *Suppositi*, became a formal goal of later generations of Italian *commediografi*, who sought 'a fusion of increasingly numerous and disparate sources, displaying sure technique of construction' (p. 33). The corollary principle that plots should be complicated was reinforced by the vogue for Aristotle's *Poetics*, and Dolce, though sometimes disdainful of Aristotelian strictures, at least as interpreted by pedants, felt the necessity of intertwining primary and secondary plots, each with recognition scenes and reversals, and all culminating in marriage. Such a procedure was later codified by theoreticians such as Girolamo Ruscelli, Dolce's great rival in Venice, who notes in 1554, when this opinion was already entrenched, that 'from the first act through the fourth and often midway through the fifth, Comedy should proceed by ever-increasing upheavals, differences, intrigues'; trans. by Clubb, p.33).[39]

Dolce's plot complications, however, have not always found favour among later critics. Salza, for example, concludes his summation of the play's plot lines with the following statement: 'Una quantità di tipi e di caratteri ha saputo introdurre il Dolce in questa sua *Fabrizia*, che supera, a parer nostro, il *Ragazzo*, come commedia di tipi, mentre nello svolgimento non può non notarsi una lentezza inopportuna. L'aver voluto intessere fra di loro due intrecci ha interrotto l'organismo principale della commedia' (Dolce knew how to introduce a large number of character types in his *Fabritia*, which in our opinion surpasses the *Ragazzo* as a comedy of types, while one cannot but notice an inappropriate slowness in its development. The desire to entwine two plots with each other interrupted the main component of the comedy; p. 135). But this, of course, is exactly what Dolce wanted to do; to have done otherwise would have opened him to the criticism directed against Machiavelli's *Mandragola* – namely, that the play is too simple to be worthy of imitation.[40] And the two plots provide for a pleasing variety of comings and goings, although, without doubt, several brief scenes could be cut without damaging the play's development.

As for other modern opinions of the play's worth, Marvin Herrick, in his brief summary of Dolce's comedies, says that '*La Fabritia* can hardly be identified with any earlier comedy, ancient or modern, yet the main action suggests a parallel with the *Eunuch* of Terence and the ridiculous Doctor of Law might well be the brother of Bibbiena's Calandro or of Machiavelli's Nicia.' His conclusion is that 'it is a lively play, set in Mantua, abounding in local color and allusions to contemporary life' (*Italian Comedy*, p. 115). Giorgio Padoan is less generous, calling the play 'scadente' (shoddy). He, too, finds Terence to be the source of Dolce's inspiration, citing both the *Eunuch* and the *Hecyra* for the two plot lines, but feels that the characters are restricted to comic types who are unbelievable ('confinati nel generico e nell'improbabile'). Not even the pedant stands out from the century's prevailing type, coming across as much less colourful than Aretino's pedagogue (*Commedia*, p. 191). While Padoan's criticism is surely too harsh, his assessment of the pedant as not too colourful is, on the whole, accurate; however, one might cite as a more lively model not only Aretino, but Dolce's own *Ragazzo*, where the pedant is a delight. The only unbelievable character is Messer Athanagio, who is relentlessly characterized by his avarice, a quality shared also by Dottor Pomponino, the pedant.

For Ferrini, finally, who mentions the play in his discussion of the *Ragazzo*, the pedant is a buffoon, who has almost assumed the character of a mask, prefiguring what will happen in the *commedia dell'arte*. Similar to the pedant in Aretino's *Marescalco* (significantly, both have the same name – Dottor Pomponino), Dolce's figure establishes his authority based on his literary merits, but his citations of other authors are such that the public has no difficulty mocking him (p. 476). Ferrini seems to conflate Dolce's two pedants, since Dottor Pomponino uses much less Latin than the *Ragazzo*'s pedant and rarely cites other authorities.[41]

While the *Fabritia* is not necessarily written at the level of the *Ragazzo* (Salza, for example, notes that the *Fabritia* contains thirty-six monologues and that, consequently, the action develops at an awkward length and with a tedious pace), the play does have its fine touches and surpasses the earlier work in its depiction of character, as Salza himself admits (p. 136). Even here, one might accentuate the positive and say that the numerous monologues and brief scenes add to the sense of a finely entwined structure, with characters coming and going, some just missing the others, some fleeing, some chasing, some meeting just when necessary, and so forth. The number of scenes in each act (11, 14, 18, 22, and 12) illustrates the hectic aspect of the play, which seems slow only because of its length.

But more than this, the play offers an interesting portrait of many customs of the time. In fact, Herrick seems closer to the truth with his reference to the play's many 'allusions to contemporary life' than the other critics who emphasize either character types or the masks of the *commedia dell'arte*. As proof, let me mention just a few of the elements of local colour that enliven the *Fabritia*. To facilitate the discussion I will first provide a summary of the play's two plot lines.

Fabritio, son of avaricious Messer Athanagio (and brother of Lisetta, one of the main characters of the secondary plot), has fallen in love with a slave girl being offered for sale by Luppo, *Ruffiano*. M. Athanagio's avarice comes to the fore, both when he refuses to help Fabritio buy the girl and when he asks Messer Roberto for a dowry to be returned. M. Roberto's son Giulio had married Lisetta, but was immediately sent away on business without having once enjoyed his wife, and was then reported drowned in a shipwreck off Ragusa. Now, M. Athanagio wants to find a new husband for Lisetta.

Lisetta, meanwhile, is pregnant, having been forced by an aunt (who was supposed to protect her) to sleep twice with a youth, who then gave her a ring as a sign of his affection, all this before her marriage to Giulio. Her nurse, the *Balia*, tries to protect her, but Lisetta is disgraced and must leave home to give birth to her child.

The pedant, Doctor Pomponino, has also been attracted by the beauty of the slave girl and would like to buy her, but is reluctant to spend the necessary money. He asks the parasite Melino to help him, but Melino is looking out only for himself and for Fabritio, since the young man is much more generous with his money. Eventually, the parasite will trick the pedant out of a meal, three hundred gold florins, and a gold-brocade coat.

Another figure involved in the affair is a servant of M. Athanagio – the Moor. After first refusing to aid Fabritio (just to torment the youth), he promises to help him steal the necessary funds from his master, since he knows liberal Fabritio will inherit his stingy father's money some day. Before the play's end, the Moor will trick M. Athanagio out of the dowry (which is then lost to the police) and will help Fabritio steal a string of pearls from his father in order to pawn them for the clothes to disguise the Moor as a rich merchant and Fabritio as a Turkish girl. Fabritio, in disguise, will be introduced into the Ruffian's house, from where he will flee with the girl.[42]

By the end of Act III, Fabritio's attempts to get the funds to buy the slave girl are foiled when his father comes across the Moor (who got the dowry by trickery) before the money can be handed over; the Moor's ruse – namely, that the money is plague-ridden – results in its seizure by the police. The parasite Melino, in turn, has taken advantage of the stupid pedant. As for the secondary plot, Giulio, thought dead, has returned to learn to his despair that his wife, Lisetta, is pregnant.

Over the course of Act IV, the Balia has trouble finding a midwife for Lisetta, who is about to give birth; the pedant is mocked by his servant and tricked by the parasite; the Ruffian is deceived by the Moor into accepting a disguised Fabritio into his household; M. Athanagio goes mad over the loss of his pearls; and the Ruffian and Pedant get into an argument over money.

Act V, of course, results in a resolution of all these plot lines, including what happens to the dowry seized by the police. Nothing is left hanging. Fabritio and the slave girl flee from the Ruffian's house and get married. Lisetta gives birth to a boy without the help of a midwife. M. Roberto and his son Giulio discover that the girl Giulio slept with before his marriage was Lisetta, his wife, so the child is his. M. Athanagio regains his senses when he learns his daughter is not disgraced. The parasite Melino learns from the Ruffian that the slave girl was actually Doctor Pomponino's daughter, so the pedant's failure to obtain her saved him from incest. And, finally, the pearls are back in the possession of the Moor, who will return them to his master, M. Athanagio, along with the dowry, which was determined not to be plague-ridden. The entwining of the two plot lines ends in a double knot, formed by two recognitions (the slave girl as the pedant's daughter, Lisetta as the girl Giulio slept with [apparently in the dark!] before he married her) and two marriages (one new, one recovered).

Dolce's reference to 'i costumi d'hoggidì' in the prologue to *Il ragazzo* (1560 edition, p. 4^r) is an expression perhaps more apt as a description for what *La Fabritia* provides, for truly the play is permeated and enlivened by references to the customs of the time. In addition, however, Dolce offers an intriguing use of a mythological figure, that of the underworld boatman Charon. Despite all the references to Charon in mythological fables, farces, intermedi, and melodramas, 'erudite forms of both comedy and tragedy seem to avoid extended portrayals of the ferryman and rarely include even minor references to him by name.'[43] Dolce is an exception, since he not only refers to Charon but sets his reference in the imagined descent of a madman. The influence, as one might expect, seems to be that of the mock-heroic depictions of descents, such as that of Luigi Pulci in the *Morgante* (2. 38–9), where the giant promises to create havoc in hell – to debeard Charon; knock Pluto off his chair; finish off Phlegethon with one sip; eat Phlegyas; and kill Tisiphone, Alecto, Megera, Erichtho, and Cerberus with one blow. Here, Messer Athanagio in his madness cries out:

Però gran Diavolo, Belzebub Archiduca dell'Inferno, manda Caronte che mi porti con la sua barca ne i paesi de' disperati ... Ma se io vi ci entro, renditi certo, che io farò più faccende, che non fece Hercole. Prima voglio mangiar Cerbero, et farmi della sua pelle un copertoio da portare al tempo delle nevi. Dapoi ridurre in un fastello, Isifone, Tantalo, et le Furie: et gettarli tutti nell'Oceano. In ultimo voglio dare un cavallo a Proserpina; et tenerla a miei bisogni per fantesca da cucina. (V, 6; p. 60^r)

[Therefore, o great devil, Belzebub, Archduke of Hell, send Charon so he may bear me in his boat to the countries of those without hope ... But if I go there, you can be sure that I'll do more deeds than Hercules did. First I want to eat Cerberus, and make of his skin a large cover to wear when it's snowing. Then I'll tie Ixion, Tantalus, and the Furies in one bundle, and throw them all in the ocean. And lastly, I want to give a horse to Proserpina, and keep her as a kitchen maid for my needs.]

The humour, of course, lies not only in the exaggerations, but in the inconguity of the deeds.

Apart from his use of classical mythology, particularly as seen in the popular imagination, Dolce has filled his play with a wide variety of events and practices taken from the everyday life of the time. Among the more interesting are the institution of slavery, here seen through the selling of girls captured in war (see I, 1; p. 6^v, where reference is made to a girl sold as one sells a beast, and I, 6; p. 10^v, where we learn the asking price is a thousand florins; *et passim*), and the treatment of young women in general. In the latter respect, Dolce deals with such subjects as dowries (I, 2; p. 7^v, where we learn that a dowry of two thousand gold florins was paid – using five hundred in clothes and jewels, and the rest in cash – and that the whole is to be returned since the husband died before consummating the marriage), the selling of young girls for sexual favours (I, 7; pp. 11^r–12^r, where Lisetta, motherless at thirteen, was sent to be raised by an aunt, who sold not only her, but also her own daughters), unwanted pregnancies (I, 7, and, for a description of morning sickness and other effects of pregnancy, II, 9; p. 22^r), the attempted deception of parents (II, 6; p. 20^r, where we see the ruse of Lisetta being possessed by a devil), abortions (I, 7; pp. 11^{r-v}), the tossing of aborted foetuses into the toilets (IV, 2; p. 42^r), and the practice of using midwives to help with childbirth (IV, 1; p. 41^r and IV, 16; p. 53^v, where reference is also made to a woman, the *sventraiuola*, who performs Caesarean sections).

The relationships between men and women, and in particular the *questione della donna* (see II, 3; p. 18^v, where both sides of the question are argued), also come up for discussion. The social commentary includes a description and criticism of the practices of marriage brokers, the *sensale* (II, 3), as well as an attack on the behaviour of men, who are accused of being so afraid of an annoying wife ('la seccaggine della moglie') and the vexation of children ('il fastidio de' figliuoli') that they give themselves to adultery, rape, incest, sacrilegious acts, and worse (p. 18^r).

Women are not spared in this critique, although the criticism of them is expressed from a dubious source – the mouths of men who love freedom and think all women are alike. For these misogynistic men, women are prideful, arrogant, wicked, cruel, lustful, and insatiable. They assassinate their husbands, poison their children, and fill the house with bastards. All disturbances, sorrows, discord, enmity, conflicts, fights, wounds, and death proceed from them, since there is no worse animal in the world than woman (pp. 18^{r-v}). The discussion becomes personal in a later monologue of Messer Athanagio, who calls his pregnant daughter a 'puttana' and expresses through a proverb the social conflict that 'chi non prende moglie è incolpato, et chi la prende è tormentato' (he who doesn't take a wife is blamed, and he who takes one is tormented; II, 9; p. 22^{v}).[44]

The social criticism extends as well to a variety of professions, regions, nationalities, classes, and races. Jewish moneylenders are referred to more than once (e.g., I, 3; p. 8^{r}), and are seen as being avaricious (II, 7; p. 21^{r}), excessively cautious, traitors, and Christ-killers ('questi uccide Christo') (III, 17; p. 38^{r}).[45] Servants are evil (see Moro in I, 1; p. 8^{v}, who 'per meno d'un carlino [assassinerebbe] il paradiso' [for less than a carlin would assassinate paradise]), as seen additionally in these words:

... perchè tutte le ghiottonerie, gli intrichi, i garbugli, le giunte, gli assassinamenti, et le ladrarie stanno meco, come le paure con la notte, il Sole col giorno, i pulici con la state, il freddo col verno, et i fiori con la primavera. (I, 4; p. 8^{v})

[... because all the gluttonies, the intrigues, the muddles, the cabals, the assassinations, and the thefts come along with me, just as fears with the night, the sun with day, fleas with summer, the cold with winter, and flowers with spring.]

Part of the reason for their evil lies in how servants are treated. In Act III, scene 11, Moro laments that a servant who works hard to please his master is treated worse than a beast, as if God had created the master with a different soul from the servant's, and as if Sir Adam was made from sugar and the rest of us from mud ('Poi è gran peccato, che un servo s'affatichi per far piacere al padrone, perchè essi ci tengono da peggio di bestie; quasi che Domenedio gli habbia fatti nascere con altra anima che non habbiam noi; et Messer Adamo impastati di Zucchero, et di ambracane, et noi altri di fango'; p. 23^{r}).

Elsewhere, the nobles come in for a more gentle dig. As Messer Athanagio says, nowadays nobility without money, even if virtuous, is like a beautiful house without a roof, unfit for anyone to live there ('hoggidì la nobiltà et la virtù senza danari è, come una bella casa senza tetto, che nessuno vi può habitar dentro'; I, 4; p. 19^{r}).

As regards other nationalities and regions, the Spanish are always sighing and lamenting (I, 5; p. 10^{r}), while the different cities of Italy all have their own characteristics. In one speech, where the predominant motif is encomiastic (at times, perhaps, tongue-in-cheek), the Ruffiano Luppo and his servant Invola wonder whether they might have had better luck selling their slave in a city other than Mantua (I, 9). To each of the servant's suggestions, Luppo responds with doubts: the people of Ferrara, while liberal, are more concerned with virtuous works than with lust, because of their good rulers; the Florentines are interested in other markets; in Rome, the youths study great things, and there is no place for women; the Neapolitans have little to spend, and the few men who are rich expect to win women using perfumes, sonnets, the doffing of hats, and other Spanish usages; in Genoa, the men do not even care about their wives; in Milan, the people have other things to think about; the Bolognese love and want to be loved in return, but because liberality is natural to them, they give things rather than buy them; and, finally, the Venetians are kind and courteous, but do not throw their money away (pp. 13^{r-v}).

More open to being mocked are a variety of professions. In addition to the marriage broker, who speaks ill of his own profession ('Fra tutte le arti, o industrie, o mestieri, che chiamar li vogliamo, nessuno ve ne è certamente peggior del mio' [Among all the arts, or industries, or jobs, call them what you will, there is certainly none worse than mine]; II, 3; p. 18^{r}), the following professions come in for veiled or open criticism:

- teaching: 'Dottore per lettera, et bufolo per volgare' (Doctor in Latin, and clumsy ox in the vernacular; II, 8; p. 21^{v})
- oratory: 'l'arte Parasitica dell'Oratoria' (the parasitic art of oratory), something praised as practical for gluttons, since they can either say what great men want to hear or keep silent (IV, 18; p. 40^{r})
- usury: 'ella hoggdì si può far senza conscienza di peccato, et senza riprensione' (one can practise it today without conscience of sin and without reprehension; IV, 2; p. 41^{v})
- alchemy: used to counterfeit coins ('farsificar monete' [*sic*]; ibid)
- lawyers: who get rich quickly by taking money from the people they defend as well as from their adversaries (p. 42^{r})
- notaries: who acquire wealth by falsifying legal documents and changing the number ten into a thousand (ibid)
- fortune-telling: an art with which one can easily take money from the hands of a thousand foolish men and women (ibid)
- making cosmetics: an art more useful than all the others (ibid)
- abortionists: their job saves the hospitals money (ibid)

– doctors: knowing only two pages from Galen and Avicenna, one can take money from the healthy and the soul from the sick, since 'a questi tempi ogni ignorante è tenuto Dottore' (nowadays any ignoramus is thought to be a doctor; p. 42^v)
– poets: who do poorly, since people no longer appreciate virtue, and the poets themselves are not as learned as Bembo or as witty as Aretino (ibid).

And at worst, if one knows none of the above arts, one can become a boatman or a priest (p. 42^v) (who sometimes buy boys [p. 46^r]), or even a dog breeder ('nudrir cagnuole'), as they do in the French city of Lyons (p. 45^v).

Other aspects of the life of the time that are revealed in the play include the love of sugary sweets, such as the Sicilian honey-and-nut treat the 'pignocate' (*pignoccata*; II, 23; p. 25^v), and good wine (II, 1; p. 17^r), and of toys for children, such as the Salta Martino, a jumping toy made from part of a nutshell with a spring and a toothpick, that Turchetto plays with while mocking the pedant (IV, 3; p. 43^v),[46] the *commedia dell'arte* ('le più nuove Comedie, che mai s'udissero recitare da i bufoni di Vinegia' [III, 9; p. 32^r]), and less pleasant aspects such as the debtors' prison (II, 12; p. 24^r), the death penalty by hanging for thieves (II, 11; p. 23^v), the cops (III, 1; p. 31^r), and counterfeit money (II, 14; p. 30^r).

In short, while called a 'comedy of types,' the *Fabritia* might just as easily, and perhaps more appropriately, be called a 'comedy of manners.' Along with the *Ragazzo* and some of the Plautine adaptations, such as the *Captain*, where the language sparkles with wit, the *Fabritia* deserves to be read at leisure and appreciated, for its many virtues outweigh the play's faults. If nothing else, the work stands out among the comedies of the time as a *speculum consuetudinis*, and as such will not fail to interest the student of the Renaissance.[47]

As a writer of comedies, Lodovico Dolce can justly be placed among the brighter lights of the century, whether or not one agrees with Salza that it was perhaps in this form, above all others, that the author succeeded in winning the highest honours for himself (p. 152). What is clear is that Dolce's three *rifacimenti* and two original works of comedy add to his lustre as one of the outstanding and truly versatile men of letters in the sixteenth century.

4

Between Lord and Lady:
The Tyrant's Captain in Dolce's
Marianna

Dolce as Tragedian

Dolce's fame as a writer in the cinquecento is closely tied to his works of tragedy; in that genre he was active both in producing translations of Euripides and Seneca, works which in some cases might better be called *rifacimenti*, and in writing original plays based on classical and other sources.[1] As his contemporary Carlo Zancarolo wrote to him: 'Tutte le sorte dei poemi v'hanno qualche obbligo et precipue quello delle tragedie nelle quali riuscite felicemente, avete grazia e spirito' (cited by Cicogna, p. 103). Active from 1543, when his adaptation of Seneca's *Thyestes* was first published,[2] to 1567, one year before his death, when his version of *Le troiane* was recited for the second time in Venice,[3] Dolce stands out as one of the more important mid-century tragedians. Federico Doglio, in fact, calls Dolce 'l'autore tragico più notevole [dopo Padre Stefano Tuccio] del nostro secondo '500' (the most notable tragic author in Italy [after Father Stefano Tuccio] of the second half of the sixteenth century; p. lxii). But Tuccio's tragedies were in Latin, and of influence primarily on the *teatro gesuitico* of the latter half of the sixteenth century,[4] while Dolce's works, first appearing twenty years earlier than Tuccio's, were at the forefront of the theatrical productions of the time. Doglio goes on to note that 'le tragedie del Dolce, specialmente la *Marianna*, per i loro caratteri di suggestiva teatralità furono tra i grandi successi del loro tempo, e rilanciando, dopo il periodo giraldiano, la formula del teatro ad effetto, giovarono alla fortuna della nostra tragedia' (Dolce's tragedies, especially the *Marianna*, because of their suggestively theatrical characters, were among the great successes of their time and, relaunching, after the Giraldian period, the formula of theatre for effect, helped the fortune of our tragedy; p. lxiii). Dolce himself, despite his avowed modesty, saw his works as worthy companions to those of Trissino, Rucellai, Giraldi, Speroni, and Aretino.[5]

Regarding his versions of classical authors, Dolce often confessed that his goal was to offer, not a strict translation, but a reworking of the traditional material *in imitation of* the ancients. As Cicogna paraphrases him, 'Dice rifiutare l'ufficio di semplice traduttore: che non si contentò solo di tradurre, ma in più luoghi ha allargato ed ampliato' (he says he refused the obligation of a simple translator: that he was not content just to translate but in numerous places enlarged and amplified; p. 94). What Dolce took from his sources, as he says in his dedicatory letter of 12 January 1559 to the Venetian senator Marc'Antonio da Mula, was the *inventione*, the *testura* ('tessitura,' or basic plot structure), and some of the *sentenze*.[6] Perhaps his reluctance to present the works as accurate 'translations,' particularly those from Euripides, lies in part in his awareness that his Latin originals (assuming with Cicogna that Dolce knew little or no Greek) were not always themselves accurate translations of the Greek.[7]

The distinction between translation and *rifacimento* is often signalled by the language of the title page in the Giolito and Sessa editions, where we find one play 'tratta da Seneca,' another 'tradotta da Seneca.' Such is the case for the *Thieste*.[8] In the 1560 edition of Seneca's tragedies (*Le tragedie di Seneca, tradotte da M. Lodovico Dolce*) containing ten tragedies in verse: *Hercole furioso, Thieste, Tebaide, Ippolito, Edipo, Troade, Medea, Agamennone, Ottavia,* and *Hercole etheo*), we find works that Dolce considered closer to the original, whereas in the edition of his own tragedies of the same year published by Giolito (*Tragedie di M. Lodovico Dolce*), we find works Dolce considers his own ('hauendo io alquanti anni a dietro composte le presenti Tragedie, togliendo le inuentioni, le sentenze, e la testura da gli antichi' [I myself having composed the present tragedies some years earlier, taking the ideas, maxims, and plot structure from the ancients]; p. 3^v).[9]

The same holds true for the *Troiane*, published by Giolito in 1567, where Dolce says that he 'fece sua' Seneca's *Troiane* (which appears in the translated work of 1560 as the *Troade*). The 'original' work (written 'senza obbligarsi a cosa di Seneca' [without feeling any obligation to Seneca]) was performed in Venice, in 1566, by the company of Giovanni de' Martini. Carmelo Musumarra offers a reason why the translators of the sixteenth century might have thought of their works as original: They were eliminating the great distance that separated the original literary work from the public.[10]

At any rate, as regards the translations acknowledged by Dolce, we have the following four works of Euripides: *Hecuba* (1543), *Ifigenia [in Aulide]* (1551, recited in Venice), *Medea* (1557), and *Giocasta* (1549, from *The Phoenician Women*, performed in Venice),[11] and the ten tragedies of Seneca mentioned above. In this alone, Dolce deserves praise.[12]

As far as staged representations of his original works, two plays, *Marianna* and *Le troiane*, had a notable success. The *Marianna* was recited for the first time in the house of Sebastiano Erizzo in 1565 and the second time in the palace of the Duke of Ferrara (now the Fondaco dei Turchi). In the first instance, the leader of the *recitanti* was the famous Antonio Molino, better known as Il Burchiella.[13] Cicogna informs us that, even though it was performed without scenic backdrops and without music, it gained the applause of more than three hundred gentlemen spectators. At the second performance, in the Duke's palace, in full costume and with scenic arrangements and music, the recitation was hindered by the size of the crowd in attendance, although a third staging, in the same location, came off with great success. And as for the *Troiane*, written at the insistence of Giorgio Gradenigo according to Dolce's dedication, the play was performed by the company of Giovanni de' Martini before an audience of illustrious Venetian citizens on 21 March 1566.[14]

What is significant is that all of Dolce's work in this field was intended for performance. His success finds further confirmation in the fortune his adaptations found in other countries. The *Giocasta*, for example, was presented at Gray's Inn, in English translation, as early as 1566 (Doglio, p. lxiii n), and appeared in print in the translation of George Gascoigne and Francis Kinwelmarsh, along with Ariosto's *I suppositi*, with Italian and English on facing pages, in 1573.[15]

With this background in mind, I would like to turn now and in the next chapter to two of Dolce's plays of varying originality, first to the *Marianna*, which I will analyse in the context of the tragic topoi of the theatre of the time, and then, in chapter 5, to the *Didone* (1547), a play whose thematic material, derived from Book 4 of Virgil's *Aeneid*, was of interest to other authors of the cinquecento, including Alessandro Pazzi de' Medici, whose *Dido in Cartagine* was published in Rome in 1524, and G.B. Giraldi, who composed his *Didone* and a *Lettera sulla Didone* in its defence no later than 1543.

The World-View of Cinquecento Tragedy

While the study of Italian Renaissance comedy has undergone a resurgence over the years, interest in and appreciation for Italian tragedy have lagged behind in comparison with the efforts expended on the theatre of other countries, particularly Spain, France, and England.[16] The excuse offered, in part, is that Italy had no Shakespeare, no Lope de Vega or Calderón, no Corneille or Racine. But this inferiority complex and subservience to the major tragedians of other European countries is perhaps misguided and certainly futile. Although scholars have modified the severe judgment of Romantic critics like Symonds, who emphasizes the 'essential feebleness' of Italian tragedy in the cinquecento,[17] justice has not been adequately rendered to at least one of Dolce's tragedies, the *Marianna*, a work of unusual dimensions. Performed in Venice in 1565, the *Marianna* is developed with more vitality than is customarily conceded and contains intriguing themes and well-developed characters.[18]

Although Dolce's play was written after the diffusion of Aristotle's *Poetics* (a work which reinforced the identification of tragic character with figures of the highest rank),[19] the *Marianna* offers a dramatic figure characterized more by nobility of spirit than by that of birth, the tyrant's captain. The captain manifests not only an inner conflict that would appeal to the Romantic imagination but also a greater range of emotions than perhaps some cinquecento critics might allow as verisimilar.

Dolce, moving beyond the self-consistency recommended by Aristotle and Horace, a condition interpreted as limiting the representation of contrasting feelings within one character,[20] depicts the captain as a figure torn between duty (his allegiance to an evil ruler) and human rights (his concern for a victimized woman). This conflict acquires yet greater significance when seen in relation to the world-view inherent in almost all cinquecento tragedy.

The tyrant's captain functions in a world of unnatural disorder, a world which is meaningless apart from a proper background of cosmic order by which to judge it. The concept of a rationally ordered and harmonious universe was very much a part of the collective mind of the Renaissance, from its expression in the poems of Lorenzo de' Medici in 1474[21] to its appearance in the prose works of Fray Luis de Granada in 1582, who finds order subsumed in a pomegranate.[22] The natural *ordo rerum*, established and controlled by providential design in the Christian tradition reaffirmed by the Counter-Reformation, was seen with greatest clarity in the movement of the celestial bodies.[23] This conception of order, so common to the time that it needed little explicit reference,[24] is evident in the imagery not only of the two plays in question, but of such representative tragedies as Trissino's *Sofonisba* (1515), Rucellai's *Rosmunda* (composed around 1515), Giraldi's *Orbecche* (1541), Sperone's *Canace* (1542), and Torelli's *Merope* (1589). In order to understand better the world in which the tyrant's captain moves, and his own significance, let us examine briefly the imagery of these five plays, before approaching Dolce's *Marianna*.

In the sixteenth century, the Humanist conception of the world, usually seen as orderly, sane, and secure, gave way to various degrees of pessimism. The harmony of the world was threatened by man's perversity. The Chorus in Trissino's *Sofonisba* at one point invokes the sun to bring more serene days, contrasting celestial harmony with the earthly disorder caused by wars. The sun is apostrophized as being 'infinite and eternal' and as bringing with its 'sure voyage' day after evening, and summer, autumn, and winter after spring.[25] Since the ups and downs of fortune, as pagan Scipione notes (in close to Christian terms), do not spare even those dear to the gods (lines 1160–3), and the present is full of plundering, anger, wrongs, wounds, and deaths (lines 622–4), man's only hope is to trust in providence, for the future, as the last lines of the play tell us, resides with divine power, whose unknown manner makes all foresight futile.[26]

Giovanni Rucellai's *Rosmunda*, a *tragedia di fin lieto*, begins in a kingdom where, because of war, natural law has been subverted. The new king, Albuino, has forbidden the rite of burial to the dead. Rosmunda, aware that her father, King Comundo, has been slain, is consumed by her desire to find and bury him before she herself crosses the river Styx. The women of the Chorus, for their part, perturbed by the unhappy condition of Rosmunda, lament not only the instability of earthly happiness, but also their own loss of freedom. Addressing the divine mind which governs all in the eternal order, they imply that it would be unnatural for God to care for the lower orders of being and not for humans, higher on the scale. The entire passage is a well-constructed elaboration of the motif of order:

> O divin'alta mente, che governi,
> Rotando il cielo attorno,
> Le volubili sfere, e ciò ch'è in quelle;
> E col vago variar de' moti eterni
> Rivolgi in un sol giorno
> Il Sol, la Luna, e le minute Stelle;
> E tante cose belle:
> La luce al dì, e poi l'ombra alla sera;
> E fai tornar com'era
> Ogni stagion, con ordin sempiterno,
> Sempre la rosa il Maggio, il ghiaccio 'l verno:
> Signor, che desti 'l senso agli animali,

E insin nelle piante
Ponesti con tant'ordine la vita;
Increscati de' miseri mortali,
Ai quali 'l tuo sembiante
Donasti, e l'alta mente a te unita;
Sia la mia voce udita. (p. 157)

[O lofty divine mind, which rules, with heaven rotating around, the ever-moving spheres and that which in them lies; and with the graceful variation of eternal motions turns in a single day the sun, the moon, and the small stars; and so many beautiful things: [brings] light to the day, and then shadow to the evening; and makes every season return as it once was, with everlasting order, always the rose in May, ice in winter: Lord, who gave consciousness to animals, and even in plants placed life with so much order, have pity on mortal miseries, [mortals] to whom you gave your image and the lofty mind united to you; may my voice be heard.]

From the heavens, to the seasons, to the ladder or chain of being, to the correspondence of macrocosm and microcosm, of God to man – all are motifs central to the world picture of the Renaissance.

The Chorus, in its final speech in Act III, returns to the motif of the *ordo rerum* in order to stress the instability of earthly things. Kingdoms are like spiders' webs broken by any breeze, while the thread by which mortals hang from the celestial spheres can be broken in a thousand ways (pp. 176–7).[27] Rosmunda herself is an example and a victim of ever-varying fate (p. 175). The Chorus, having enumerated the celestial correspondences (from the highest heavens to the spheres of fire, air, earth, and water), concludes that heaven cannot be held by human knots (p. 177).

The moral distance from God's purity to the evil of the world is emphasized in the Chorus's prayer concluding Act IV: 'Dalla tua *alta* sfera / Pon mente chi *quaggiù* t'onora e cole' (From your *high* sphere, think of those *down here* who honour and adore you; p. 188, my emphasis). If graceful spring follows cold winter, and after rain, the sun, why, they ask, is our grief eternal? (pp. 187–8). The answer, of course, is that nothing on earth is eternal.

In Giraldi's *Orbecche*, Oronte also comments on the instability of human fate (III, 5), but the comparison of heaven to earth is made by the Chorus. Behind their ideas, expressed at the end of Act IV, lies the concept of the earth as a reflection, a microcosm, of the universe. The order inherent in nature is reflected in the elaborate metrical structure of the Chorus's speech, composed of eight identical stanzas of ten verses (rhyming AbcBDaCDeE) of which the first five stanzas, despite the editor's punctuation, are syntactically a single period.[28] Giraldi begins by apostrophizing 'faith' (in the sense, perhaps, of cosmic order) and then, six stanzas later, asks why it is that man is the only one to break its law. In the intervening verses we find a long exposition of how faith binds all contrary things so that nothing ever varies from the order established by nature. Even heaven preserves the accustomed law, for all the spheres, from the lowest to the most sublime, regulate themselves by the motion of the first.[29]

Giraldi enumerates the elements and their appropriate places, noting how all created things fit into an eternal scheme of generation, death, and rebirth. In verses reminiscent of Trissino's, Giraldi adds that this is why spring follows winter and then brings summer and autumn.[30] Against this background of order preserved by faith, Sulmone, the impious tyrant, is seen as an example of those who wish to destroy faith's holy name. As such he is unnatural. Orbecche, who kills the tyrant, asks the sun how it could look on the tyrant's deeds of cruelty without fleeing. Sulmone, having transgressed against the universal law of faith, deserves to die, a sacrificial victim to the gods, in order to restore order. But Giraldi's ultimate message is that the good found on earth, more specifically man's happiness, is slight compared with that of heaven. As the Chorus says in its last speech, mortal felicity is vain and fleeting, a shadow of the eternal. He who discerns the truth will direct his thoughts to immortal happiness found in heaven, where God governs a11.[31]

Speroni expresses his ideas on the *ordo rerum* through Venus, who delivers the prologue in *Canace*. The queen of the third heaven castigates those of low intellect who imagine heaven to be lacking in perfection because all goods on earth are imperfect. Human beings think, she says, that they can raise themselves to heaven and discern clearly the thoughts and decisions within the lofty and secret natures of eternal substances ('I consigli e le menti / Per entro le nature alte e secrete / Delle sostanze eterne'), but instead they are incapable of even preserving peace on earth.[32] Acting most often according to passion, rather than reason, humankind is bound to the material order of nature, which tends towards chaos and confusion, and is thus subject to causality. The few individuals who submit themselves to the higher order of nature, to just law and reason, strive to attain love, harmony, and peace.

Pomponio Torelli opens his tragedy *Merope* with an image central to the concept of order, or its lack, that of Merope as a ship having lost its sailor.

The disorder characteristic of the realm of Messene is emphasized indirectly when the Chorus, full of hope, praises the god Love, who from chaos and disorder ('perpetua guerra') created order with variety, whence the world with so many forms is beautiful. Later, the Chorus, employing atmospheric and climatic images, compares the happy past to the grievous present (the queen, for example, has a cloudy heart and heavy lashes and the sun of her eyes distills itself in tears),[33] only to find respite in the natural order these meteorological images suggest: Phoebus will not always remain below the earth; ice and frost give way to pleasing flowers.[34] Torelli avoids, through images, the usual phraseology of day following night and spring following winter.

At the close of Act I, the Chorus, like Trissino's, addresses the sun ('pure eye of the sky'), asking it to clear away all clouds. Despite the fact that events on earth and in its depths are stormy, God, they claim, will bring justice and peace (pp. 323–4). That the tyrant Polifonte is a force of disorder is made manifest in Act II in a speech on law and justice. As he says to his captain, 'the laws of which you speak so much have no power over princes' (p. 338). Establishing himself outside of nature and not subject to eternal laws, the tyrant, instead, is a source of discord and chaos. The realm, lacking a just prince, is unnatural, a river without water, a ring without a jewel (p. 374).

As in other tragedies of the Counter-Reformation, the references to the fallaciousness of human foresight are numerous. The Chorus, addressing Jove, asserts that, though his infinite power is known, his designs are hidden in shadowy depths: 'È nota l'infinita tua possanza; / Ma tuoi consigli son celati, e chiusi / Fra più profondi, e tenebrosi abissi' (p. 335). Others lament inexorable fate. At the end of Act IV the image of a sailor (the sea of course is the image *par excellence* of instability and disorder) once again appears. The Chorus, praising hope, refers to the wearied sailor who, after a storm, finds consolation in a small star. But even at this moment the sound of arms brings doubt. The outcome is good, however; the tyrant has been killed, order restored. As the wise counsellor says, in closing the play on an atmospheric note, 'Phoebus, crowned with green, triumphal laurel, spreads everywhere his rays of gold' (p. 399).

From earthly storms to the celestial sun, from disorder to order: this is the essential movement characteristic of *tragedie di fin lieto*, the movement sought but lost in *tragedie orribili*. Within this scheme the tyrant is a figure who has transgressed cosmic law. The chaos he creates is directly opposed to the rational order inherent in the universe. His subjects, unable on their own to establish harmony in the realm, and unable to fathom the hidden designs of the divine, exist on hopes, so often fallacious. If consolation is to be found, it is in the awareness that there is a natural order of things, an order, furthermore, controlled by the unknown but all-knowing mind of the gods.

La Marianna of Lodovico Dolce

The thematic background of Dolce's *Marianna*, the stage upon which the tyrant's captain acts, is essentially the same as that represented in the cinquecento tragedies mentioned above. The manner in which the captain fulfils his duties, the ends he endeavours to effect, the hazards he faces, are all a direct result of his living in a realm of chaos and of being a figure who seeks to establish order.

In turning to the *Marianna*, one finds an initial situation of disorder. Pluto, in the second prologue,[35] furnishes the first indication of this by sending Jealousy to Herod in order to drive him to madness and to cause chaos and ruin throughout the realm. The unnatural state of the world is here subsumed in the instability of Herod's mind. As Marianna says in the first speech of Act I, even the sun hides his rays behind the clouds. The thematic implications of the image are obvious. Herod's hatred has passed all natural bounds. Not only has he killed her grandfather and brother to solidify his throne, but now, she adds, he treats her like an enemy. When the tyrant's captain, Soemo, enters, we learn the secret for which he has risked his life in telling Marianna: Herod had left orders that, if he were to be killed while on a trip to Egypt, Marianna herself should be slain. Soemo realizes that he merits to some extent a 'bloody death' just for having failed to obey Herod, although, as he says, 'certo obbedir è cosa indegna / A signor, che comanda offici ingiusti' (certainly it is an unworthy thing to obey a lord who commands unjust deeds; pp. 216–17). Marianna recognizes his 'sincere love' which led him to reveal the impiety of cruel Herod, and praises his faith and good counsel (p. 217).

Encouraged, Soemo relates Herod's suspicions concerning a possible conspiracy by his children, suspicions which have increased on his return as a result of seeing Marianna so perturbed. The captain tells the queen of his own attempts to dispel Herod's doubts by protesting his own fidelity and by depicting Marianna's anger as feminine resentment; she is either angry at having been enclosed in the castle during his voyage or has heard a false tale of Herod and a concubine (pp. 219–20). Alone, Soemo fears Herod's anger and laments his indiscretion. At best he should have kept quiet and, if Herod were killed in Egypt, then have refused to carry out his orders. But, as he says, 'sì mi parve un tal mandato ingiusto, / Che tener non potei le labbra chiuse' (such an order seemed so unjust to me that I could not keep my lips closed; p. 223).

Soemo's predicament is a result not only of his divided loyalties – his duty to serve Herod, his concern for Marianna – but also of his sense of moral values, which is greater than his master's. Though a figure of low social standing, he is in reality noble in spirit. Moreover, he functions as a force of reason striving for light and harmony in a world of blind and chaotic madness. The Chorus, giving voice to Soemo's desires, closes the first act by asking for the return of the sun, symbol of order and happiness.

Despite Soemo's efforts to bring about a reconciliation, in Act II a counter-figure, the tyrant's sister Solome, persuades Herod that Marianna is plotting his death. A victim both of his sister's evil and of his own *pazzia*, Herod accuses Marianna, who responds with counter-accusations, and also castigates him for having loved only her body. Marianna finds temporary respite after the cupbearer who has aided Solome's plot confesses, in an unexpected and very effective reversal, to his lie. But the captain is less fortunate. The king's trusted eunuch Beniamino informs Herod of his captain's breach of promise. This is enough for the tyrant to imagine a love affair between his wife and the captain. The Chorus, in closing Act II, laments the fugacity of mortal happiness and sounds the Golden Age theme so common to the Renaissance.[36] Tracing the decline of man from the biblical 'first youthful age' down to the present, the Chorus concludes that it is not fate or cruel fortune which torments humans, but our wickedness alone: 'E non il Fato, o la crudel Fortuna, / Ma sol malvagità ci sferza e preme' (pp. 249-50). The blame for evil is laid squarely on each individual.

The impossibility of communication between Herod and Marianna underlies the action in Act III. Marianna's only source of consolation is that in time God will right the disorder of the earth; if the unjust escape punishment in this life, they will find it in the next. It is the queen's mother Alessandra, however, who comments on the inscrutability of God's providence and on the necessity of living so as to please him (p. 253).

When Herod orders his men to seize both Alessandra and Marianna, a Counsellor, a figure who shares with Soemo the duties and characteristics of Rucellai's captain, attempts to dissuade him, proffering examples of good conduct. Passion, the *Consigliere* notes, referring to sight, can make you see in error ('vi può far veder torto'; p. 256). But, despite refuting the king's arguments and pointing out at great length the fallacy of his conjectures (all in an excellent speech entirely lacking in adulation), the Counsellor is unable to open 'blind' Herod's eyes, since the tyrant himself thinks he sees clearly (pp. 256–60).

A second scene of confrontation, this one between Herod and Soemo, follows immediately. It is a scene handled with masterly skill. The characters of both men are developed with subtle touches and remain well defined. The pace is excellent, with unusually well-maintained suspense. Especially felicitous are the initial speeches of direct attack and parry, where Herod notes Soemo's paralysis, his inability to speak, his pallor, his 'gesti sbigottiti' (gestures of dismay), and where the captain in his vague response displays the struggle to compose his mind ('Signor, qual volta io penso a la gran forza, / Che la fortuna ha ne le cose umane' [Lord, whenever I think of the great power which fortune has in the affairs of men]), followed by Herod's incisive comment 'Tu pigli da lontan la tua risposta' (you begin your response from afar; p. 263). Soemo's conclusion, after an exculpatory speech of forty-seven lines, that he has erred, but that his error is worthy of pardon (p. 265), is true on both accounts. However, his hopes of finding pity on earth, mirroring that shown by the 'King of Heaven,' are to be deluded. Herod, a bad theologian, like so many tyrants, exonerates himself for his actions on what to him seem equally solid grounds – on justice of the type practised by the 'King of the Elements' when he refused to pardon the first error of our 'ancient father' (p. 268).

The Chorus, in its final speech of Act III, laments the condition of those who serve a tyrant, thus accentuating the precarious position of someone like Soemo. The anti-tyranny and anti-court motifs of the Chorus are continued in Act IV in a speech by the messenger, who announces Soemo's death and relates his last protestations of innocence. Herod's next concern is Marianna. Having shown her Soemo's head and hands before ordering them to be cast to the dogs, Herod now condemns his wife to death. When their two children beg for Marianna's life, Herod calls them sons of Soemo and orders both youths to be strangled in front of their mother. Furthermore, the soldiers are to behead Alessandra in Marianna's presence (pp. 288–93). Again, the Counsellor, who continues Soemo's role, is unable to change Herod's mind.

The final ode of the Chorus in Act IV returns to the Golden Age theme of a past characterized by order and goodness which has degenerated into a present where men gain the throne through ruthlessness rather than through innate worth.[37] Following an encomiastic reference to Venice, which will bring back the happy age of gold, the Chorus passes to a Christian motif. Addressing God, they pray: 'E se di qualche errore / punir vuoi, Padre, il popol tuo che langue, / Punisci noi, Signore, / Nè pera l'innocente e real sangue' (And if for some error you wish to punish your people, who are languishing, Father, punish us, oh Lord, and let not innocent and royal blood perish; p. 299). But their hopes are as futile as were the actions of Soemo and the Counsellor. It is only after the deaths of the queen, her two children, and her mother that the tyrant finally repents, in Act V, blaming jealousy for his deeds. His new-found compassion, however, in the messenger's words, has arrived too late (p. 304). The details of the deaths, presented in a powerful speech, acquire greater dramatic force in that Herod now listens to them as a new person, aware of and lamenting his own cruelty.[38] Grief-stricken, he blames, not fortune, but his own evil as the cause of his loss. The fatal lack of communication between husband and wife now extends beyond the grave ('Marianna, io ti chiamo, e tu non m'odi' [Marianna, I call you, and you don't hear me]). As Herod himself notes, in hell he will have lost his beloved Marianna for eternity. The final speech of the Chorus, only nine lines long, and perhaps the play's weakest, ends the tragedy with an abrupt moral lesson: Since anger is the cause of incomparable evils, one should not allow the reins of reason (reminiscent of Dante's 'il fren dell'arte') to fall from the hand ('non vi lasciate uscir di mano / Il fren de la ragione'; pp. 315–16).[39]

In Dolce, the captain, belonging to the long tradition of those who offer advice to the prince, performs a service comparable to the role of the courtier advocated by Castiglione. He functions as a counsellor, striving to temper the excesses of a tyrant in order to produce a state of order and equilibrium. His position is rendered especially precarious, despite his strong character, by his divided loyalties and resultant missteps. And, like the Italians of the cinquecento, he fails in his attempts to control outside forces, largely because he is able to employ only words against physical power. The truly tragic message of this play, in which the anti-tyranny theme is so strong, seems to be that only God is powerful enough to thwart the forces of evil. If any victory is to be gained, it is only by those who trust in Divine Providence. Mankind, represented in the figure of the captain or the counsellor, fails in its attempt to establish an image of celestial order on earth. The insistence in *Marianna* on humanity's own evil rather than on the ineluctable force of an external fate is significant. The earth, as a result of man's fall, is no longer a faithful microcosm of celestial order; the Golden Age in the structure of this play is indeed irretrievable.

Although the play deals with a lofty figure who falls because of a tragic flaw (jealousy which leads to insanity), the situation of the other characters is no less to be lamented. Those who suffer include not only the evil (personified in the tyrant who experiences the loss of someone dear) and the good (personified in women or in the young and innocent), but also the minor characters – the Chorus, the counsellors, and the captain. The last suffers because of his inability to act effectively to stop others from suffering. One of the tragic aspects of this play lies, then, not merely in the fall of a lofty individual, but in the failure of society as a whole. But, at least the captain, though unable to bring about a condition of harmony, perhaps in part because of his 'flaw' (divided loyalties and reliance on words against tyrannical force), stands out for his efforts to create order out of disorder. For this effort alone, though lowly by birth, he becomes ennobled in spirit, and thus is truly worthy of the label 'tragic hero.'

5

From Imitation to Emulation:
Dolce's Classicism and the Fate of
Infelix Dido in Cinquecento Tragedy

Greek tragedy of the classical period derived many of its elements from earlier epic, in particular from the *Iliad* and the corpus of myths provided therein, although the *Odyssey* also provided paradigms for tragic (and comic) plots.[1] What better example, then, following the recommendation of Aristotle that tragic poets should draw their material from epic, than for Dolce and his predecessors in the sixteenth century to have recourse to Virgil's great poem, the *Aeneid*,[2] and to integrate into their works female characters and the themes of love and madness, dear also to tragedians such as Euripides?[3] When they do so, they re-enact a pattern, familiar in the Latins, regarding the transmittal of tragic myth from one language to another. That is, the first works of transition are usually close imitations, at times sheer translations, of the original, while later works are more independent, despite the requirements of adhering to the general framework of the original story. In Rome, so far as can be judged from the extant fragments, the first imitators of Euripides – writers such as Ennius, Pacuvius, and Accius – followed their Greek models rather slavishly. With Seneca's works, however, we find tragedies that, while parallel to Greek plays in so far as their themes are concerned, not only demonstrate greater independence in the use of common material, but also contain original elements.

In Italian literature, this movement from slavish imitation to independent emulation can be seen in the three most significant tragedies of the cinquecento to deal with the story of Dido – the *Dido in Cartagine* of Alessandro Pazzi de' Medici, composed in 1524 and apparently circulated only in manuscript; the *Didone* of Giambattista Giraldi Cinthio, probably written before 1541 and performed at the Court of Duke Ercole II of Este in 1543 (which is also the date usually cited for Giraldi's *Lettera sulla*

'*Didone*,' addressed to the Duke in defence of his play);[4] and the *Didone* of Lodovico Dolce, performed and published in 1547, apparently the most successful of the three plays in the sixteenth century itself.[5]

As developed by Virgil, Dido's story contains its own inherent drama, seen primarily in the conflict between love and duty, which evolves into a juxtaposition of the feminine *querelle* of abandonment and a masculine defence based on heroism and the demands of destiny. Feminine discourse (love, ease, and peace) and female perceptions (marriage sanctioned by the gods) duel with masculine discourse (duty, fame, and war) and male perceptions (cohabitation with no legal bonds). When Dido refers to 'conubia nostra' (IV, 316), for example, Aeneas responds that he never entered such a compact ('nec coniugis unquam / praetendi taedas aut haec in foedera veni' [IV, 338–9]).[6] He counters her protestations of love for him with his love of country (IV, 347), her emotional outburst with his calm logic, suppressing, with masculine steadfastness, his pain (IV, 332). In place of Dido's suicide, Aeneas offers what can only appear to the modern reader as a rather weak metaphorical self-sacrifice, renouncing his love on the altar of duty. These built-in structures of contrast must surely have appealed to the tragedians of the cinquecento.

The contrastive thematics, in fact, are evident from the episode's first moments, where Dido is seen both as a woman 'of surpassing beauty' (I, 496) and as a queen dispensing justice. The conflict becomes more obviously internal in Book 4, where the drama is that within Dido's soul, as decency (*pudor*) wrestles with love. Individual desire (self-fulfilment) duels with Dido's universal fame (duty to one's people). That masculine discourse will win out over feminine becomes clear when authorial judgment goes against the goddess Juno herself. The scene of the *innamoramento*, referred to by Juno as 'sure wedlock' (126), concludes with condemnation: Dido 'calls it marriage and with that name veils her sin!' (172).

The internal conflict becomes external once Mercury reminds Aeneas of his duty. As a woman about to be abandoned, Dido is allowed a full range of emotions, couched in forms that run the gamut from accusations of betrayal, logical appeals to reason, and pleas, to unrestrained rage and ultimate vindictiveness. When the queen learns of Aeneas's guile and accosts him, her lengthy speech, full of exclamations, rhetorical questions, and pleas, is perhaps the high point of the dramatic conflict inherent in the story. What makes the speech so intense is the artistic control with which Virgil expresses Dido's passion. To look at just the beginning of the speech, Dido's first three questions are framed with the accusatory vocatives 'perfide' and 'crudelis,' while the middle question itself is a well-balanced triad: ' "nec te noster amor nec te data dextera quondam / nec moritura tenet crudeli funere Dido?" ' (' "Can neither our love keep thee, nor the pledge once given, nor the doom of a cruel death for Dido?" '; 307–8). An abrupt exclamatory question – ' "quid?" ' – gives her the breath to launch a longer question, again with repeated words and parallel structures, before a brief, plaintive ' "mene fugis?" ' (' "From me dost thou flee?" '; 314). The entreaty that follows, anchored with an artistically structured triple plea (' "per ... has lacrimas dextramque tuam ... / ... / per conubia nostra, per inceptos hymenaeos" ') (' "By these tears and thy right hand ... by our marriage, by the wedlock begun" ' [314–16]), ends with a vain wish: If only a child had been born to her, if only there were a tiny Aeneas playing in her hall to remind her of him, she would be able to bear his flight (327–30).

The reference to motherhood, Dido's vain longing for a child, crystallizes the motifs of gender and shows Dido, at least in the context of biological determinism, at her most human. Aeneas, at least, has a son; in fact, this is one of the forces that draws him away to gain a new empire. Dido's love will be fruitless. From this point on in the story, having bared her soul, she can open herself no more. There is no greater appeal she can make, no other outlet for her love.

Given the inherent drama of the Virgilian model, who could have hoped to surpass the master? The answer is obvious. No one. So what, then, might have motivated the tragedians of the cinquecento to employ Virgil's great story, other than the Aristotelian recommendation to avail oneself of the material of epic poetry? Perhaps the answer is simple, since a parallel exists in our own time. The form of tragedy had the same relation to epic as the form of a movie's screenplay has to a novel worthy of adaptation. In this sense, the interests of Renaissance society correspond to the demands of the marketplace of today.[7] The important question is perhaps not why (although that, too, is intriguing), but exactly how and with what degree of success the tragedians of the cinquecento adapted the classical material to produce works of interest to their own time.

Alessandro Pazzi de' Medici

In preparation for the rehearsal of a play, the English actor Charles Laughton once told James Garner to 'take the risk of being bad.' I am reminded of the expression when faced with Alessandro Pazzi de' Medici's *Dido in Cartagine*, the first work to dramatize Virgil's story. One takes the risk of being bad in the hope of attaining greatness. Unfortunately, in Pazzi's case, the risk did not pay off.[8] Still, the author must be praised for his intentions, if nothing else. But his tragedy, composed in 1524, also stands as a noteworthy example of experimentation in metrics, preceding in time the *Nuova poesia* of Claudio Tolomei (1538–9) and going beyond Alberti's efforts to reproduce the Latin dactylic hexameter and Dati's work with Sapphic odes.[9] As Angelo Solerti notes, all these poets sought to distance themselves from the sonority of the rhymed hendeca-syllable. In this, Pazzi was successful, although the result failed to please his readers.

Learned in both Greek and Latin, translator of Aristotle's *Poetics* (published in 1536 in Latin with facing Greek text, but possibly completed as early as 1526, the date of the dedicatory letter), Pazzi aimed in his Italian works at a verse that would best reflect the meters of Greek and Latin poetry. As he wrote in his preface to both the *Dido in Cartagine* and the *Ifigenia in Tauride*: 'mi pare necessariamente si debba ricorrere ad una specie di metro non molto dissimile alla prosa, nel quale sia non dimeno occultamento numero, et symmetria poetica, il che dico essere in questa specie di versi, et in ogni altra più et meno, nella quale sia observatione et legge determinata; purchè la quantità delle sillabe non exceda la forma del verso, perchè tal numero et symmetria si causano da quella uniformità observata continuamente' (it seems necessary to me that one ought to have recourse to a kind of meter not very different from prose, in which nevertheless there is a hidden rhythm and poetic symmetry, which I say is in this kind of verse, and in every other kind more or less, in which one finds observation and a fixed law, as long as the quantity of syllables does not exceed the form of the verse, because rhythm and symmetry result from that uniformity being continuosuly observed; pp. 50–1). In fact, his solution – a twelve-syllable line which can be *piano, tronco,* or *sdrucciolo* – is not without its merits, since iambic trimeter, a triple repetiton of $x - u -$ (where x is either short or long),[10] was recited in the classical period without music, and Pazzi's verse, which he admits will strike his readers as awkward, is best read as prose.[11]

Pazzi's wrote his tragedies following an extensive study of Euripides, whom he read in a countryside villa while fleeing the plague in Florence.[12] As to the subject-matter, Pazzi says he followed Horace's precept that tragic material is best derived from Homer, as opposed to invented: 'mi missi in tale idioma a comporre la Tragedia Didone in Carthagine, observando il precepto Oratiano, il quale più appruova nella sua mirabile poetica gli argumenti tragici tractati da Homero, che il fingere nuove persone, et nuovi casi' (I set myself to compose in such an idiom the tragedy *Dido in Carthagine*, observing the precept of Horace, who in his marvellous poetics prefers tragic subjects drawn from Homer to the invention of new characters and new events; p. 46). In Dido's case, of course, Pazzi's Homer was Virgil, from whom, as he admits, he took as much as he could: 'in gran parte in epsa Tragedia ho imitato Vergilio adiungendo molte cose pertinenti alla exornatione, et dispositione del poema. Dal qual confesso ingenuamente haver tolto il più che ho potuto' (in large part in this tragedy I imitated Virgil, adding many things pertinent to the embellishment and dispositon of the poem, from whom I confess to have taken as much as I could; p. 47). His justification is that Virgil himself did the same, imitating not only Homer, Hesiod, and Theocritus, among the Greeks, but also Ennius and Lucretius, among the Latins, and, for the Dido episode, the fourth book of Apollonius of Rhodes's *Argonautica* (p. 47).[13]

Following the example of Trissino's *Sofonisba* and Greek tragedy, Pazzi does not divide his play into acts. The 1767 verses, however, have subdivisions demarcated by long speeches of the chorus.[14] He begins *in medias res* and thus is able to observe the unity of time, with the action transpiring over the course of twenty-four hours.[15] Since the story was so well known, Pazzi does not hesitate to announce in the prologue the resolution of the play. While possibly lessening the dramatic impact, the procedure is difficult to criticize, especially when one considers that modern play- and moviegoers often see the same work more than once, deriving pleasure from each occasion. Pazzi, instead, in an attempt to create conflict, expands on Virgil and has both Jarba and Pygmalion attack Dido. As Robert Turner notes, 'cette guerre est une des principales données de la pièce' (this war is one of the work's main motifs; p. 17), but, as he also notes, Pazzi had several classical, late-medieval, and Renaissance sources for the rage of Jarba, including Ovid, Silius Italicus, Boccaccio, Guido da Pisa's *Fiore d'Italia*, Ravisius, and Niccolò Perotti.[16] The significant point, however, is not the fact that Pazzi had antecedents, but that he is less adept at developing internal conflict, preferring the more obvious, external clash of enemy forces.[17]

Seneca's influence, in its most rudimentary form, is also evident throughout the play. The Chorus's speeches, for example, are full of *sententiae*, each verse of which is prefaced by a quote mark as an aid to the reader, with aphorisms along the lines of 'Ah quanto dolore / 'morde la conscientia a chi senza freno / 'seguendo quel che li piace, non si possede?' (Ah how much grief gnaws the conscience of one who without restraint, following what is pleasing, does not control oneself?; p. 62). Both

Giraldi and Dolce will expand the *sententiae*, more successfully, into longer moralizations.[18]

Having touched on the twin motifs of restraint and pleasure in the first episode, Pazzi attempts to dramatize this opposition through dialogue. The Chorus announces Anna, and for the first time we have an actual exchange between characters, a scene in which logical Anna portrays herself as the voice of reason, a discounter of dreams, capable of providing a reasoned defence of her sister, while enamoured Dido embodies the voice of passion, a believer in dreams, who succumbs to self-accusation. The dominant motifs are fear and loathing.[19] The ensuing dialogue between the two sisters, eight verses of stichomythia in imitation of both Euripides and Seneca (where the one-line exchanges are employed for scenes of intense emotion or strong argumentation), presents the dramatic opposition of *furor* and *ragione*, with Anna saying such things as 'Regina il troppo amore al furore è presso' and 'Revoca la ragione, et ripiglia il freno' (Queen, excessive love borders on madness ... recall reason and take up the reins), to which Dido responds, 'Il freno d'ogni mio arbitrio tiene altri hor mai' and 'Preda legata sono da insolubili lacci' (By now someone else holds the reins of my will ... I am a prey bound by unloosable nets; pp. 68–9).

Having established these thematic oppositions through speech, Pazzi now sets in motion the play's action. But his skill at advancing the story line is pedestrian and leaves much to be desired. He plods in Virgil's steps, methodical and prosaic, unfolding events with a lack of imagination; in his translation, Virgil's concise verses lose all their intensity.[20] To make matters worse, during the exchanges between Dido and Aeneas, the Chorus intersperses comments that seem to function in part as *didascalie* – stage directions or subtitles that interpret events for us and tell us what we should see. After Dido's first plea, for example, the Chorus says: 'Come potrà costui non piegarsi a questi / sì dolci preghi et sì pietose parole? / Ma lasso il non cangiarsi nel volto gli occhi / non pur mover, mi tengon molto dubbiosa' (How can he not bend to such sweet prayers and such pitiful words as these? But, alas, his unchanging face and eyes that do not move keep me in great doubt; p. 77). And when Aeneas responds, the Chorus tells Dido that 'già tremon le tue membra, già non sostenghono / gli occhi sdegnosi, il volto del Re superbo' (already your body trembles, already your disdainful eyes cannot bear the face of the proud king; pp. 79–80). Clearly, the effect is somewhat amateurish.

The narrative moments continue, with the Chorus describing events as related by Virgil, and with the author attempting to create action through vibrant language.[21] Despite this, the scenes remain static on the whole, and lacking in dramatic intensity. In the third episode, for example, another of Pazzi's contributions to the story, Mercury informs Jarba that Aeneas is leaving, then promises to take him, unperceived by others, to see first the Trojans' departure, then Dido's palace.[22] The scene, though brief, creates no tension, and the same can be said for the twenty-verse stichomythia between Dido and Anna, after the latter returns with the news of her failure to detain Aeneas.[23]

Finally, Jarba's decision to kill his ally Pygmalion in an attempt to win Dido's hand (an original motif) provides for a Senecan (or Euripidean) conclusion to the play.[24] In one of the work's more interesting moments, Dido accepts Jarba's offer of marriage, affirming that 'ciascun de' cedere / a quel che 'l ciel dispone' (each one must yield to what heaven disposes; p. 112), and soon after we find her accepting her brother's head and hands from a messenger. Her lack of emotion (she accepts the gruesome remains as a 'grato dono') has amused modern readers, among them Emilio Bertana (see Turner, p. 28). Dido's death itself takes place off stage, with Barce narrating her final words to the Nuntio so he can inform Jarba.

On the whole, Pazzi has done his best to dramatize the Virgilian story, integrating Euripidean and Senecan elements in an attempt to create greater horror. While he has embellished the plot with a few original notes, his play is noteworthy more as an experiment in meter than for its poetic beauty or dramatic innovations. The narrative source has not been fully assimilated, as seen in the use of banal speeches to advance the action, a preponderance of description, a recourse to a facile external conflict, and a rather shallow characterization of the protagonists. Accused of being a pedestrian translator of Virgil and a learned imitator rather than creator, criticized for his rough verses and lack of elegance, he nevertheless deserves praise for taking the first step towards unifying the motifs of Greek and Latin tragedy with those of Latin epic, and for introducing the story of Dido into sixteenth-century Italian tragedy.

Giambattista Giraldi Cinthio

As P.R. Horne, in his study of *The Tragedies of Giambattista Cinthio Giraldi*, notes, Giraldi, through a misreading of Aristotle, gave invented stories the primacy over traditional material (pp. 34–5), so it is no surprise to find among his nine tragedies only two – the *Didone* and the *Cleopatra* – that are based on traditional material. The reason for writing these works was simple: The subjects were suggested to Giraldi by the Duke of Ferrara. As a consequence, with regard to the *Didone*, we find what Horne has called a 'pedestrian imitation' of Virgil, though Giraldi's style, I would add, is not nearly as awkward as that of Pazzi (p. 75). The tragedian follows the *Aeneid* quite closely, adding little of his own to the plot, in part because he felt constrained not only by his material, but also, as Horne notes, by Aristotle's dictum that tragedy and epic do not differ as regards subject-matter: to write a tragedy based on a narrative poem, one needs merely to cut up the plot and distribute its parts among the appropriate characters of the play. It is because of this conception of the interchangeability of the two forms that Giraldi, in his *Lettera sulla Didone*, justifies the appearance of supernatural creatures like Venus and Juno (criticized by the Greek lecturer Francesco Porto) simply because they appear in the original source.[25]

Another feature of his play that Giraldi felt needed defending was the great number of characters. As Horne points out, of the twenty characters 'only six have a proper part in the action, and many of them, particularly some of the messengers, could easily be suppressed' (p. 87). The majesty of the theme and the importance of tragic spectacle won out over principles of economy. In his *Lettera sulla Didone*, Giraldi justifies the number simply by saying they are necessary to the plot. He also defends writing in verse; the division of the play into acts and scenes (here Giraldi cites the example of the Romans); the monologues (necessary to show the intimate thoughts of great characters); and the length of the play, which was nearly six hours long at the request of Duke Ercole.

In his *Discorso intorno al comporre dei romanzi, delle comedie, e delle tragedie* (1544), Giraldi recommends, among other things, that the action be shown, not told, and that the playwright observe the unity of time. The action of the *Didone*, in fact, even though Giraldi starts at the beginning and not *in medias res*, takes place during the course of one long day. Later critics have not always recognized this fact. Robert Turner, for example, says that, since Euripides' *Heracles* was not limited to one day and Aristotle permitted this licence, Giraldi allows the action of the *Didone* to take place over the course of two days (p. 33). But this is not true, and Giraldi goes to great pains to attest the opposite, with character after character talking about all that has happened 'hoggi' (today).[26] It seems, in truth, as if he is proud of the fact that he has compressed so much action (from the goddesses' initial conflict, through the hunt and *innamoramento* of Dido and Aeneas, to their separation and Dido's eventual suicide) into one day. The result, however, stretches the limits of verisimilitude.

Following a detached prologue, in which Giraldi tells his audience what he has taken from Virgil and what the thematic hinges are,[27] the play opens with a monologue of Juno that combines plot features from Virgil and Seneca. The background is Virgilian (derived from *Aeneid* I, 27–54), the technique Senecan (Juno initiates the action in *Hercules furens* with a 124-verse speech). As regards the dialogue between Juno and Venus, Robert Turner mordantly says, 'L'absence de parallèles et l'extrême maladresse du dialogue indiquent qu'elles sont l'œuvre originale du Giraldi' (the lack of parallels and the extreme clumsiness of the dialogue indicate that these are Giraldi's original notes; p. 38).[28] His criticism is that Giraldi is too prolix (pp. 38–9), but, speaking of the play as a whole, one might respond that the length is less objectionable than the endless repetitions, particularly of words of lamentation, as the play draws near a close.[29]

Giraldi is adept at developing his minor characters. Their discourse functions both as a vehicle of self-definition and as a commentary on the character and actions of the protagonists. Achates, for example, functions as a wise counsellor and, following his failure to dissuade Aneas from accompanying Dido on the hunt, comments on Aeneas as no longer being himself: 'In tal maniera hor vinto è da Didone, / Ch'egli, come huomo effeminato, e molle, / Tutto è sotto l'arbitrio di costei, / Come tener fanciul sotto la Madre' (He is now won over by Dido to such an extent that, like a soft, effeminate man, he is completely under her will, like a tender child under a mother; pp. 54–5). The harshness of Achate's speech, his sarcasm, should perhaps be seen not so much as a reflection of a Renaissance attitude towards men (in which any man under a woman's thrall might be considered effeminate), but rather as a self-characterizing feature that further delineates the counsellor and his role. Dido's priest comments on her failings in a similar fashion. She has taken as her guide 'disio folle' while ignoring both 'divino voler' and the dishonour to her (p. 56). The minor characters serve as moral guideposts along the way, in case we have failed to note the errors of the protagonists.[30]

Another dramatic technique of interest is the use of asides, most obvious perhaps in Act III, but evident throughout the play. Quite often, as the action develops, characters literally withdraw to one side of the stage, interspersing their comments with those of another individual who is unaware of their presence. In effect, both figures on stage speak directly to the audience, thus creating a sensation of ironic displacement. Another feature worthy of note is a speech of a servant of Dido, who echoes Ovid's *Heroides* and the *Amores* (II, xviii, 21–6) by referring to other men who have abandoned women, such as Jason did to Medea, Theseus to Ariadne, and Demophoon to Phyllis (III, 5, 77).[31]

Giraldi's use of the Chorus represents an advance over that of Pazzi. Rather than spouting simple *sententiae*, the Chorus quite often develops thematic motifs at some length. One of the more intriguing examples is the clear exposition of Neoplatonic thought at the end of Act III, which recalls themes developed by people like Pico della Mirandola (our ability to rise or fall to any level) and Ficino (the ascent of the soul to union with the divine). The speech is developed with an engaging use of figurative language, from the first reference to God as 'il Motor eterno de le stelle' to man as a chameleon (pp. 82–3).[32] The increasing fervor of the speech reminds one of the ascesi of Pietro Bembo's hymn at the end of the *Cortegiano*. Here, inspired by 'bel desio,' the soul detaches itself from the earth, striving to return to its native place: 'E cerca ad uno, ad un gli eterni chori, / Tutta infiammata di celesti ardori' (and searches one by one the eternal choirs, completely inflamed with celestial ardor; p. 84). Finally, not content among those sublime spirits and 'accesi di charità immensa' (fervid with immense charity), the soul becomes one with God, after which it returns to inspire others on the same voyage (p. 85).[33] The beauty of the speech is diminished only by the five-verse coda, with its moral tag that anyone who has a pure mind 'non sente amor, com'hor Didone, insano, / Nè si lascia ingannar da disir vano' (does not feel mad love like Dido now, nor lets oneself be deceived by vain desire; p. 86).

The Chorus's lengthy speeches at the end of each act provide Giraldi with an opportunity to inject the spiritual concerns of the time, even if sometimes expressed in the code of a pagan world. The speech at the end of Act I is another good example, with its message that 'erri, chi pone in mortal cosa speme' (he errs who places hope in a mortal thing; p. 34).[34] Dolce will take advantage of the same technique, though his message will be less optimistic.[35] The significant point is not that these moralizations derive from the classical world (where similar motifs are sometimes found) or that they necessarily represent or betray a personal mental world (although I think in Dolce's case they often do), but that they reflect the tastes, sensibilities, and ideology of the time. The necessity of a moralizing conclusion requires the author not so much to preach (which is the obvious form, particularly in Dolce's play) as to mirror back to the audience their own concerns and expectations. The psychology behind the choral odes, then, is not so much personal as collective, and as a consequence the themes developed are quite often those of the Counter- or Catholic Reformation.

Other more original notes are, unfortunately, less felicitous. To cite merely one example from the end of the play, Giraldi, in an attempt to foreshadow Dido's death, has Anna report on a strange event that took place earlier that day. A disbeliever in dreams in Act I, Anna has suddenly changed, now afraid 'che questo non ne sia segnalato espresso / Di qual che inevitabile ruina' (that this might not be a clear sign of some inevitable disaster; p. 118). But what is this event that has the features of a fable? Having gone to the river to wash herself, Anna saw a wolf howling in pain because of an injured paw. The wolf approached a shepherdess, who at first fled in fear, then returned when she saw that, 'più di un mansueto Agnello / Fra le sue pecorelle il Lupo stava' (milder than a lamb, the wolf stayed among the sheep; p. 117). The *pastorella* removed a thorn from the wolf's paw, after which it assumed its usual mien and tore the girl to shreds. Barce's response is of the utmost banality, especially when one considers that within the context of the play this is a real event: 'Un'animo affannato sempre al peggio / Rivolge tutto quel, ch'occorrer vede; / Ma, nel ver, tanto non vi dee attristare / Questo incontro, e più tosto vò che noi / Lo ci arrechiamo à bene' (A distraught soul always turns what it sees occur to the worst; but, in truth, this encounter should not sadden you so much, and I prefer us to take it as something good; p. 118). The good interpretation of the event, for Anna, is that it refers to what has already happened to the two of them. Of course, we readers/spectators know the *lupo* is Aeneas, and Dido the poor *pastorella*. The author is so intent on the event as augury that a consideration of how one would react in the face of this reality is the farthest thing from his mind.

The play's conclusion, finally, despite the original scene with Dido's dying body on stage, is equally disappointing. The moral of the play, as the Chorus tells us in the final speech (introduced by 'dunque,' possibly the ugliest word in Italian poetry), is to beware of evil fortune and fallacious love: 'Dunque chi questo vede / Per ischifare, e l'uno, e l'altro errore, / Volga al verace ben subito il core' (So then, they who see this, in order to avoid both the one and the other error, let them turn their hearts immediately to the true good; p. 128).

That Duke Ercole was attracted by two classical stories with female characters (Dido and Cleopatra) is a tribute to the courtly environment of Ferrara, where strong women held an important place.[36] Given Giraldi's feminist sympathies, it is not surprising to find that Aeneas has been turned into a courtly lover, characterized by his (un)gentlemanly behaviour, and Dido into a passionate women, who becomes a deserted mistress: As Horne says, 'The hero is emasculated; the heroine is a pathetic creature lacking a truly regal stature' (p. 84). This state of affairs is best seen in the episode where Dido accosts Aeneas. Giraldi, like Pazzi, translates the *Aeneid* for Dido's plea (Act IV, scene 1), taking twice as many verses to emphasize the pathos of Dido's situation, but then amplifies the twenty-nine lines of the original, where Aeneas calmly defends himself, with sixty-five lines of self-justification. Horne criticizes the excess, noting that Aeneas has become a 'perfect gentleman ... [who] cannot bring himself to ride roughshod over the feelings of the woman he is leaving behind' (p. 83). In Giraldi's version, Aeneas both protests his love for Dido and is touched by her grief, to the extent that he says more than once that his own heart is breaking.[37] As opposed to the stern hero of the *Aeneid*, 'Giraldi's courtly hero ... seeks a graceful way of deserting his lady without causing any hard feelings' (p. 84). The implication in Horne's analysis of the play is that this represents a 'weakening' of the original, but one might argue instead that Giraldi has simply humanized the figure. In Virgil, Aeneas, for all his heroic steadfastness, comes across, at least to the modern reader but also very likely to some of Virgil's contemporaries, as a cold man. Unfortunately, Giraldi's portrayal of the figure runs to the opposite extreme.

For a play written contemporaneously with the *Orbecche*, the *Didone* is surprisingly lacking in the conventions of Senecan drama. There is no attempt to create a violent or horrific atmosphere, with ghosts from hell and human atrocities. What remains of Seneca is the tendency towards moralization. That tragedy had a moral function to play in general was not new with Giraldi, but what was new, according to Horne, was the manner in which the lesson was conveyed in most of his plays, specifically those *di fin lieto*: Giraldi 'is not content with putting generalized sententious comments into the mouths of the chorus and the characters; he also points the moral of the play as a whole by using the spectacle of poetic justice. In other words, in order that the spectators may be persuaded to follow good and eschew evil, they are shown virtue triumphant and vice punished ...' (p. 38). It is because of this that the happy ending is so crucial to Giraldi's conception of tragedy.[38] As regards the *Didone*, however, the nature of the plot itself, with its truly tragic ending ('O historia miserabile,' as Anna says in Act V, scene 4, 'qual mai / Si vide tragedia di più tristo fine?' [Oh wretched story, what tragedy with a sadder end was ever seen?]), limited the poet, as regards his moralization, to the speeches of his characters and the chorus.

Lodovico Dolce

One of the first things one notes when approaching Dolce's tragedies – and, in particular, his prologues, whether detached or part of the play –

is that the fellow knew how to write. If one feels the need to criticize, one might say that he wrote too easily. He has a natural fluidity and facility with language, so much so that his works sometimes seem hastily done. Still, they are usually a pleasure to read, especially when compared with some of their rougher antecedents.

As regards his tragedies, Dolce himself admitted that the form was more difficult than that of comedy, where stock figures facilitated the creation of character and where the writer did not have to worry so much about the majesty of speech and action. The topic of the popularity of tragedies and the difficulty of writing them comes up for discussion in the prologue of his *Medea*, where Dolce first speaks of fortune in bitter terms, and then contrasts the two theatrical forms. Since fortune provides so much material for works dealing with themes such as death, war, and sorrow, tragedies have come to be the dominant form for scenic representation. While seeming to protest the audience's demand for tragedy (so popular that comedy has been neglected) and the difficulty of the endeavour (tragic characters seem to require greater depth), the poet may simply be emphasizing his own skill as a writer, since he clearly feels worthy of wearing both the comic sandal and the tragic cothurnus.[39]

Despite their obvious differences and varied difficulty of composition, comedy and tragedy share a common goal. In his dedicatory letter for the *Hecuba*, dated 16 June 1543 and addressed to Cristoforo Canale, Dolce traces the origins and aims of both forms. The origin of theatre is found in the diversity brought about by fortune. The fact that fortune's ups and downs affect everyone caused the ancients to use comedy and tragedy for didactic purposes, with the ultimate goal being to direct the viewer's thoughts from the instability of earthly goods to the stability of heavenly pleasures.[40] As in almost all Dolce's works, the importance of edification is emphasized. By using a 'pleasing veil' under which they disclose, little by little, a better life, poets are able to provide moral instruction and lead us to the higher truth represented by God.[41]

In turning to the *Didone*, one notes immediately the establishment of both background and atmosphere. Unlike Giraldi, who used a separate prologue, Dolce's prologue is delivered by Cupid, disguised as Ascanius, and is thus an integral part of the play's action. His speech is Senecan in its violence and cruelty. After defining his dual nature, Cupid says he wishes to see Dido in hell, because Juno has treated his brother Aeneas so badly. To bring about this end, Cupid will descend to the depths of Styx and bring back the shade of Sychaeus, in order to drive Dido to madness.[42]

In both Dolce and Pazzi (where Sychaeus delivered the prologue and filled in the *antefatto)*, the action begins the evening before Aeneas's departure, but in Dolce's play, Dido herself fills in the *antefatto* at the beginning of Act I, reminding her sister Anna of the prior year's events. When she mentions how she fell in love with Aeneas, encouraged by Anna, Dolce makes a point of clarifying what most other authors before him left unquestioned – namely, that Dido herself was innocent because she was freed of her marital ties to Sychaeus following his death (p. 5$^\mathrm{v}$). (In Giraldi, I should note, Dido also dies innocent, but that is because the poet casts the blame on Anna.) In Dolce, as Dido herself says, it would have been 'sciocchezza grande / A consumar il fior de' miei verd'anni / Senza gustar alcun soave frutto' (a great stupidity to consume the flower of my green years without tasting some sweet fruit; p. 5$^\mathrm{r}$). Virgil's oft-mentioned 'culpa' has become almost a virtue, although a worldly one, and Dido herself has become more a woman of the time.

Dido's lengthy, initial speech is one of feminine pride, in which she traces Pygmalion's treachery, her flight, the foundation of Carthage, her refusal to marry Jarba (who is angered 'de l'ingegno, e de l'ardire, / Che in sesso feminil vide mostrarsi' [at the wit and daring that he saw demonstrated in the female sex]), Aeneas's arrival, and the moment of their *innamoramento* in the cave. Now, she is bothered by a dream she had at dawn. When Anna tells her one should not believe all dreams, and then asks what it was about, Dido unfolds a story that is original to Dolce and that establishes the play's contrastive atmosphere. In her dream, Dido saw herself in a beautiful green meadow through which a silvery stream flowed. Seated beside her, her 'heart and soul' crowned her hair with a green garland he had woven. His words were so sweet the winds became calm, the day bright and clear, so much so that she seemed to be in heaven. Suddenly, a dark cloud turned day to night, leaving her in what she thought was a blind hell. A ray of light illuminated the area around her, only her consort was gone. Going in search of him, she found instead a ditch of blood. She heard a voice tell her to enter, since her Sychaeus was waiting for her, and at this she woke (pp. 6$^\mathrm{v}$–7$^\mathrm{r}$).

Her dream, in which the contrast of light and darkness vaguely recalls the same motif in Pazzi, seems to combine the two traditional roles assigned to dreams in literary texts – prophecy and commentary, with the former being the dominant mode. The atmosphere of the dream recalls the pastoral (whether in lyric, dramatic, or narrative form) and its use of the elements of fable. I think of dramatic works such as Angelo Poliziano's *Favola di Orfeo,* where the idyllic is transformed to the tragic, or of the prose narratives found in works such as Jacopo Caviceo's *Libro del peregrino* and Sannazzaro's *Arcadia*, where strange, dreamlike events occur, then turn suddenly awful, or where we move from a beautiful landscape, a *locus amoenus*, to a lament for the death of a shepherd.[43] Here, the movement is from light to darkness to blood.

Having established the background and the atmosphere, Dolce focuses on structures of contrast, a technique reminiscent of Virgil.[44] Unlike Pazzi, who tried to create dramatic tension in part through physical action (i.e., by having Jarba and Pygmalion attack Carthage), Dolce finds conflict in thematic oppositions. Among the motifs that dominate the play, one finds reason vs madness (*ragione/pazzia, intelletto/furor*), faith vs deceit (*fede/inganno, fido/perfido*), honour vs dishonour, virtue vs wealth (*merto e virtù/oro e ricchi panni*), mercy vs cruelty (*pietoso/impietoso*), life vs death, liberty vs servitude, and a just ruler vs a tyrant.[45] Unlike Giraldi, Dolce does not feel constrained to include the bickering goddesses as characters, nor the figure Rumour. He seems more concerned with believable action, with human motives, and with the story's moral overtones.[46]

As an example of the contrastive thematics that underlie human motives, in the second scene of Act II one finds a lengthy discussion between Aeneas and Achates regarding the uncertainty of life (p. 11^v), duty and the pull of contrary desires (where, as in Giraldi, Aeneas is seen in turmoil; p. 11^r), the 'honesto' as contrasted to 'quel, che piace,' the debt owed to Dido, and other related motifs. Of secondary interest is Aeneas's recounting of Mercury's message to him. The god fortells the future not only of Rome, but also of 'un'altra gran città ... / ... in mezo l'acque' (another great city in the midst of water), where a golden age will flower. The motif, an encomium of Venice, is a recurrent one in Dolce's works.[47] Here he writes of the city 'Ove la pace sempre, ove l'amore, / Ove virtude, ove ogni bel costume / Terranno il pregio in fin, che duri il mondo. / Quivi la bella Astrea regnerà sempre / Coronata i bei crin di bianca oliva' (where peace always, where love, where virtue, where every beautiful habit will be esteemed as long as the world endures. Here beautiful Astraea will reign forever, her beautiful hair crowned with white olive; p. 11^v). In the context of the tragedy's contrastive thematics, the list is intriguing (though typical), since it both alternates and unifies what might seem conflicting values, such as love and virtue, although this love is a positive force, not mad passion. The technique, of course (if we are meant to find any conflict in the terms), is common in Golden Age thematics, where the lion lies down with the lamb. Whatever the case, the love extolled here stands in contrast to the passion that rules Dido.

At the conclusion of Act II, the Chorus refers again to the weakness of human intellect in the face of the stars – 'Perche forza divina / Humana forza di gran lunga avanza' (because divine force far surpasses human force; pp. 14[r]–15[v]) – then notes that joy comes drop by drop, sorrow like a wave.[48] The pessimistic note would have appealed to Leopardi: 'Dura legge mortale, / Per che si nasce a tale, / Per viver sempre in guai: / Beato chi più tosto s'avicina / Al fine, a cui camina / Chi prima è nato, o nascerà giamai' (Harsh mortal law because one is born to such, to live always in woe; blessed is the one who soonest approaches the end, to which moves he who first was birthed or ever will be born; p. 15[v]). In Act IV, the thematic contrast between reason and madness is again well developed, as Dido first grieves over her lost love – emphasizing not the effect of a woman's wrath on a man, as the Chorus had done, but miserable plight of the abandoned women themselves[49] – then rages against Aeneas. Of interest is the series of *adynata* employed by the poet when Dido seeks out a priestess to help win back Aeneas. To those mentioned by Alessandro Pazzi, Dolce adds more, utilizing all the topoi passed on from Virgil, even though some of woman's abilities seem more typical of Orpheus than of an old priestess who has promised either to heal amorous wounds or to inflame sane minds with eternal love.[50]

By the end of the play, Dido herself has come to recognize where the blame for human action lies. Talking in her mind to Sychaeus, she starts to blame fortune, then adds the following disclaimer, typical of Dolce's moralism in dealing with those who allow reason to be swayed by passion: 'Ma indegnamente la fortuna incolpo, / Indegnamente amor; ch'io sola errai, / C'havea ragione, havea intelletto, e mai / Non dovea consentir a le lusinghe / D'Amor, che non potea l'empio sforzarmi' (But I blame fortune undeservingly, undeservingly love, since I alone erred, since I had reason, I had intellect, and should never have consented to the flatteries of Love, since the impious one could not force me; p. 33[r]).

Aside from the thematics, Dolce demonstrates throughout the play both his fidelity to the original story as narrated by Virgil and his freedom to invent. The encounter between Dido and Aeneas, for example, follows the Virgilian pattern.[51] The power of the speech in the original source seems to have intimidated the tragedians of the cinquecento, who fear to compete with the Virgil's forceful conciseness, but Dolce, at least, does not translate word for word. Here, in imitation of Virgil's 'nec te noster amor nec te data dextera quondam / nec moritura tenet crudeli funere Dido?' (307–8), we read: 'E non vi possa ritener l'amore, / Che in me vedete, e conscoete a prova, / Ne la data a mè fè con questa mano: / Ne'l veder anco a manifesti segni, / Che me, partendo, condannate a morte' (And can not the love that you see in me and know by experience hold you, nor the faith pledged to me with this hand, nor seeing yet with manifest signs that in leaving me you condemn me to death?; p. 22^r). For Virgil's 'mene fugis' and the artistically structured triple plea that he places in Dido's mouth ('"per ... has lacrimas dextramque tuam ... / ... / per conubia nostra, per inceptos hymenaeos"' [314–16]), Dolce writes:

> Voi me fuggite, me; che data in dono
> V'hò, quanto al mondo havea di bello e caro,
> L'honestà, la città, la propria vita.
> Ma, se da l'amore mio vi cal si poco;
> Vi prego Enea per queste istesse amare
> Lagrime, ch'io quì spargo, e per cotesta,
> C'hor tocco, forte e vincitrice mano;
> Poi, ch'altro a me non ho lasciato bene;
> Per li communi abbracciamenti nostri,
> Per le pur hora incominciate nozze
> (Se ricevuto beneficio alcuno
> Da Dido havete, e qualche cosa cara)
> Che vi mova a pietà de la ruina
> Del nuovo regno ... (pp. 22^{r-v})

[You flee me, me, who gave you as a gift everything in the world that is beautiful and dear – decorum, the city, my own life. But if you care so little for my love, I beg you, Aeneas, because of these same bitter tears that I shed here, and for this strong, conquering hand that I now touch, since I have nothing left to me of good, for our shared embraces, for the nuptials just now begun (if you have received any benefits at all from Dido, and something dear) that you let the ruin of my realm move you to pity ...]

Though tied closely to his source, Dolce's poetic idiom is less clumsy than Pazzi's and more fluid (though perhaps less elevated in tone) than Giraldi's.

The action of Act V provides a good example of the merging of both the traditional and the new. At one point, the Messenger arrives with a bloody sword and describes an encounter with a sorceress, a sacrifice to the gods, and Dido's last words before she killed herself. The Chorus responds briefly with the requisite note on the caducity of beauty ('O caduca beltade, / Come misera, come / Picciol momento ti consuma, e perde' [O fleeting beauty, how wretched; what a brief moment consumes and wastes you; p. 37^v]), after which the Messenger offers the sword to the Prefect, who as the highest official in the state will take over the government following his confirmation by Anna. The Prefect promises to be a just ruler, then says he will avenge Dido with the blood of Trojans, since nothing is more pleasing to the gods than the death of a tyrant ('perchè nessun liquore / È a Dio più grato, o vittima più cara, / Che quella d'un tiran crudele, et empio' [p. 38^r]). The anti-tyranny theme, as we saw in chapter 4, is one dear to Dolce.

Elsewhere, Dolce is possibly more innovative, although one might object that his original features are Senecan in origin. Act II, for example, presents us with several novelties, among them the first scene, with Cupid and the shade of Sychaeus, where the god wraps a snake he has taken from Megera around Sychaeus, knowing it will terrify Dido when she sees her dead husband. Though the tone is Senecan, the idea may derive from Virgil (*Aeneid*, VII, 346ff.) or Ovid (*Metamorphoses*, IV, 452ff.), both cited by Turner (p. 64). But one might add that the Attic tragedians had often taken advantage of the snaky-haired Erinnyes (Tisiphone, Alecto, and Megera) to hound individuals (e.g., Oedipus) guilty of crimes. The chthonic serpent, of course, manifests the aggressive power of the underworld gods, the dark forces in mankind, and, in this instance, since taken from Megera, represents perhaps a personification of the pangs of conscious. Sychaeus clearly expresses his rancour at Dido's behaviour, referring to her as 'costei / Rubella d'honestà, di fe, e d'Amore' (she, enemy of decorum, of faith, of love; p. 10^v). Within the context of the traditional story, Dolce's additions are original features.

As regards Dolce's use of Senecan horror, Act III is perhaps the play's high point. Here, Barce describes Dido's offering to the gods and the bad omens that resulted, including wine turning to blood.[52] More horrific than that, however, is the encounter with Sychaeus's ghost in the temple where his ashes are kept. Dido first hears his voice, then sees 'L'ombra di lui con spaventoso aspetto. / Havea la barba, i crini, il viso, e i panni / Tinti di sangue, e tutti molli e brutti' (his shade with a dreadful look. His beard, hair, face, and clothes were tinged with blood, and all moist and ugly; p. 16^r), at which point an unseen hand wraps a snake around Dido's neck 'che con molti nodi / Lo cinse errando, e sibilando pose / La testa in seno; e la vibrante lingua / Quinci e quindi leccò le poppe e 'l petto; / Poi via disparve, e non le fece oltraggio' (which wound tight around her neck with many knots and, hissing, placed its head in her bosom; the flickering tongue licked her breasts and chest here and there, then slipped away and didn't harm her; pp. 16[r]–17[v]). The precise and detailed description and the morbid sensuality of the snake's action all add to the play's dramatic intensity.

Turning to the minor characters, one notes that, as in Giraldi, they function as commentators and judges of morality, but here the situation is both more complex and more dramatic, for the Nuntio and the Chorus present and argue opposite sides of the case. The Nuntio, for example, having overheard the Trojans' preparations for departure, informs Dido of this, and then, following her departure, launches into a speech against flattery, confiding in the Chorus about the difficulty of telling the truth to one's lord, for few in lofty seats wish to hear the truth. 'Anzi quasi a ciascun, che stato regge, / De' falsi adulator la turba è grata' (On the contrary, the crowd of false adulators is pleasing to everyone who rules a state; p. 18[r]). The speech against flatterers quickly passes into a condemnation of Dido, then of Aeneas. The queen's so-called marriage displeased not only the Nuntio, 'de la vil plebe nato' (born of the common people), but also most of the realm's honoured citizens. And Aeneas was low-born and a traitor to Troy. The Chorus refutes the Nuntio's claims, concluding that Aeneas is famous for having defended Troy for ten years. The statement provides the Nuntio with a chance to criticize fame. Nothing under the moon is 'più bugiarda' and 'più fallace' (more lying and more false; p. 19[v]). And, as regards Dido, he refuses to believe that her 'errore' came about as a result of 'ragione alcuna.' What follows at this point is a contrapuntal movement, where the Nuntio describes the incident at the cave and the Chorus counters each of his claims with a more positive interpretation. Of significance is that Dolce's moralization is not limited to the speeches of the Chorus at the conclusion of each act, but extends to those of the other characters.

The procedure is evident in the scene immediately following the conflict between the Messenger and the Chorus. Aeneas and Achates arrive, with Aeneas wondering how to tell Dido he is leaving. As in Virgil, he hesitates over the best course of action, but not in fear. And his concerns never extend to the maudlin, as do Giraldi's. This Aeneas is a more heroic figure, recalling Jove's command, even though he is aware he may cause Dido's death. His only note of pity is the statement 'N'andrò, come colui, che va col piede, / Ma il cor dal suo camin resta lontano' (I'll leave, like he who goes with his foot, but his heart remains far from his path; p. 20[r]). But the conflict, again, does not remain merely internal. It flares up very effectively, this time between major and minor characters. When the Chorus denounces Aeneas, saying his actions are not worthy of him,

Achates tells them to mind their own business. The ten-verse exchange that follows is an excellent use of stichomythia for dramatic conflict:

CORO: Gia non è cosa honesta il romper fede.
ACHATES: Non è tenuto a quel, c'huom fa per forza.
CORO: È peccato ingannar semplice Donna.
ACHATES: Si pecca a indur a far le cose ingiuste:
CORO: Ingiusta è quei, che'l beneficio nega.
ACHATES: Beneficio non è, se apporta danno.
CORO: Danno io dirò, se haver la vita è danno.
ACHATES: Meglio è morir, che viver con vergogna.
CORO: Vergogna è l'esser Re di questo stato?
ACHATES: È, quando a miglior stato il ciel dispone. (p. 20$^\mathrm{v}$)

[CHORUS: Of course it is not honest to break one's faith.
ACHATES: A man is not held to that which he does through force.
CHORUS: It is a sin to deceive a simple woman.
ACHATES: One sins in inducing to do unjust things.
CHORUS: Unjust is he who denies a benefit.
ACHATES: It is not a benefit, if it brings harm.
CHORUS: Harm I will call it, if having life is harm.
ACHATES: Better it is to die, than to live with shame.
CHORUS: Shame is it to be a King in this state?
ACHATES: It is, when heaven disposes a better state.]

Angered by this, the Nuntio says that everyone, both the *popolari* and the *cittadini*, sinned by not driving the Trojans from their shores the moment they landed (p. 21$^\mathrm{r}$). The dramatic conflict intensifies, in part, one feels, because we have a plebeian talking to a noble. As always in the Dolce, however, the representatives of the common people represent moral right. Here, the Nuntio concludes with a political note (relevant to Dolce's own time, when Spanish domination was everywhere increasing) that it is only just that he who makes himself a servant of foreign peoples should suffer ('Ma così va, così è ragion, che pianga / Chi di Barbare genti si fa servo' [p. 21$^\mathrm{r}$]). Aeneas's only response is suggest to Achates that they leave, since it is unworthy to contend with 'huom negletto e vile' (a man sloven and base). As the Nuntio tells us when he departs, he himself leaves because *reason* has to give way to *force*.

Among Dolce's other innovations is the addition to the story of two new characters (mentioned above), the Prefect and a Counsellor, who appear at the conclusion in Act V. Again, as with the Messenger, the poet utilizes these figures to express his moral judgments. The Prefect, for example, talks about servitude ('Che la libertà tutti i thesori avanza' [since liberty surpasses all treasures; p. 34ʳ]) and how bitter it is to serve an unworthy prince. Recalling the good old days when Sychaeus was still alive, the Prefect launches into a speech where the contrastive leitmotifs are liberty vs servitude, virtue vs wealth, individual merit vs nobility, and reward for the good vs punishment for the bad. Now, he concludes, when such a lord is needed, cruel Love has darkened the light and the intellect of Dido. It is through these marginal characters, then, that Dolce's own poetic personality comes to the fore. Free from the restraints of Virgil's *auctoritas*, he espouses motifs of interest to himself and his contemporaries. Whether these are simply the topoi of the age or a matter of personal taste is less significant than the fact that he chooses to express these ideas in the form of a judgment, delivered by representatives of a sane, non-noble, citizen class, in the context of a world deprived of these values, and consequently headed for ruin. As the Counselor sums up, 'È di servo, e fedel debito officio / Di supplir, dove manca il suo Signore' (It is the duty and obligation of a faithful servant to make up for where his lord is lacking; p. 34ʳ). We are not too distant from the social criticism of Carlo Goldoni, though Dolce never openly mocks the nobility. In fact, he goes on to make a distinction not so much between social rank as between good and evil, and his point is that one serves the state not for reward or praise but out of love and a sense of duty. This is true patriotism.

The author's final addition to the traditional story is Anna's death by hanging. The tragedy, however, is not limited to the two sisters; the citizens will soon feel the results of Dido's error. Bitias tells of the recent arrival of a soldier with his hands, ears, and nose cut off, a man who announces Jarba's vengeance and the Getulian carnage, then dies. The message seems to be that the actions of rulers, especially their deeds of folly, are felt by all their subjects.[53] With this, the Chorus concludes the play with an eight-verse speech, advising the audience to submit to fate. The message is surprising, whether one interprets it as a statement of pagan belief or as a veiled reference to predestination: 'Quel dì, che'l miser huomo / Veste quà giuso l'alma / Di questo corporal velo, / La sù con lettere salde, e adamantine / È discritto il suo fine. / Però a i fati cedete / Voi, che felici, o sventurati sete: / Ch'ogni cosa mortal governa il Cielo' (The day that a wretched man clothes his soul down here with this corporeal veil, up there his end is written down with firm, adamantine letters. Therefore you who are happy or unlucky cede to the fates, since heaven governs every mortal thing; pp. 39^r–40^v). The final chorus seems one of the play's weakest, as is often the case for other tragic poets as well. It is almost as if the author visualizes his audience begin to fidget and decides to wrap things up quickly. Clearly, the final speech of the Chorus is not the place for lengthy philosophical exortations.

While these three tragedies by Pazzi, Giraldi, and Dolce have been considered by most critics to offer little of interest, each has its intriguing features and innovations of undeniable significance. The authors' motivations in writing may differ – from Pazzi's desire to pass the time in a stylistic exercise of metrical innovation through Giraldi's goal to satisfy his patron with a work of stylistic and rhetorical elegance, to Dolce's more practical concerns with a stageable play of natural ease and fluidity – and the results vary in quality, but each work merits a rereading, not the least for its historical interest as a representative of the development of a theatrical motif that will find its greatest success with Metastasio. Without these antecedents and their later imitators, his *Didone abbandonata* might not have been written. All three plays, whatever their individual quality, are noteworthy experiments in the transferral of epic material to tragedy. In this they carry on and renew a hallowed tradition that begins in Greece with the first practitioners of the genre.

In talking of these three works and their common source, one can state that we move in less than twenty-five years from a rapport of filiation in Pazzi (or intertexuality, in the classic sense of the word as used by Julia Kristeva) to one of continuity (or genealogy, as used by Paolo Valesio) in Giraldi, to one of relationship (or transtexuality, as used by Gérard Genette) in Dolce, where, however, the ties to Virgil's epic are manifest rather than hidden.[54] Clearly, despite the authority of the classical source (bordering on tyranny), each author attempts to write to the best of his ability and to be original within the constraints of the genre and of other forces at work on the author, such as the pressures of limited time (a factor that had to concern Dolce, given his myriad endeavours), considerations of the patron or audience, and so forth. Even the author most closely tied to Virgil, Alessandro Pazzi, strives for a measure of originality, though he attains it only as regards form. Giraldi, who feels constrained by his material to offer his audience a faithful reworking of the classical material, attains a somewhat greater freedom of expression, although his expanded version of the story has earned him the censure of both his contemporaries and later critics. And Dolce, writing in a form that requires (he says) more effort than comedy, manages not only to maintain the same freedom of expression, but to attain some degree of dramatic intensity.

In all three authors, Dido's drama lies not so much in action – an orderly progression of physical events (although these do occur) – as in the expression of forceful, female emotions. As Lawrence Lipking says of the abandoned woman in general, 'No feelings are too strong or too shameful for her to express. Hysteria, carnality, self-loathing, infatuation, fury, abasement, longing – these are her daily bread' (p. 20). Though in the story of Dido as presented by our three authors and their classical source, the masculine discourse of heroism may prevail in the end over the feminine discourse of romance, these plays dramatize the contest and thus literally give voice on stage to a woman who would otherwise be silent.

6

'Non Mai Stanco di Giovare': The Prose Dialogues and Treatises

In his dedication to Dolce's posthumous *Giornale delle historie del mondo* (1572), Guglielmo Rinaldi refers to our author as 'gentilissimo, et non mai stanco di giovare' (most noble, and never tired of helping; p. 3ʳ). The epithet truly applies to the compiler of the prose works studied in this chapter. Each of these works, whether original or a translation, attests to Dolce's praiseworthy goal of popularizing the élite culture of the time, rendering its more obscure aspects accessible to a much wider audience. While the sceptical might claim that Dolce wrote works of this sort simply for money (for, as Ruscelli wrote in his *Tre discorsi a M. Lodovico Dolce* [p, 15], there were 'lettori studiosi ... che spendono denari in comprare et tempo in leggere i libri' [studious readers ... who spend money in buying and time in reading books]), such is not the case. True, he lived off his efforts, but he was also aware of their significance to the public. In the 'Preface to the Readers' in his summary of Aristotle's philosophy (*Somma della filosofia di Aristotele*), Dolce, justifying his work as a popularizer of culture, wrote:

L'abbreviare e ridurre in compendio i buoni autori è di grandissimo profitto agli studiosi: perciochè nei grandi volumi la memoria si perde, e prima che 'l leggente pervenga alla fine, si scordano le cose lette ... Laonde non fia di picciolo profitto il vedere i gran libri di Aristotele rapportati in una convenevole brevità ... I quali tutti libri si apprendono con gran difficultà nelle scole: et in tal forma ridotti, possono esser facilissimi a ciascuno.

[Abbreviating and reducing good authors to a compendium is of very great profit to students, because in large volumes one's memory gets lost, and before the reader reaches the end, everything read is forgotten ... Therefore it may be of no small profit to see the great books of Aristotle recast in a convenient brevity ..., all of which books one learns with great difficult in schools; and reduced in such form, they can be very easy for everyone.]

The culture of the second half of the cinquecento abounded in *rifacimenti* and *sunti*, in notebooks (*zibaldoni*), in historical works, moral treatises, esoteric philosophical works, and similar encyclopedic endeavours. What is significant is that Dolce is aware of the profound modifications to culture brought about by the new technologies of the time, above all the printing presses, which facilitated the diffusion of knowledge.

As a promoter of knowledge for the masses, then, Dolce feels free, even in a translation, to 'improve' on the original, supplying his own examples for greater clarity, modernizing, interpreting and amplifying abstruse concepts, adding rhetorical ornaments, warming through a fluid and friendly style the cold text of the original. The range of his 'improvements' is noteworthy. Dolce's attention to his responsibilities as a promulgator of culture results at times in a sort of ideal conversation with the text he is translating. To cite one example, in his dedicatory letter to Giovan Giacomo Leopardi, the Count of Monte Abate, accompanying his translation of Guglielmo Guilleo's *Discorso ... sopra i fatti di Annibale* (1551), Dolce affirms his right to prove as false Guilleo's arguments concerning Hannibal's greatness – namely, that he was superior to those who conquered him.[1] In effect, the translator interjects himself into the text and argues with it. Nothing is accepted without question.

When not contesting the ideas present in his source, Dolce adds to them. In his version of the *Congestorium artificiose memorie* of the German Dominican Johannes Romberch, first published in 1520 and translated in 1562, Dolce expands the text at the point where Romberch treats the places of Hell: 'For this (that is for remembering the places of Hell) the ingenious invention of Virgil AND DANTE will help us much. That is for distinguishing the punishments according to the nature of the sins. Exactly.'[2] As Frances Yates notes in *The Art of Memory*, the fact that one may regard Dante's *Inferno* as a system for memorizing orders of places comes as a great shock. 'It would take a whole book,' she writes, 'to work out the implications of such an approach to Dante's poem,' adding soon after that,

if one thinks of the poem as based on orders of places in Hell, Purgatory, and Paradise, and as a cosmic order of places in which the spheres of Hell are the spheres of Heaven in reverse, it begins to appear as a summa of similitudes and exempla, ranged in order and set out upon the universe. And if one discovers that

Prudence, under diverse similitudes, is a leading symbolic theme of the poem, its three parts can be seen as *memoria*, remembering vices and their punishments in Hell, *intelligentia*, the use of the present for penitence and acquisition of virtue, and *providentia*, the looking forward to Heaven. In this interpretation, the principles of artificial memory, as understood in the Middle Ages, would stimulate the intense visualisation of many similitudes in the intense effort to hold in memory the scheme of salvation, and the complex network of virtues and vices and their rewards and punishments ... (p. 95)

In addition to rendering Romberch's scheme more intelligible to Dolce's contemporaries, our author can be honoured for having inspired a reader four hundred years later.

Elsewhere, Dolce's attempts at improving his orginal source consist of a modernization of elements to render the text more meaningful. Usually, this entails the substitution of contemporary examples of artists (those dear to Dolce) for earlier figures. One example, typical of similar substitutions in other works, can be found in Dolce's unacknowledged translation of Camillo Leonardi's *Speculum lapidum* (first edition, 1502; translation, 1565). In Book 3, which deals with engraved stones, Leonardi treats both ancient and modern sculptors, mentioning several outstanding representatives for each of Italy's major cities. In Rome, he cites 'Ioannes Maria Mantuanus,' in Venice 'Franciscus Nichinus Ferrariensis,' in Milan 'Leonardus Mediolanensis' (p. 48^r), after which he goes on to mention that Italy also has great painters, such as Melozzo, Giovanni Bellini, Perugino, and Andrea Mantegna. While elsewhere translating Leonardi's personal comments and observations word for word, as if they were his, here Dolce deletes most of the original examples and expands at great length with his own favourites. As he says:

Et a nostri tempi habbiamo havuto, et habbiamo Scultori a quegli antichi non inferiori: come il divino Michele Agnolo Scultore, e pittore parimente, M. Giacopo Sansovino, M. Danese Cataneo, e M. Alessandro, giovane di gran spirito, polito e leggiadro Maestro, et altri. Come nella Pittura Maestri similmente singolarissimi, come Leonardo Vinci, Giovan Bellino, l'istesso Michele Agnolo, Rafaello d'Urbino, il Mantegna, Antonio da Coreggio, il Parmegianino, Titiano, et altri ancora: come Paolo Verone, il Tintoretto, e M. Gioseppe Salviati. (pp. 67^v–68^r)

[And in our times we have had, and have, sculptors not inferior to those ancients: like the divine Michelangelo, sculptor and painter alike, M. Jacopo Sansovino, M.

Danese Cattaneo, and M. Alessandro, a youth of great spirit, refined and graceful master, and others. As in painting [we have] similarly singular masters, like Leonardo da Vinci, Giovanni Bellini, the same Michelangelo, Raphael of Urbino, Mantegna, Antonio da Correggio, Parmigianino, Titian, and still others, like Paolo Veronese, Tintoretto, and M. Giuseppe Salviati.]

The canon of excellent painters has changed, with the addition of the great masters of the high and late Renaissance. In fact, the only painters Camillo Leonardi and Dolce revere in common are Leonardo, Giovanni Bellini, and Andrea Mantegna.

Examples abound of Dolce's tendency to interpret abstruse concepts, a trait which usually finds him citing a Latinate form (derived from his original), and then defining it in the vernacular in a secondary clause introduced by 'cioè.' These range from the simple – 'albo, cioè bianco' – to the more complex – 'ruota, o diciamo bossolo marineresco,' where Dolce explains that the wheel referred to in the original corresponds to a modern compass or *bussola nautica* (*Libri tre ... delle gemme*, pp. 24^r, 54^r).

As for his tendency to amplify the original through rhetorical ornaments, one might cite not so much a specific example, since all his translations illustrate this feature, but his poetics of 'traduzioni artistiche.' In the dedicatory letter accompanying his translation of Seneca's *Thyestes* (the *Tieste* of 1543), addressed to M. Giacomo Barbo, Dolce affirms that it is proper to criticize those writers who put their ideas into writing 'senza saperle ne disporre, ne ornare, ne con qualche piacevolezza dilettare l'animo di chi legge' (without knowing either how to arrange them, or adorn them, nor how to delight the mind of the reader with pleasantries). If this is difficult, how much more so to translate another person's ideas in such a way that one offends neither the intellect of the reader nor the ear of the listener. The task is not to be underestimated, he says; the result not to be poorly esteemed, since the translator's duty is to produce a work that is easily read. To do so, the translator must almost create a new language or take on a new nature, and must above all else have both good judgment and eloquence of expression.[3]

Dolce, it is safe to say, rightfully includes himself among those who possess these skills. Unfortunately, not all critics, including many of our own age, have understood his intent, perhaps in part because Dolce's contemporaries were equally blind. In a letter accompanying his translation of Pedro Mexia's *Vite di tutti gl' imperadori romani da Giulio Cesare insino a Massimiliano* (1558), Dolce feels compelled to defend himself against accusations of being an unfaithful translator, once again justifying his approach on the grounds of a fluid style. His additions, in fact, simply reflect his desire to observe 'la proprietà della nostra pura e dolce favella' (the propriety of our pure and sweet speech).[4]

His graceful versions of arcane texts continue to prove of aid to scholars writing today. Two examples may suffice. Who would not rather read Dolce's beautifully rendered version of Camillo Leonardi's *Speculum lapidum* when faced with the cramped and heavily abbreviated script of the Latin original? Only a glutton for punishment. Frances Yates, when dealing with Johannes Romberch's *Congestorium artificiose memorie*, prefers the 'more agreeable' version of Dolce's Italian translation (*Art of Memory*, p. 115). As she says, 'The crabbed Latin of the German Dominican is transformed [by Dolce] into elegant Italian dialogues,' and the resultant work, modelled on Cicero's *De oratore* (one of the speakers is Hortensio, recalling Cicero's Hortensius), has the polished surface of classical rhetoric, expressed in the 'dulcet tones of Dolce's "Ciceronian" Italian, in a modern-looking dialogue form' (p. 163).[5]

As a final introductory note having to do with utility, let me return to Dolce's *Giornale delle historie del mondo*, where one finds an intriguing example of his desire to entertain and instruct the masses. The *Giornale* is a calendar with notable historical and literary events listed for each day of the year. The effect is similar to that of today's newspaper columns usually headlined 'On This Day' or 'In Our Pages' and listing important events that have occurred over the last century on that particular day of the week and month. Dolce's compendium, however, is not limited to events of recent memory; it ranges from his own time to the origins of civilization. As such, rather than a work of historical analysis, it stands as an amusing source of cursory knowledge, and responds to a taste similar to the modern desire to read books of lists or of things the educated person should know.

To illustrate Dolce's technique, I will cite the entries for one person (Michelangelo) and for one day (18 January). My task is rendered easier by two tables, one a very thorough listing of the names mentioned in the calendar (Petrarch, for example, shows up four times, Poliziano, Bembo, and Michelangelo twice each), the other, a list of the authors cited in the *Giornale*. In addition, at the start of each month, Dolce explains the origin of the name itself, then provides variants derived from the calendars of other cultures.

This is what he has to say about Michelangelo:

XIIX Di Febraio. XII. Kal. Mart.
L'anno 1563. passò di questa a miglior vita la gloriosa anima di Michel'Angelo Buonaroto, in Roma. Il cui cadavere fu portato alli XI, di Marzo in Fiorenza: ove furongli fatte solennissime essequie dall'Academia delli Scoltori, et Architetti. (p. 66)

[**18 February. Twelfth Day before the Kalends of March.**
The year 1563. The glorious soul of Michelangelo Buonarroti passed from this to a better life, in Rome. His cadaver was taken on the 11th of March to Florence, where most solemn funeral rites were given to him by the Academy of the Sculptors and Architects.]

VI Di Marzo. Pridie non. Mart.
L'anno 1474. Nacque il Divino Michel'Agnolo Buonarota, nel Casentino, dove Lodovico, suo padre, era all'hora Podestà, huomo perfettissimo nelle tre più belle arti, Architettura, Scoltura, et Pittura. oltre a ciò, di perfettissimo giudicio nella Poesia Toscana, onde fu detto da alcuni, Nuovo Apollo, et Nuovo Apelle. Visse novant'anni; et, se havesse havuto a vivere tanto più de gli altri, quanto era da più, non sarebbe morto mai. Benche si può ben dire, ch'egli hora gloriosamente viva, havendo lasciate dopo se tante segnalate opere, che danno altrui maraviglia incredibile. (p. 91)

[**6 March. Day before the Nones of March.**
The year 1474. The Divine Michelangelo Buonarroti was born, in the Casentino, where Lodovico, his father, was then the Podestà, a most perfect man in the three most beautiful arts, Architecture, Sculpture, and Painting. In addition to that, of most perfect judgment in Tuscan poetry, whence he was called by some a New Apollo and a New Apelles. He lived ninety years, and if he had been required to live for as long a time as he was better than others, he would have never died. Although one can truly say that he now lives gloriously, having left behind him so many remarkable works that fill others with incredible marvel.]

As an example of a daily entry, I cite the following, chosen at random:

XIIX. Di Gennaio. XV. Kal. Febr.
L'anno dopo Christo 1256. Lodovico, Duca di Baviera, avolo di Corradino Svevo, fece morire Maria, sua moglie, per cagione di adulterio, senza ascoltare ragione. Fece anche la Cameriera, come consapevole, gettarla giù di una Torre. Oltre a ciò uccise una vergine, della famiglia Prennebergense, nobile.

L'anno 1379. Il s. Galeotto Malatesta hebbe Cesena in Vicariato perpetuo da Papa Bonifacio nono.

L'anno 1547. Morì in Roma Pietro Bembo, Cardinale, huomo di cognitione di cose, et di eloquenza prestante. (p. 28)

[18 January. Fifteenth Day before the Kalends of February.
The year after Christ 1256. Ludwig, Duke of Bavaria, grandfather of Conradin the Swabian, had his wife, Mary, killed because of adultery, without listening to reason. He also had the maid, who was aware of the situation, thrown down from a tower. In addition to that, he killed a virgin of the nobile Prennebergense family.
The year 1379. The lord Galeotto Malatesta received Cesena as a perpetual vicariate from Pope Boniface IX.
The year 1547. Cardinal Pietro Bembo died in Rome, a very learned man of outstanding eloquence.]

Those who would criticize the work as useless from a historical point of view have failed to understand its purpose.[6] It does not take much curiosity to be interested in the *Giornale*, if for no other reason than the pleasure of seeing what else happened on one's birthday, or what else one might commemorate on any given day. Furthermore, for those of a more practical bent, the publisher has left space for the addition of new events, as they occur. In the copy of the work available to me (Special Collections, University of Arizona library), someone, in fact, has done just that, penning in his or her own additions to the calendar.

Having seen the variety of ways that Dolce employs his sources (from contesting the ideas in the work he is translating to supplying his own examples in the place of ones considered out-of-date, from amplifying the original for greater clarity to adding rhetorical ornaments), we can now approach Dolce's dialogues and treatises, several of which are translations. Given this fact, whether acknowledged or not by Dolce, my focus, of necessity, will fall, not on the work's originality (or its lack), but on its utility; not on the author's fidelity to an original source, but on his communication of knowledge, in an eloquent and highly readable vernacular, to those who are 'sanza lettere' (unlearned in Greek and Latin), to borrow Leonardo da Vinci's self-descriptive phrase.

Wives and Ill-Married Husbands

The two works to occupy us here are part of four titles in two volumes published by Curtio Troiano d'i Navò in Venice. The first volume is a rather inelegant work, giving indications of having been released either in haste or with a lack of care. The title page lists three works by Dolce, none, however, with his name, each separated by a blank space, followed by the date MDXXXVIII (1538).[7] There are no indications as to place or publisher, and the third title contains a misprint. The titles read: *Paraphrasi nella sesta sa / tira di Givvenale: nel / laquale si ragiona del / le miserie de gli huo / mini maritati. // Dialogo in cui si parla / di che qualita si dee tor moglie, et del / modo, che vi si ha a tenere. // Lo epithalamio di Ca / Catullo nelle nozze di Peleo et di Theti.* The dedicatory letter to 'M. Titiano pittore et cavaliere' preceding the *Paraphrasi* is dated 10 October 1538, from Padova, and is signed 'Lod. Dolce.'[8] The second work, the dialogue on wives, is prefaced by an unsigned dedicatory letter 'Al magnifico M. Federico Badoaro suo signore,' dated 1 February 1539, from Venice, and runs for a total of thirty-two pages. Again, the title appears without an author, though changed now to read simply *Dialogo del modo di tor moglie.*[9]

The second volume, published by Curtio Navò a few years later, shows greater care.[10] The title page, reading: *Dialogo piacevole / di Messer Lodovico Dol / ce: nelqvale Messer / Pietro Aretino / parla in difesa d'i male / aventvrati mariti*, contains the publisher's emblem – a rampant lion clutching a winged dragon from behind – followed by 'Per Curtio Troiano d'i Navò M.D.XXXXII' (1542). The dedicatory letter to Giorgio Zorzi, written by Curtio Navò, informs Zorzi that 'come, ch'io mal volentieri soglia publicar le fatiche d'altri senza volontà del suo autore: nondimeno essendo venuto alle mie mani il presente Dialogo di Messer Lodovico Dolce, giudicandolo soggetto piacevole et degno d'essere veduto, ho preso da me medesimo autorità di farlo imprimere' (even though I am not accustomed to publish willingly the labours of another without the author's will, nevertheless, the present dialogue of Messer Lodovico Dolce having come into my hands, judging it a pleasing subject worthy of being seen, I have taken upon myself the authority of having it printed).

Before focusing on the dialogues dealing with wives and ill-married husbands, both written within the span of three or four years, I would like to mention in passing a third work of greater renown, Dolce's *Dialogo della institution delle donne, secondo li tre stati che cadono nella vita humana*, a work first published in 1545 by Gabriel Giolito de' Ferrari in Venice. Unjustly reputed to have been solely a plagiarization of the *De institutione foeminae Christianae* (1538) by the Spanish philosopher Juan Luis Vives,[11] the dialogue, 'one of the most celebrated works devoted to women of the sixteenth century,' has been well studied in recent years from a more equitable point of view.[12] Taking into account different social levels and roles, Dolce rejects the common opinion that learned women are less chaste than unlearned, and advocates that women destined to rule should undertake a nearly complete humanistic program of studies, including the whole Latin curriculum and the major vernacular authors, but excluding the Greek as too weighty. In this area, as in so many others, his work functions as a prototype of what is to come in the latter cinquecento.

In his late twenties and early thirties, then, Dolce produced three works dealing with the relationships between the sexes, only the last of which won him some measure of fame in this genre. My task will be to examine the lesser-known, preparatory works, both of which belong to a different current than that of the *Dialogo della institution delle donne*, which is dedicated to praising the nobility and excellence of women, while at the same time educating them regarding the norms of comportment for virgins, married women, and widows.[13] The earlier works, in contrast, more openly demonstrate the influence of the misognynistic current, though the first tries to sum up both sides of the issue.

'Io voglio, che hoggi parliamo de le donne' (p. Hiii^v) – these words, from Dolce's *Dialogo del modo di tor moglie*, are those of Madonna Flaminia, one of eight young women and three youths whom the narrator, a young man named Fronimo, comes upon one holiday as the *brigata* is about to eat lunch on a hillside overlooking the city of Bologna. Madonna Flaminia's wish, that the group talk about women, will be met, although most of the talking, as in Castiglione's *Cortegiano*, will be done by the men.[14] The dedicatory letter would lead us to believe that the conversation to follow fails to come to a conclusion, for the writer informs Federico Badoaro that he himself must resolve 'questa controversia nata pur'ora (benché di vita indegna)' (this controversy born just now [though unworthy of life]). Such a conclusion, however, would be inaccurate, for the work's tripartite structure is vaguely reminiscent of Bembo's *Asolani*, where the final section deals with spiritual love.

The controversy alluded to in the dedicatory letter is mirrored in the work's structure, which consists primarily of two long narrative sections (each mostly a long speech with some authorial interventions), followed by a more traditional dialogue form with two principal interlocutors – Marcello and Fronimo – and only one authorial comment (the introduction of a third speaker, Philotimo) until the final line of narration.[15] Following an introduction that sets the scene in a *locus amoenus* reminiscent of the idyllic settings of the *Decameron* and the *Asolani* (accompanied by praise of Bologna that recalls Castiglione's celebration of Urbino in the *Cortegiano*), all described in a mellifluous tone with a few well-placed superlatives (*delicatissimi, bellissimi, honorevolissime*) and reading as if it were Boccaccio at the top of his form, one finds what almost seems to be an exculpatory note for the text found earlier in the volume, Dolce's translation of Juvenal's misogynistic sixth satire. I say 'seems to be' on the assumption that the author (Dolce) and the narrator (Fronimo) are to be identified as one. Here, when Madonna Flaminia accuses Fronimo of holding an opinion against women, exclaiming 'che domine v'hanno fatto le donne?' (What on earth have they done to you?; p. Hiii^v), he responds that he has never been opposed to women, nor spoken ill of them:

Io sono più à le donne, che à niuno obligato: io di loro nacqui senz'alcun dubbio: elle mi formarono, qual mi vedete: elle mi potevano storpiare: elle mi dierono il primo nutrimento: elle mi insegnarono i costumi: e poi una donna con la sua invitta honestà me fece apparare d'essere huomo ... (pp. Hiii^v–Hiv^r)

[I am more obliged to women than to anyone. I was born from them without a doubt. They formed me just as you see me. They could have maimed me. They gave me the first nourishment. They taught me manners. And then a woman with her unconquered honesty made me learn to be a man ...]

With this preamble, the group, having proposed for discussion the question 'se si dee pigliare la moglie, o nò' (whether one should take a wife or not), chooses one of the young men (unnamed and never used) as judge, Madonna Flaminia as the ruler ('la reggente'), Madonna Emilia as the administrator ('la procuratrice'), Marcello as the person speaking against the question, and Fronimo in favour. These practical matters are all accompanied by a lively discourse, including the interjection of one impatient youth who gets fed up with the delay and says, 'oh voi m'havete fastidito con queste vostre parole del dare, e de l'havere: spendete il tempo, il fiato, e la giornata senza prò: venite hoggimai à 'l fatto: se si deve pigliar moglie' (Oh you've annoyed me with these words of yours about giving and having; you waste time, your breath, and the day for nothing. Get down now to the facts: whether one ought to take a wife; p. Hiv^v).

But again, before the discussion gets under way, Emilia establishes a practical point – namely, that, as regards the husband, they are *not* talking about stupid youths or weak old men, *not* the unhealthy of body, *not* soldiers always off fighting, *not* merchants always dealing, *not* fools, philosophers, astrologers, doctors, or poets, but about a man of decent age, above all noble, literate, and wise with respect to himself and others. With this proviso, the men are left to decide the question, but the comment serves to inform us in advance that, if from the point of view of men some women are not ideal wives, then neither are many men ideal husbands, and that includes philosophers and poets, the people who usually argue these issues! A salutary note indeed.

The subject-matter of the two presentations that follow brings to mind the critical commonplace that the delight one experiences in reading a work of literature derives in part from the sense of novelty, in part from the sense of recognition. As for the latter, Marcello, the youth who is ordered to speak against marriage, claims that 'per non acquistarmi la vostra malavoglienza, io non dirò alcuna cosa di mio capo, ma secondo, che una volta mi ricordo haver letto in un libro' (in order not to gain your ill-will, I won't say anything of my own, but only according to what I remember once having read in a book; p. Ii[r]).[16] The sense of recognition for the modern reader, of course, moves in both directions; that is, while admittedly much of the work brings to mind the earlier treatises on love and marriage, later authors also reflect elements in Dolce's work, whether derived from him or from others writing in this tradition.[17]

Adriana Chemello, in discussing Dolce's *Institution delle donne*, makes a point that applies here as well, although perhaps not to the same degree. In the cinquecento, the weight of convention dominates the universe of signs to the extent that intertexuality becomes a constant. Each work is one part of a continuing serial, with some simply mirroring the model, as the function of the author disappears.[18] Dolce's contribution, while it adheres to a model of imitation common to the time, consists in an intelligent rewriting of the 'già detto,' with the aim not only of rendering the material more elegant, but of filtering it through a lens that is both more modern and secular (where 'secular,' I might add, stands in opposition to such things as the 'religious,' or spiritual, tone of Neoplatonic thought), in order to reach a wider class of readers, not all of whom belong to the aristocratic élite. To a new audience, all material is new. What matters is not who originated the thought, but whether or not the thought is worth passing on. Nevertheless, despite the traditional patterns followed by Dolce, the presentations have several details taken from common life that serve to detach them from the writings of his predecessors.

Marcello's discourse begins by touching on the theme of liberty, which he opposes to matrimony, a form of slavery – of the wife to the husband and of the husband to the wife – that resembles and only ends in death (p. Ii[r]),[19] after which he moves on to woman's importunity, summed up in her tongue, which never stops, and her (sexual) appetite, which is never sated. Two brief anecdotes meant to be humorous are then narrated, after which Marcello presents a cynical picture of what awaits a tired husband when he returns home. The portrait of the domestic scene in satiric-realistic tones is a procedure employed later with particular success in the *Galateo* of Giovanni Della Casa. Here, we learn that the wife, after her husband has gone to bed to rest his tired limbs, continues to annoy him by starting new arguments and raising new issues, thus ruining his sleep for good.[20] Like priests who never tire of asking for offerings, wives are always asking for 'what is owed them,' and after having asked ten, a hundred, nay even a thousand times, they turn around and tell the husband he hasn't done anything, and that he should start over again. The concluding exclamation is: 'oh dio, che ingorda voragine si pò a questa assomigliare?' (Oh God, what voracious chasm can one compare to her?; p. Iij'); even the beasts are more discrete, since they conjoin once and are satisfied.

From sexual appetites, we move to another domestic detail – the spending habits of wives, here introduced through the *praeteritio* of 'Io voglio tacere de le gravissimie spese' (I wish to keep silent about their very heavy spending). A long list of things to buy follows ('veste, cinte, ornamenti, gioie, anella, catene, maniglie, ventagli, vasi, unguenti, odori, belletti, gibellini, schiavi, nani, cavalli, carrette, cocchi, gondole, et istrumenti da pelarsi, da far ricci i capelli, e d'altri simili infiniti' [garments, belts, ornaments, jewels, rings, chains, handles, fans, pots, ointments, perfumes, cosmetics, bodices, slaves, dwarves, horses, carts, red dyes, gondolas, instruments to remove hair, to make hair curly, and infinite other similar things]), after which Marcello launches into an internal dialogue between a wife and her luckless husband, the whole quite entertaining and characterized by a comic tone of low realism. All the ills that matrimony bring are amply covered, often by means of hyperbolic repetition.[21] Marcello's conclusion is that a celibate life makes a celestial life that much easier. The more lustful a creature is (like the sparrow or lettuce, which seeds quickly), the sooner it dies. With wives, the other divine gifts – 'la prontezza de lo ingegno, il thesoro de la memoria, e la lunghezza de la vita' (the quickness of wit, the treasure of memory, and the length of life; p. Iiij^v) – all disappear.

Within Marcello's presentation, we find not only dramatized scenes with narrated dialogue, but also the use of what I will call an antagonistic interlocutor (reminiscent of Machiavelli's use of the same in the *Prince*). Quite often we find expressions such as 'mi risponderai' (you will reply to me), 'qualch'uno dirà ... io vi rispondo' (someone will say ... I reply to you), 'alcuni arguiscono ... per risposta brevemente dirassi' (some infer ... one will briefly say in response), 'so bene che sia qualch'uno che dirà ... io rispondo' (I know well that someone will say ... I reply), 'Alcuno mi potrebbe gittare in occhi ... io ho detto altre fiate' (Someone could throw in my eyes ... I have said other times), all used to enliven the discourse, since each person speaks at great length without interruption.

Fronimo's rebuttal is once again a retouching of what someone else has already said. His first humorous comment, in fact, is that Marcello might have told us what the author of the book he quoted had to say in response to these misogynistic comments, and saved Fronimo himself the effort.[22] Fronimo's argument is based on the statement that there is nothing so perfect that it does not have some defects, with examples drawn from the sun, moon, stars, fire, air, earth, water, iron, gold, silver, victory, science, virtues, men, and bees (p. Ki^r). What he will try to prove is that, in marriage, there is more good than bad.

Each of Marcello's points is rebutted, beginning with 'marriage as servitude.' For Fronimo, given that man is a political animal, what better conjunction can there be than that of two souls? What sweeter thing is there than to have 'una perpetua compagna de la vita' (a perpetual companion in life), with whom one can speak as if to oneself? Marriage, for all its defects, is a 'commune concordia' (p. Ki^v). As for the other vices of wives mentioned by Marcello, Fronimo says these are true of some evil women, but not of all. To those who say wives are quick to do ill, he replies that this is a result of their husbands' injustice (p. Kii^r). If raised well, women, like men, turn out well. In opposition to Medea, Procne, Clytemnestra, Messalina, and other infamous women (none, incidentally, mentioned by Marcello), one can list the Lucretias, Portias, Hypsicrateas, Zenobias, and other glorious women, including virgins who killed themselves to remain pure.

Fronimo's justification of infidelity is of a practical (rather than moral) sort. If a tender virgin is married to an impotent old man and she happens to fall in love with another, the fault is not hers but that of those who attempt to marry her off and of the man who takes her. Marriage itself is justified as a thing of virtue through the Aristotelian principle of the golden mean. Just as liberality is the midpoint between the extremes of avarice and prodigality, or strength between daring and timidity, so between virginity (we cannot all be virgins or life will not continue, Fronimo notes) and incontinence stands a certain modest conjunction – the institution of matrimony.[23]

Having established this, Fronimo continues to respond point by point to Marcello's attack. As regards 'temperate sex,' for example, he finds a justification in its medicinal benefits (p. Kiij^r).[24] Virginity, in turn, is as much to be blamed as sterility. With this and the other contrary positions routed, Fronimo next turns to an approvation of marriage as an institution ordained by God. Good wives take care of the possessions acquired by their husbands; they spend only for the good of the family; they help their husbands in illness. In opposition to Marcello's depiction of the tired husband returning home to squabbles, Fronimo paints a domestic scene of sweetness, then mentions the joy of wedding celebrations, the delight in seeing a beautiful girl, especially when nude (with the classical example being Helen), and the inexpressible pleasure of sexual conjunction. Love is loftier than all else and makes all food sweet; love lifts one from extreme sadness to extreme joy. A wise man will love *not* girls, *not* horses, *not* mules, dogs, birds, factories, possessions, and so forth, but his wife – 'la moglie, la consorte, la compagna de la vita, e de la fortuna' (p. Kiv^r). To those who say one can find these advantages with a concubine (in addition to being able to leave her any time one wishes), he responds that there is no comparison between a concubine and a legitimate wife. The concubine loves money, not the man.

Examples of wives who were willing to die for their husbands follow (including Indian wives who join their dead husbands on the funeral pyre), after which Fronimo celebrates the fruits of marriage, particularly well-raised children. With this, he launches into a hymn to matrimony (beginning 'O Matrimonio, felice e santo') reminiscent of Bembo's hymn to love in Book 4 of Castiglione's *Cortegiano*. But this hymn, despite Emilia's assertion that we can all go home happy now, does not conclude the work. Instead, Marcello and Fronimo begin a true dialogue that continues for eleven more pages, with very occasional narrative incursions. Among the interesting points brought up for discussion are the names of those writers who have criticized wives, including Juvenal, Boccaccio, Ariosto, il Manganello, and il Burchiello, all of whom are castigated for specific comments or actions (p. Li^v). Fronimo also turns the table by mentioning many who have spoken well of women.

At this point, the focus of the dialogue changes when Philotimo, the youth who had proposed the question, says he himself has decided to get married and wants to know how to choose a wife. If he could, he would like one more accomplished than Castiglione's woman of the court (p. Liij^v).[25] Fronimo's response is that she should be just like the husband. The wife is a companion, not a slave to her spouse. As regards beauty, that of the soul is more important, although he takes the time to describe both in some detail. Her ears, for example, should not be so small that they disappear, nor so large that they seem those of an ass (p. Liv^v). Physical beauty, however, is fragile and not to be esteemed in comparison to the beauty of the soul, which increases with age. During the discussion, several complaints are lodged against the customs of the time, in particular against arranged marriages, which make it difficult to judge a woman's beauty of body or of soul (though those ugly in body but beautiful in soul deserve to be loved no less), and mixed marriages, where nobles and non nobles are joined 'hoggi in questa nostra Italia' (today in this Italy of ours; p. Mi^{r-v}).[26]

The dialogue as a whole is an entertaining work of lively spirit, written with skill. While the discussion lacks both the numerous classical exempla of Francesco Barbaro's *De re uxoria* and the intellectual rigour of a work like Giovanni Della Casa's *An uxor sit ducenda*, it also avoids the dry tone of both those works. If one were to compare Dolce's dialogue to books on the market today, it would resemble not so much an arid academic tome as a work of pop psychology. At the same time, the work's more practical elements and its occasional comic motifs are leavened by the idyllic setting and tone of gentle discourse. To teach one must also entertain.

If Dolce, through Fronimo, seems to apologize at one point in his *Dialogo del modo di tor moglie* for the misogynistic tone of his preceding translation of Juvenal's sixth satire, the procedure is more overt in his *Dialogo piacevole ... nelquale Messer Pietro Aretino parla in difesa d'i male aventurati mariti* of 1542. In this latter work's dedicatory letter of 10 August 1542, which follows the dialogue, since the publisher placed his own letter at the beginning, Dolce tells the 'magnifica Signora Madonna Leonora Silvia' that he does not doubt he will gain more blame than praise for the work. In part, he has written the truth, he says, but for the rest he should have been more temperate. Where he told the truth was in his discussion of those wretches who are cuckolded by women, but at the same time his words of criticism were excessive, since one also finds women who are honest and virtuous (p. 18^{r}). His request for forgiveness is shrewdly and humorously worded, in that those who are innocent will understand that he was not speaking of them and forgive him, the implication being that those who are guilty deserve the vituperation. At the same time, he promises another work (surely his *Institution delle donne*), which will make amends for his error.

The dialogue's two interlocutors, Aretino and Piccardo, meet on a pleasant spring day just after Piccardo's return from Rome, where all the cardinals are sad because of the death of Contarini. Wishing to ignore unpleasant things, Aretino asks about 'our Carlo, courtier of the Muses,' only to learn that he has been cuckolded by his beloved Giulia (p. 2^v). Again, the speeches are filled with witticisms. Giulia, for example, has produced in Carlo a metamorphosis more beautiful than any of Ovid's, transforming him into one of those animals that the ancients called 'hirci' and the moderns 'becchi' (goats). Her job was easier than Diana's in changing Actaeon into a deer since her husband was already a perfect animal, lacking only horns. How she did this is 'una novella, la più piacevole che mai s'udisse' (a story, the most pleasing ever heard). What follows is a comic narration of Giulia's seduction by a young doctor hired by her impotent husband to make her fertile. The comic tone is evident from the first line, where the husband and wife are described as two extremes, Giulia being beautiful and Carlo more ugly than one of the Baronci, since his breath also stinks (pp. 2^v–3^r). The tale ends in court, after Carlo catches the two *in flagrante delicto*. The doctor, to the laughter of the onlookers, wins the case by showing that no other remedy existed.

Aretino's response is to say that he will prove that neither being called a cuckold nor being made one is worthy of blame. He begins by explaining the origin of the term 'becho,' an animal so gentle that it cares not if another mounts its mate ('la sua donna capra') in front of its eyes (p. 4^r). A man who is cuckolded by his wife deserves no blame, since this would imply that a man's reputation came from women, who are imperfect creatures incapable of taking away another's good name, just as the sun receives no blemish in penetrating the ugliness of the earth (p. 5$^{r–v}$). Here, unlike the earlier dialogue, no one defends women, for Piccardo responds that everyone would concede this point.

The virtues of men and the vices of women are presented through examples, beginning with classical figures (Cesare, Marc'Antonio, Catone, Pompeo Magno, Servio Sulpitio, Marco Crasso, Aulo Gabinio, Domitiano, Claudio Imperadore) whose dignity and fame were not lessened due to their having unfaithful wives (p. 6$^{r–v}$). The wickedness of women exceeds the number of grains of sand in the sea or stars in the sky. Pagan Roman law is exhalted over Christian, since Romulus allowed a husband to leave a wife caught in adultery (p. 7^r). In making his points, Aretino employs internal dialogue, narrating the discussions held in his house at other times and attributing speeches to various contemporaries (e.g., Giulio Bragadino, a Venetian patrician; Fortunio Spira, an orientalist from Viterbo; Francesco Maria Molza [1489–1544], a well-known *letterato* from Modena; Giulio Camillo [*ca* 1480–1544], praised elsewhere by Aretino as a writer of letters; the Florentine Benedetto Varchi [1503–1565]; Francesco Gussano [Cusano], a translator of Homer who dedicated the first book of the *Iliad* to Aretino; Ludovico Ariosto [1474-1533]; and Bernardino Daniello [died 1565], a translator of Virgil's *Georgics* and commentator of Dante and Petrarch), some of whom cite as authorities the ancients, ranging from Plato to Terence. As a result, the tone is one of unrelenting, unmitigated criticism and (to the modern reader at least) renders the dialogue displeasing rather than 'piacevole.' The most that one finds in opposition is an occasional weak 'Non so, se io 'l creda' (I don't know if I believe that).[27] Surprisingly, Aretino at one point even cites 'il mio compare Messer Lodovico Dolce,' saying he always has on his lips that Ovidian verse 'Casta est, quam nemo rogavit' (She is chaste whom no one solicits) and quoting other sayings of his at some length (pp. 8^v–9^r). In turn, Piccardo tells Pietro to tell Messer Lodovico (Dolce) what he thinks about having wives in common.

Another of the dialogue's features is the use of misogynistic anecdotes and *facezie*, some appearing in other collections and thus common to the time (see, for example, the stories on p. 9^v, dealing with trees from which wives have hanged themselves). The usual lists of women who were good (Penelope, Lucretia) and bad (Clytemnestra, Medea, Pasiphae, Myrrha, Pandora, Eve, Eriphyle, Circe, Scylla, Niobe, Medusa, Biblis, Semiramis) appear, with the good stories called fables, the bad stories called true (pp. 10^r, 12^{r-v}). The diatribe against women continues at length, with whole pages given over to Aretino's invective, and the occasional one-line response of Piccardo, which is usually something like 'Così penso io anchora' (I think so, too; p. 11^r). Similes and allegorical fables are employed to make his point.[28] Women are compared to harpies gorged on the blood of men, with claws of avarice, and stinking of vices; every evil under the sun is attributed to them; they are criticized at length for their treachery, including the use of make-up and hair colour to hide the truth. All are said to be alike, at least as regards lust (p. 12^v). The onslaught is so overwhelming that finally Piccaro has to ask Pietro to say no more, for fear of giving rise to suspicion.

Aretino, in reponse, claims to be a friend and servant of women, and speaks, not out of hatred, but only to tell the truth (p. 13^r). Having said that, he launches into another assault. And so goes the dialogue for another ten pages, in the midst of which Piccardo again warns Aretino that what he says makes him suspect. Pietro responds with the same I'm-a-friend-of-women clause (p. 15^r), this giving him the excuse for more vituperation, much of it repetitive, including references to the same classical figures mentioned earlier and another lament that modern laws do not permit husbands to leave unfaithful wives (pp. 16^{r-v}).

Only two interesting notes are sounded. The first is Aretino's assertion that Petrarch's Laura was dishonest, and that the poet, after spending a happy night with her, would rush back to write pages of praise.[29] Piccardo's response is one of agreement, after which he adds that the same could be said of Dante's Bice, Cino's Selvaggia, and many others. The second item of some novelty is Aretino's concluding pronouncement that anyone who believes that the vice of a woman can offend the virtue of a man is 'più Heretico di Luthero' (more of a heretic than Luther; p. 17^v). And what is the presumed point of all this? As the title says, it is simply to defend cuckolded husbands from the calumny of others. Apparently, Dolce would agree with those who claim the best defence is an attack. In this case, the author truly had cause to apologize.

Memory

An indication of the nature of Dolce's *Dialogue on Memory* can be found in the dedicatory letter to Philip II, dated 1 October 1562.[30] There, Dolce says he has had other opportunities to honour him with greater works, 'che dalla lingua Latina io portai nel Volgare' (which I brought from Latin into the vernacular), but has picked this small volume instead (p. 2^r). Though subtly, the author has pointed to the trait that characterizes the present work: it, too, like the other works referred to soon after, is a translation from Latin to Italian, and specifically from the Latin of the German Dominican Johannes Romberch, who published his *Congestorium artificiose memorie* in 1520.

According to Frances Yates, Romberch's treatise was 'one of the fullest and most widely cited of the printed memory treatises,' though she herself prefers the more agreeable translation of Dolce (*The Art of Memory*, pp. 82–3 and 115n). A significant representative of the main strand of memory treatises descending from the scholastic emphasis on memory, Romberch's book combined all three classical sources – not only the *Ad Herennium*, but Cicero's *De oratore*, and Quintilian, while at the same time integrating into the Dominican memory system other more modern writers like Petrarch, who is frequently cited, Peter of Ravenna, and Thomas Aquinas (pp. 114–15).[31]

Romberch divides his *Congestorium artificiose memorie* into four parts; the first an introduction, the second on places, the third on images, and the fourth an outline of an encyclopedic memory system. As for the place systems, he establishes three different types: the cosmos (his design for the spheres of the universe reappears in Dolce), the signs of the zodiac (where

Metrodorus of Scepsis is cited as the authority as found in Cicero's *De oratore* and in Quintilian, with an additional reference to the images of all the constellations provided by Hyginus), and, finally, real places in real buildings (as found in the more normal, mnemotechnical method). This section of the book also contains visual alphabets, all of which are reproduced by Dolce.[32] The last part of Romberch's book outlines an ambitious program to memorize all the sciences (theological, metaphysical, and moral) as well as the seven liberal arts, through the use of images, with each subject to be placed in a memory room.

Dolce's purpose in translating Romberch is clear from a statement he makes in the dedicatory letter, where he explains that he is writing to engage and beguile those youths who are desirous of new things (p. 4[v]). The dialogue takes place between an older man, who does most of the talking, Hortensio, and a youth by the name of Fabritio. The stimulus for the discussion is a practical matter. Fabritio understands things well, but soon after forgets all about them, a complaint common to students then and now. In contrast, Hortensio speaks of those great men of antiquity with fabulous memories, people like Seneca, who could repeat two thousand names in the same order as recited by someone else (p. 5[v]). Memory, he says, is 'certo bellissimo dono di Natura' (certainly a beautiful gift of nature), but unfortunately it is fragile and subject to many mishaps, including the fact that if it is not helped by art, it slips away, rendering vain all our labours and all our reading (pp. 5[v]–6[r]).[33] With this in mind, Hortensio promises to tell Fabritio what he has learned from reading others, and will add a few items from his own imagination, all with the aim of helping him (p. 6[r]).

Since memory is such a significant gift, it is incumbent upon both sexes, and all classes and kinds of people, from religious to secular, from scholars to anyone with a profession, to develop it (p. 7[r]). Citing ancient authorities, Hortensio provides a definition of memory (p. 8[r]) along with a diagram of the head showing the location of imagination, fantasy, memory, thinking, and so forth (p. 9[r]), before dealing with the best way to improve one's retention, which is not with medicine, but with places and images (p. 8[v]). This, the so-called '*memoria artificiale*,' requires diligence and art, for which Petrarch is cited as an authority (pp. 8[v]–9[r]).

The difference between memory and reminiscence is made clear (i.e., between what today we would call voluntary and involuntary memory), after which Hortensio lists the seven types of people who are not apt to learn – the 'mal disposti,' those 'di tardo ingegno,' those who waste time, the 'spensierati,' 'gli amalatici, o languidi e tormentati da i dolori' (the poorly disposed, those of slow wit, those lost in the clouds, the ill or languid and tormented by suffering; p. 9^v). Provided you are capable of learning, you need three things to use your memory well: a good disposition of the soul, since memory is one of its faculties; a sound body, since memory uses one's senses; and a body in conformity with the soul. And, as Petrarch tells us, along with these three qualities, one needs three other conditions, – namely, freedom from other tasks, a mild manner, and sobriety (p. 10^r).

This last term brings to the pages of this dialogue a criticism of excessive drinking, in which all the resultant evil effects are described, from vomiting to bad breath to dizziness (p. 10^v). Memory is damaged, not only by this, however, but also by excessive eating or by eating foods that are hard to digest, such as meat and hard-boiled eggs (p. 11^r). Beyond diet, one needs moderation in other aspects of life as well. Too much sleep is bad for one's memory, as are an excess of heat or cold, extremes of passion, carnal use, and similar extravagances. Despite the medieval sources, these strictures have a distinctly modern ring to them.

With this established as a base, Hortensio begins a long presentation on places, images, and order, a discussion that includes distinctions between imagination, images, and signs (p. 14^r). Having placed the images of things in an orderly fashion in different places, one can easily recall them in any order desired (p. 13^r). To facilitate the process, however, one needs to use imagination, first of external things, such as hills, valleys, rivers, and woods; next, of things that are invisible, such as heaven, hell, and purgatory; and, finally, of things made by art, such as houses, palaces, and monasteries (p. 16^r).

Along with the theoretical background, specific practical recommendations are made. As regards the number of places needed, for example, Hortensio says that for beginners it should not be too many (p. 17$^{r–v}$), perhaps ten images for the major places, and in each anywhere from four to ten rooms (p. 18^r). In each of these rooms, there are four corners plus the door, or four walls plus the centre. As for the selection of the major places, it helps to travel and see a lot (pp. 18^v–19^v). And if you can't go in person, you can always read about other places, visualizing them in your imagination (p. 19^r).

This discourse brings up other matters, such as the division of the world into three major continents – Europe, Africa, and Asia (p. 19^v) – and these in turn have their own divisions, which are then provided to us: the countries of Europe, Asia, and Africa (pp. 20^r–23^r). Geography and cosmography both help memory; without them, one fails to understand either history or sacred letters (p. 23[r]). In addition to all these places, one can employ for 'comuni luoghi' things such as the twelve signs of the zodiac and lists of animals in alphabetical order (p. 24[r]). That Dolce is translating from the Latin is obvious from the location in his alphabetical list of 'Orso' (from the Latin 'ursus'), which follows 'Tigre.' Sometimes the scheme seems more elaborate than the items one wants to memorize, but the artificial techniques are simply a means for encyclopedic memorization.

Having dealt with effectual reality ('i luoghi effettuali'), Hortensio moves on to more abstract places ('i luoghi imaginarij') – such as features of the sky, hell, purgatory, and paradise. Combinations of consonants and the five vowels in order are also useful, as, for example, the letter *n*, one might find *Navigante*, *Negromante*, *Ninfa*, *Notaio*, and *Nuntio* (p. 38[r]). Here, as elsewhere, the young Fabritio's brief comments serve more as dividing points between topics than as substantive additions to the dialogue. Matters of interest to the reader are almost always expressed by Hortensio. Following a definition of images and a listing of their synonyms ('spetie, Idoli, simolacri, simiglianze, figure, forme, Idee, et imagini'; p. 41[r]), we move to alphabets, where we find several illustrations of Giacomo Publicio – letters along with objects that are similar to them (pp. 53[r]–56[r]). Other alphabets with appropriate objects follow, including the Greek (p. 59[r]) and an alphabet with animals that resemble letters (p. 59[v]), as well as a list of women's and men's names by letter (p. 60[r]). Words are created to help memorize things ('Saligia' might thus be the equivalent of the following vices: 'superbia, avaritia, lusuria, ira, gola, invidia, accidia'). In such a practice, one finds the origin of things like the musical scale (p. 73[r]). The important element is always the 'colleganza,' the relationship tying images to other images (p. 74[r]).

Other techniques are detailed, including putting lists of things and names into a story, and the use of similarities. For example, Hortensio says that, when he hears Dante's name, he thinks of Petrarch, Bembo, Capello, Veniero, and Tasso (p. 79[r]). Grammar brings to mind Niccolò Perotti, Aldo Manuzio, and others in that profession (p. 79[v]). Astrological signs are useful memory devices, as are also the images painted by famous painters, if we know them well. In both examples (poets and painters), Dolce again modernizes his source. Here, for example, he mentions Titian and puts in a plug for his own publisher:

Come chi volesse raccordarsi della favola di Europa, potrebbe valersi dell'esempio della pittura di Titiano: et altretanto di Adone, e di qual si voglia altra favolosa historia, profana, o sacra: eleggendo specialmente quelle figure, che dilettano, e quindi sogliono la memoria eccitare. A che sono utile i libri con figure, come per lo più hoggidì si sogliono stampare nella guisa, che si possono vedere nella maggior part di quelli, che escono dalle stampe dell'accuratissimo Giolito. (p. 86ʳ)

[As one who wanted to remember the fable of Europa could make use of the example of Titian's painting, and the same for Adonis, and any other fabulous history whatsoever, profane or sacred, chosing especially those figures that delight, and thus usually stimulate memory. For which purpose, books with figures are useful, such as those on the whole published nowadays, something one can see in most of those that come from the press of the most careful Giolito.]

As another example of modernization, in the examples of hybrid creatures like the Chimera that can be broken down into their component parts, we find Ariosto's hippogryph (p. 88ʳ).

Hortensio begins his final presentation on ways to learn the sciences and the liberal arts. We find terms from the fields of philosophy and dialectics laid out using scales; ways to learn the books of the Bible using images for each; techniques for memorizing numbers and mathematics, with specific examples for merchants (among which we find the publisher of the present dialogue, 'Messer Marchiò Sessa, honoratissimo Mercatante di libri' [p. 117ʳ]); the use of playing cards (pp. 117ᵛ–18ʳ); and, finally, of chess (pp. 118ʳ⁻ᵛ). The concluding words of Fabritio might well apply to all of Dolce's readers: 'Io del tuo ragionamento rimango molto sodisfatto: e te ne ho per questo un'obligo quasi infinito, sperando col mezo de' tuoi raccordi in breve dottorarmi, e comparere ancora io a cicalar nelle corti' (I remain quite satisfied with your discourse, and because of it I have almost an infinite obligation to you, hoping by means of your recollections to gain before long my doctor's degree, so I can hold forth in the courts). This, then, is Dolce's aim – the dissemination of knowledge with a practical use – and his motivation is his desire to help those who wish to improve themselves. His reward, as that of any teacher, is the gratitude of those kept for too long outside the sacred precincts of hidden wisdom.

For Every Noble and Singular Mind: The Treatise on Gems

An examination of Dolce's career as an original author and critic would be incomplete without a reference to his work as a scholar and translator of scientific treatises. In this area, as in so many others, he performed a notable service to the field of humane letters. I concentrate here on the

Trattato delle gemme (1565), as one example of many. Though usually referred to as a work 'based on' Camillo Leonardi's *Speculum lapidum* (1502), the treatise is, in fact, a word-for-for word translation of the original, the only major changes I detected being the one cited in the introduction to this chapter (the updating of contemporary painters and sculptors) and a new dedication to the work as a whole.[34] In contrast to the Latin original, however, with its cramped script and numerous abbreviations, Dolce's version, as mentioned earlier, must have appeared as a welcome relief, particularly to the common reader, as, for example, for a sixteenth-century goldsmith with an interest in jewels, someone more concerned with content than with whether or not the author has produced an original work.

Dolce, in fact, does not hesitate to list the numerous sources for the knowledge being divulged, translating as his own Leonardi's assertions that the content of the book is not original but owes its derivation to others, both ancient and modern, and that the work as a whole is more a compilation than anything else (pp. 4^r, 23^r).[35] The list of sources, which includes works of scientific knowledge extending beyond mere lapidaries, reads as follows:

Dioscoride, Aristotele, Hermete, Evase, Serapione, Avicenna, Giovanni Mesue, Salomone, Fisiologo, Plinio, Solino, Alberto Magno, Vicenzo historico, il Lapidario, Helimanto, Isidoro, Arnaldo, Iuba, Dionigi Alessandrino, Therel[,] Rabano, Bartolomeo di riva Romana, Marbordio Vescovo[,] l'Ortolano[,] il libro delle Pandete, Cornucopia, Chirando, e 'l libro della natura delle cose. (pp. 23^{r-v})[36]

Dolce sees himself, then, as simply continuing a process common to any encyclopedist.

As Carla De Bellis notes in her study of Camillo Leonardi, the work itself, combining practical and speculative elements from alchemy, astrology, and magic, not only offers a mirror of how much of this ancient culture reached the Renaissance, but also shows us what elements were still considered useful or believable (p. 69). One notes with some surprise that this happens to be almost all of them. The *Speculum*, in fact, is characterized by the acceptance of the most primitive and barbaric beliefs of magic (considered more on practical than on speculative terms) and by an astonishingly archaic manner, attributable in part to the author's pedestrian repetition of his sources. Dolce's translation, however, surrounded as it is by his many other works of cultural dissemination, needs to be looked at from a slightly different, more modern perspective.

As De Bellis notes, the translation gains special significance, in part because it illustrates the anxiety felt by individuals in the cinquecento both to define themselves and to catalogue, and thus systematize, knowledge. To these motivating forces, one might add the necessity, felt so strongly in the High and Late Renaissance, of creating a new ethical framework to replace that of the late Middle Ages, undermined in the quattrocento by those humanists who were interested less in God and the life to come, and more in the world around them.

The text, then, whether the original effort of Camillo Leonardi or the *volgarizzamento* of Dolce, is a compendium, a work of synthesis that merges the lapidary culture of the Middle Ages (based, in turn, on earlier works) with the contemporary interest in medico-magical arts. Leonardi himself was both a doctor and an astrologer, having worked in Pesaro with the celebrated astrologer Lorenzo Bonincontri, a widely travelled man who in the mid-fifteenth century lived in Naples, where he was a member of the young Pontano's literary circle; who then spent time in Florence, where he read Manilio's *Astronomicon* and joined Ficino's Accademia; and who served Pope Sixtus IV in Rome, where he joined the academy of Pomponio Leto (De Bellis, p. 68). The cultural interests of both men, reflected in the *Speculum*, tended, then, towards the esoteric, with the goal not only of rediscovering the original *prisca sapientia*, but also of unveiling that knowledge for others (p. 69). In this, Dolce was again of service, and the genre of gem books (like so many other genres) owes a debt of gratitude to him.

Most scholars who deal with the more esoteric arts of the Renaissance or who compile literary histories tend to gloss over this plagiarized treatise. To take a different approach, one concentrating more on content than on authorship, perhaps it might be useful to cover as succinctly as possible the material as presented in Dolce's treatise, approaching the text from the point of view of a curious reader rather than that of a critic concerned only with originality.

Quantunque le Gemme siano comunemente prezzate, come dice il nostro gentilissimo Poeta, dal Volgo avaro e sciocco; e questo per lo guadagno, ch'esso ne trahe: nondimeno per la bellezza e virtù loro, elle debbano essere istimate da ogni nobile e pellegrino ingegno. (p. 4^r)[37]

The *Trattato delle gemme* is divided into three books, dealing with the formation and physical qualities of jewels, the powers infused in them by the stars, and the magical and astral figures inscribed on jewels with their associated powers. The authorities cited with the greatest frequency in the nine chapters of Book 1 – where the most common terms are ones like 'matter and form,' 'cause and accident,' 'extractive heat and constrictive cold,' '*virtù minerale* and *virtù animale*' – represent the Aristotelian tradition, ranging from Aristotle himself (who discusses 'dry exhalation' and 'moist exhalation' at the end of Book 3 of his *Meteorologica*) to the Persian philosopher and physician Avicenna (who wrote in Arabic), to the Spanish-Arabian Averroes, and the Scholastic philosopher Albertus Magnus (particularly the *Libri mineralium*).[38]

Having set aside gold and silver, minerals which liquefy with heat, the author deals primarily with gems and precious stones, which are divided into two types – those that are either of a muddy or an oily substance (i.e., of the earth) or those in which the watery element predominates (p. 6^r). The effect of climate (where a hermetic source is alleged) and of geographical location (where the source is Solomon's book of precious stones) are also significant:

... sono diverse sorti di pietre, e si generano i diversi luoghi: perciochè alcune sono prodotte nel mare, alcune in diverse terreni, alcune ne' fiumi, alcune ne' nidi de gli Augelli, alcune ne i ventricoli degli animali, et altre nelle rene de' Dragoni, di serpenti, e di altri simili animali. (pp. 9^v–10^r)

[There are different kinds of stones, and different places generate them: because some are produced in the sea, some in different lands, some in rivers, some in the nests of birds, some in the stomachs of animals, and others in the kidneys of dragons, serpents, and similar animals.]

In addition, some are formed in the air, from exhalations of the earth mixed with the air's humid viscosity (p. 10^r). Aristotle, Pliny, and Albertus Magnus are cited for the phenomenon, after which the author provides a contemporary example ('a nostri tempi' – i.e., in Leonardi's time, not Dolce's): a large stone that fell from the clouds in Lombardy. Book 1 concludes with a presentation of the various qualities of stones, including clarity and opacity, softness and hardness, lightness and heaviness, and with a discussion of false and genuine jewels. Lesser gems are sometimes tinted, we learn, to make them seem more precious (p. 16^v).

In Book 2, the author concentrates on specific gems, dealing first with the question of whether or not they have powers (*virtù*), here citing numerous ancient authors (among them Solomon, Pliny, Solinus, Ptolemy, and the Hermetic Corpus), personal experience (a magnet attracting iron), and the authority of the ancient philosphers (Orpheus, Plato, Democritus), all in order to affirm that precious stones do have powers and that they proceed from the stars, since inferior things are governed by superior (p. 21^v). Concerning the powers themselves, the author cites, among others, Solomon, who claims that 'alcune fanno gli huomini essere amati: altre saggi: altri invisibili ... alcune estinguono i veleni' (some make men be loved, others wise, others invisible [and] some destroy poisons; p. 19^r). Having said this, and perhaps having recognized the danger of such an allegation or the difficulty of proof, the author quickly adds that, while the foregoing ideas can be supported to a certain extent, they are not truly philosophical (p. 21^v). As a corrective (which will then be ignored), he cites the more judicious comment of Albertus Magnus: 'Alberto Magno, che fu raro e gran Filosofo, seguendo la forza naturale, pone, che la virtù delle pietre viene dalla stessa specie e forma di esse pietre' (Albertus Magnus, who was an exceptional and great philosopher, when dealing with natural forces, holds that the virtue of the stones comes specifically from what kind they are and their form; p. 22^r). It is at this point, perhaps for further protection from those opposed to magic, that the author provides a list of all the sources employed in Book 2, as mentioned above.

The book's final two chapters, 5 and 6, provide alphabets – first of the colours of stones, with at least one representatives for each colour,[39] then of the gems themselves, with a detailed description of each,[40] including its name, where it is found, its colour, the different types (if more than one), the best kind, and 'ultimamente, come cosa più disiderata dall'huomo, diremo le virtù loro, accioché conosciamo, che ogni cosa prodotta da Dio, è a beneficio de gli huomini: a cui dobbiamo rendere infinite gratie, poscia che non solo ha cura dell'anima, ma anco del corpo nostro' (lastly, as the thing most desired by man, we will mention their powers, so that we may know that every thing made by God is for the benefit of men: [God] to whom we ought to render infinite thanks, since he cares not only for the soul but also for our body; pp. 28^{r-v}).

Book 3, according to Leonardi, is the most difficult, since an explication of the figures engraved on gems by the ancients requires a knowledge of astrology, magic, and necromancy. Though he claims that he himself has no knowledge of these *scienze*, he will collect what he has found spread here and there in different books of learned writers, 'accioché queste cose di tanta nobiltà non periscano, et i lettori ne habbiano quel gusto, che se ne può havere' (so that these things of such nobility not perish, and the readers may gain from them whatever pleasure as can be found therein; Dolce, p. 67^r). In chapter 2 of Book 3, where Leonardi traces the great sculptors of antiquity and the best painters and sculptors of his own age, Dolce makes his greatest change to the original text, updating the list of contemporary artists (for which see the introduction to this chapter), before moving on to the images engraved on stones. The images themselves can be formed in three ways, as Albertus Magnus tells us: first, they may be marked with colours by nature (King Pyrrhus had an agate depicting the nine muses and Apollo with his lyre, all made by nature, while Camillo Leonardi – and thus Dolce after him! – has seen one with seven trees in a plain); second, they may be formed like a cameo by nature, as when rocks stick to other rocks or when parts of a stone wear away; and third, they may be transformed by art.[41]

Leonardi points out that sculptured or engraved gems acquire greater virtue, and that this virtue derives from the stars. The author is careful to qualify this point with a reference to free will, translated by Dolce as follows: 'Come somigliantemente diremo la volontà dell'huomo esser libera, ma con la ragione è condotta a far cose degne et honorate, che senza non sarebbe' (as similarly we say the will of man is free, but with reason it is led to do worthy and honourable things, which otherwise it would not have done; p. 70^r). The will is free, then, until the body is used to effect it, and the body is subject to the stars, although the soul may overcome the body's influence. Like a body, precious stones may have many powers, which are then reduced to one by the sculptor. Regarding the durability of this power, Leonardi disagrees with Albertus Magnus, who claims that the stone's *virtù* may disappear with time, and cites in opposition Haliozacle, Guido Buonetto [Bonatti], and other astrologers, who say that the *virtù* derived from the stars remains in the stone, even if the image is effaced (pp. 71^{r-v}). Having established this point, he moves on to discuss first universal, then particular *virtù*. Universal images are those like the zodiac that have the same power no matter what stone they are engraved on, while particular images are the planets, constellations, and those of magic.[42]

In chapter 7, Leonardi again worries about the judgment of the Church. Dolce translates: 'E, perchè non paia, che le parole mie travijno dalla chiesa Catholica, quando io dico, che alcuna pietra con la cotal figura habbia virtù di produrre tale, o tali effetti, non creda il lettore, che l'huomo sia necessitato a far quello; perciochè sarebbe errore' (And, so that it not

seem that my words stray from the Catholic Church, when I say that a
certain stone with such a figure has the power to produce such an effect
or effects, let the reader not believe that man is forced to do that, because
that would be mistaken; p. 73^r). With this warning – namely, that we do
have free will – we pass to the signs of the zodiac, listed three at a time,
depending on whether they are of fire (Aries, Leo, Sagittarius), earth
(Taurus, Virgo, Capricorn), air (Gemini, Libra, Aquarius), or water
(Cancer, Scorpio, Pisces). As regards the second triad of Taurus, Virgo,
and Capricorn, to cite one by way of example, the author tells us that they
are earthly and meridional; their lords or ruling planets (*signori*) are Venus
in the daytime, the moon at night, and Mars at dawn; and that, when
engraved on a precious stone, they help 'tutte le calde e humide malatie
... e in ogni putrefattion di sangue' (all the warm and humid illnesses ...
and in every putrefaction of blood). In addition, they incline the wearer
towards religion and to natural activities such as planting, seeding, and
viniculture (p. 74^r).

Following the signs of the zodiac, we move to the planets, each of which
is described as it appears on precious stones. Jove, for example, is depicted
in three ways, one of which is as a man in a chair or a cathedra with four
legs, with a wand in one hand and a ball in the other (p. 75^r). For each of
the constellations, we are told its name, how it was described by ancient
writers, in what sign of the zodiac it is placed, if it is southern or northern,
the nature of the planet, and its *virtù* if engraved on a gem. The Bear, for
example, makes the person who wears it become learned, astute, cautious,
and powerful (p. 76^r).

Just as the Latin original occasionally skips chapter numbers (although
different ones), the numbering now jumps from 10 to 14, to bring the text
into alignment with the source. In chapter 14, the author deals with magic
images, first with those from Ragel (in Camillo Leonardi 'Aragel' = Ragiel)
in his book of wings ('nel libro delle ali'; p. 80^r), then with the Hebrew
images from Chael (p. 81^v), and finally with the images or seals ('sigilli')
of Thetel. Among the interesting details are that concerning the griffin
(from Ragiel), which if sculpted on a crystal has the great power of filling
the breasts with milk (p. 80^v); the image of a horse with a crocodile above
it (from Chael), which, if engraved on a hyacinth, helps one be victorious
in civil suits (p. 82^r); and the sign of the cross on a green jasper (from
Thetel), which has the power to free the wearer from ever drowning (p.
86^v). Fifteen seals or images from the Hermetic Corpus (the 'libretto del
quadripartito' or *Kyranides*) follow, along with various ones collected from

other learned men (see pp. 93^rff.), the last of which is a winged horse and a cat. At this point the treatise comes abruptly to a close with no conclusion.

Despite Leonardi's lack of originality and Dolce's servile translation, it must be recognized that both men performed a useful function – namely, the collection and preservation of ancient knowledge, and Dolce, in particular, helped spread that knowledge to those levels of society unlearned in Latin and thus traditionally left out in the cold as far as what the Middle Ages and the Renaissance called science. These are the readers that cared more about arcane lore than they did about who made that lore available to them, the readers that Leonardi and Dolce served as a conduit. After all, that was one of the fundamental features of the Renaissance – the rediscovery and preservation of antiquity.

In concluding this glimpse at Dolce's translations of technical treatises, I might merely note that at least one stone comes in for additional comment – the heliotrope. As Dolce writes, 'se fia unta col succo dell'herba del suo nome, fa invisibile altrui. E di quì prese il Boccaccio la occasione della novella di Calandrino, che andava cercando questa pietra per lo Mergnone' (if it is oiled with the juice of the herb of the same name, it makes others invisible. And from here Boccaccio took the situation of the short story of Calandrino, who went around looking for this stone in the Mergnone; p. 42^r). With this, and the earlier Dolcean addition of contemporary sculptors and painters, one has to be content. The rest, as Dolce would say, is for our utility and, for that alone, those desirous of learning the mysterious secrets of ancient lore cannot help but be pleased.

Painting and Colours

Dolce's *Dialogo della pittura ... intitolato l'Aretino* (1557) has been translated into English and studied at some length by scholars in recent years.[43] The material of *L'Aretino* can be summed up in Roskill's words:

Three separate but somewhat overlapping elements ... make up the content of the Dialogue. First, there is art theory in the purest sense of that term: that is, the principles and properties of good painting are set forth and elucidated. Accompanying this are certain sidesteps into literary theory and also the adumbrations of a philosophical system, scattered intermittently through the argument. Then there is the *paragone* between Raphael and Michelangelo, which is resolved in terms of the principles established in the first section. Tied in with this are the subsidiary evaluations of certain other artists which follow – eight leading men of the Cinquecento, beginning with Giorgione – and the argument for Titian's greatness. Finally there is the encomium of Titian, as the great representative of Venetian (as against Roman) painting, and the outline of his career. (p. 8)

While some have emphasized Dolce's criticism of Michelangelo, finding a rationale for this in Aretino's personal vendetta,[44] elsewhere Dolce makes quite clear his admiration for the Tuscan artist.[45] Athony Blunt, however, has claimed that Dolce 'probably ... genuinely thought that Michelangelo was a one-sided artist in comparison with Raphael, and that in his later work, particularly in the *Last Judgement*, he was falling off from his earlier standard' (p. 83). Dolce's attitude, he adds, is consistent with his strictly Renaissance view, in which Mannerist idiosyncrasies are regarded as signs of decadence. As opposed to Michelangelo's *terribilità*, Dolce prefers Raphael's easy elegance. The latter painter stands, then, as an example of the perfectly balanced humanist, skilled in all areas of painting, while Michelangelo is seen as an artist who concentrates on only one aspect of that art – the drawing of the nude. While that may be true within the context of this dialogue, one needs to add that Dolce was well aware of Michelangelo's genius, demonstrated in more than one branch of the arts, as Dolce points out not only here, but in other works, such as the *Giornale delle historie del mondo*, cited earlier in this chapter.

One other element of the dialogue has come in for special emphasis – namely, Dolce's view that the educated layman was competent to judge everything except the technical aspects of a painting.[46] In response to Giovan Francesco Fabrini, the dialogue's other interlocutor, Pietro Aretino claims that 'la pratica fa il giudicio' (Roskill, pp.102, 103). Painting, like its sister poetry, is a learned pursuit, although artists themselves are more born than made. Just as 'si trovano molti, che senza lettere giudicano rettamente sopra i poemi, e le altre cose scritte' (one finds many who correctly pass judgment on poems and other literary matters without being themselves men or women of letters), so too the masses evaluate painters and other types of artists. With this affirmation, as Mario Pozzi notes (p. 2), the modern public of the artist comes into being. Dolce's argument, however, as presented through Aretino, focuses not so much on the masses (though he admits, following Cicero, that there is very little difference between the learned and the unlearned as far as their judgment is concerned), but on certain individuals of fine intelligence who have refined their judgment with the aid of literature and through practice to the extent that they can judge a wide variety of works, and in particular those that pertain to sight.

I would like to turn now to another lesser-known but nevertheless intriguing work published eight years later, in 1565, Dolce's *Dialogo ... nel quale si ragiona delle qualità, diversità, e proprietà de i colori*, a treatise on colours and their significance, with a wide-ranging focus.[47] Though the form is again that of a dialogue, the procedure is more expository, and the spirit less argumentative. In the letter 'Ai Lettori' preceding the work, Dolce justifies his subject-matter, which to some might seem 'bassa e vil,' by saying that he will use the testimony of the ancient Greeks and Latins to depart from the crowd. Not only will the work contain things not so well known, but these will be 'non inutili a chi legge' (not without use to the reader; p. 4^r).[48] Furthermore, when he has to deal with details that are very base, he does so, he claims, in the manner of Lucian and other 'festevoli scrittori' (p. 4^v), though he always interposes a moral to instruct as well as to delight.

In addition, he promises that he will cite and comment on sonnets, Latin epigrams, and other verses, in order to make of his dialogue 'una Selva di varie lettioni' (a collection of various readings). If readers finds it pleasing (something the author takes for granted), he will soon publish both a treatise on gems and a summary of Aristotle's philosophy. In all these works, the author affirms that readers will find 'cose di diporto e profitto grandissimo' (things of pleasure and of very great profit; p. 5^r). Rather than having to pour through all the works of Aristotle, for example, readers are promised a compendium that will allow them, without much effort, to use his thought in any way they wish (p. 5^r). Having brought up these works soon to be released, Dolce takes advantage of the moment to defend both the *Sommario* and his translations:

Nè debbono alcuni troppo severi riprendere il trasportar nella nostra lingua così fatte opere: perciochè non possono essi dire, che non apportino frutto a belli spiriti, che non sanno lettere Latine, e meno Greche. E 'l così riprendere è un dimostrare di portar invidia al beneficio di altrui. (p. 5^r)

[Nor should some [who are] too harsh reprove the transmission of such works into our language, for they cannot say that these works do not bear fruit for beautiful spirits who do not know Latin letters and less Greek. And to reprove in such fashion is to demonstrate that one is envious of help given to others.]

The principle of helping others is more important to Dolce than the barriers put up by the learned. He goes on, in fact, to criticize foolish pedants who strut like peacocks among the crowd, citing a line or two from the Latin poets and historians, often backwards or with some barbarism, while the readers of Dolce's own translations, whether commoners or not, often understand the material better than the pedants, and abound in greater memory and intellect. He adds that, as a result, one sometimes sees simple women reason, often with assurance, with learned men about serious matters contained in the books of philosophy (pp. 5[r–v]).

As promised, Dolce's dialogue does not deal simply with colours. While his discussion of their properties derives from Antonio Telesio,[49] as one of his interlocutors makes clear (see p. 6[v]) and as most modern critics state, much of the remaining material comes from Fulvio Pellegrino Morato's *Del significato de colori e de mazzoli* (for which see below). Telesio's treatise consists of an index, a brief prologue, twelve chapters devoted to colours (and their various shades), and an epilogue (which is called chapter 13), followed by two poems.[50] The descriptions of the colours occupy a total of only 22 pages (i.e., 11 leaves), in comparison to the 171 pages (85 leaves) in Dolce – a small fragment indeed.

In addition to Telesio, however, Dolce relied heavily on Fulvio Pellegrino Morato, a humanist who spent much of his career in Ferrara and who published a heraldic treatise on the symbolism of colours and flowers in Venice in 1535, with at least five other editions appearing prior to 1565.[51] Morato's work numbers fifty-six pages (thirty-two leaves), thus helping to account for another portion of Dolce's text. Where Dolce occasionally expands upon his sources is in the discussion of the significance of the colours, passages full of intriguing digressions, with many references to works of literature. As the main interlocutor, Mario, notes, he speaks as someone whose study is letters and not painting, which would be a topic more appropriate for Titian (p. 7[r]). The digressions become the focus of the work somewhere around folio thirty-seven, at which point a discussion of the meaning behind gifts expands into a general presentation of the meaning behind all objects of significance in life. As each object comes up for interpretation, the text expands yet further, until at times we have a miniature guidebook to life, as for example when chess is discussed, a game that came in for comment earlier in both Alberti's *Della famiglia* and Castiglione's *Cortegiano*.[52]

The scope of the work is so wide-ranging that I would like to give a more extensive indication of the work's content, lest those uninterested in colours turn away from a closer reading of this encyclopedic work, a text that might profitably serve historians of all sorts, but particularly literary, in their interpretation of Renaissance texts. Dolce begins with a discussion lacking in Telesio, first defining colour, and then light, definitions that cite the Pythagoreans, Plato, and Aristotle (pp. 7^r–8^v). Following a list of all the colours ('ponendo prima il nome latino, e poi il volgare, o sia Thoscano, o no'), Dolce presents and amplifies on the material in Telesio's *Libellus de coloribus*. We learn, for example, and this from Telesio, that in antiquity Homer's *Iliad* was bound in red, signifying the blood of battles and death, while the *Odyssey* was bound in blue, because of Ulysses's voyage on the sea, which imitates the sky's colour (p. 9^r).

Where Telesio cites Virgil's use of dark blue for Charon's boat ('ut apud Virgilium puppis Cœrulea Charontis'), a colour worn by the Greek women at funerals, since they believed the souls of the dead passed into the sky, and thus a colour connected with motifs of sadness (Caput I), Dolce adds a Petrarchan example of the word's use (p. 9^v). Similarly, in discussing another colour connected with Charon in antiquity (*caesius, cesio, blue-grey*), Dolce notes first that in antiquity the colour was connected with anger, which in Greek is *cara* and in Latin *ira*. When used for eyes, the colour thus signifies 'fiery' or 'fierce.'

E da questo così fatto horrore stimo, che prendesse il nome cariddi, e Caronte. Di cui dicendo Virgilio, che egli haveva occhi di fiamma, volle dinotar che quel vecchio, i cui occhi erano occhi di color Cesio, era horribile e crudele. Il che imitando Dante disse

Caron dimonio con occhi di bragia
Loro accennando tutti li raccoglie,
Batte col remo qualunque s'adagia.

Il che espresse mirabilmente anco Michel'Agnolo nel Caronte, ch'egli dipinse nel giudicio. (pp. 10^v–11^r)

[And from this [use of the colour *caesius* for] horror, I think both [C]harybdis and Charon took their names. Because of this Virgil, saying that he had eyes of flame, wanted to denote that that old man, whose eyes were the colour blue-grey, was horrible and cruel; for which Dante, imitating him, wrote 'Charon demon with eyes of coal / Beckoning to them collects them all, / He beats with his oar whoever delays.' Which Michelangelo also admirably expressed in the Charon that he painted in *The Judgment*.]

The reference in Telesio, of course, was only to Virgil.[53] Dolce expands the text to include not only the vernacular's greatest literary depiction of Charon, that found in *Inferno* 3, but also the most famous artistic representation of Dante's scene, that in the Sistine Chapel.[54]

Among the interesting additions is Dolce's citation of Petrarch's description of Andromeda as a 'giovane bruna,' with beautiful eyes and hair of the same colour. For Cornelio, this signifies that the young woman's hair, like her body, was black, something not praiseworthy in a human head, he says, 'che dee esser bianco' (which should be white; p. 12^r).[55] Following the discussion of the names of colours, Mario asks Cornelio about their significance (p. 19^v). From this point on, the material no longer derives from Telesio but from Fulvio Morato – (Cornelio says he will present not only what he has read in others, but also his own opinions) and the discussion expands to include such varied items as an analysis of idioms.

Among the more interesting exchanges is that concerning the expression 'esser giunto al verde' (to be broke), much of which derives from the condensed and difficult text of Morato. In addition to the three or four standard explanations for the idiom (the surface of gamblers' or bankers' tables, the lining of pockets, the base of candles), Dolce provides many more, including some that may not have been discussed by later etymologists. One explanation, mentioned earlier by Morato, derives from a practice of ancient Roman priests, who offered burning sticks to the gods on their altars, placing the dry twigs into a receptacle of green wood. The expression 'to have arrived at the green,' then, signified that nothing remained to be burnt (p. 19^v). In later times, the Romans used candles that were painted green at the base, like copper – first, because the colour resembled a green branch; second, because it took the place of the wooden green receptacle used by the ancients (p. 20^r). In support of this idea of green representing a lack, Cornelio recites a few verses from one of Petrarch's sonnets ('Già fiammeggiava l'amorosa stella'), where one finds the expression 'mia speme già condotta al verde' (my hope already brought to the green). For Dolce (through his interlocutor Cornelio), this signifies that the poet's hope had disappeared, even though he admits that others have interpreted the verse differently.[56]

As similar interpretations of the colour green come up for discussion, including a proverbial use to describe someone who has fallen into misery, the book's material (colours) slips from our consciousness. To have reached the fruit ('esser giunto alle frutte') and to have reached the nut ('esser giunto alla nocetta') are both explicated, again following Fulvio Morato's text. The fruit is the last course at a meal; the nut derives metaphorically from the crossbow, where the 'revolving nut' connected to the lockplate on the stock is the farthest that one can draw the bowstring.[57] Mario brings up yet another expression 'essere al cane,' whose origin is then discussed by Cornelio. The phrase derives from the name of some Roman citizens who were hired to dispose of the belongings of the condemned for very little or nothing. This, in turn, provides the explication of another phrase: 'Onde, quando alcuna cosa è a buon mercato, si suol dire, che ella tanto vale insino nella casa de' cani' (Whence, when something is cheap, one usually says that it's worth as much even in the house of the dogs), although some believe this refers to gambling dice as seen in the verse 'Semper dannosi prosiliere canes: Cioè; Sempre i dannosi cani usciro fuori' (always the damaging dogs came forth; p. 20^v).

If the discussion seems complete, the reader is mistaken, for Dolce, following Morato, now expounds first on similar uses of the colour green, then on a variety of possible interpretations for using the colour to signify 'broke.' Similar uses consist of the ancient custom of wearing green in sympathy for the loss of a friend or relative, especially if the person was young, thus signifying the loss of hope. Several literary examples are cited from Virgil, called a 'most diligent observer of antiquities and most excellent poet' (p. 21^r). The relations extend to the funerary relics dug up by archaeologists, to be specific, to the emerald rings found in the tombs of the ancients and to celery (*appio*), paintings of which adorned the tombs. And poets who best sang of these matters were also crowned with celery.

As for the other explanations of *essere al verde*: In cutting into melons, the closer you get to the green, the closer you are to the bitter (p. 21^v); the ancient Persians remarried their wives after the woman's death, placing on her finger an emerald as a sign of their having lost all that mattered to them. Here, in further support, Cornelio mentions first a beautiful emerald owned by Isabella da Este, Marchesana di Mantova, said to be found in the tomb of Cicero's daughter Tullia, and second the fact that Virgil mentions a figure dressed in green who appears to Aeneas in a dream. Green plants in spring, green clothes, the green parrot, green decorations in tombs, the green worn by Venetian ferrymen, the green that covered the carts of ancient matrons are all cited as used for sadness, with references to Pliny, Vitruvius, and Cassiodorus (pp. 21^v–22^r), for which see also Morato.

When Mario disagrees with Cornelio, alleging the better-known interpretation of green as the colour of hope and saying that all of Cornelio's examples and literary references support this significance, Cornelio responds, 'Credi, come a te pare: ciò a me non importa' (Believe what you want; it doesn't matter to me; p. 22^v), after which he moves on to another colour. Later, when Mario brings up divergent interpretations, Cornelio will neither disagree nor attempt to disprove what the youth says, preferring instead to move on to other material, an indication that the dialogue form is actually extraneous to the process. No argument is permitted, merely the encyclopedic accumulation of data.

To list by way of example just a few of the numerous other topics that come up for discussion, we have an analysis of the cutting of hair or of beards as a sign of grief, why the devil is painted black, the use of white for God as well as the colour's negative aspects, a discussion of clothes reminiscent of that in Castiglione's *Cortegiano* with the conclusion being that one should dress not according to the significance of the colours but according to what delights the eye and to what is worn in one's city,[58] and a wide-ranging presentation of the use of colours in conceits (e.g., if you want to show that a love is not appropriate for both parties, you can send a bitter orange, since it has a beautiful peel, but sourness within).

That some points are digressions (and apparently more original) is announced by the author himself, as when he has his two interlocutors discuss such things as 'Che dinota l'Ape?' (What does the bee signify?; p. 38^r), with the answer sometimes being somewhat far-fetched. Here, for example, the significance of the bee (that one will obtain one's desire if one pursues it) is explained by the fact that a bee is also called a 'pecchia,' and this word can be converted into the verb 'picchia' (in the sense of 'to insist'), 'cioè sta fermo e saldo, che vincerai' (that is, stand firm and steady, for then you will win).

From a bee, we move to the significance of disparate objects: a ring, an eagle, herbs, plants, chickens, chestnuts, onions, a butterfly (here the author quotes Petrarch, Bembo, and Sannazzaro), cherries, mushrooms, grain, beans, acorns, flowers, rabbits, books, melons, flies, mice, nuts, eggs, a pearl, birds, fruit, arrows, pliers, a compass, a chessboard, dogs and their behaviour (here he cites their use in Egyptian hieroglyphics to mean fertility and includes a sonnet of Giulio Camillo and verses of Virgil and Ariosto, then mentions dogs who love their masters despite being beaten), the unicorn, a horse, ox, lamb, mule, ass, lion, snakes (here he clarifies Ariosto's use of two snakes in the symbol following the text of the second edition of the *Furioso*, discusses his use of a beehive to which a peasant applies fire in the *impresa* of the first edition, exemplified by the accompanying motto 'Pro bono malum'), a camel, stork, ant, spider, key, fish, the lute (which brings up first the topic of music, and then that of great writers), monkeys, giraffes, a salad, drinking glass, and so forth.[59] Throughout these pages, Dolce first expands on his source – Morato's *Il significato de mazzoli, de herbe et altre molte cose*, a work with the brevity of dictionary entries[60] – and then leaves it behind entirely.

Paintings and emblems, including those of Aldus (p. 54[r]), Marchiò Sessa (p. 56[v]), and Giolito (p. 57[v]), are discussed at length; religious notes are sounded, as when the author rejoices that the Catholics have defeated the Huguenots (p. 64[r]); topics as diverse as sleep (p. 65[v]), the whispering game (p. 69[r]), and eyeglasses (p. 76[v]) are explicated. The Bible is praised, while Erasmus's translation of it is criticized (p. 74[r]). Readings of classical and modern authors (including whole sonnets) are given, with expositions that sometimes vary from those of other critics. Among the authors who come in for treatment are Livy, Lucan, Ovid, Juvenal, Pliny, Catullus, Propertius, Tibullus, Statius, Virgil, Dante, Petrarch, Bembo, Sannazzaro, and Pontano.

This *concordia discors* – a hodgepodge of knowledge all concerned with signification – is a cornucopia of insights that rarely fail to be intriguing, exotic, recondite, astute, or bizarre. The absolute freedom taken by the author, through Mario, who asks the questions, provokes a response within the text itself, for Cornelio exclaims at one point, 'Tu non serbi ordine alcuno in queste tue domande' (You don't keep any order in these questions of yours; p. 84[r]). But structure and order are not the controlling principles; signification is. What do things mean? That is the question that rises over and over again. And what the author provides in response are the answers as he sees them. This is his gift, knowledge and understanding. If Aristotle, in Dante's phrase, is the 'maestro di coloro che sanno' (the master of those who know), then surely Dolce, a much lesser thinker but diligent interpreter of the learned, indefatigable compiler of knowledge, generous disseminator of data for the unlearned, deserves to be called the master of those who know naught.

Conclusion

One of the witticisms related by Lodovico Domenichi in his collection of *Facetie* had to do with how the ancient authors, thought dead, may be more alive than the living. Here is how Charles Speroni translates the anecdote:

Messer Lodovico Dolce, a man of great intellect, was reading some classical authors – something that he did regularly. A friend of his went up to him and said, 'What are you doing here, hiding among the dead? It's time that you came out with us who are alive.'
'On the contrary,' he replied; 'they are still alive because they are famous; whereas you are not alive either in name or in deed, for you go on living like a beast.'[1]

The story is telling, in more ways than one. First, it offers us a picture of the way Dolce was perceived by his contemporaries – as a man of great learning, regularly engrossed in study – and, second, it provides an indication of Dolce's attitude to fame and his regard for literature, particularly the classics. These are the works that for him were truly alive and that deserved to be made available to all those desirous of knowledge, even those with no access beyond the vernacular. It was towards the latter group, a much wider audience than that of the learned élite, that many of his efforts were directed. As he knew, the true fame of an author, fame that endures through time, consists in being read by those who enjoy literature – and not all those who enjoy literature, then as now, know Greek or Latin.

As for himself, he might have envisioned a dual obligation and a dual renown. The first debt he owed was to those, whether ancient or modern, whose works he had read, enjoyed, and thought useful for others to know.

A teacher at heart, he fulfilled his debt to these authors by translating their works in a way that brought them to life for a new class of readers, thus contributing to the original works' enduring fame or to the preservation of the ideas therein embodied. For this, he might have expected the gratitude of future generations, and, as the quotes with which I began this study show, he received such a tribute for several centuries. To this, one might add his equally important reputation as an editor. Many of the classics of Italian literature, from Dante through the works of Dolce's own contemporaries, passed through his hands, often (particularly in Ariosto's case) accompanied by supplementary material to facilitate our reading. We still feel the effect of this today, even though most are unaware of it. Everyone who refers to *The Divine Comedy* rather than simply *The Comedy* indirectly recognizes the influence of Dolce's edition of 1555.

The second debt he paid, for which he might also have expected the reward of some renown, was to himself as a writer. Surely most of his contemporaries might also have envisioned this, for few others were so active with such facility in so many genres. Numerous works of his were applauded not only by the greatest authors of the century, who read, enjoyed, and were sometimes influenced by his books, but also by the greater mass of the reading public, for whom edition after edition issued from the presses of publishers such as Gabriel Giolito.[2] His prominence is reflected as well in numerous works of his contemporaries, where he is often praised (the notable exception being the criticism of his rival Girolamo Ruscelli) and sometimes even employed as an interlocutor in other writers' dialogues.[3]

While I have attempted to discuss some of Dolce's lesser-known works in this study (and other scholars have dealt at some length with the more famous of Dolce's works, such as his *Dialogue on Painting* and his *Dialogue on the Institution of Women*, to mention two), many more remain to be exhumed from the graveyard of time, works as disparate in tone, subject-matter, and intention as his stanzas on the African victory of Charles V (1535); his mythological fable in eighty-four octaves, *La favola di Adone* (1545, 1547);[4] his satirical *Capitoli*;[5] his rhymes;[6] his *Vita di Giuseppe* (1561); his youthful *Il Sogno di Parnaso con alcune altre rime d'amore* (1532);[7] his *Sonetti spirituali* (1547); the explanatory verses he wrote to accompany Francesco Marcolini's work on fortune-telling by cards;[8] his stanzas explicating the *imprese* illustrated by Battista Pittoni;[9] his lives of Ferdinand I and Charles V;[10] and the other works mentioned in passing in this study, particularly those of literary criticism, such as his *Osservationi*. For the industrious, the task of studying these works in detail will, I believe, be accomplished with profitable results.

The goal of this study has been to provide a closer look at several of the more interesting elements of Dolce's literary production as it ranges from original works to adaptations, using 'original' in both its modern and its Renaissance connotations, while at the same time also suggesting other areas deserving of greater attention (e.g., his *Paraphrasi nella sesta satira di Giuvenale*). I have not, therefore, examined in detail Dolce's work as either an editor or a translator (as Dolce understood the term), although aspects of his efforts in these areas have been mentioned either to help clarify the literary exegesis or (as in the last chapter) to demonstrate Dolce's interest in Renaissance science. His work as an editor and translator, surely to him equally important aspects of his career (since this was how he supported himself and his family), merit further study. An examination of his work in these fields would help us better understand his role, by no means insignificant, in helping both to formulate and to propagate the culture of mid to late cinquecento Italy. Few men of letters were more closely attuned to the changing moods of the time and the ever-expanding needs of his ever-expanding audience; few offer a better portrait of the multi-varied interests of the scholar/writer.

It would be superfluous to summarize the major points of each chapter in this study. Perhaps here, by way of conclusion, I might simply provide an indication of the results of categorizing Dolce's publications (original works, adaptations, translations, and editions of others), not by genre, but by the date of publication. What follows, however, is not a complete listing of everything produced by Dolce. Roughly, dividing them into decades, one can say the following:

During the 1530s, Dolce seems to have worked primarily on Ariosto (his edition of the *Orlando furioso* dates to 1535, his *Apologia* to 1539) and to have been interested most in the genre of chivalric romances. This is the decade of his adaptation of Boccaccio's *Filocolo*, published in 1532 at the age of twenty-two as *L'amore di Florio e Biancofiore*; his *Stanzas on the African Victory of Charles V* (1535) and his *Sacripante* (1535–36). At the same time, however, he translated works as varied as Horace's *Poetics*, Juvenal's sixth satire, Catullus's *Epithalamium for Peleus and Thetis*, and Ovid's *Metamorphoses*.

In the 1540s, Dolce seems to have turned to theatre as an area of new interest. Having earlier edited Ariosto's comedies, he now not only translates and adapts tragedies of Seneca and Euripides, but writes his own comedies and tragedies as well. One finds in this decade the first publication of Dolce's *Ragazzo* (1541), Euripides' *Hecuba* (1543) and *Giocasta* (1549), Seneca's *Thyestes* (1543) and *Troades* (1547), Dolce's *Capitano* and *Marito* (both 1545), his *Didone* (1547) and *Fabritia* (1549). At the same time, he continues his work on Ariosto (*Espositioni*, 1542), Boccaccio (editions of the *Decameron* and *Corbaccio*, 1541, and the *Amorosa Fiammetta*, 1542), and other classical authors, either translating (in addition to the tragedies mentioned above) or editing Sabellico (1544), Achilles Tatius (1546), Cicero (1547), Galen (1548), letters of the ancients (1548), and Philostratus (1549). This decade also saw the publication of other original works, ranging from his *Dialogue on Ill-Married Husbands* (1542) to his *Fable of Adonis* (1545).

During the 1550s, now in his forties, Dolce seems to have dedicated himself primarily to his work as a critic and editor. He published works of Lampridius, Ariosto, Giulio Camillo, Castiglione, Vittoria Colonna, Poliziano, Sannazaro, Mario Equicola, Dante, Bembo, Solinus, and the rhymes of women. Accompanying some of these editions are lives of Dante and Boccaccio. He also published his *Observations* and essays on the origin of the satire, Horace's epistles, and the *Poetics*. His translations include works of Euripides, Ovid, Horace, Appian, and Pedro Mexia. This is also the decade of his *Life of Joseph* and his *Dialogue on Painting*.

During the 1560s, Dolce's varied publications begin to show the range of his interests and what has been called his pre-encyclopedism. He continued to edit other authors, including Cicero (three editions of the *Dialogo dell'oratore*) and contemporary authors, among them Poliziano, Bernardo Tasso, Burchiello, Sebastiano Erizzo, Domenico Delfino, and Giuseppe Orologi. His translations include works of Furio Ceriola, Sextus Rufus, Seneca, Cicero, Mohammed II (Sultan of the Turks), Joannes Zonaras, Aristotle (actually a summary of his philosophy), Anatholius Desbarres, Antonio Ulstio, and Virgil. He adapted two Spanish works in his *Palmerino* and *Primaleone*, and a tragedy of Seneca in his *Troiane*. He wrote lives of Charles V and Ferdinand I, as well as one of Ovid. These are the years of several of his dialogues (on memory, colours, and jewels) as well as of a discourse on rhetoric. He revised his *Observations*, wrote stanzas for a book of *imprese*, and published another work on Ariosto (his *Modi affigurati*) and perhaps his most original work of tragedy, the *Marianna*.

At the time of his death, Dolce had several works ready for the press or in various stages of preparation. Most noteworthy were his long poem on Achilles and Aeneas, his incomplete poem on the early deeds of Orlando, his encyclopedic *Giornale delle historie del mondo*, and a translation of Homer's *Ulysses* and the *Batracomiomachia*.

Truly, then as now, taking into account all his imperfections and those of the age, this is a worthy career for any man or woman of letters. Without his unstinting efforts, the history and development of Italian literature would surely be the poorer. In addition, if what others have said about him is accurate, Dolce was also a good man, for after 'indefatigable' the adjectives used most often to describe him are 'pacifico' and, of course, 'dolce.' In such a contentious age, these are simple but high words of praise indeed.

Notes

1: 'Miserabile Insieme, e Glorioso'

1 'Ma vie n'est pas intéressante; mais il peut arriver que, d'ici à quelque temps, on trouve dans un coin d'une ancienne bibliothèque, une collection de mes œuvres. On sera curieux, peut-être, de savoir qui était cet homme singulier qui a visé à la réforme du théâtre de son pays, qui a mis sur la scène et sous la presse cent cinquante comédies, soit en vers, soit en prose, tant de caractère que d'intrigue, et qui a vu, de son vivant, dix-huit éditions de son théâtre' (My life is not interesting, but it may happen that sometime in the future someone will find in the corner of an old library a collection of my works. One will perhaps be curious to know who was that singular man who aimed at the reform of his country's theatre, who put on stage and under the press 150 comedies, whether in verse or in prose, both of character and of intrigue, and who saw, during his life, 18 editions of his theatre [translation mine, as are all in this study, unless otherwise indicated]). Of course, in Goldoni, one sees both feigned humility and pride. I quote from *Mémoires de Monsieur Goldoni pour servir à l'histoire de sa vie et à celle de son théâtre*, in Carlo Goldoni, *Opere con appendice del teatro comico nel Settecento*, p. 7.

Full citations for all sources in this study are supplied in the bibliography.

2 See E.R. Curtius, *European Literature and the Latin Middle Ages*, pp. 83–5 and 407–9. Dolce, himself, it should be noted, valued the immortality provided by the written word, although his reference to 'glory' occurs in a letter thanking Aretino for immortalizing him by including a letter addressed to Dolce in one of Aretino's collections. Dolce writes: 'M'è dunque cara la lettera e 'l Sonetto a me indirizzato e posto in compagnia delle lettere scritte a tanti Principi e uomini, che meritano grandemente. M'è cara dico nella guisa, che debbono esser care quelle cose, che danno la immortalità tanto

desiderata e bramata da coloro; i quali sanno quanto dolce cibo sia il frutto della gloria; e quanto il restar vivi dopo morte sia più prezioso tesoro, che vivendo senza questa speranza posseder quante ricchezze sono al mondo' (The letter is dear to me and the sonnet addressed to me and placed in the company of letters written to so many princes and men, who thoroughly deserve it. It is dear to me, I say, in the same way these things ought to be dear that give the immortality so desired and longed for by those who know what sweet food is the fruit of glory, and how remaining alive after death is a more precious treasure than living without the hope [but] possessing as many riches as there are in the world; *Lettere scritte a Pietro Aretino* [Bologna: Gaetano Romagnoli, 1874], photostatically reproduced in the *Scelta di curiosità letterarie inedite o rare dal secolo XIII al XIX*, dispensa 132 [Bologna: Commissione per i testi di lingua, 1968], vol. 1, part 2, letter 366, pp. 288–9).

3 As Paul F. Grendler notes, the term *poligrafo* is commonly used by literary historians in a pejorative sense, referring to 'tradesmen of the pen' who earned their living by writing with little concern for accuracy, truth, or plagiarism (*Critics of the Italian World. 1530–1560: Anton Francesco Doni, Nicolò Franco and Ortensio Lando*, p. 12). In Dolce's own time, the attitude towards these writers, and Dolce in particular, was often quite different. In a letter to Dolce dated 1 September 1541, Pietro Aretino refers to him as 'born for the common good, like good men' ('voi sete nato a comune utilità, come gli uomini buoni'; *Lettere. Il primo e il secondo libro,* ed. Flora, Book II, Letter 279, p. 797).

Despite his achievements, Dolce appears in reality to have been a modest man. In a letter dated March 1546, Aretino begins with a question: 'Sapete di ciò che io mi maraviglio, compare M. Lodovico? Del come la vostra singulare modestia per essere sì grande non ritiene in sé tutte le forze di quello ingegno con che avanzate ogni altro intelletto' (Do you know what makes me marvel, [my] friend M. Lodovico? How your singular modesty, though so great, does not contain within itself all the force of that intellect with which you surpass all other intellects; Aretino, *Lettere*, ed. Procaccioli, Book IV, Letter 394; vol. 2, p. 718).

4 'può più tosto essere ammirato che agguagliato': *Isole più famose* (1590), cited in Emmanuel Antonio Cicogna, 'Memoria intorno la vita e gli scritti di Messer Lodovico Dolce letterato veneziano del secolo XVI,' p. 184. This memoir (found on pp. 93–200) remains one of the fundamental sources of much of our knowledge regarding Dolce. A more recent, much-abbreviated summary of Dolce's life and character can be found in Mark W. Roskill, *Dolce's 'Aretino' and Venetian Art Theory of the Cinquecento,* but the fullest modern source is Claudia Di Filippo Bareggi's impressive cultural and social

history, *Il mestiere di scrivere: Lavoro intellettuale e mercato librario a Venezia nel Cinquecento*. G. Romei's article in the *Dizionario biografico degli italiani* is disappointingly brief as regards Dolce's life, and haphazard as regards his works. Romei cites the standard historical surveys (those by Crescimbeni, Quadrio, and Tiraboschi) and often relies on them and other cited sources for information, which is sometimes mistaken. Regarding Dolce's translation of Camillo Leonardi (for which see chapter 6 of this study), Romei claims Dolce 'in parte si rifà allo *Speculum lapidum* di Camillo Leonardi da Pesaro' and 'Come fonte, il D. cita soltanto Aristotele' (p. 400), both incorrect. With minor exceptions, Dolce translates word for word and lists more than twenty-five sources in one paragraph alone. Romei repeats the standard literary judgments (as a poet, for example, Dolce is a 'mediocre versificatore'; p. 404), apparently without having read some of Dolce's works discussed in the article. The failure to approach Dolce with thoroughness and on his own terms results in a reference to 'incoerenti premesse' (p. 404), a term that might more accurately describe Romei's entry on Dolce rather than Dolce himself.

5 'merita d'esser annoverano [*sic*] frà gli huomini nelle Lettere famosi, poiche si mostrò d'altissimo ingegno in qualsivoglia genere delle dilettevoli discipline; ... riuscì particolarmente nelle traduzioni, nelle quali più certamente, che in altra cosa, essendo riuscito mirabile, da quelle ne trasse lode immortale a se stesso, et utilità grandissima a professori della Toscana favella.'

Ghilini goes on to say: 'Having a great desire to gain honour and aware of his quick wit and ease of assimilation, he set himself to learn everything he judged appropriate for the perfection of an uncommon and noble intellect; but weighed down by poverty, he never had the strength to free himself from its powerful grasp. As a result, always humble and abject, he never succeeded in rising to the level of his worthy thoughts, and he appeared to his compatriots as an example of human misadventure, both wretched and glorious to the end of his unlucky days, shaming with his misfortunes his century, which he honoured with the merit of his varied and delightful knowledge' ('Havendo egli gran disiderio d'avanzarsi ne gli honori, e vedendosi d'un'ingegno prontissimo, e facilissimo all'imparare, si mise ad apprendere tutto ciò, che giudicava esser alla perfezione d'un peregrino, e nobile intelletto conveniente; ma oppresso dalla povertà, non hebbe mai forza di potersi liberare dal suo potente braccio; perciò stando sempre humile, et abbietto, non potè mai alzar le ali per conseguir il volto de' suoi honorati pensieri, et apparve nel cospetto de' suoi compatrioti un'esempio dell'humana disavventura miserabile insieme, et glorioso fino all'ultimo de' suoi poco fortunati giorni, vituperando con le disgrazie il secolo, che tanto honorò co'l valore della varia, e dilettevole sua dottrina'). Following a long list of Dolce's works, Ghilini adds: 'from which works one sees the perfect genius of Lodovico Dolce, truly sweet, nay, most sweet, both in prose and in poetry, being in one and the other a wide ocean of Tuscan eloquence' ('da' quali componimenti si vede l'ingegno perfetto di Lodovico Dolce, veramente dolce, anzi dolcissimo, così nella prosa, come nella Poesia, essendo stato, e nell'una, e nell'altra un'ampio Oceano di Toscana eloquenza'): *Teatro d'huomini letterati aperto dall'abbate Gerolamo Ghilini, academico incognito*, p. 148.

6 '[L]e tante sue fatiche recaronlo al sommo della stima universale, e il posero tra i più chiari letterati del secolo, con quel famoso elogio che non v'era l'impresa che resistere potesse alla felicità della sua penna': *Istoria della volgar poesia*, p. 121.

7 'Se nel Dolce si palesò una fecondità d'ingegno, ed una infaticabilità nello scrivere straordinaria, per cui à luogo fra gli storici, oratori, grammatici, retori, filosofi, fisici, etici, tragici, comici, epici, lirici, e tra gli editori, traduttori, raccoglitori, commentatori, d'altra parte in nessuna cosa riuscì egli con eccellenza.' Cited in Cicogna, 'Memoria intorno la vita e gli scritti di Messer Lodovico Dolce,' p. 94. Muratori's comment shows up in Tiraboschi, *Storia della letteratura italiana*, who is then cited by Pierre-Luis Ginguiné when he writes that 'he was above all one of the busiest and most fecund authors who ever wrote. Grammarian, rhetorician, orator, historian, philospher, tragic poet, comic, epic, lyric, satiric, editor, translator, tireless commentator, he attempted all genres but excelled in none' ('ce fut surtout un des auteurs les plus laborieux et les plus féconds qui aient jamais écrit. Grammairien, rhéteur, orateur, historien, philosophe, poëte tragique, comique, épique, lyrique, satyrique, éditeur, traducteur, commentateur infatigable, il s'essaya dans tous les genres, mais il n'excella dans aucun'; *Histoire littéraire d'Italie*, vol. 4, p. 532). Later critics seem to disparage Dolce, following the example of Muratori and other earlier critics, often without having read the works under discussion. It is ironic that so many critics accuse Dolce of plagiarism when they themselves merely repeat what others have said, often using almost the exact words and usually without acknowledgment.

8 'Se il Dolce non fu in tutto un corretto scrittore, fu amante però della lingua toscana, in cui scrisse varie cose lodevolmente, e fu uomo senza prosunzione e boria, che scrisse solo per giovare ad altrui, non per desio di comparir maestro, come il Ruscelli e il Muzio, i quali se molte cose seppero di lingua, di molte altre non ebbero perizia punto ...': *Dialoghi della lingua toscana* (1821), p. 368, cited in Bartolommeo Gamba, *Serie dei testi di lingua e di altre opere importanti nella italiana letteratura, scritte dal secolo XIV al XIX*, s.v. 'Dolce,' p. 405. In the words of Marco Foscarini, 'No one brought greater

benefits to the Italian language than Lodovico Dolce, numbered therefore among the principal grammarians and illustrators of our native speech' ('Nessuno arrecò alla lingua italiana comodi maggiori quanto Lodovico Dolce, annoverato perciò fra i principali grammatici e illustratori del natio parlare'; *Della letteratura veneziana ed altri saggi*, p. 177).

As for Ruscelli and Muzio, Tommaso Garzoni pointed out that the former was one of those 'correctors' who correct others for their own mistakes, as pointed out to him by Muzio when Ruscelli criticized Dolce. See *La piazza universale di tutte le professioni del mondo*, Discorso XXX, 'De' correttori o censori,' in Tommaso Garzoni, *Opere*, p. 542.

9 'Spicca l'abilità di quell'uomo, che se in tutte le guise del comporre non toccò sempre il segno della perfezione, tanto di buono però in ogn'una vi sparse da potersi arguire, ch'era in facoltà sua il divenir sommo, ovunque egli si fosse preposto di mettere stabilmente la propria industria': *Della letteratura veneziana*, pp. 477–8.

10 '... ditegli ch'el suo Sacripante, non meno leggiadro che innamorato, mi ha fatto passare un pezzo di caldo questa estate senza noja,' adding that Dolce 'è un de li principali ornamenti di questa nostra età' (is one of the principal ornaments of our age): Veronica Gambara in a letter to Pietro Aretino in 1536, cited in *Della nuova scielta di lettere di diversi huomini et eccellenti ingegni* (Venice: n.p., 1582), vol. 2, p. 48.

'Certo che Iddio vi ha concesso una sì egregia qualità di natura, che nessuno vi può simigliare ... Veloce, fertile e generoso è il vivo spirito dello intelletto che vi detta ciò che parlate, notate e pensate': Aretino, *Lettere*, ed. Procaccioli, Book IV, Letter 394; vol. 2, p. 718, letter dated March 1546. Aretino adds: 'la locuzione è in voci scelte e ornate, con una innocenza sì pura e candida ne lo esprimere i suoi concetti, che ogni maniera di dire, ancora che magnifica e splendida, è vinta dalla nitida e tersa leggiadria de la lingua vostra dolcissima. Ne i sensi e ne l'ordine mirabilmente dimostrate che ne lo scrivere di voi non apparisce difficoltà né oscurezza. Anzi pare che ogni cosa si narri in sua grazia e a caso' (The locution is in selected and ornate words, with an innocence so pure and candid in expressing its concepts that every manner of speech, even though magnificent and splendid, is conquered by the clear and terse gracefulness of your most sweet tongue. As regards the meaning and arrangement [of words], you show wonderfully that in your writing there appears no difficulty or obscurity. On the contrary, it seems that every thing is narrated gracefully and spontaneously.) This is high praise, indeed, and accurate as well.

'... Dolce fu veramente gentil poeta, perciocchè era tenero e delicato nel suo stile, facile ne' concetti, et purgato nella lingua, et pronto nel verso': Sansovino, cited by Cicogna, 'Memoria intorno la vita e gli scritti di Messer

Lodovico Dolce,' p. 106. Francesco Sansovino (1521–1583) was the son of the sculptor and architect Jacopo Sansovino.

Many contemporary and later authors cite Dolce in their lists of the outstanding poets of the age. Tommaso Garzoni (1549–1589), for example, lists Dolce among egregious authors of comedy in his work of erudition called *La piazza universale di tutte le professioni del mondo* ... (1665 ed.), p. 547, as well as one of the authors of treatises on vernacular grammar (see the Venice 1601 edition, p. 86). Pietro Aretino, in a letter of 2 November 1536 to Veronica Gambara, mentions being a courier between her and Pietro Bembo, and then refers to a letter from Dolce to Gambara, adding that Dolce, 'thanks to his recent virtues, would not inappropriately be added as third among you' ('per merito de le sue nuove vertù, non si disdirebbe d'entrar terzo fra voi'; *Lettere* 77, ed. Erspamer, p. 170; ed. Flora, Book I, Letter 78, p. 97). Elsewhere, in a letter of 25 November 1537 addressed 'Al Bevazzano' (Agostino Beaziano), Aretino lists Dolce in conjunction with Ariosto ('Né si trova altro che un Ariosto e un Dolce al mondo'; Letter 251, ed. Erspamer, p. 517; ed. Flora, Book I, Letter 251, p. 313; *Lettere*, ed. Procaccioli, Book I, Letter 94; vol. 1, p. 290) and in his list of poets from the letter 'Il Parnaso in Sogno' dated 6 December 1537 and addressed to Gianiacopo Lionardi (Letter 282, ed. Erspamer, p. 584; ed. Flora, Book I, Letter 280, p. 351; ed. Procaccioli, Book I, Letter 103; vol. 1, p. 313 – for which see also Christopher Cairns, *Pietro Aretino and the Republic of Venice*, ch. 10, 'The Dream of Parnassus, Aretino's Heritage and the Poligrafi,' pp. 231–49). In a letter to Girolamo Molino, dated October 1549, Aretino lists Dolce (along with Bembo, Castiglione, and others) as an author worthy of imitation (ed. Procaccioli, Book V, Letter 585; vol. 2, p. 922). Dolce, it should be noted, published his *Sogno di Parnaso* in terza rima in 1532. For a reference to a letter of Gambara's praising Dolce, see ed. Flora, Book I, Letter 129, p. 158. Aretino also writes to Dolce regarding not only Gambara's letter of praise, but one of Vittoria Colonna (Book I, Letter 296, p. 372). He says, in part, 'Né so che più bel vanto possa dare chi nascerà di voi, che il dire d'esser discesi da tale che la Marchesa di Pescara e la Contessa di Correggio non si sdegnò di mentovargli il nome con tanto honore' (I don't know what more beautiful boast one who will be born of you can make than to claim to be descended from someone whose name the Marquise of Pescara and the Countess of Correggio did not disdain to mention with so much honour) and recommends that Dolce save them as gems of glory (17 December 1537). Many of these letters are also available in *The Letters of Pietro Aretino*, translated by Thomas Caldecot Chubb.

11 *Renaissance Thought and Its Sources*, p. 10.

12 For a list of Dolce's voluminous production, see the bibliography of primary
sources. Other *poligrafi* of the time, in particular Pietro Aretino, marvelled at
Dolce's productivity. In a letter addressed to Dolce (Letter 278; 7 December
1537), Aretino says, 'In verità, che non vi esce cosa de l'ingegno che non
corresponda al cognome vostro e a la spettazion in cui poneste il mondo il
primo giorno che si vide come la natura vi ha posto lo stile e la invenzione
ne la fantasia e ne la penna. Io non so come la vena non vi secchi nel comporre di tante opere. A me parve già d'esser quello che sputasse i libri interi
interi, ma sete pur voi che così fate' (In truth, nothing comes out of your
mind that does not correspond to your last name and to the expectation in
which you placed the world the first day that one saw how nature placed
style and invention in your fantasy and in your pen. I don't know how your
inspiration does not dry up in composing so many works. I used to think
that I was the one who spit out completely whole books, but it is you who
do so; ed. Erspamer, pp. 569–70; Book I, Letter 281, in *Lettere*, ed. Flora, p.
354). In another letter of November 1545, Aretino refers to Dolce's 'fermo e
senza mai perder dramma di tempo istudio vostro sollecito' (firm and
solicitous study, never losing a dram of time) and to 'la infinita moltitudine
de le composizioni che ci fate intratanto' (the infinite multitude of the
compositions you are making for us in the meantime; *Lettere*, ed. Procaccioli,
Book III, Letter 334; vol. 1, p. 663).
13 See *Grande dizionario enciclopedico*, s.v. 'Dolce.'
14 The most notable exception is Nino Borsellino, who speaks at moderate
length of Dolce's work as a critic, in the volume edited by him and Marcello
Aurigemma, *Il Cinquecento: Dal Rinascimento alla Controriforma*, vol. 4, part 1,
pp. 457–9.
15 *Critics of the Italian World*, p. 67. The five prose works to which Grendler
refers are the *Dialogo della pittura intitolato l'Aretino*, *Osservazioni*, *Vita di Carlo
Quinto*, *Vita di Ferdinando Primo*, and the *Imprese*.
16 Interestingly, while Grendler cites the numbers provided by Cicogna for
translations (forty-five) and studies of other writers (twenty-eight), he
ignores Cicogna's accounting of Dolce's original works. Where Grendler
talks of five original prose works, Cicogna lists twenty ('Memoria intorno la
vita e gli scritti di Messer Lodovico Dolce,' pp. 140–51), in addition to
nineteen original works in verse (pp. 152–67), and fourteen works either
unpublished or of uncertain authorship (pp. 168–72). The correct number for
the original works lies somewhere between those reported by Cicogna and
those acknowledged by Grendler.
17 For which see the three-volume *Studi sul 'Palmerin de Olivia.'* Volume 3
contains the *Saggi e ricerche* of various scholars, among which is Franco

Bacchelli's 'Il ''Palmerin de Olivia'' nel rifacimento di Lodovico Dolce,' pp. 159–76.

18 Benedetto Croce, in criticizing Bernardo's description of duels, has this to say of Dolce: 'Il fastidio che reca il poema di Bernardo Tasso è tanto che può far sì che si leggano quasi con piacere e approvazione quel paio di romanzi della serie dei *Palmerini* che il letterato buono a tutto, Ludovico Dolce, mise similmente in poema sull'esempio dato da lui. Il Dolce, per lo meno, non ha pretese di alta letteratura né di eroica tensione, e racconta con certa disinvoltura di verseggiatore che ha nell'orecchio l'Ariosto' (Bernardo Tasso's poem is so annoying that it makes one read with pleasure and approbation the pair of novels of the *Palmerini* series that Lodovico Dolce, the good-for-everything man of letters, put in poetic form, following the example given by him [Tasso]. Dolce, at least, has no pretense of lofty literature or of heroic tension, and narrates with a certain ease of a versifier who has Ariosto in his ear; p. 322). And later he adds, 'Anche i racconti di duelli e combattimenti non hanno la impacciata pesantezza e la vana verbosità di quelli di Bernardo Tasso' (Also the stories of duels and battles do not have the clumsy heaviness and the empty verbosity of those of Bernardo Tasso, p. 323). See 'Gli ''Amadigi'' e i ''Palmerini,'' ' in *Poeti e scrittori del pieno e del tardo Rinascimento.*

19 For the translation into English, see *History Workshop: A Journal of Socialist Historians* 9 (Spring 1980), 5–36. The interpretive method (one that Freud learned from Morelli) is 'based on taking marginal and irrelevant details as revealing clues,' keys 'to a deeper reality, inaccessible by other methods' (p. 11).

20 The controversy surrounding Dolce's year of birth derives from the date traditionally listed (1508) and Bareggi's conclusion based on Dolce's stating his age as forty-eight when interrogated by the Holy Office in 1558 (pp. 39, 51n). The traditional date derives from the dedication to Erasmo di Valvasone written by Francesco Sansovino for an edition of Dolce's *Trasformazioni*, published on 24 March 1568, where Sansovino says Dolce died earlier that year (probably in January) at the age of sixty ('Morì il Dolce quest'anno d'età d'anni 60, e fu seppellito in S. Luca di Venetia'), and the date computed from that, 1508, appears in a manuscript biography found in the Museo Correr, Venice, *Cod. Cicogna*, 3001/I, Biografie, vol. 16, p. 124, first cited by R.P. Niceron, *Mémoires pour servir à l'histoire des hommes illlustres* (Paris: Briasson, 1736), vol. 22, p. 270.

   As regards the later date, 1510, in the trial against Alfonso di Ulloa, Dolce was questioned at his home on 22 March 1558, declaring his age to be forty-eight. See Bareggi, *Il mestiere di scrivere*, pp. 206–8, 233n, who cites the

Archivio di Stato, Venice, *Sant'Uffizio*, B. 14 'processo ad Alfonso de Ulloa.' One would have to assume that Dolce's indication of his age would be more accurate than that of a friend, his colleague Francesco Sansovino.

21 For a study of political and social rank in Venice, see Andrea Zannini, *Burocrazia e burocrati a Venezia in età moderna: I cittadini originari (sec. XVI–XVIII)*, pp. 63 *et passim*, and Robert Finlay, *Politics in Renaissance Venice*, p. 46. Basically, below the patriciate class of nobles and above the lower classes was an intermediate level of *cittadini originari*, third-generation citizens (i.e., ones who could prove that their father and grandfather were Venetian citizens). As an indication of the family's social status, one might cite the facts that one of Dolce's cousins, Gasparo Spinelli, was a pharmacist, and Dolce himself was godfather for both Pietro Aretino and the jeweller Gaspare Ballini (Cicogna, 'Memoria intorno la vita e gli scritti di Messer Lodovico Dolce,' p. 108).

As for the Dolce family itself, according to the Archivio di Stato, Venice, *Storia veneta*, V, Misc. cod. I, T. Toderini, *Cittadini veneti*, c. 749, they may originally have come from Lombardy, but had been in Venice for a long time. Elsewhere, we read that the family was 'honorata e famosa in Venetia, per l'antica nobiltà dell'ordine popolare, ma in que' tempi tanto decaduta dalla prima prosperità che erano sforzati que' pochi che di essa erano avanzati a trattenersi con la notaria e con servizio del Palazzo, e questo mezzo con l'insegnare a leggere alla gioventù' (honoured and famous in Venice, because of the ancient nobility of the popular rank, but in those times so fallen from earlier prosperity that those few who remained of them were forced to occupy themselves with the notarial profession and with service in the palace, namely teaching youths to read; Biblioteca Municipale, Venice. A. Zeno, *Appunti genealogici e biografici di famiglie venete*, 1578, c. 230^r, in *Mss. It*, VII, 351 (8385).

We know little for sure about Dolce's financial condition. Tassini (Archivio di Stato, Venice, *Storia veneta* II, Misc. cod. I, T. Tassini, *Cittadini veneti*, c. 779) says, 'Avevano case da stazio a San Salvatore e case in altre contrade. Possedettero pure, ed anzi secondo alcune cronache, fabbricarono il palazzo ai Gesuati, conosciuto oggidì sotto il nome di Sceriman. Facevano per arme una dolce o donnola, oppure un scudo diviso da una fascia con una dolce [an animal] sopra e l'altra sotto la fascia mediana' (They had stables at San Salvatore and houses in other districts. They also owned, and rather built, according to some chronicles, the palace at the Gesuati, known today under the name Sceriman. For their coat of arms, they made a *dolce* or weasel, or else a shield divided by a band with a *dolce* above and one below the median band). Most likely this refers to another branch of the family. As Bareggi notes, there is no declaration of this in the Savi alle Decime and it seems too obvious of a fiscal evasion for Lodovico not to have claimed so much and such well known property (*Il mestiere di scrivere*, p. 39).

22 Two brothers, Piero and Giovanni Battista Dolce, took advantage of the funds donated by them for the War of Candia in 1648 to ask for the privilege of nobility for the family. They mentioned that the family had resided in Venice for over three hundred years and that, among the family's illustrious personages, was included Ludovico Dolce as an 'insigne letterato' (Biblioteca Nazionale, Venice, *It.*, VII, 626 [8047], Aggregazione di Famiglie alla Nobiltà Veneta per la guerra di Candia, cc. 47^r–50^v; Bareggi, *Il mestiere di scrivere*, pp. 39, 51n).

23 Other jobs that Dolce's status would have permitted included work as a notary, scribe, guard, accountant, boatman, licenser, messenger, broker, measurer, porter, weigher, doorman, and supervisor (Finlay, *Politics in Renaissance Venice*, p. 47).

24 *Teatro d'huomini letterati*, p. 148. Grendler claims that 'Dolce, Sansovino, and Domenichi were born higher in the social scale [than Doni, Franco, and Lando] and enjoyed the advantages of wealthier parents' (*Critics of the Italian World*, p. 68). He goes on to note that, although Dolce's father died when the boy was only two, Dolce enjoyed the patronage of wealthy patricians. Still, while this patronage, particular that of the Cornaro family, supported the boy during his years at the Paduan Studio, he was constrained like the other *poligrafi* to work for a living thereafter.

25 Roskill provides an edition and translation of Dolce's dedicatory letter in his study of *L'Aretino* (pp. 196–9).

26 For Dolce's studies in Padua, both Cicogna and Bareggi cite Nicolò Comneno Papadopoli, *Historia Gymnasi Patavini*, vol. 2, p. 221, ch. 24, anno 1568 (with no other bibliographical indications). Papadopoli says that Dolce studied in Padova with Gerolamo Ruscelli, Celio Secondo Curione, and Ludovico Castelvetro.

27 For an introduction to the press of Gabriel Giolito, see Salvatore Bongi, *Annali di Gabriel Giolito de' Ferrari da Trino di Monferrato, stampatore in Venezia*, as well as the chapter by Amedeo Quondam, ' "Mercanzia d'onore," "Mercanzia d'utile": Produzione libraria e lavoro intellettuale a Venezia nel Cinquecento,' and the works cited there, particularly pp. 61–2, notes 14–17. The claim that Dolce worked as a teacher does not seem to be supported by archival documentation. Claudia Di Filippo Bareggi, who says that 'perhaps' he may have taught, can only quote from Dolce's comedy *Il ragazzo*, where a pedant is described at some length (*Il mestiere di scrivere*, p. 273). One might conclude that, if indeed Dolce did work as a private tutor, he found the job distasteful.

28 But, as Cicogna himself goes on to ask, 'But who would believe it? He was never able to reach that degree of celebrity, attained by others of his time, both writers of poetry and prose' ('Memoria intorno la vita e gli scritti di Messer Lodovico Dolce,' p. 94). In the field of letters, it takes propitious fortune as well as ability to rise to the top, and at times some are chosen for fame who deserve it less than those who fall by the wayside.

29 Bareggi quotes Ruscelli's mean-spirited comment in his *Tre discorsi a M. Lodovico Dolce*, p. 5, where Ruscelli, his competitor and critic, says that Dolce's income derives from 'm. Gabriello [Giolito], a spese del quale ... vivevate, et vivete voi' (*Il mestiere di scrivere*, p. 257). According to her research, the highest salary paid to those who worked as *letterati* for lords in various courts was 100 scudi a year, with food and lodging included ('con provisione di 100 scudi d'oro l'anno, tavola, cavallo, servitor pagato' [Luca Contile, *Lettere* (Pavia: Bartoli, 1564), vol. 1, pp. 185^{r-v}] letter dated Venice, 20 March 1559; Bareggi, pp. 246–7). But others received anywhere from 50 scudi a year (Ruscelli) to 40 scudi a year (Toscanella) (p. 247). As for those in the Republic of Venice who worked for the presses, Bareggi found no precise references, although it appears that working on clandestine editions paid more (p. 248). Among the fourteen intellectuals studied by Bareggi, only Dolce appears to have made his living solely from his work for the press (p. 255).

All the other testimony points to the fact that the Dolces had to work of necessity, being 'dell'ordine della cancelleria, et per conseguenza buoni et honorati cittadini veneti, discendenti da altri fedeli et di buon nome, di mediocre fortuna' (of the rank of the chancellery, and, as a consequence, good and honoured Venetian citizens, descendants of others who were faithful and of good name, of average patrimony; Museo Correr, Venice, *Mss. PD.* 613 c/IV, Carte spettanti alla famiglia Dolce, f. 95^v, no. 47).

30 Antonio Brucioli, Nicolò Franco, Francesco Sansovino, Gerolamo Parabosco, Giuseppe Betussi, Ludovico Domenichi, Anton Francesco Doni, Ortensio Lando, Gerolamo Ruscelli, Francesco Baldelli, Alfonso di Ulloa, Tommaso Porcacchi, Orazio Toscanella, and Lodovico Dolce.

Bareggi provides a table showing quantitatively, year by year, the different works to which these authors put their hands in Venice alone, separating original works from translations, and editions from translated editions. She notes that these authors were often *volgarizzatori* and *rimaneggiatori* of the works of others, reducing, summarizing, and sometimes plagiarizing, and adds that 'il concetto stesso di opera originale prende qui contorni incerti e sfuggenti' (the concept itself of original work here acquires uncertain and fleeting outlines; *Il mestiere di scrivere*, p. 54). The criterion she employs, then, is to respect, not the exigencies of the modern critic, but those of the cultural world of the time. A book that was reworked is counted as original if it took a huge effort of re-elaboration. Only obvious plagiarized works are not counted. First editions are counted separately from *ristampe*, and only works that date from 1526 (Brucioli's first) to 1599 are considered.

31 Given the nature of her work, Bareggi does not undertake a critical reading of any of the texts she enumerates. Her focus on statistical analysis accounts, perhaps, for the negative judgments she expresses concerning Dolce's work. As regards his original books, for example, she says, 'Anche nel caso del Dolce occorre sottolineare che, strettamente parlando, non fu quasi mai un autore di opere originali in senso proprio' (In the case of Dolce, too, it is necessary to point out that, strictly speaking, he was almost never an author of original works in the proper sense; *Il mestiere di scrivere*, p. 98n). And elsewhere she says that Dolce began as an original author, 'una strada che non gli fu poi congeniale' (a route that turned out to be not congenial to him; p. 59). In this, she relies in part on the judgment of Tiraboschi, whom she cites as a particularly harsh critic.

32 Bareggi points out that most of Dolce's work for presses other than Giolito concentrated on literature, clearly a matter of personal preference and taste. When he went to work for Giolito, instead, he appears to have divided his time between literature, in which he was the press expert, and history, in addition to other more minor genres (see *Il mestiere di scrivere*, pp. 288–9). What is difficult to determine is how much choice he exercised and whether or not he was 'indotto e condotto, se non veramente costretto' (induced and led, if not actually constrained) to occupy himself with other sectors. One must remember, however, that publishers, while 'gentilhuomini,' were not so much men of letters as merchants experienced in matters of printing. Publishers assay the market, but, in varying degrees, they also rely on their editors for what reaches the marketplace.

33 Bareggi, *Il mestiere di scrivere*, p. 99n. One of Dolce's characteristics pointed out by Bareggi is that he did not limit himself to the great authors; 'curò infatti un numero molto elevato di autori contemporanei medi, piccoli e anche francamente oggi sconosciuti, con una attenzione quasi da *talent scout*' (he edited a very high number of contemporary authors who were average, slight, and also frankly unknown today, with the attention of a talent scout; p. 59). She refers to authors like Giulio Camillo Delminio (*ca* 1480–1544), Vittoria Colonna, Sebastiano Erizzo, and many collective works, including editions of letters, lyrics, and stanzas of various sorts.

34 Bareggi points out that Dolce's career is emblematic of that of the other authors she studied. That is, a general rule applied to all of them: their collaboration with a press developed gradually and was never limited to that press alone. In Dolce's case, his first publication came in 1532, but his

first edition with Giolito dates only to 1542, a decade later. Following that, his numbers slowly increased: two books out of six in 1542, four out of five in 1543, five out of eight in 1545 (*Il mestiere di scrivere*, p. 286). Only after 1547, when nine out of ten titles appeared under Giolito's imprint, did Dolce work primarily for one press. Giolito absorbed most of Dolce's work from that date down to 1563, after which Dolce's work was split among various presses. In 1565, for example, Giolito published seven of the thirteen items that appeared under Dolce's name; and, in 1566, that number had diminished to only three (all reprints) out of sixteen titles (p. 287).

35 The attitude of the *poligrafi* towards borrowing from others is perhaps best expressed by Pietro Aretino in a letter to Dolce dated 25 June 1537. There, in speaking against pedants, he writes: 'Dicamisi: non ha più ingegno il ladro che trasforma l'abito che ruba in foggia che portandolo non è dal padron conosciuto, che quello che per non saper pur ascondere il furto ne viene impiccato?' (Tell me: doesn't the thief have more intelligence who transforms the stolen outfit in such a fashion that, in wearing it, he is not recognized by the owner, compared to one who, because he doesn't know how to hide his theft, is hanged? *Lettere*, ed. Flora, Book I, Letter 156, p. 192).

36 Grendler, in discussing the life of the *poligrafi* in his *Critics of the Italian World*, (see especially pp. 10–14), refers to Doni's quadripartite classification of writers: 'In the highest place were those who wrote original works, second were the translators, third were the commentators who clarified the works of the learned, and finally there were the compilers and editors ...' (p. 66). As Grendler notes, most *poligrafi*, constrained by their economic situation, produced works in all four categories. Grendler contends that Dolce was more of a hack than an original author, but the numbers he gives to justify his opinion are not entirely accurate. Dolce produced more original works, as will be shown later, than usually acknowledged by literary historians.

37 Grendler discusses the significance of popularizations of history in his article 'Francesco Sansovino and Italian Popular History, 1560–1600,' originally published in *Studies in the Renaissance* 13 (1966), 139–80, and now ch. 1 in *Culture and Censorship in Late Renaissance Italy and France*.

38 Aretino's expression is 'de la fama gran tromba' (*Lettere*, ed. Procaccioli, Book VI, Letter 643; vol. 2, p. 1004). The letter dates to September 1552.

39 Charles V (1500–1558), emperor from 1519, abdicated in 1556 in favour of his son Phillip II (1527–1598, King of Spain from 1556) and his brother Ferdinand (1503–1564, King of the Romans from 1521, King of Bohemia and of Hungary from 1527, and emperor from 1556).

40 Another example of a time-saving work that also deals with history is

Dolce's posthumous *Giornale delle historie del mondo* (1572), discussed briefly in chapter 6 below. Dolce organized the major historical events of the past (births, deaths, wars, battles, peace treaties, and so forth) in a day-by-day fashion, allowing one to follow the development of illustrious deeds in an abbreviated chronological outline or, with the aid of the eighty-six-page index, to check such things as the significant dates in the lives of major figures.

41 Roskill (in *Dolce's 'Aretino'*) cites as support the following (all of which derive from Cicogna, 'Memoria intorno la vita e gli scritti di Messer Lodovico Dolce,' pp. 117, 119, 125ff., 129, and 144–6): Dedication of Dolce's *Paraphrasi nella sesta satira di Giuvenale* (Venice 1538), addressed to Titian from Padua; letter to Federico Badoaro from Padua, 3 April 1542, in B. Pino, *Della nuova scielta di lettere ...* (Venice: Aldus, 1574), vol. 2, p. 186; dedication of the *Ecuba* to Cristoforo Canale, dated Padua, 16 June 1543, and dedication of the *Tieste* to Giovanni Barbo, dated Padua, 1 August 1543; letter from Dolce to Giolito, dated Padua, 1 August 1544, and included in the second Giolito edition of the *Orlando furioso*; dedication of Dolce's translation of *Le istorie veneziane di Marco Antonio Sabellico* to Nicolò Gabriele, dated Mantua, 1543; letter to Fortunato Martinengo from Tivoli, dated 3 December 1544, in *Lettere di diversi* (1547), vol. 1, p. xv; letter to Paolo Manuzio, sent from Pieve di Sacco on 14 February 1545, in B. Pino, *Della nuova scielta di lettere ...*, vol. 1, p. 379; and various letters sent to Paolo Crivelli from the same place in 1545, ibid., vol. 2, pp. 194, 196ff., 200, 323.

Upon consideration, however, one has to question Roskill's statement that Dolce 'evidently moved quite extensively around Italy' (p. 6). The distances between most of the cities cited above are quite small, of course.

42 Roskill mistakenly says the letter is one of Dolce's (*Dolce's 'Aretino,'* p. 50, n5). The letter, written from Dolce's son-in-law Fortunato Martinengo, may be found in *Lettere di diversi*, published in Mantua by Venturin Ruffinello in 1547, vol. 1, pp. xvi–xvii. Fortunato Martinengo, a count from Brescia, founded the Accademia dei Dubbiosi in 1551, which lasted until 1553, when Martinengo died. Dolce and the count exchanged letters beginning as early as 28 January 1540, when Dolce wrote to Martinengo. From Martinengo, we also have a letter from Padua, dated 23 December 1541, in which it appears he married a daughter of Dolce's. Bareggi adds a note of caution, suggesting that Martinengo might have been referring, via a *gioco di parole*, to one of Dolce's comedies (see *Il mestiere di scrivere*, p. 190n). In Ruffinello's collection there appear two other letters of Dolce (pp. XV[r–v] [dated Tigoli, 3 December 1541] and pp. XXXV[r]–XXXVI[r] [Venice, 14 June 1546]), as well as one other from Martinengo (pp. XVI[v]–XVII[v] [Brescia, 1544]).

43 Francesco Sansovino wrote to Dolce on 11 June 1542, from San Domenico di Bologna, giving him a precise report on that city (published in *Lettere di diversi eccellentissimi signori*, cited by Cicogna, 'Memoria intorno la vita e gli scritti di Messer Lodovico Dolce,' p. 185).

44 The quote derives from an introductory poem found in the 1536 edition of the *Sacripante*, where Dolce adds: 'Sta da te lunge ogni discordia et guerra / di ch'arse già l'Italico terreno: / Né si trovi o mia patria intoppo o freno / Al tuo Leon, ch'ogni animal atterra. / In te la bella Astrea chiaro et lucente / Ritien suo seggio; e in te verdeggia eterna / La cara libertà, c'huom più desia. / Si piaccia al ciel, quando il mio giorno sia, / Ch'io chiuda in te quest'occhi, né dolente / Contrario al buon voler corso discerna' (May every discord and war, from which Italian soil has already burned, remain far from you; nor may your Lion, which fells every animal, find, o my country, hindrance or restraint. In you, beautiful Astrea maintains her clear and shining seat; in you, dear liberty, which everyone most desires, remains eternally verdant. May it please heaven, when my day is done, that I close my eyes in you, and not perceive a grievous course contrary to goodwill; p. Aiij^v). Astrea, of course, often invoked in Golden Age motifs, is the goddess of justice.

45 The letter reads in part as follows: 'Gli impressori cominciarono a darlo alle stampe, prima che io avessi posto fine al primo libro, onde ne fu bisogno di compartire il lavoro dì per dì, in modo che loro pienamente servisse; da che ne nacque, ch'io non poteva rivederne carta; sì avvenne ancho, che per non lasciare il volume imperfetto, fui sforzato a seguitarlo nel tempo, che ... io mi sentiva aggravato da moltissima febbre. A questo s'aggiungono diversi errori avenuti nello imprimere ... Laonde volentieri lo haverei riveduto & corretto; chè per aventura lo havrei saputo & voluto fare; ma essendo già il libro stampato, se io mi avedrò, che 'l filo & la testura del tutto non dispia-cerà a gli intendenti, da capo tornerò l'opra a l'incude per ripollirla ... Ma se io per aventura, per la bassezza del mio ingegno, non potrò condur la mia traduttione a quella perfettione che io desidero, ne avverrà almeno che da alcuni si conoscerà quella delle Historie Vinitiane del Sabellico non esser mia; non havendo io, come molti sanno, fatto altro che la prefattione, & alcune poche carte tradotte nel principio dell'opera' (The typographers began to give it to the printers before I had finished the first book, so it was necessary to partition the work day by day in order to keep them busy. As a result, I was not able to check the pages. In addition, in order not to leave the volume imperfect, I was forced to continue at a time when ... I was weighed down with a high fever. To this were added various errors that occurred in printing ... Therefore, I would willingly have checked and

corrected [the pages], because I would have known about it and would want to do so. With the book already published, if I find out that the thread and weaving of the whole is not entirely pleasing, I will put the work back on the anvil to polish it ... But if, by chance, because of the baseness of my intellect, I cannot bring my translation to the perfection I desire, let others realize, at least, that the translation of Sabellico's *Venetian Histories* is not mine, since, as many know, I prepared nothing other than the preface and a few pages translated at the start of the work; cited by Bongi, *Annali di Gabriel Giolito de' Ferrari*, vol. 1, pp. 253–4).

46 See also Bernard Weinberg, *A History of Literary Criticism in the Renaissance*, s.v. 'Dolce,' and *Il Cinquecento: Dal Rinascimento alla Controriforma*, Borsellino and Aurigemma, eds., pp. 457–9.

47 Laura Terracina laments Dolce's treatment in the dedicatory letter to her *Quarte rime*, addressed to Giovanni Alfonso Mantegna, even though a year later she sent her *Discorso sopra il principio di tutti i canti d'Orlando furioso* to Dolce, accompanied by eight verses. Dolce had asked to edit her *Rime*, then sent the manuscript to the press with more errors he introduced. Similarly, Bernardo Tasso, in a letter to Girolamo Ruscelli dated 4 March 1557, complains about the poor job Dolce did in editing the fourth book of his lyric poems (see Bongi, *Annali di Gabriel Giolito de' Ferrari*, vol. 1, pp. 472–3). The word play 'dolce-amaro,' as one might expect, was common. Stefano Guazzo, for example, in a letter to Annibale Guasco dealing in part with the various forms of Italy's languages, reports that some have accused 'Dolce d'amarezza' (*Lettere*, 1592, p. 433). For a recent study dealing in part with Dolce's involvement with the publication of lyric anthologies in the cinquecento, see Louise George Clubb and William G. Clubb, 'Building a Lyric Canon,' pp. 332–44.

48 In 1539, Federico Badoer (1519–1593) became a magistrate and, in 1547, ambassador to Urbino, later serving in the same capacity in Vienna and Madrid. A founding member of the Accademia della Fama, he was later accused and tried for having caused the academy's financial difficulties. Domenico Venier (1517–1582), a poet as well as patrician, was among the founding members of the Accademia Veneziana in 1558.

For Dolce as a source of books for his many friends and contacts, including Paolo Manuzio, Jacopo Marmitta (secretary of Veronica Gambara), and Benedetto Varchi, see Bareggi, *Il mestiere di scrivere*, p. 179. Cicogna provides a brief summary of forty-four letters written by Dolce ('Memoria intorno la vita e gli scritti di Messer Lodovico Dolce,' pp. 143–8).

49 Bareggi notes the cordial esteem and frequent contacts between Dolce and

figures of the highest rank, from Bembo and Titian to Domenico Venier and Federico Badoer (*Il mestiere di scrivere*, pp. 166–7). Dolce's letters, though respectful in tone, demonstrate a level of friendship that permitted him even to offer advice, of a literary sort at least, to Venetian patricians. As for a collection of his own letters, Dolce seems to have refused to publish one, as seen in a letter to Fortunato Martinengo where he writes: 'et quanto alle mie il nostro da bene et virtuoso m. Gasparro [Gioielliere] ha pensato, ch'io facessi quello che non mi venne mai in animo di dover fare. Io conosco né lettere né cosa alcuna di mio esser degna di stampa, et se fin qui alcuna n'è uscita fuori, tutto che nescit vox missa reverti, pure mi affaticherò d'ammendar di qui inanzi questo errore, et non lasciare uscire più' (and, as regards mine, M. Gasparro – a good and virtuous man – thought that I should do what had never come to my mind to need doing. I know of no letters or anything else of mine deserving of being published, and, if up to now some have come out, although the spoken word cannot be recalled, I will work hard right now to amend this error, and to let no others come out; Tigoli, 3 December 1544; *Lettere di diversi* [Mantua: Ruffinello, 1547]).

50 Bareggi points out that almost all the dedications of cinquecento editions are to individuals who comprised the dominant class of the time – gentlemen and gentlewomen, important churchmen, and figures of international fame (namely emperors, kings, princes, granddukes and dukes, politicians, military leaders, and the like), indicating that matters of income were more important than simple friendship or cultural affinity. Interestingly, among the few exceptions she mentions, one finds Dolce, who dedicates more than one work to his readers, a dedicatory form, however, that in his works often stands alongside the more traditional dedication to an individual (*Il mestiere di scrivere*, pp. 267–8, 281n).

51 Piccolomini's letter contains the following appeal: 'Molto magnifico et honoratissimo Signor mio, perché Gabriel Zerbo mi ha riferito come si deva recitar in Venetia in questo carnovale una comedia di mio et che Vostra Signoria ha stretta dimestichezza con quelli signori che son sopra a tal cosa, mi farebbe cosa grata che quella vedesse ... di far d'haver un bollettino in nome mio, accioché per il favor di quello non mi sia negato l'esser ammesso dove la detta comedia si recitarà' (My most magnificent and most honoured lord: Gabriel Zerbo has informed me that a comedy of mine will be recited in Venice this *carneval* and that your lordship is quite familiar with those lords who are in charge of this. I would be grateful if you could see ... that a ticket in my name be made available, so that, as a result of this favour, I may be admitted to where the comedy is being recited; *Della nuova scielta di lettere*

di diversi huomini et eccellenti ingegni [Venice: n.p., 1582], vol. 2, pp. 395–6 [Padua, 17 February 1541], cited in Bareggi, *Il mestiere di scrivere*, pp. 181 and 191n).

For Bembo, Dolce served as an intermediary for favours requested of Aretino – in one letter a sonnet against one of Bembo's detractors, in another letter selections from Aretino's *Capitoli*. In the later case, Dolce even volunteers to come transcribe the selections if Aretino has only one copy. See *Lettere scritte a Pietro Aretino*, as cited in note 2, above, vol. 1, part 2, Letter 359, pp. 274–5, and Letter 363, pp. 285–6.

Varchi wrote to Dolce asking for his help in getting Luigi Alamanni (1495–1556) into the Accademia degli Infiammati (ibid, Letter 364, p. 286).

52 *Lettere scritte a Pietro Aretino*, vol. 1, part 2, Letter 367, p. 291.

53 Of the fourteen letters from Dolce to Aretino, published by Marcolini in 1551, only three are dated (1537, 1540, 1549). For an edition of the letters, see *Lettere scritte a Pietro Aretino*, as cited in note 2, above. The letters were originally published in *Lettere scritte al signor Pietro Aretino da molti signori, comunità, donne di valore, poeti, et altri eccellentissimi spiriti. Divise in due libri* (Venice: Francesco Marcolini, 1551).

Dolce used Aretino in his *Dialogo della pittura ... intitolato l'Aretino* (1557) and his *Dialogo piacevole ... nelquale Messer Pietro Aretino parla in difesa d'i male aventurati mariti* (1542), while Aretino employed Dolce in his *Ragionamento delle corti* (1538) and cited him in the *Marescalco* (1533 version). Trajano Boccalini also has Dolce speak in his *Ragguaglio* V (1624 edition, p. 16) on 'qual sia la più preclara legge politica della Veneta Repubblica' (what political law of the Venetian republic is most illustrious). Giuseppe Orologi employs Dolce as an interlocutor (discussing art and literature with Girolamo Ruscelli) in his philosophical work *L'inganno*, and Anton Francesco Doni has a 'Dolce' as interlocutor in his 'Mondo Risibile' from the first book of his *I mondi*.

54 In a letter addressed to Bernardino Daniello, dated Venice, September 1545, Aretino laments his lack of Latin ('sempre mi son doluto del non essere interprete de lo idioma latino'), adding 'Ma a la mia ignoranza in ciò supplisce la dottrina del mio eccellente Compare unico M. Lodovico Dolce' (but my ignorance in that is made up for by the knowledge of my excellent friend, the unique M. Lodovico Dolce; *Lettere*, ed. Procaccioli, Book III, Letter 291; vol. 1, p. 615). See also note 55, below.

55 According to Paul Larivalle, Dolce probably edited the third Marcolini edition (called 'edizione seconda') of Aretino's Lettere in August 1542. See *Lettere di, a, su Pietro Aretino nel fondo Bongi dell'Archivio di Stato di Lucca*. Aretino himself, in letters to Dolce, both attests to his lack of schooling in

Greek and Latin (*Lettere*, ed. Flora, Book I, Letter 250, pp. 311–12; *Lettere*, ed. Procaccioli, Book I, Letter 93; vol. 1, pp. 288–9) and thanks Dolce for offering to edit the second book of his letters (ed. Flora, Book II, Letter 179, pp. 797–8; ed. Procaccioli, Book II, Letter 175; vol. 1, pp. 469–70). In this letter of 1 September 1541, Aretino specifically says: 'vi mando il libro, con arbitrio però che ci potiate e aggiugnere e scemare né più né meno che a l'altezza del vostro fedel giudizio parrà e di scemarci e di aggiugnerci' (I send you the book, with the freedom to add or delete neither more nor less than seems appropriate to the loftiness of your faithful judgment; ed. Procaccioli, p. 470).

Aretino refers to Dolce, who is 'gently blossoming at this moment' in Act V of the *Marescalco*. See Aretino, *The Marescalco (Il marescalco)*, p. 98.

56 For the relationship between Dolce and Aretino, see Christopher Cairns, *Pietro Aretino and the Republic of Venice*, pp. 59–62, and for his contributions to Aretino's works, pp. 64, 84–5. The term 'Nicodemite,' employed by Cairns, is usually applied in Italy to those who continued to live as Catholics while leaning towards Protestantism. Aretino's Erasmian convictions (and their possible sources) are discussed at length by Cairns, but see, in particular, pp. 64, 66, 81, 83, 124, and 139. As for Erasmus himself, while some of his works were criticized as early as the mid-1520s, organized and extensive opposition to his works did not occur until after the collapse of the Ratisbon colloquy in 1541, which marked the failure of the policy of reconciliation (Paul F. Grendler and Marcella Grendler, 'The Survival of Erasmus in Italy,' 1–2). One of Dolce's correspondents, Pietro Carnesecchi, an avowed Protestant, was imprisoned and eventually executed as a heretic in the 1560s.

Dolce wrote to Aretino on 22 February 1540, offering to send him the 'Proverbi di Erasmo' that he had requested through another and adding that 'ella gli potrà vedere con suo commodo; e serbargli insino che io manderò per essi' (you can examine it at your ease and keep it until I send for it; *Lettere scritte a Pietro Aretino*, vol. 1, part 2, Letter 358, p. 273).

57 *Lettere scritte a Pietro Aretino*, vol. 1, part 2, Letter 307, pp. 269–70.

58 Another pastime revealed by Letter 307 is Dolce's habit of reading. Though far from Venice ('in questa mia lontananza') he carries with him several books that, as he says, 'mi fanno sovente cara e dolce compagnia' (often provide me with sweet and dear company; pp. 270–1). Elsewhere (*Lettere scritte a Pietro Aretino*, vol. 1, part 2, Letter 361, p. 277), Dolce refers to being in a garden with other gentlemen, reading Aretino's comedy, *Il marescalco*.

59 Dolce's bitter polemic with his one-time friend Girolamo Ruscelli of the rival Valgrisi Press is discussed by Cicogna, 'Memoria intorno la vita e gli scritti di Messer Lodovico Dolce,' pp. 94–6, 98–9, and Bongi, *Annali di Gabriel*

Giolito de' Ferrari, vol. 1, pp. 299, 354–5, 363–4, 398–400. For the conflict with Nicolò Franco, see Cicogna, p. 109, and Cairns, *Pietro Aretino and the Republic of Venice*, pp. 40–1n. For a violent letter attacking Franco, see Pietro Aretino, *Lettere*, ed. Flora, Book II, Letter 124, pp. 593–7. Other polemics in which Dolce engaged are mentioned in chapter 2 of this study. I call Ruscelli a former friend of Dolce based on what Ruscelli himself writes in his *Discorso primo*: 'come da quattro anni, ch'io sono in questa felicissima città, hebbi, come sapete, fin da principio la conoscenza vostra laquale si fece poi strettissima conversatione; e passavano poche settimane, che alcune sere la gentilezza vostra non vi guidasse ò solo ò accompagnato, à passarne meco gran parte. Et senza entrare à ricordarvi, se con parole, et con quegli effetti, che la confidenza vostra, et le forze mie mi posero in occasion, io vi dimostrassi piu d'una volta l'amorevolezz mia' (I've been in this most happy city for four years and made your acquaintance, as you know, right from the start, which then became an intimate conversation. Not too many weeks passed before you were spending a large part of several evenings, either by yourself or with others, in my company. And there is no need to remind you whether, with words and with those actions that your trust and my efforts made possible, I showed you, more than once, my affection; *Tre discorsi*, p. 4).

60 *Lettere scritte a Pietro Aretino*, vol. 1, part 2, Letter 361, p. 278, undated but certainly written in June 1536.

61 Dolce goes on to criticize Franco's command of Latin. 'E non s'accorge il buffolo; che non sa comporre dieci parole insieme, che stiano bene: perchè egli non sa l'ortografia: e non la sapendo, per ragione ne seguita, che egli non sappia grammatica ancora. E che ciò sia vero: in dieci righe ha seminato venti errori: che in tre luoghi egli ha scritto *giudicio* per t: dove ogni semplice fanciullo sa che questa voce si scrive per c e non per t: derivandosi da *iudico* verbo latino, che per c si scrive' (And the buffoon does not realize that he does not know how to put ten words together correctly, because he does not know how to spell, and not knowing orthography, it follows that he does not know grammar either. And to prove that: he made twenty errors in ten lines, in three places writing *giudicio* with a *t*, when even a simple child knows that this word is written with a *c* and not a *t*, since it derives from the Latin verb *iudico*, written with a *c*; Bongi, *Annali di Gabriel Giolito*, vol. 1, p. 281). As for Franco's criticism of Dolce, he says he wants only one thing – these few words: 'ciò è che l'opere mie sono state lodate, e leggonsi da uomini, a i quali egli non è degno non pure di essere discepolo, ma di servir per famiglio' (that is, that my works have been praised and are read by men to whom he is unworthy of being a disciple or even a servant; pp. 282–3).

For Dolce to get published, he did not have to pass off as his the works of a better poet, as Franco attempted to do with sonnets from the Marquise of Pescara (Vittoria Colonna) (p. 283). Finally, the letter reveals Dolce's own attitude towards fame and excellence. As he says, 'il lodarsi da se medesimo è cosa da pazzo' (praising oneself on one's own behalf is a crazy thing), for it is works that make one famous, not talk ('le opere, i buoni frutti dello ingegno rendeno l'uomo famoso'; p. 279).

62 The latter translation was extremely successful. Paul Grendler, in his discussion of average print runs in the Renaissance, notes that Giolito (who first published the *Trasformationi* on 1 May 1553 [not 1543, as Grendler cites it]) sold more than 1,800 copies of the work in four months, and hastened to issue another printing before the end of the year: *The Roman Inquisition and the Venetian Press, 1540–1605*, p. 11. The work was also reissued by Giolito in 1555, 1557, 1558, and 1561; by Francesco Sansovino in 1568; and by Domenico Farri in 1570.

For a discussion of Ruscelli's attack, see Bareggi, *Il mestiere di scrivere*, pp. 296–301.

63 Charles V (1500–1558) began to abdicate his titles in 1555 and 1556, delegating his authority in Germany to his brother Ferdinand. His son Philip II received Spain, America, Sicily, Naples, and The Netherlands. Charles himself retired in 1556 to the monastery of Yuste. Among the many works celebrating his life is one by Dolce, for which see the bibliography, under *Vita dell' invittiss. e gloriosiss. imperador Carlo Quinto*.

64 *Il mestiere di scrivere*, pp. 39 and 51n. Bareggi cites the Museo Correr, Venice, *Mss. Cod. Cicogna*, 2991, II/35, Origini delli teatri.

65 According to a document in the Archivio di Stato in Venice (*Storia veneta* II, Mss. cod. I, T. Tassini, *Cittadini veneti*, c. 779; and see also Archivio di Stato, Venice, *Avogaria di comun*, cittadinanze originarie, B. 361 rosso), Ludovico had three children.

According to Cicogna ('Memoria intorno la vita e gli scritti di Lodovico Dolce,' p. 174), a genealogist, Marco Barbaro, reports that Ludovico had three brothers (Daniele, Angelo, and Agostino). Another genealogist, Alessandro Capellari, says his son was named Agostino and he had a daughter who married Francesco Duodo in 1594. Capellari, however, does not know who Dolce's father is, unlike Barbaro, who reports his name as Fantino. Capellari also errs in reporting Dolce's death date as 1558. Bareggi expresses caution as regards Martinengo's status as Dolce's son-in-law, noting that the reference to a daughter might be to one of Dolce's comedies (*Il mestiere di scrivere*, p. 190n). Martinengo, in fact, did write to Dolce about a copy of his comedy *Il ragazzo*, which Dolce had sent him, but the letter, from

Brescia in 1544, is one of lament. It reads, in part, as follows: 'Mi scordava di dirvi che venendomi a caso fin l'altro dì alle mani alcune lettere a stampa, io ve ne lessi una, che già io feci in risposta di una vostra, nella quale mi fate dono della comedia vostra del *Ragazzo*. S'io me ne meravigliai et dolsi non ve 'l potrei dire, per havere visto in stampa una mia lettera, la qual cosa non tende ad altro fine che a mostrare le mie inettie et grosserie: oltre a l'haverla letta così corrotta, come erano tutte l'altre, che non v'era una parola che stesse bene' (I forgot to tell you that by chance I came across some letters in print just the other day. I read one that I wrote in response to one of yours, in which you gave me a copy of your comedy *Il ragazzo*. I could not tell you how shocked and upset I was at having seen a letter of mine in print, one that has no other aim than showing my ineptitude and coarseness, and then to have read it so corrupted, as were all the others, to the extent that not a single word fit well; *Delle lettere di diversi autori raccolte per Venturin Ruffinelli*, Mantua, 1547, p. XVII^v). Dolce's letter of apology (he laments that the works were 'lacerate' rather than 'stampate') was also published in the Ruffinelli collection, p. XV.

66 Anton Francesco Doni lists Dolce as having been one of the Accademici Pellegrini in his *Zucca*, p. 119, while Francesco Saverio Quadrio, in his *Della storia e ragione d'ogni poesia*, notes both the Pellegrini (vol. 1, p. 108) and the Pastori Fratteggiani (vol. 7, p. 11). (The Accademia della Fratta was named after its location in Fratta Polesine di Rovigo.) Bareggi notes that Benedetto Varchi wrote to Dolce about the Accademia degli Infiammati, referring to it as 'nostra accademia' (*Il mestiere di scrivere*, p. 150n). For the letter from Varchi, see *Della nuova scielta di lettere,* vol. 2, p. 51 (and cf. II, p. 578), or *Lettere volgari* (Venice: Manuzio, 1544), pp. 159^v–160^r. The Accademia degli Infiammati was located in Padua, where Dolce most likely attended the university. There is no indication that Dolce belonged to the most prestigious, but short-lived, of academies – the Accademia Venezia or della Fama – founded by his friend Federico Badoer in 1557 or 1558. That academy came to an inglorious end in 1561 (Bareggi, pp. 126 and 148n).

   For the Accademia della Fratta, see also M. Maylender, *Storia delle accademie d'Italia* (Bologna: Cappelli, 1929), vol. 1, pp. 56–7.

67 See Bareggi, *Il mestiere di scrivere*, p. 129.

68 The 'intriguing but unexplained detail' of Dolce's arrest, as Roskill puts it, was finally clarified in 1978 by Giorgio Padoan, *Momenti del Rinascimento veneto*, pp. 302 and 307n. Padoan cites the Archivio di Stato, Venice, Consiglio dei Dieci, *Parti comuni*, Reg. 12, ff. 10^r–11^v for the order.

69 A.S.V., Consiglio dei Dieci, *Parti comuni*, Filza 21, doc. 121. Dolce's appeal was accepted by the council as noted in the *Parti comuni*, Reg. 12, f. 28^r of 23

May 1537. Padoan writes that 'Lodovico Dolce era uscito di casa "circa a un hora di notte" (cioè alle sette di sera) con il "proponimento di andare a Padoa" quando fu arrestato a Santa Croce, già presso "alle barche"' (Lodovico Dolce had left home 'at about one hour at night' (that is, at 7 in the evening) with the 'intention of going to Padua,' when he was arrested at Santa Croce, already close 'to the boats'; p. 307n.). As both Padoan and Cicogna before him note, Dolce was visited in jail by Domenico Venier, according to a letter Dolce wrote to Federico Badoer (Paolo Gerardo, *Novo libro di lettere*, p. 12).

70 The letter reads in part as follows: '[Q]uanta securtà io prenda nell'amore, che ella mi porta, le dimostro ora con pregarla, che voglia per quella usata cortesia antica, e perpetua cittadina del suo animo, trovarmi tanto di favore appresso il signor Ambasciador di Mantova, o d'Urbino, che si cavasse de prigione un mio servitore, che iersera vi fu posto per esser stato trovato contra il suo costume con una spada, venendo di Mestre, dove io lo aveva mandato per alcuni miei servizii' (How much security I get from the love you bear me I show you now by praying, because of that habitual courtesy, ancient and perpetual citizen of your mind, that you gain favour for me with the ambassador of Mantua or Urbino, so that one of my servants might be let out of prison, where he was placed yesterday evening, for having been found with a sword, against his custom, coming from Mestre, where I had sent him to do some work for me; *Lettere a Pietro Aretino*, vol. 1, part 2, Letter 370, p. 294).

71 Arrivabene ended up being denounced by Pietro Manelfi, an ex-Lutheran, converted in 1551, and with him all the other reform groups in Italy known to Manelfi (Bareggi, *Il mestiere di scrivere*, p. 197).

72 Crivelli worked with Dolce and took Dolce's place during his absences from the city, such as in the winter of 1545, when Dolce stayed in a 'piccolo Castello, detto Piove di Sacco discosto da Padova dieci miglia, molto vago, e molto gentile; sì per la qualità dell'aere dolce e temperato, come del terreno non men fertile che dilettoso,' where he often loved to go by boat, driven by the 'fiato d'un fresco venticello' (small castle, called Piove di Sacco, ten miles from Padua, very graceful and pleasing, both because of the quality of the air, sweet and mild, and of the earth, no less fertile than delightful; *Lettere scritte a Pietro Aretino*, vol. 1, part 2, Letter 307, pp. 269–73).

73 *Della nuova scielta di lettere*, vol. 2, 217–18.

74 Alfonso di Ulloa was a Spaniard born in Cáceres in 1529. His father, Francisco, fought for the emperor Charles V and in 1552 came to Venice as a secretary of the Spanish ambassador Diego Hurtado de Mendoza. As for Alfonso, following a short career in the military, where he worked for the

Gonzaga, he returned to Venice, where he worked as a translator of Spanish texts and, possibly, as a spy for King Philip II (Bareggi, *Il mestiere di scrivere*, pp. 36 and 83).

75 See the Archivio di Stato, Venice, *Sant'Uffizio*, busta 14, cited in Bareggi, ibid, p. 50n, and see also ibid, pp. 206–8.

76 Felipe de la Torre was an Aragonese who travelled widely in France and the Spanish Low Countries. He was in close contact with Protestants, among them Perez de Pineda, the editor of Valdés and a Spanish translator of sacred texts, and Martin Lopez, who hired him as a tutor for his son Martin Junior, who then went on to become the intermediary between the Calvanists of Antwerp (Anversa) and the French Huguenots. De la Torre's work was dedicated to King Philip II and earned him the title of royal chaplain. His *Institutione* is not to be confused with the *Institutione del prencipe christiano* of Antonio de Guevara (1480?–1545), translated by Mambrino Roseo da Fabriano and edited by Dolce for Giolito in 1553. See Bareggi, *Il mestiere di scrivere*, p. 233n.

77 Archivio di Stato, Venice, *Sant'Uffizio*, busta 14, processo ad Alfonso de Ulloa. See Bareggi, *Il mestiere di scrivere*, pp. 207–8, 233n.

78 Bareggi reports the particulars of the case, citing the Archivio di Stato, Venice, *Sant'Uffizio*, busta 20. The relevant documents have also been edited by Salvatore Bongi, in *Annali di Gabriel Giolito de' Ferrari*, vol. 1, pp. LXXXV–CXIII.

79 The *De statu religionis et reipublicae Carlo V imperatore Commentarii* of Johannes Sleidanus was published in Strasbourg in 1555 and reissued clandestinely in Italy by Lorenzo Torrentino (the Dutchman Laurens Leenaertsz van der Beke, ducal printer in Florence) in 1556. Sleidanus, who became the official historian of the Schmalkaldic League in 1545, had been strongly influenced by Calvinist ideas. Bareggi provides the date that the book was placed on the index (*Il mestiere di scrivere*, p. 233n), citing F.H. Reusch, *Die Indices librorum prohibitorum des sechzehnten Jahrhunderts* (Tübingen, 1886), p. 162. The Schmalkaldic League was a military alliance of German princes opposed to Charles V's efforts to convert Protestants back to Catholicism; Charles went to war against the League in 1546 and defeated them in 1547.

80 Cicogna, 'Memoria intorno la vita e gli scritti di Lodovico Dolce,' p. 110. In a dedicatory letter presenting Dolce's *Enea* to Francesco de' Medici, heir of Cosimo I, dated 1 February 1568, the publisher Varisco says Dolce died a few days earlier. Another letter referring to Dolce's recent death is that of Francesco Sansovino, who dedicated Dolce's *Trasformazioni* (a translation of Ovid's *Metamorphoses*) to Erasmo di Valvasone on 24 March 1568. Sansovino says Dolce died at the age of sixty in that year, adding that Dolce *'fu* uago &

dolce nelle sue cose.' I quote from the facsimile editon published in New York and London by Garland Publishing, 1979, with introductory notes by Stephen Orgel: *Le trasformationi di M. Lodovico Dolce tratte da Ovidio con gli argomenti et allegorie al principio & al fine di ciascun canto*, p. 2.

2: Between Ariosto and Tasso

1 Regarding the 'ottava rima,' for example, Dolce writes: 'Il Boccaccio (come fu detto; e secondo, che egli stesso afferma) ne fu inventore, e primo in essa materia di arme, come fu la Theseide, discrisse. Dapoi nella seguente età alcuni bassi ingegni, parendo loro questo modo di rimar facile, in cantar diverse menzogne e favole di Orlando e de' Paladini le adoperarono, di maniera, che per lungo tempo in queste non si raccolsero cose degne di esser lette. Dopo vario tempo un Francesco Cieco da Ferrara vi scrisse pure in soggetto de' Paladini assai comportevolmente. Compose anco Luigi Pulci il Morgante. Ma costui fu poscia lasciato a dietro dal Boiardo sì di stilo, come d'inventione. Indi il Politiano altamente cantando, primo adornò così fatta maniera di versi, di dottrina, di vaghezza, e di leggiadria: et aperse la strada, per la quale felicemente caminando l'Ariosto, pervenne a tant'altezza, che non solo si può dire, ch'egli le Stanze illustrasse, ma che le habbia ridotte a quella perfettione, alla quale tra' Latini Virgilio, e tra Greci Homero ridussero il verso Hessàmetro ...' (Boccaccio [as has been said, and as he himself affirmed] was the inventor of the octave and the first to describe in that form matters of arms [epic material], such as in his *Thesiad*. In the following age, some base minds, thinking this manner of rhyming was easy, adopted it to sing diverse lies and fables of Orlando and the Paladins, in such a manner that for a long time nothing was written in octaves worthy of being read. After a while, Francesco Cieco da Ferrara wrote in octaves about the Paladins, in a very bearable manner, as did Luigi Pulci in the *Morgante*. But he was later left behind by Boiardo, both as regards style and invention. Then Poliziano, in lofty song, first adorned this type of verse with doctrine, loveliness, and grace, and opened the way along which Ariosto, happily walking, came to such loftiness that one can say that not only did he illustrate the stanzas, but that he brought them back to the perfection that Virgil among the Latins and Homer among the Greeks brought the hexameter; *I quattro libri delle osservationi* [Venice: Altobello Salicato, 1573], pp. 235–6). Interestingly, recent studies of this metrical form take similar approaches. See, for example, A. Limentani's 'Struttura e storia dell'ottava rima.'

Earlier, Dolce had employed heroic poetry to make a grammatical point, commenting on Ariosto's reasons for changing the first verse of the *Furioso*

('quando al Retto si dà l'Articolo, necessariamente a tutti gli obliqui si debba darlo' [when one uses an article in the direct form, it is necessary to use it in the indirect]):
Onde prudentemente levò l'Ariosto quel primo verso della sua opera.

'Di Donne, e Cauallier gli antichi amori;

e pose in quella vece,

Le Donne, i Cauallier, l'arme, e gli amori,

non solo per volgere il primo nel terzo obliquo, imitando Virgilio, et alludendo a quel di Dante,

Le Donne i Cauallier, gli affanni, e gli agi;

ma per serbar questa regola, alla qual prima non haueua hauuto pensiero.' [Whence Ariosto prudently removed the first verse of his poem – 'Of women and knights the ancient loves' – and replaced it with 'the women, the knights, the arms, and the loves,' not only in order to turn the first into the third oblique, imitating Virgil and alluding to Dante's 'the women, the knights, the worries, the comforts,' but in order to follow this rule, about which he first had not thought] (p. 45).

2 Ettore Bonora calls the polemic 'significativa' (*Critica e letteratura nel Cinquecento*, p. 232) and refers the reader to V. Cian, 'Varietà letterarie del Rinascimento. II. Una polemica dantesca nel secolo XVI: il Bembo, il Dolce ed il Gelli.'

3 See G. Fontanini, *Della eloquenza italiana ... libri tre novellamente ristampati*, pp. 391–2.

4 See his posthumous *L'Achille et l'Enea* (Venice: Gabriel Giolito, 1570) in fifty-five cantos of *ottava rima* and his *L'Ulisse* (Venice: Gabriel Giolito, 1573), also in *ottava rima*. Appended to this latter work is Dolce's translation of the *Batracomiomachia*. Citing Apostolo Zeno, Cicogna notes that *L'Achille et l'Enea* is not strictly a translation, being quite different from *L'Enea*, published a few days after Dolce's death ('Memoria intorno la vita e gli scritti di Messer Lodovico Dolce,' p. 152). In reality, however, the work follows Homer and Virgil quite closely, although Dolce extends the story down to the time of the Caesars. As Cicogna also points out, *L'Ulisse* is not so much a translation as 'una storia tratta dall'Odissea' (ibid, p. 121).

5 Joel Elias Spingarn notes that 'critical activity in nearly all the countries of

western Europe seems to have been ushered in by the translation of Horace's *Ars Poetica* into the vernacular tongues. Critical activity in Italy began with Dolce's Italian version of the *Ars Poetica* in 1535 ...' (*A History of Literary Criticism in the Renaissance*, p. 171).

6 Cited in Bernard Weinberg, *A History of Literary Criticism in the Renaissance*, vol. 1, p. 144. Dolce's 'discorso' can be found in *I dilettevoli sermoni, altrimenti satire, e le morali epistole di Horatio ... insieme con la poetica. Ridotte da M. Lodovico Dolce dal poema latino in versi sciolti volgari. Con la vita di Horatio. Origine della satira. Discorso sopra le epistole. Discorso sopra la poetica.*

7 'Prefazione antica di Lodovico Dolce,' in *L'Amadigi di M. Bernardo Tasso, colle vita dell'autore e varie illustrazioni dell'opera ...*, vol. 3, p. iii (Bergamo: P. Lancellotti, 1755).

8 The fame of Ariosto, Dolce notes, 'è da riportarsi al giudizio comune: il qual solo è quello, che toglie e dà la riputazione, e la immortalità a qualunque Poema' (is due to common judgment, which is the only thing that takes away and gives fame and immortality to any poem; p. xii). Ariosto himself, in requesting permission to publish from the Doge of Venice, noted that he wrote 'per spasso et ricreatione dei Signori et persone de animo gentile' (for amusement and recreation of lords and people of noble mind) as well as 'per sollazzo et piacere di qualunche vorrà et che se delecterà di leggerlo' (for the solace and pleasure of anyone who wants to and enjoys reading it); cited in Umberto Renda and Piero Operti, *Dizionario storico della letteratura italiana*, p. 73; see the letter in *Lettere di L.A.*, a cura di A. Cappelli [3d ed., Milan, 1887]).

   Dolce's preface is also discussed by Giulio Ferrario, in *Storia ed analisi degli antichi romanzi di cavalleria e dei poemi romanzeschi d'Italia ...* , pp. 354–5; in Nino Borsellino and Marcello Aurigemma, eds., *Il Cinquecento: Dal Rinascimento alla Controriforma*; and briefly by Bonora (*Il Cinquecento*, pp. 162–3).

9 Borsellino and Aurigemma, eds., *Il Cinquecento*, p. 311. For Ariosto's reception in the cinquecento, see Daniel Javitch, *The Canonization of* Orlando Furioso.

10 I quote from the *Apologia* in the 1540 edition of Ariosto's *Orlando furioso*, published in Venice by Mapheo Pasini, here pp. II, v^r, and II, vi^r.

11 'Chi è, che non sappia esser stato sempre licito in qual si voglia età a gli scrittori e di versi o di prose di porre alle volte nei Poemi e scritti loro alcuna parola nuova e non mai dagli antichi usata; quando quella tal parola sia acconcia ad esprimer il concetto di colui, che scrive? Niuno certamente; se non sciocchissimo' (Who does not know that in every age it has always been permitted to writers, both of verse and of prose, sometimes to place in their

poems and writings a new word, never used by the ancients, when that word is appropriate to express the concept of the person who is writing? No one certainly, if not very foolish; p. II, iii^r).

12 We find in Spanish, for example, the 'Exposición de todos los lugares difficultosos' by Alfonso de Ulloa in his translation of Ariosto (Venice: Giolito, 1553), also translated by Hieronimo de Urrea (Lyon: Bastano di Bartholomeo Honorati, 1556).

13 Weinberg quotes Dolce's theoretical statement from the preface 'A i lettori' as follows: 'Ciascuno, che disidera, che i suoi componimenti siano volentieri letti e lodati da gli huomini giudiciosi e dotti, dee senza fallo procacciar di scriver regolatamente, ornatamente, figuratamente et artificiosamente' (Anyone who wishes that his compositions be willingly read and praised by judicious and learned men must without fail endeavour to write in an ordered manner, ornately, figuratively, and with artifice; vol. 1, p. 174). As well as the admonitory statement pointed out by Weinberg, one might note the emphasis on being read by others.

14 See Fontanini, *Della eloquenza italiana* ..., p. 378. Dolce speaks elsewhere of other works of Ariosto, as, for example, his comedies in verse. See *Le osservationi* (1573 ed.), pp. 192–3.

15 Renda and Operti, *Dizionario storico*, p. 401. Cicogna, however, following Jacopo Paitoni and Apostolo Zeno, lists the epic among Dolce's original works in verse ('Memoria intorno la vita e gli scritti di Messer Lodovico Dolce'). The claim is that the epic is different from the *Enea* translated by Dolce and published in Venice by Giovanni Varisco in 1568 (pp. 127 and 152). Both Cicogna and the *Dizionario storico* list the first edition of the combined work as that of 1572. Gamba (no. 1359) gives 1571 (or 1572). The University of Chicago's Regenstein Library, however, has a 1570 edition of the poem, as does Trinity College, Cambridge.

   Dolce's disdain for Trissino, incidentally, is expressed in his *Osservationi* (1573 ed.), p. 186.

16 Luigi Groto, il Cieco d'Adria, wrote to Dolce, as Fòffano notes, 'pregandolo di porre "in capo o a piè del Bojardo che andava riformando a guisa d'orsa'' (cioè leccandolo, lisciandolo colla lingua) certi versi' (*Il poema cavalleresco*, p. 41). See also Ferrario, *Storia ed analisi degli antichi romanzi di cavalleria e dei poemi romanzeschi d'Italia*, vol. 2, p. 215.

17 L. Dolce, *Stanze composte nella vittoria africana nuovamente avuta dal sacratissimo imperatore Carlo V* (Rome, 1535), in V. Vivaldi, *La Gerusalemme liberata studiata nelle sue fonti (azione principale del poema)*, p. 13.

18 'Note sul dissolversi della forma rinascimentale. Dall'Ariosto al Tasso,' pp. 174–90.

19 *Angelica ed i 'migliori plettri.' Appunti allo stile della Controriforma*, p. 24. Leo, perhaps to bolster his arguments dates the Sacripante to around 1520, based on a prophetic reference in the poem itself to that date (pp. 12 and 42 n17). But Dolce would have been ten (or, at most, twelve) years old at that time, and thus very precocious indeed. Leo claims that Dolce speaks of Ariosto as still alive in canto X, 3ff., where Dolce lists the illustrious writers and leaders of his time. But several of the figures listed as if alive were dead before Dolce was born, such as Pontano (†1503), and, for others, such as Fortunio (†1517), the present tense is also used. Following Leo's logic, the poem would have to have been written at least as early as 1517, when Dolce was seven (or possibly nine)! But when Dolce refers to the death of the Marchese di Pescara, if the reference, as seems likely, is to the Ferrante d'Avalos, Marchese di Pescara, who married Vittoria Colonna and who died in 1525 after leading the imperial army to victory in the Battle of Pavia, the reference effectively destroys an early dating.

20 My source is *Il primo libro di Sacripante di Messer Ludovico Dolce, nuovamente ristampato* (colophon: Venice: Giovan'Antonio de Nicolini da Sabio, 1536). The first edition, published in Venice by Francesco Bindoni and Mapheo Pasini, also dates to 1536. An earlier, shorter version, the *Cinque primi canti di Sacripante*, was published, against the poet's wishes, in Venice in 1535.

21 Ulrich Leo, in discussing the punishment of Angelica, which he claims represents 'il motivo quasi dominante' of Dolce's incompleted poem (*Angelica ed i 'migliori plettri,'* p. 35), seriously and mistakenly impugns Dolce's moralism, at one point going so far as to insinuate that, with the punishment of Angelica, 'il Dolce soddisfece il proprio sadismo e quello dei suoi lettori' (Dolce satisfied his own sadism and that of his readers; p. 35), and that the *castigo*, for Dolce and others, was an 'occasione adatta per presentare scene lubriche o sadiche' (suitable opportunity to present lubricous and sadistic scenes; p. 25). Yet, the very scene where Angelica is whipped, to use Leo's adjective, 'sadisticamente' (p. 22), is an allegorical trial, with King Time as the judge who punishes Angelica for having disdained love (VIII, 51–65). As the king notes, evil derives from disdain: 'Perchè da ciò, come da largo rio, / Deriva quel, ch'ogni virtute infetta; / Quel peccato, che tanto offende Dio, / Che da voi ingratitudine vien detta' (because from that [disdain], as from a broad stream, derives that sin which infects every virtue, which so much offends God, which is called ingratitude by you; VIII, 55). It is also difficult to forget that this scene, which is a vision beheld by Marphisa and Selannio (when they 'awaken' from blows to the head which have left them unconscious), is prefaced by the poet's prayer to God for Marphisa: 'Padre del ciel, deh non lassar; che 'l fine / Sia de la tua

fedel sì brutto e presto. / Serbala a più honorate discipline; / Che per te mora, et il morir fia honesto' (Heavenly Father, for pity's sake, don't allow the end of your believer to be so ugly and so soon. Save her for more honoured tasks, so that she may die for you, and her death may be honourable; VIII, 49). Marphisa and Selannio in fact, as *faithful* lovers, will leave this allegorical court at peace with the fierce king (VIII, 69).

The moral substraum of Dolce's poem is quite evident. One must also remember that Dolce, in discussing the function of the poet, emphasized not only the goal of providing delight, but also the accompanying moral intention: 'L'ufficio del Poeta è di imitare le attioni de gli huomini: e il fine *sotto leggiadri veli di morali et utili inventioni* dilettar l'animo di chi legge' (The duty of the poet is to imitate the actions of men, and the goal [is] to delight the mind of the reader with moral and useful inventions under lovely veils; *Le osservationi*, cited in Weinberg, *A History of Literary Criticism in the Renaissance*, vol. 1, p. 421, my emphasis).

22 The description is reminiscent of Dante's Charon (see *Inferno* III, 99, 109) and may be, as well, a reference to Michelangel's 'Last Judgment,' which depicts Charon, in Dantesque fashion, with his oar over his shoulder. If so, the two works are roughly contemporary, the *Sacripante* dating to 1535–6, the 'Last Judgment' to around 1534–41. More likely, however, Dolce is thinking of traditional depictions of demons.

23 I, 41. All quotations are from the *Furioso* in Ariosto, *Opere*, ed. Giuliano Innamorati.

24 Dolce's early use of Bembian schemes is significant, for, as Roberto Battaglia notes, it is only towards the middle of the cinquecento that the motif of love as expressed in epic poems consolidates itself in the form dictated by Bembo. Battaglia's example is Bernardo Tasso's *Amadigi* ('Note sul dissolversi della forma rinascimentale,' 176–7).

25 *Teatro italiano antico*, V (Milano: Società Tipografica de' Classici Italiani, 1809), pp. 249–50.

26 An awareness of the poet's seriousness invalidates the critical statements of Ulrich Leo who comments: 'Ma già il Dolce – il cui unico elemento controriformista è la falsa verecondia – ha di nuovo ridestato dal ben meritato riposo della tomba, la povera vecchia Alda, chiamandola finanche Aldabella (*Sacripante* II, 64; IV, 12)' (But of course Dolce – whose only Counter-Reformistic element is false modesty – has again reawakened from the well-deserved rest of the tomb poor old Alda, even calling her Alda the Beautiful; *Angelica ed i 'migliori plettri,'* p. 45 n43).

27 Cf. Sannazzaro's maga in *Arcadia*, ch. 9.

28 Cf. Venus's kingdom in Boccaccio, *Teseida* VII, 50–69, and Poliziano, *Stanze per la giostra* I, 70–91. In Dolce, the realm also contains a Dantesque stream of forgetfulness (*Sacripante* V, 79).

29 Carandina, more powerful than Circe or Medea (*Mambriano* I, 32), also imprisons those she loves in her magic castle, constructed with the aid of infernal beings, including Charon.

30 The idea of entitling one's poem after an enemy of the French is a tradition dating back, in Italy, to the *Ancroja regina*, first published in Venice in 1479.

31 Bernardo Tasso places Dolce among the illustrious poets in his list in the *Amadigi* (1560), canto 100, while, in a different genre, Giambattista Giraldi Cintio also lists Dolce among the illustrious, praising him in a terzina at the end of the *Hecatommithi* (1565).

32 The clause 'e mille e mille ingegni' shows that Dolce considered Erasmus and Melancthon, not as Lutherans, but as scholars. Prior to the early 1540s, Erasmus enjoyed enormous prestige in Italy, both as a man of vast classical learning and as a teacher. As Christopher Cairns notes, Aldus published at least eight works by him between 1508 and 1521, Gregoriis another nine between 1522 and 1526, and Zoppino at least four more from 1526 to 1529. See *Pietro Aretino and the Republic of Venice*, pp. 57–8 and *passim*. See also Paul F. Grendler and Marcella Grendler, 'The Survival of Erasmus in Italy'; and, for the fertility of the educational treatises of Erasmus, Eugenio Garin, *L'educazione in Europa, 1400–1600*, pp. 152–9. The first Italian index to ban Erasmus's works was that of Siena in April 1548, with the initial Papal Index dating to the spring of 1555 (Grendler and Grendler, p. 3). With the latter Index, even purely scholarly works of the northern heresiarchs were banned as pernicious to the faith. Dolce's praise of Erasmus is tempered in later years. In his *Life of Charles the Fifth*, Dolce says, 'È lodato per uno dei più dotti e belli ingegni Erasmo se non si fosse egli imbrattato nel morbo Lutherano; onde furono dalla Chiesa più volte et ultimamente dannate tutte le sue opere' (Erasmus is praised for having one of the most learned and beautiful intellects were he not to have soiled himself with the Lutheran disease, as a result of which all his works have been condemned many times and recently by the Church; in Pedro Mexia, *Le vite di tutti gl' imperadori romani da Giulio Cesare insino a Massimiliano tratte per M. Lodovico Dolce dal libro spagnuolo del nobile Cavaliere Pietro Messia. Aggiuntavi la vita dell'invitissimo Carlo Quinto imperatore, discritta dal medesimo M. Lodovico Dolce*, p. 97).

33 Boiardo breaks off his poem with the following octave: 'Mentre che io canto, o Iddio redentore, / Vedo la Italia tutta a fiama e foco / Per questi Galli, che con gran valore / Vengon per disertar non so che loco; / Però vi lascio in

questo vano amore / De Fiordespina ardente a poco a poco; / Un'altra fiata, se mi fia concesso, / Raccontarovi il tutto per espresso' (While I sing, O God redeemer, I see Italy all in flames and fire because of these Gauls, who with great valour come to devastate I know not what place; therefore I leave you in this vain love of Fiordespina, burning bit by bit. Another time, if it is permitted to me, I will narrate the whole explicitly; III, ix, 26). All quotations of Boiardo's works are from *Orlando innamorato, sonetti e canzoni di Matteo Maria Boiardo*, vol. 2.

34 I would agree with Ulrich Leo when he writes that 'A me è sempre parso che si tenda ad esagerare la differenza tra buoni e cattivi poemi' (It seems to me that one tends to exaggerate the difference between good and bad poets), claiming that 'Il Dolce e l'Aretino hanno tuttora una grazia rinascimentale e suonano a volte come il maestro stesso' (Dolce and Aretino still have a Renaissance grace and sound at times like the master himself; *Angelica ed i 'migliori plettri,'* p. 13).

35 Sacripante, of course, is also one of the characters in Boiardo's *Innamorato*, and is first seen there in love with Angelica: 'Egli era innamorato oltra a misura / Della donzella, e lei lui poco amava' (He was enamoured beyond measure with the damsel, and she loved him little; I, ix, 41).

36 Pandragone is also a figure from Boiardo's *Innamorato* (I, x, 12ff.; xv, 16, 23ff.; xvii, 55.

37 As briefly mentioned earlier, one woman, Hersilia, an example of fortune's ups and downs, narrates a story similar in certain respects to that of Alatiel (*Dec.* II, 7), although possibly based on Spanish sources (*Sacripante* VI, 85–110). Captured at sea by 'gente Pyrata,' Hersilia (a married woman) was passed from the King of Algiers, who wanted to marry her, to a knight, Tanardo by name, who takes her to Catania. There she is imprisoned by a Sicilian who desires her, but is sent instead to a cousin in Spain. In Valencia, King Marsilio wishes to give her to a nephew, but she is accused of trying to poison the King and is sentenced to be burned. The men who are to carry out the King's orders wish to enjoy her first, but she is freed at last by Rinaldo. Hersilia, however, another of Dolce's examples of fidelity, laments the fate of her spouse more than any of her own ills (VII, 5).

38 All quotations are from *Le prime imprese del conte Orlando di M. Lodovico Dolce ... con argomenti et allegorie per ogni canto ...*, p. ij^v.

39 The poem, however, has its own merits, as noted by Ferrario: 'La narrazione è chiara ed assai animata, la locuzione mediocre ma naturale, i caratteri bastantemente sostenuti. Alcuni *episodj* sparsi nell'azione, i quali non mancano d'interesse, e la varietà degli avvenimenti, fanno che non si legge

senza diletto questo poema ... Il *Dolce* lo scrisse per avventura con minor fretta e più accuratamente degli altri suoi poemi' (The narration is clear and very animated, the locution mediocre but natural, the characters sufficiently sustained. Some interspersed episodes, which are not lacking in interest, and the variety of the events make it so that one does not read this poem without delight; *Storia ed analisi degli antichi romanzi di cavalleria e dei poemi romanzeschi d'Italia*, vol. 2, pp. 262–3). The appeal of the poem is attested in part by its translation into Spanish: *El nascimiento y primeras empresas del Conde Orlando*, trans. Pero Lopez Henriquez de Calatayua (Vallodolid: Diego F. de Cordova y Oviedo, 1595).

40 Boiardo writes: 'Tutte le cose sotto della luna, / L'alta ricchezza, e' regni della terra, / Son sottoposti a voglia di Fortuna: / Lei la porta apre de improviso e serra, / E quando più par bianca, divien bruna; / Ma più se mostra a caso della guerra / Instabile, voltante e roïnosa, / E più fallace che alcuna altra cosa' (All things under the moon, lofty riches, and realms on earth, are subject to Fortune's will: she opens the door suddenly and closes it, and when she most seems bright, she becomes dark. Yet more, she shows herself unstable in case of war, revolving and ruinous, and more deceptive than any other thing; I, xvi, 1).

41 The first octave of Dolce's poem, incidentally, shares much with that of the youthful Tasso's *Rinaldo* (1562), written in the same period of time. Compare the following two octaves, first Tasso's: 'Canto i felici affanni e i primi ardori / che giovinetto ancor soffrì Rinaldo, / e come il trasse in perigliosi errori / desir di gloria ed amoroso caldo; / allor che, vinti dal gran Carlo, i Mori / mostrâro il cor più che le forze saldo; / e Troiano, Agolante e 'l fiero Almonte / restâr pugnando uccisi in Aspramonte' (I sing the happy travails and the first ardours that Rinaldo suffered while still young, and how a desire for glory and loving heat drew him into dangerous errors, where, conquered by the great Charles, the moors showed their hearts to be stauncher than their forces; and Troiano, Agolante, and the fierce Almonte were killed fighting in Aspramonte; I, 1), and then Dolce's: 'Canto le prime imprese, i primi affanni / Di quel famoso e sempre invitto Conte, / Ch'a Saracin per lungo spatio d'anni / Domò l'orgoglio e la superba fronte. / Dirò come fanciullo in brevi panni / Sciolse lo spirto a l'Africano Almonte, / E di sue spoglie adorno il Re Agolante / Vinse, e uccise il padre d'Agramante' (I sing the first deeds, the first travails, of that famous and always unconquered count, who tamed the pride and proud forehead of the Saracens for a long span of years. I will tell how, as a child in short clothes, he freed the spirit of the African Almonte, and, adorned with his spoils, he conquered King Agolante and killed the father of Agramante; I, 1).

42 Cantos I–IV are based loosely on the *Reali di Francia* (Book VI, chs. 52–70),
while canto V begins with material, again much transformed, from the
Aspramonte. Other sources include the French *Girard de Viane*. Dolce's poem,
though based on traditional material, is original. Compare, for example,
L'Aspramonte in prose of Andrea da Barberino, I, chs. 32–7, to Dolce's poem,
canto XV. Dolce dramatizes certain features for moral effect. In the *Aspramonte*, Carlo allows Almonte time to arm himself, after which the pagan
thanks him for his graciousness (ch. 38). In Dolce, Carlo helps Almonte arm
himself (Christian charity), but, once armed, the pagan calls him a fool: 'E
disse, o sciocco Re chi t'ha insegnato, / Ch'al nimico si debba esser cortese'
(And he said, o foolish king, who taught you that one ought to be courteous
to the enemy; XV, 34). Dolce is not mocking Carlo, as so many of the mock-
heroic poems do, but is contrasting his *virtù* to the pagan's *viltà*. Dolce's
version, on the whole, is much abbreviated compared with his sources, but
the changes are instructive.

    The same can be said of Dolce's use of *I Reali di Francia*. Cf., for example,
Carlo's dream in *Reali* VI, 64, and *Prime imprese* IV, 38–42). Dolce adds
classical parallels (Caesar, Philip, Constantine) and emphasizes that dreams
are signs from God.

43 Carlo, for example, who orders Milone and Berta (caught in bed together) to
be burned, seems as cruel as Herod. Prudent Namo fails to mitigate his
anger, much as Soemo fails to allay Herod's suspicions and violence. Namo,
in a second speech (I, 78–80) following a dream of Carlo, speaks much like
Soemo and the wise counsellor in the *Marianna*.

44 See *Prime imprese* VII, 25, and, for the Boiardian reminiscence shared here
with *Prime imprese* XIII, cf. *Orlando innamorato* I, xvi, l. Other references to
fortune bring to mind Dantesque, Boccaccian, and Machiavellian sources. In
canto IX, for example, Almonte decides that 'chi non piglia / Fortuna,
quando puote, e in mano ha il crine; / In van dietro le corre e si distrugge /
Che non ritorna più, quand'ella fugge' (he who does not grasp Fortune,
when he can, and has her hair in his hand, in vain runs after her and ruins
himself, for when she flees she returns no more; 33). Neither Dante's 'ne'
biondi capegli, / ... , / metterei mano' (I would put my hand in her blonde
hair; 'Così nel mio parlar voglio esser aspro') nor Boccaccio's 's'i avessi in
mano gli capegli avvolti' (if I had her hair twisted in my hand; *Rime*, pt. 2,
xv) is perhaps as appropriate a reminiscence as Machiavelli's depiction in
the *Principe*, ch. XXV, 9, or that in his *Capitolo*, 'Dell'Occasione,' where
Fortune says, 'Li sparsi mia capei dinanti io tengo: / Con essi mi ricuopro il
petto e 'l volto / Perch'un non mi conosca quando io vengo' (I hold my
spread hair in front of me. With this I cover my breast and face, so that no
one may know me when I come).

Unknown to Machiavelli, but attesting to the earlier origin and popularity of this particular image of Fortuna/Occasio, is a Goliardic poem found in the *Carmina Burana*, a collection of about two hundred poems compiled by a Benedictine monk at the monastery of Beuron in Bavaria in the late thirteenth or early fourteenth century, but not published until 1837. In the poem 'Fortune plango vulnera' we read: 'Verum est, quod legitur, / fronte capillata, / sed plerumque sequitur / Occasio calvata' ('Truer words were never writ: / "Seize her by her forehead's hair; / the back of her scalp is all bare!" '). I quote from *Carmina Burana, cantiones profanae*, ed. Carl Orff, original text with introduction by Judith Lynn Sebesta and a new translation by Jeffrey M. Duban, p. 15.

45 In the early cantos, for example, the Maganzesi are depicted as traitors (e.g., in II, 44), whereas later we are told they had not yet become traitors (IX, 20). Likewise, after speaking of Agolante's children at length in the early cantos (e.g., I, 5–6), Dolce identifies both them and Agolante again, as if for the first time, in canto V, 50–9.

46 Dolce writes that Guarnier 'deliberò di vendicar la morte / del padre sopra Carlo e la sua corte' (decided to avenge the death of his father on Charles and his court; V, 6), just as Ariosto claims that Agramante 'si diè vanto / di vendicar la morte di Troiano / sopra re Carlo imperatore romano' (boasted the he would avenge the death of Troiano on king Charles, Roman emperor; I, l).

47 And cf. *Rinaldo* XII, 63, where Tasso writes: 'Non è sempre l'istesso il lor viaggio, / né sempre fanno ancor l'istesso suono; / perché sì come or punta or taglio n'esce, / diverso il suono ed il cammin riesce' (Their journey is not always the same, nor do they make the same sound, because just as now a thrust now a slash comes out, so the sound and the path turn out different).

48 Defeated by Ruggero, Galaciella renounces her pagan beliefs and is baptized (VIII, 39), but eventually marries Ruggero (VIII, 66–7). As 'I primi frutti del lor casto amore' (the first fruits of their chaste love; IX, 2), she bears twins, the Ruggero and Marfisa rendered famous by Ariosto.

49 I refer, not to the first encounter of Tancredi and Clorinda (*Lib.* I, 47) nor to that of VI, 26, but to the splendid vision of III, 21, in which Clorinda's helmet is dislodged by Tancredi's lance 'e le chiome dorate al vento sparse' (and her golden hair spread in the wind).

50 Dantesque reminiscences occur throughout Dolce's poem. To mention just the first canto by way of example, Berta's foreboding dream (stanza 31) recalls that of Ugolino (*Inf.* XXXIII, 28–36) and her brother Terigi, a trusted *scudiero* of Milone (the name in Pulci belongs to a squire of Orlando), is described with words used by Pier della Vigna (*Inf.* XIII, 58–60): 'Questa volgeva del suo cor la chiave' (I, 38). Dante's image of flowers recovering

from a frost under the sun (*Inf.* II, 127–30), imitated nearly verbatim by Boccaccio (*Filostrato*, pt. II, lxxii, 6), is imaginatively transformed by Dolce to flowers which recover from heat under the rain: 'Come, quando al Leon passando il Sole / Fende il duro terren col raggio ardente, / Arso fioretto con la pioggia suole / Ritornar più che pria fresco e ridente: / Così tempra l'incendio, onde si duole, / La Donna, e ristorar tutto si sente / A conforti fedel de la Nutrice, / Sperando del suo amor gioir felice' (Just as, when the sun passes through Leo and splits the hard earth with burning ray, a burnt flower is accustomed with rain to return fresher and more smiling than before, so the woman tempers the fire that causes pain, hoping to rejoice happy at her love, and feels herself completely restored by the faithful comfort of the wet-nurse; I, 40).

51 The variations, of course, are endless. Luigi's brother, Luca Pulci, in his epic on Ciriffo Calvaneo, puts the following words in the mouth of the future mother of Ciriffo, Massima, who falls in love in Rome with Antandro, the son of the future mother of Constantinople: 'Et guardando più volte il nobil viso, / Giurato harei, ch'io fussi in paradiso' (And gazing at his noble face, I would have sworn that I was in Paradise; Giunta ed. of 1618, p. 8). In his *Rinaldo*, Tasso employs the traditional idea, with originality, to describe Floriana, queen of Media, enamoured of his hero: 'Lampeggia come 'l sol nel chiaro umore, / ne gli umidi occhi un tremulo splendore' (a tremulous splendour flashed in her wet eyes like the sun in clear liquid; IX, 79).

52 For example, in Book III of *L'Italia liberata dai goti*, we read of 'L'angel Nettuno' who appears 'col tridente in mano'!

53 Earlier versions of portions of this chapter have appeared in print as 'Lodovico Dolce and the Chivalric Romance' in *Studies in the Italian Renaissance: Essays in Memory of Arnolfo B. Ferruolo* and as 'Between Ariosto and Tasso: Lodovico Dolce and the Chivalric Romance,' in *Italian Quarterly*.

3: 'I Costumi d'Hoggidì'

1 Cited by Abd-El-Kader Salza, in *Delle commedie di Lodovico Dolce*, p. 27.

2 *Les six premières comédies facecieuses de Pierre de Larivey Champenois a l'imitation des anciens grecs, latins et modernes italiens*, in *Ancien théâtre français, ou collection des ouvrages dramatiques les plus remarquables depuis les mystères jusqu'a Corneille publié avec des notes et éclaircissements par M. Viollet Le Duc*, vol. 5 (Paris: P. Jannet, 1860). The first edition of these comedies (of which *Le Laquais* is the first) was published in Paris by Abel l'Angelier in 1579. See Salza, *Delle commedie di Lodovico Dolce*, p. 72.

3 *Il ragazzo: Comedia di M. Lodovico Dolce* (Curtio de Navò et Fratelli, al Leone, MDXLI). This play, dedicated to Fortunato Martinengo (di villa 16 agosto

1541), was favourably received and apparently recited several times. Salza says it was recited for sure on Fat Thursday in 1542 in Mantua, according to Ippolito Capilupi, secretary of Francesco Gonzaga (letter of 25 February 1542, to Don Ferrante di Guastalla, cited in A. D'Ancona, *Origini del teatro italiano*, 2d ed. [1891], vol. 2, p. 438: Salza, *Delle commedie di Lodovico Dolce*, p. 28).

4 The first joint edition dates to 1560 (*Comedie di M. Lodovico Dolce, cioè, Il ragazzo, Il capitano, Il marito, La Fabritia, Il ruffiano*) and is dedicated by the author to Prospero Podacataro di Cipro, a professor at Padua in 1546, in the school of *Diritto Civile* (Civil Law). Each comedy in this edition (from which all later citations are taken, unless otherwise noted) is paginated separately.

5 *Italian Comedy in the Renaissance*, p. 112.

6 While the title page of the first edition says the play was 'tratta dal Rudente di Plauto,' Salza quotes Dolce's dedicatory letter of 1 November 1551 to the abbot Scipione Gesualdo, where the poet says he has just finished the work, 'fabrica non meno della mia penna, che di quella di Plauto, o di altro che piacevolmente la fece comparere tra huomini di villa' (a product no less of my pen than of that of Plautus, or of another who made it appear pleasingly among men in the countryside; Salza, *Delle commedie di Lodovico Dolce*, pp. 136–7). The 'altro' referred to is Ruzzante, from whom Dolce, according to Salza, 'ha non solo preso qualcosa, ma tutta la commedia, senza ricorrere in alcun modo a Plauto, chè altrimenti si sarebbe avveduto della contaminazione fatta dal comico padovano nella *Piovana*' (took not only something, but the whole comedy, without recourse to Plautus at all, because otherwise he would have become aware of the additions made by the Paduan comic in the *Piovana*; p. 137). While Ruzzante's play is a reworking of Plautine material, Dolce's is almost an exact translation of *La piovana*, including the prologue, where Ruzzante (through Garbinello) humorously protests the newness of the work, even though made of old wood.

7 Ruzante, *La piovana*, testo originale a fronte, a cura di Ludovico Zorzi, introduzione di Mario Baratto, p. 5.

8 See the introduction of Mario Baratto to *La piovana* (' "Pavano" e "Latino": *La piovana* e il problema dell'imitazione'), p. v. The plot of Ruzzante's play follows quite closely that of the Plautine *Rudens*, with some traces of the *Mercator*, the *Pseudolus*, and Terence's *Heautontimoroumenos*. Giorgio Padoan also notes the influence of Ariosto's *Cassaria* (one scene of which is borrowed in its entirety), in addition to the general but extensive influence of Terence (*Commedia rinascimentale veneta*, p. 126). Padoan, however, goes on to say that, though the *Piovana* is usually considered a free translation of Plautus (as defined by Beolco in his request for publication rights), Ruzzante has impressed his own personal dimension on the play: 'Non di traduzione

si deve parlare, ma di rifacimento che perviene all'originalità' (p. 127). For
Ruzzante's infusion of the rustic spirit of comedy into a classical mould, see
also Radcliff-Umstead, *The Birth of Modern Comedy in Renaissance Italy*,
pp. 219–23.

9 The fact that the Latins borrowed from the Greeks was a common excuse
given by cinquecento poets who imitated Plautus and Terence. Ercole
Bentivoglio, in the prologue of his *Fantasmi*, excuses himself for having used
Plautus (the *Monstellaria*) by saying that, after all, the Latins used the Greeks.
Giovanmaria Cecchi does the same in the prologue of his *Dote* (taken from
Trinummus); cited in Salza, *Delle commedie di Lodovico Dolce*, pp. 20–1. Louise
George Clubb points out the range in attitude towards ancient comedies in
Italian Drama in Shakespeare's Time, p. 32, and Douglas Radcliff-Umstead
traces the revival of Plautus and Terence in *The Birth of Modern Comedy in
Renaissance Italy*, especially ch. 2, 'The Emergence of the Erudite Comedy.'

10 The *fanciullo* asks the audience: 'che vorreste più tosto voi huomini una
Donna vecchia, o una giovane? senza dubbio tutti rispondereste la giovane:
et così all'incontro le Donne anteporranno sempre i giovani a gli attempati.
Che più? vedete la Primavera, quanto per rinovarsi allhora la terra d'herbe
et di fiori, è grata equalmente a tutti: et la stagione, nella quale caggiono le
foglie de gli alberi, dispiace insino alle bestie' (What would you men rather
have, an old woman or a young one? Without doubt, all would respond, the
young one. And thus, on the contrary, women would favour the young over
the aged. What more? You see spring, which is pleasing to all because the
earth is renewed with grasses and flowers; and the season when leaves fall
from trees displeases even the beasts; p. 5^v).

11 Herrick cites Giraldi Cinthio's comments regarding the correctness of
unrhymed verse for comedies but the inappropriateness of *sdruccioli*, not
suited for the common crowd 'among whom a *sdrucciolo* does not happen
once a day' (p. 114). For a discussion of the controversy over prose and
verse, see Salza, *Delle commedie di Lodovico Dolce*, pp. 22–7.

12 *Il marito*, in *Comedie di M. Lodovico Dolce, cioè, Il ragazzo, Il capitano, Il marito,
La Fabritia, Il ruffiano*, p. 2^r.

13 As Salza notes (in *Delle commedie di Lodovico Dolce*), Dolce wrote from his
residence in Pieve di Sacco in 1545 (la Domenica di carnovale) to his friend
Paolo Crivello in Venice, saying 'la mia comedia *ha mutato viso*: et le è nata
un'altra sorella: penso che ve ne nascerà la terza' (my comedy has changed
faces, and another sister has been born to her, and I think a third will be
born from her; *Della nuova scielta di lettere di diversi nobiliss. huomini ... Con un
discorso ... di M. Bernardino Pino*, II, p. 218). According to Salza, Dolce was
referring to the *Capitano*, which was possibly first written in prose, then

changed to verse, and to the *Marito*, and perhaps to others not written (or to one of the last two – *La Fabritia* or *Il ruffiano*). In a letter of 26 February [1545], Dolce added: 'la mia comedia del *Capitano* holla ridotta in essere, che io estimo che non vi dispiacerà: udite gran parola. La seconda è detta il *Marito*, et è in buona parte il soggetto dell'*Anfitrio* di Plauto' (I've reduced my comedy of the *Capitano* in size, such that, listen to this, I think it will not displease you. The second is called the *Marito*, and it derives in large part from the *Anfitrio* of Plautus; Salza, p. 12). He asked his friend to check with Trifon Gabriele regarding the best way to write comedies, that is, if they should be in verse or in prose, and, if in verse, if this should be the *endecasillabo piano* or *sdrucciolo*. Crivello wrote back soon after (*Della nuova scielta*, II, 351, dated 19 February, which Salza says is 'certamente erronea' since Crivello is responding to Dolce's letter of 26 February [unless that one has an incorrect date]), saying Giolito was prepared to publish the work. Crivello complimented Dolce: 'Se non fusse ch'io son solito molte fiate di vedere simili miracoli di voi, io mi sarei stupito nello intendere, c'habbiate fatto la seconda comedia appresso la prima, et forse anco la terza in tanto spatio di tempo ch'apena sarebbe stato bastante a trascriverle; ma non si può desiderar cosa sì grande di voi che il vostro intelletto non sia atto a produrla maggiore' (If I was not accustomed to seeing similar miracles from you many times, I would have been astonished at learning that you have written a second comedy after the first, and perhaps a third, in a span of time barely enough to transcribe them. But one cannot desire something great from you without your intellect being capable of producing something greater; Salza, p. 13).

On 10 March (1545) Dolce wrote Crivello, explaining that the reason for composing his comedies in verse was, in addition to the example of the ancients for whom comedy was a poem, the authority of Ariosto, who used 'molto acconciamente il verso sdrucciolo' (Salza, p. 13). This verse seemed appropriate to Dolce for comic compositions because it added dignity to the form. Still, the opinion of Trifone was so authoritative for Dolce that he withdrew his reasons and decided to write his later comedies in prose.

14 'Ah, valentuomeni, ah, uomeni da ben tuti, n'abiè paura, e agnon tasa, che a' sentirí una noela bela e nuova. E de sta nuova a' v'in seguro mi; che l'è puoco che l'è fata, e daspò fata, l'è stà int'un banco arsarò, e no è mé pí vegnúa fuora nomé adesso. L'è ben vera che l'è fata de legname vegio; mo de questo a' in dessè essere pí continti, che a' sarí pí seguri de bontè. ... E se 'l ve paresse d'aver aldío un'altra fià sta sfilatuoria, no v'in para stragno, che 'l no se pò né dire né fare che 'l no sia stò pí fato. ... Né no ven che negun abia robò negun, con se pensa qualcun, che an questa sia stà robà; ché a' no

la mostressamo a tanti, mo a' la tegnissemo asconta. Se uno catesse int'un cofanazo vegio una de quele gonele che se solea portare al tempo de antighitè passò, e che 'l pano fosse bon, mo la sisa fosse desmetúa; se del pano el ne fesse cassiti e zupariegi e corsiti per i vivi, e la sisa el la lagasse per i muorti, seràvelo robare questo? Mo a' crezo de no, el serave conzar per i vivi e no tuor a negun de i muorti; ché la sisa sera' d'i muorti e 'l pano d'i vivi, e a sto muò no ghe manchera' gniente, e no ghe mancando gniente, el no ven robò' (Ruzzante, *La piovana*, pp. 5, 7). Unless otherwise indicated, all translations into English are mine.

15 Dolce dedicated the *Capitano* to the Abbot of Gonzaga with a letter of 15 April 1545, but when the work was brought out along with the *Marito* in 1547 by Giolito, the dedication was changed to read 'al virtuoso fanciullo M. Tiberio d'Armano.' This youth was apparently the son of Pietro d'Armano, a well-known actor in Venice (see D'Ancona, *Origini*, vol. 2, p. 450 n3), who first performed Dolce's tragedy *La Didone*. In the same year (1547), in fact, Tiberio d'Armano dedicated the first edition of the *Didone* to the Venetian senator Stefano Tiepolo and, in doing so, tells us that he himself played the role of Ascanio when his father performed the play in Venice during the prior carnival (1546), 'avendo il padre mio ... aperto la strada ad altrui di avvezzar le orecchie, corrotte per tanti anni dai giuochi inetti di certi moderni comici, alla gravità tragica' (Salza, *Delle commedie di Lodovico Dolce*, p. 79).

16 Fulvio appears first in Ariosto's *La Lena* (1528–9), and Fulvia as early as Bibbiena's *La Calandria* (1513), where, however, she is Calandro's wife.

17 In Plautus, the parasite Artotrogus says 'By Pollux, if only / You'd really tried, you'd have transpenetrated your arm / Through hide and guts clear down to elephant marrow' (I, 1; translated by Peter L. Smith, in Plautus, *Three Comedies*, p. 20).

18 My comments derive from a seminar on cinquecento comedy taught by Professor Clubb at Berkeley in the fall of 1973, but see her refinements on these ideas in her book *Italian Drama in Shakespeare's Time*, especially the chapter 'Italian Renaissance Comedy.'

19 For early representations in translation of Plautus and Terence in Venice, see Giorgio Padoan, *La commedia rinascimentale veneta (1433–1565)*, pp. 48–51.

20 Salza's analysis, mostly an attempt to compare elements of Dolce's play to those found in other cinquecento comedies, is found in his *Delle commedie di Lodovico Dolce*, pp. 11–69, with a brief discussion of *Il ragazzo*'s fortune in France, in particular in Pierre Larivey's *Laquais* (pp. 70–8). For Ferrini, see '*Il ragazzo di Ludovico Dolce: Rilettura.*'

21 *Commedie del Cinquecento*, vol. 2, ed. Ireneo Sanesi (1912), reprint ed. Maria Luisa Doglio (1975), here p. 207. All future references to this text are to the 1975 edition.

22 Salza is hesitant in his judgment. He writes, 'Nei particolari forse, a parer
   nostro, il Dolce ha migliorato la favola, benchè in essa possano parere un
   difetto gli amori dello Spagnuolo e di Camilla, che acquistano tanto im-
   portanza, quanta ne ha la burla a M. Cesare' (In the details perhaps, in our
   opinion, Dolce has improved the story, although the love affair between the
   Spaniard and Camilla might seem a defect, since it acquires as much importance as the trick played on M. Cesare; *Delle commedie di Lodovico Dolce*,
   p. 36).

23 'Lo scopo, che probabilmente il Machiavelli ebbe presente, di rappresentare
   una famiglia, in cui per poco entra il disordine, a causa dei capricci d'un
   padre che è sempre stato modello, e di mostrar come si può formare una
   buona famiglia, viene a mancare del tutto nel Dolce, che vuol solo far
   divertire lo spettatore e nella molteplicità delle azioni cerca guadagnarsene
   l'attenzione' (The aim that Machiavelli probably had in mind of depicting a
   family that falls into disorder because of the caprices of a father who has
   always been a model, and of demonstrating how one forms a good family, is
   lacking entirely in Dolce, who wants only to delight the spectator and tries
   to garner attention from the multiplicity of events; ibid).

24 'Ma in quest'ultima scena la corruzione è più raffinata, e più piacevolmente
   l'autore s'intrattiene a descriver minutamente i particolari, al solo scopo di
   solleticare la naturale immoralità del pubblico; il Machiavelli è più rude,
   quasi crudele, perchè egli non vuole che l'attenzione e il riso degli ascoltanti
   si fermi con diletto su quella scena nauseante' (But in this last scene the
   corruption is more refined, and the author dwells more pleasingly on
   minutely describing details, with the only goal of exciting the public's
   natural immorality. Machiavelli is more severe, almost cruel, because he
   does not want the attention and the laughter of the listeners to linger with
   delight on that nauseating scene; ibid, p. 37).

25 Doria's first and last sentences will serve as illustration: 'Io non risi mai più
   tanto, né credo mai più ridere tanto; né, in casa nostra, questa notte si è fatto
   altro che ridere. ... Io mi voglio tirare da parte per vedergli, e avere materia
   di ridere di nuovo' (I never laughed so much, nor do I think I'll ever laugh
   this much again. In our house tonight we haven't done anything but laugh. I
   want to withdraw in order to see if there is more material for laughter). I
   quote from the text edited by Aldo Borlenghi, *La Mandragola e Clizia* (Milan:
   Rizzoli–BUR, 1959), p. 135.

26 For a study of the figures mentioned, see Vincenzo De Amicis, *L'imitazione
   latina nella commedia italiana nel XVI secolo*, pp. 142ff., cited in Salza, *Delle
   commedie di Lodovico Dolce*, p. 41.

27 Salza notes that one of Dolce's satirical *capitoli* laments the fact that a graceful boy fled from his house and went to Padua ('Capitolo d'un Ragazzo a M.

Anselmi'). In the cinquecento, boys were commonly employed as servants and pages, and, in some cases, for sexual purposes. Salza cites Berni's verses to the effect that boys were safer, if one wished to avoid certain diseases: 'Attenetevi al vostro ragazzino, / Che finalmente è men pericoloso' (p. 58, citing *Il primo libro delle opere burlesche* [Utrecht, 1771], pp. 30ff.). Dolce's boy, it should be noted, at least from what he himself claims, while beautiful and learned, while keeping him warm in bed on cold nights, while in looks similar to a 'donna di palagio,' was nevertheless morally pure. His preoccupation, in fact, is that the boy not stray from the correct path and fall into the hands of a hypocrite who lives off of innocents.

28 Neither author is mentioned as a possible source in Louise George Clubb's study *Giambattista Della Porta*, although she rightly notes that the *Fantesca*'s sources are heterogeneous, and that many of the play's situations 'can claim kinship with dozens of earlier Renaissance comedies' (p. 160).

29 See *La commedia rinascimentale veneta (1433–1565)*, pp. 189–96. While discussing Dolce's comedies, Padoan also notes his frenetic activity as a translator of both Seneca and Euripides, as well as the great success of all Dolce's tragedies, whether original, *rifacimenti*, or translations (see especially pp. 194–5).

30 Interestingly, the author pretends to have revealed the plot without realizing it until afterwards. Here is how Dolce summarizes the play's action: 'Lo autor, cioè colui che l'ha ritratta dal vero, ha voluto intitolarla *Il Ragazzo*: non senza cagione, per ciò che avrete a veder tre diversi inganni in un medesimo tempo fatti a un vecchio il quale, invaghito d'una giovane di cui s'era innamorato il figliolo, credendo trovarsi la notte con lei, gli è condotto innanzi un ragazzo in abito di fanciulla, tanto simile all'amorosa che ciascuno che lunga dimestichezza non avesse con lui avuto se ne sarebbe ingannato. Il figliolo gode del suo amore; la figliola se ne fugge con uno suo amante; e la fante ancora ella, fuggendo, invola al vecchio certi argenti. Il fatto si scopre e i travagli sono grandi. Finalmente, succedendo da tutte le parti onorato matrimonio, conosciuto il ragazzo esser fratello di colei, tornata la fante con gli argenti a casa, le feste si raddoppiano da per tutto. Così, non me ne avedendo, io v'ho detto l'argomento della comedia' (The author, that is, he who drew it from the truth, wanted to entitle it the *Ragazzo*, not without reason, given that you'll see three different tricks played all at once on an old man, who, taking a fancy to a girl with whom his son had fallen in love, believing himself to be with her at night, is given a boy dressed as a girl, so similar to his beloved that anyone not being very familiar with him would be deceived. The son enjoys his love; the daughter flees with her lover; and the maid-servant, fleeing also, steals certain silver

items from the old man. The deed is discovered and the travails are many. Finally, with an honourable marriage on all parts, the boy having been recognized as her brother and the maid having returned home with the silver, the festivities are redoubled everywhere. Thus, not realizing it, I've told you the plot of the comedy; p. 208).

In reality, the question of the stolen silver is resolved somewhat differently. While the maid does return with the silver, she and the parasite leave up in the air what is going to happen to it. After having hinted that they should share in the joy, they tell the spectators not to wait around to see them knock on the door and return the stolen items, implying they are going to keep them. Marvin Herrick, in his brief summary of the play, seems to have accepted what Dolce says in the prologue (the 'servant returns the silver'), without noticing what actually occurs in the play's final scene (*Italian Comedy*, p. 114).

31 See '*Il ragazzo* di Lodovico Dolce: Rilettura,' pp. 471–2, where the critic, after noting that most of Dolce's original works are dramas, says that he wrote under the influence of Aretino. 'Come questi, dipinse alcuni aspetti della realtà contemporanea nel suo teatro e ironizzò sulla condizione della classe media di quegli anni e sui cortigiani' (Like the latter, he painted some aspects of contemporary reality in his theatre and wrote ironically about the condition of the middle class of those years and about courtiers).

I would note that those who compare Dolce to Aretino usually have only the vaguest of notions and the most common of parallels to cite. These can be summarized as follows: Like Aretino, Dolce is a modern. Dolce's *Ragazzo*, like Aretino's *Marescalco*, plays with the Plautine motif of a boy substituted for a girl. (The two works, however, are quite different.) Dolce's wise servant, Valerio, has the same name as the wise servant in Aretino's *Cortigiana*. Dolce and Aretino have a few verbal patterns in common.

Herrick is one of those who cite Aretino's earlier play as a possible source for Dolce (see *Italian Comedy*, p. 114). If the reference to an Aretine influence is made to lessen Dolce's achievement, such a claim should be taken as spurious. Since I do not deal with Herrick's comments in the text, these being quite brief, let me merely note here the critical ambivalence of his conclusion regarding the *Ragazzo*: 'Dolce made many changes in the ancient plot, but his comedy remains largely derivative. It is a pretty good play, however, and Larivey adapted it in his *Laquais*' (ibid).

Another critic has taken a different perspective from both Ferrini and Herrick, seeing instead the possibility of Dolce's having had a hand in helping construct Aretino's pedant. I refer to Christopher Cairn's *Pietro Aretino and the Republic of Venice: Researches on Aretino and his Circle in Venice,*

1527–1556, especially ch. 3, 'The *Marescalco* and the Italian Renaissance Pedant,' pp. 49–68.

32 Ferrini writes: 'Così, il dottore [Pomponino in the *Fabritia*] è parte della satira alla vuota erudizione, legata al potere di rapporti economici e di prestigio, ma senza una base socialmente definibile. Tale satira ha la sua espressione anche nel Pedante del *Ragazzo*, ma, sia il dottore sia il Pedante sono essenzialmente personaggi buffoneschi' (Thus, the doctor is part of the satire on empty erudition, tied to the power of enormous relations and of prestige, but without a definable social base. Such a satire is also expressed in the pedant of the *Ragazzo*, but the doctor and the pedant are essentially buffoonish characters; '*Il ragazzo* di Ludovico Dolce,' p. 476).

33 My contention would be simply that Dolce reflects a humorous verbal pattern used by Aretino and other writers of comedy. Ferrini's attempt to pump up the phrase's significance is ironic, since he has just referred to the pedant's inflated language. Here is what he has to say about the parallel: 'nelle parole della fantesca Belcolore, d'improvviso, l'orizzonte si allarga a tutta la città, che trascorre sotto lo sguardo dello spettatore, descritta attraverso luoghi traducibili in precise indicazioni visive, tali da potersi raffigurare nella scena in prospettiva; una città dipinta nei suo simboli ideali, ma rintracciabili, seguendo l'accurata citazione, nella realtà di una Roma non del tutto generalizzata e non del tutto di cartapesta. In tal modo, nella *Cortigiana*, la strada entra prepotentemente nella rappresentazione, in funzione della satira contemporanea e per dare spazio ai personaggi, che si alternano e s'incontrano in un moto incessante di tipi e di linguaggi diversi' (In the words of the maid-servant Belcolore, suddenly the horizon is enlarged to all the city, which flows under the gaze of the spectator, described through places translatable in precise visual indications, such as to permit their recognition in the scene in perspective, a city depicted in its ideal symbols, but traceable, following the accurate citation, in the reality of a Rome not entirely generalized and not entirely papier-mâché. In such a way, in the *Cortigiana*, the street enters overbearingly into the representation, as a function of contemporary satire and in order to create space for the characters, who alternate and meet each other in an incessant movement of types and different languages; ibid, p. 476).

34 'La polemica aretiniana contro determinati aspetti del potere ha una ripresa originale in alcune battute isolabili nel teatro dolciano, ma gli spunti, interessanti nel senso della satira, sono spesso note smagate, quasi del tutto assorbite dalla rapidità del gioco teatrale ...' (The Aretinian polemic against particular aspects of power is renewed in original fashion in some isolatable exchanges in the theatre of Dolce, but the starting-points, interesting as

satire, are often weak notes, almost completely absorbed by the rapidity of
the theatrical game; ibid).

35 The expression derives from Carlo Dionisotti, 'La guerra d'Oriente nella
letteratura veneziana del Cinquecento,' p. 213.

36 'Nel *Ragazzo*, il Dolce non ha soltanto dato spazio ai casi descritti sia pure
con facilità narrativa, ma ha considerato la commedia anche come un
meccanismo ben riuscito, sovente aperto ad impressioni, annotazioni e
soluzioni nuove. Come altri commediografi del '500, ha avuto soprattutto la
sensazione e forse la consapevolezza di creare scene da attuare e recitare con
l'ironia di un osservatore esterno, che consideri il teatro in un modo sepa-
rato, riflesso in quello reale, così come la realtà può riflettere il teatro in un
gioco intellettuale, del quale sono dimostrazione alcune battute poco usuali
dei personaggi ...

L'autore si riconosce, dunque, attivo in una situazione letteraria e storica,
divenuta sempre più statica, dopo i primi indizi di crisi, che si concluderan-
no con una involuzione dalle conseguenze sociali di un progressivo irrigidi-
mento e di un sempre maggiore isolamento delle classi al potere da quelle
popolari' (Ferrini, '*Il ragazzo* di Ludovico Dolce,' p. 479).

37 The military terminology, common also to Machiavelli's *Mandragola*, where
Ligurio is the captain (IV, 9), and the *Clizia*, where Cleandro compares the
lover at some length to a soldier (I, 2), is most likely of Plautine derivation,
perhaps through an intermediary. Giorgio Padoan (*Commedia rinascimentale
veneta*, p. 126n) says the military metaphors in Ruzzante's *Piovana* derive
from Plautus (they are 'di filiazione plautina') with a possible Ariostean
suggestion ('ma fors'anche per suggestione ariostesca'). In Dolce's case, all
these authors might be cited as possible sources, though the relationship is
not one of servile imitation, and the imagery is common enough in sixteenth-century Italy.

38 The exchange dealing with Petrarch's poetry is quite funny:

PEDANTE: Onde ben disse il lipido e laureato Francisco Petrarca poeta
florentinus nel principio d'una sua tersa cantilena: 'Roma, quamvis il mio
parlar sia indarno.'
FLAMMINIO: *Domine*, parmi che dica 'Italia,' non 'Roma.'
PEDANTE: 'Roma' vuol dire.
FLAMMINIO: Il comènto dice Italia.
PEDANTE: Forsi che tu non hai veduto quello che ha elaborato lo acume del
mio ingegno.
FLAMMINIO: Questo è vero. Ma quel 'quamvis' non è parola fiorentina.
PEDANTE: Ella è latina, che importa piú.

PEDANT: Whence the limpid and laureated Francesco Petrarca, Florentine poet, said it well in the beginning of one of his polished cantilenas: 'Rome, even though my speech may be in vain.'
FLAMMINIO: Master, I think he says 'Italy,' not 'Rome.'
PEDANT: He means 'Rome.'
FLAMMINIO: The commentary says Italy.
PEDANT: Perhaps you haven't seen what the acumen of my wit has elaborated.
FLAMMINIO: That's true. But that 'quamvis' is not a Florentine word.
PEDANT: It's Latin, which is more important.

The same type of comic misquotation is employed when the pedant cites Sannazzaro (II, 9).

39 Girolamo Ruscelli, *Delle comedie elette*, 'Annotazioni,' p. 182.

40 The criticism is that of Girolamo Ruscelli: 'La onde il quarto e il principio del quinto, ne' quali suole essere la maggiore intentione de gl'intrichi, procedono tutti quietamente, e di bene in meglio; che per certo in quanto al soggetto è cosa da fuggirsi in una Comedia': 'Annotationi,' in *Delle comedie elette*, p. 183, cited and translated by Louise George Clubb in *Italian Comedy in Shakespeare's Time*, pp. 33–4.

41 Despite this mocking of literary authorities, Dolce, as Ferrini notes, was a man of wide culture, who recognized the stabilizing influence on comedy and on 'academic' language of figures like Pietro Bembo and Pietro Aretino, both cited in *La Fabritia*. The citation, however, comes from the mouth of Invola, the servant of Luppo ruffiano (the panderer), and not from the pedant.

42 Other minor characters include the pedant's boy, Turchetto; a *sensale*, or marriage broker; Invola, the Ruffiano's servant; and a Captain of the Court accompanied by two policemen (*due sbirri*).

43 R. Terpening, *Charon and the Crossing*, p. 201.

44 In Act III, scene 15, Giulio, upon learning that his wife is pregnant by what he thinks is another man, also laments marriage and the evil nature of women (pp. 36^v–37^r).

45 The vice most criticized in the play seems to be that of avarice, typical of old men in general, and in particular of both the Greek Athanagio and the pedant from Bergamo. See Act II, scenes 5 and 7, among others. As Fabritio tells the parasite in scene 7, he may resemble his father in features, but he will not be like him in habits ('Melino, io posso somigliare a mio padre nel viso, ma sappi, ch'io non lo somiglierò ne i costumi'; p. 21^v).

46 Turchetto mocks his master by pretending to be blind. The brief fragment in
Act IV, scene 3, can serve as an indication of the humour that runs throughout the play, here created in part by the inane repetition and by the loud
calls of Turchetto:

TURCHETTO: Il Domine è quà: voglio finger di non vederlo. Chi saprebbe
insegnarmi il mio padrone?
M.POMPONINO: Tu non mi vedi perde giornate?
TUR.: Chi me lo insegna? chi me lo insegna il mio padrone?
M.P.: Dove riguardi bufolo: vogliti in quà; che mi vederai.
TUR.: Il mio da ben padrone, il mio da ben padrone chi me lo insegna?
M.P.: Questo bestiolo dee esser divenuto cieco et sordo, che non mi vede ne
sente.
TUR.: O padrone amoroso, padron savio, padron dotto dove sete voi?
M.P.: Io son quà Asinetto, io son quà Babbuino, io son quà civettina.

[TURCHETTO: The master is here. I'm going to pretend I don't see him. Who
could show me my master?
M. POMPONINO: You don't see me, you day waster?
TUR.: Who can show him to me? Who can show me my master?
M.P.: Where are you looking, you fool? Turn this way and you'll see me.
TUR.: My good master, who will show me my good master?
M.P.: This stupid beast must have become blind and deaf. He can't see or
hear me.
TUR.: O loving master, wise master, where are you learned master?
M.P.: I'm here, little ass; I'm here, blockhead; I'm here, flirt.]

47 In her article 'La realtà sociale nel teatro rinascimentale,' Gloria Rabac–
Čondrić makes the point that critics have not analysed cinquecento theatre
sufficiently in depth with an eye towards reconstructing the customs of the
people and the life of the time (pp. 508–9). Her essay, like my presentation of
Dolce's *La Fabritia*, aims to correct in part this lack of emphasis, but she
ignores Dolce, mentioning, to varying degree and without much detail,
Ariosto, Machiavelli, Ruzante, Aretino, Caro, Cecchi, Giannotti, Grazzini,
and the Dalmatian writer Marin Držić.

4: Between Lord and Lady

1 For a general introduction to the genre of Renaissance tragedy, see Marco
Ariani, *Tra classicismo e manierismo: Il teatro tragico del Cinquecento* and his

introduction to *Il teatro italiano*, vol. 2: *La tragedia del Cinquecento*, pp. vii–lxxxii; Emilio Bertana, *Storia dei generi letterari italiani: La tragedia*; Ettore Bonora, 'La Tragedia'; Louise George Clubb, *Italian Plays (1500–1700) in the Folger Library*; Benedetto Croce, 'La tragedia,' pp. 305–37; Federico Doglio, *Il teatro tragico italiano: Storia e testi del teatro tragico in Italia*; Marvin T. Herrick, *Italian Tragedy of the Renaissance*; Carmelo Musumarra, *La poesia tragica italiana nel Rinascimento*; Ferdinando Neri, *La tragedia italiana del Cinquecento*; and E. Paratore, 'Nuove prospettive dell'influsso del teatro classico nel '500,' pp. 9–95.

For the influence of Euripides, see A. Dal Pra, *L'influenza di Euripide nel teatro tragico italiano dei secoli XVI, XVII e XVIII*; and Agostino Pertusi, 'Il ritorno alle fonti del teatro greco classico: Euripide nell'Umanesimo e nel Rinascimento,' pp. 205–24. For Seneca's influence, see Marco Ariani, 'L'*Orbecche* di G. B. Giraldi e la poetica dell'orrore'; Rosario P. Armato, 'The Play Is the Thing: A Study of Giraldi's *Orbecche* and Its Senecan Antecedents'; P. Bilancini, *G.B. Giraldi e la tragedia italiana nel secolo XVI*; C. Guerrieri-Crocetti, *G.B. Giraldi ed il pensiero critico del secolo XVI*; P.R. Horne, *The Tragedies of Giambattista Cinthio Giraldi*; Jean Jacquot, *Les tragédies de Sénèque et le théâtre de la Renaissance*; and A. Angelo Milano, *Le tragedie di G.B. Giraldi*.

2 The *Thieste* included in the *Tragedie di M. Lodovico Dolce, cape, Giocasta, Didone, Thieste, Medea, Ifigenia, Hecuba, di nuovo ricorrette e ristampate* (Venice: Gabriel Giolito, 1560), a reprint of the 1543 and 1547 version, is clearly a *rifacimento* (as opposed to the direct translation of the same play, also published in 1560 in *Le tragedie di Seneca, tradotte da M. Lodovico Dolce*). The major changes consist in the deletion of some of the more abstruse mythological references and the use of a more poetic, discursive Italian.

3 *Le troiane, tragedia di M. Lodovico Dolce, recitata in Vinegia l'anno MDLXVI*. Cicogna lists this work among Dolce's original works in verse, claiming that it is different from the *Troiane* published in Dolce's translation of Seneca (1560). The difference is apparent from the title, which in the edition of translated plays appears as *Troiade*. The *Troiane*, instead, is a much freer *rifacimento*, though still clearly based on Seneca. There is a clear expansion of material; the choruses and *intermedi*, among other additions, are Dolce's own. The *intermedi*, incidentally, were accompanied by music at the play's first performance in 1566.

4 See B. Soldati, *Il collegio Mamertino e le origini del teatro gesuitico* (Torino, 1908), cited by Doglio.

5 In the prologue to his *Ifigenia* (1551), published at the end of the play in *Le tragedie di M. Lodovico Dolce* (1560) as 'La Tragedia,' after tracing the origins of the form ('Io son colei, ch'addimandaro i Greci / Tragedia; e nacqui alhor,

ch'in terra nacque / La Tirannide iniqua, e incominciaro / A estinguersi la fe, l'honesto, e'l vero' [I am she, whom the Greeks called Tragedy, and I was born when evil Tyranny came to life on earth, and faith, honesty, and truth began to die out]) and after mentioning the better practioners of the art (Sophocles and Euripides) and the fact that 'a me non piacque / D'habitar sopra il Tebro' (I didn't like living near the Tiber; perhaps a reference to Seneca?), goes on to praise the authors of *Sofonisba* (Gian Giorgio Trissino, 1515), *Rosmunda* (Giovanni Rucellai, 1516), *Antigone* (translated by Luigi Alamanni, 1533), *Orbecche* (Giovan Battista Giraldi Cinthio, 1541), 'lo scelerato amor di Macareo,' i.e., *Canace* (Sperone Speroni, 1542), and *L'Horatia* (Pietro Aretino, 1546).

Following these figures, Tragedy was lacerated by those of lesser abilities, until she decided to have recourse to Euripides 'e togliendo / Il bel, che mi fe nobile e honorata, / Lo diedi a un vostro cittadino e servo [Dolce himself]; Perche con altra lingua, et altra forma, / Com'egli suol, l'appresentasse a voi. / Quinci havete veduto pianger mesta / L'infelice Giocasta: hora vedrete / Dolersi del suo error misero padre, / E lamentarsi ad un madre e figliuola' (and taking the beautiful, which made me noble and honoured, I gave it to one of your citizens and servants, so that with another tongue and another form he might present it to you, as he is accustomed. Here you have seen sad, unhappy Giocasta cry. Now you will see a wretched father lament his error, and a mother and daughter lament).

6 I quote from *Tragedie di M. Lodovico Dolce, cape, Giocasta, Didone, Thieste, Medea, Ifigenia, Hecuba, di nuovo ricorrette e ristampate* (1560), p. 3^v.

7 Still, as Cicogna notes ('Memoria intorno la vita e gli scritti di Messer Lodovico Dolce,' p. 94), Benedetto Varchi did praise Dolce's translations from Euripides, though, of course, he says he prefers the original Greek. Cicogna says that 'ad ogni modo dà le seconde laudi al Dolce, – al qual Dolce (prosegue), non meno che all'Alamanni la fiorentina, dee non poco la lingua toscana' (at any rate, he gives the second praise to Dolce – to which Dolce [he continues] the Tuscan language owes not a little, no less than the Florentine does to Alamanni). For Varchi's comments on Dolce's tragedies, see the *Hercolano*, pp. 250–1. For Dolce's approach to translation, see also Angela Paladini, 'La tragedia secondo Lodovico Dolce,' pp. 38–42.

For the arrival in Italy of Euripides' works, see Agostino Pertusi, 'Il ritorno alle fonti del teatro greco classico: Euripide nell'Umanesimo e nel Rinascimento,' particularly pp. 206–11, and for the Latin translators pp. 211–16. Pertusi recognizes the significance of the *volgarizamenti*. As he says, 'Euripide è reso attuale, ridiventa un tragico di moda, rappresentato di nuovo nei teatri e applaudito, non certo per opera dei grecisti che l'hanno tradotto in latino, ma dei poeti italiani che non sanno il greco e che si servono delle traduzioni latine approntate dai grecisti' (Euripides is made current, becoming a fashionable tragedian, staged anew in theatres and applauded, by no means because of the Hellenists who translated him into Latin, but because of the Italian poets who know no Greek and avail themselves of the Latin translations prepared by the Hellenists; p. 217).

8 The *Thieste* of 1543 is reputed to be an 'original' work, while that included in the 1560 edition of Seneca's plays is a translation. By way of comparison, however, let me cite, first, Seneca (in both Latin and English); then, Dolce's translation of Seneca, published in 1560 in *Le tragedie di Seneca*; and, finally, the *Thieste* in the 1560 edition of Dolce's tragedies (a reprint of the 1543 version):

Seneca: 'Quis inferorum sede ab infausta extrahit / avido fugaces ore captantem cibos, / quis male deorum Tantalo vivas domos / ostendit iterum? peius inventum est siti / arente in undis aliquid et peius fame / hiante semper?' ('Who from the accursed regions of the dead haleth me forth, snatching at food which ever fleeth from my hungry lips? What god for his undoing showeth again to Tantalus the abodes of the living? Hath something worse been found than parching thirst midst water, worse than ever-gaping hunger?' [*Thyestes*, tr. Frank Justus Miller, vv. 1–6])

Dolce's translation: 'Qual furor mi costringe / A uscir fuor de l'inferno, / Ove mai sempre in darno / Io cerco le vivande, / Che mi fuggon di bocca. / Qual Dio mi riconduce / A riveder le case / Hor de la gente viva? Si può trovar quì sopra / Pena maggior, c'havere / Fame continua e sete?'

Dolce's *rifacimento*: 'Qual mi toglie furor? qual empia forza / Dal cieco Regno de l'eterno pianto? / Dove per doppia mal di tempo in tempo / Il desiato frutto, e l'acqua chiara / Da le mie labbra s'allontana e fugge? / Qual Dio, per crescer doglia al mio tormento, / Di novo a riveder Tantalo adduce / I lieti alberghi de la gente viva? / Deh puossi quì trovar pena maggiore, / Ch'arder sempre nel cor di fame e sete?'

Clearly, the *rifacimento* is simply a freer translation, the additions at times redundant, serving merely to fill out the lines, which change from *settenari* in the translation to *endecasillabi* in the reworking. Nevertheless, as Angela Paladini notes 'se a noi appare una libera traduzione – all'autore certamente doveva apparire opera assolutamente originale' (if to us it seems a free translation, to the author certainly it must have seemed an absolutely original work; ' "Ornamenti" e "Bellezze," ' p. 40).

9 Today, most classical scholars deny Seneca's authorship of the *Octavia*, accepting as his only the nine other extant tragedies.

10 Musumarra writes, 'Un grande distacco s'era operto, durante lo svolgimento letterario del genere tragico, tra autori e pubblico, ed era un distacco che i poeti sentivano di dover eliminare, almeno in parte, facendo salve le esigenze retoriche degli uni e quelle realistiche dell'altro. Per questo molti autori tragici del sec. XVI tradussero le tragedie greche con la coscienza di creare opera originale, e sostituirono il proprio nome a quello del primo autore' (A large gap had formed, during the literary development of the tragic genre, between authors and the public, and it was a gap that the poets felt they needed to eliminate, at least in part, while preserving the rhetorical exigencies of one side [the authors] and the realistic needs of the other. This is why many sixteenth-century authors translated Greek tragedies with the consciousness of creating an original work and substituted their own name for that of the first author; *La poesia tragica italiana nel Rinascimento*, p. 70).

11 As Cicogna notes ('Memoria intorno la vita e gli scritti di Messer Lodovico Dolce,'), we have a letter of Carlo Zancarolo, dated 5 March 1549, in which he laments not having been able to attend the representation of the *Giocasta*.

12 Agostino Pertusi discusses Dolce's translations of Euripides in 'Il ritorno alle fonti del teatro greco classico,' pp. 219–21. As he notes, 'si può ritenere per certo che le tragedie euripidee del Dolce non sono vere e proprie traduzioni, ma rimaneggiamenti poetici secondo il gusto del tempo e attraverso le versioni latine' (one can certainly maintain that Dolce's Euripidean tragedies are not actually true translations, but poetic rearrangements following the taste of the time and the Latin version; p. 220). His final judgment mirrors that of Ferdinando Neri: 'Quanto alle tragedie del Dolce io credo che si possa sottoscrivere il giudizio del Neri: anche se l'autore "a noi moderni" è "reso un po' antipatico ... da quella sua sfacciata prontezza nel voler far di tutto, nel rimaneggiare tutto, nell'imporre sonori titoli ed attributi ad alcuni lavoracci affrettati, e compiuti soltanto per il commercio, non era privo d'ogni gusto, e nella drammatica giungeva a sentire la forza di alcuni caratteri." In ogni caso ... gli si deve riconoscere il merito di aver introdotto rappresentazioni più o meno regolari di tragedie "classiche" a Venezia' (As for Dolce's tragedies, I believe that one can subscribe to Neri's judgment: even if the author seems 'a bit antipathetic to us moderns because of his brazen willingness to want to do everything, in rearranging everything, in placing sonorous titles and attributes to some sloppy works done in haste and only for commercial reasons, he was not lacking in taste, and in dramaturgy he managed to grasp the strength of some characters.' In any case, one must pay him the merit of having introduced more or less regular stagings of 'classical' tragedies in Venice; *La tragedia italiana del Cinquecento*, p. 221).

13 Dolce edited one of Burchiella's poems written in octaves – *I fatti e le prodezze di Manoli Blessi Strathioto* (Venice: Gabriel Giolito, 1561) – and praises him in the dedicatory letter to Giacomo Contarino. Burchiella, Dolce tells us, was a dancer, singer, poet, and musician, as well as a merchant fluent in several languages. Along with his brother Armonio, he instituted an Accademia di Musica in Venice (Cicogna, 'Memoria intorno la vita e gli scritti di Messer Lodovico Dolce,' p. 136). See also the article by Gino Damerini, 'Il sodalizio artistico di Lodovico Dolce con Antonio Molino detto il Burchiella per la Marianna e le Troiane.'

14 Cicogna cites Dolce's comments regarding those in attendance, who were 'egregi cittadini, parte de' quali con sommissima laude di dottrina e di eloquenza trattano le diverse cause che occorrono dinanzi ai tribunali ed alle corone de' giudici, e parte ancora esercitano diversi ufficii civili onorata-mente' (eminent citizens, some of whom deal, with highest praise for their knowledge and eloquence, with cases in front of the courts and before judges, and others of whom carry out, with honour, diverse civic functions; 'Memoria intorno la vita e gli scritti di Messer Lodovico Dolce,' p. 160, from the dedicatory letter to Giovanni de' Martini). Cicogna claims the play was performed by Antonio Molino and Giorgio Gradenigo (see pp. 103 and 160), but the dedication attests otherwise.

15 *Jocasta: a tragedie written in Greke by Euripides; translated and digested into acte by George Gascoygne and Francis Kinwelmarshe of Grayes Inne, and there by them presented, 1566* (half-title, pp. [71]–164), in George Gascoigne, *A hundreth sundrie flowres bounde up in one small poesie* ... (London: Imprinted for Richard Smith, 1573). The *Giocasta* in Italian is Dolce's version of Euripides' *Phoenis-sae (The Phoenician Women)*.

16 A quick search of various databases, such as that of the Modern Language Association, reveals that, for Italian drama of the Renaissance, at least 90 per cent of the works deal with comedy and other related forms.

17 'Lacking dramatic instinct, these Italian scholars might have redeemed their essential feebleness by acute analysis of character. Their tragedies might at least have contained versified studies of motives, metrical essays on the leading passions. But we look in vain for such compensations. Stock tyrants, conventional lovers, rhetorical pedants, form their *dramatis personae*': John Addington Symonds, *Renaissance in Italy: Italian Literature*, Part II, p. 114. The English critic later adds: 'These tragedies were the literary manufacture of scholars, writing in no relation of reciprocity with the world of action or the audience of busy cities. Applying rules of Aristotle and Horace, travestying Sophocles and Euripides, copying the worst faults of Seneca, patching, boggling, rehandling, misconceiving, devising petty traps instead of plots,

mistaking bloodshed and brutality for terror, attending to niceties of diction, composing commonplace sentences for superfluous Choruses, intent on everything but the main points of passion, character, and action, they produced the dreariest *caput mortuum* of unintelligent industry which it is the melancholy duty of historians to chronicle' (pp. 116–17).

18 An earlier version of this section appeared in print in both English and Italian, in *Forum Italicum* 15/2–3 (1981), 153–70, and in *Il Rinascimento: Aspetti e problemi attuali*, Atti del X Congresso dell'Associazione Internazionale per gli Studi di Lingua e Letteratura Italiana, Belgrade, 17–21 April 1979, ed. Vittore Branca, Claudio Griggio, Marco e Elisanna Pecoraro, Gilberto Pizzammiglio, Eros Sequi, pp. 651–65 (Florence: Olschki, 1982).

19 According to the Aristotelian theorists and commentators of the Counter-Reformation, tragic figures must be of the highest rank (*praestantiores*), since the seriousness of tragedy requires dignified figures. From the moral nobility of Aristotle, however, cinquecento critics passed to the more narrow nobility of illustrious birth, influenced perhaps by a long line of writers from Theophrastus to Evanthius-Donatus to Isidore of Seville. See Joel Elias Spingarn, *A History of Literary Criticism in the Renaissance*, pp. 63–5.

20 See Marvin T. Herrick, *Comic Theory in the Sixteenth Century*, pp. 145–6. According to Baxter Hathaway (*The Age of Criticism: The Late Renaissance in Italy*, pp. 144–5), Robortelli commenced his treatment of the idea that a figure should be exemplar or universal with Aristotle's recommendation that character traits be heightened. The tragic poet should provide an absolute example of the trait to be described, such as wrath. Rather than delineating an individual with exact particulars, one should look to nature for ideal types.

21 Lorenzo writes of world-order in *Capitolo* I, among other places (cf. *Selve d'amore* I, 9). His most telling terzine are the following four: 'Bellissimo Architetto, il mondo bello / fingendo prima nell'eterna mente, / fatto hai questo all'immagine di quello. // Ciascuna parte perfetta esistente / nel grado suo, alto Signor, comandi, / che assolva il tutto ancor perfettamente. // Tu gli elementi a' propri luoghi mandi, / legandoli con tal proporzione, / che l'un dall'altro non disiunghi o spandi. // Da te, primo Fattor, la vita piglia / ogni animale ancor di minor vita, / benché più vile: questa è pur tua famiglia' (Most beautiful Architect, envisioning first in your eternal mind the beautiful world, you made this one in the image of that. O lofty Lord, you command each part, existing perfectly in its place, to accomplish everything perfectly. You send the elements to their proper place, binding them with such proportion that none is disjoined or scattered from the other. From you, first Maker, every creature takes its life, even the lesser forms of

life, although baser: this is still your family; I, stanza 7–9 and 17; *Tutte le opere: Scritti spirituali*, pp. 51–2.

22 In his *Introducción del Símbolo de la Fe*, Fray Luis de Granada discusses the 'granada' in dealing with the 'admirable providencia para la conservación de las frutas' (admirable providence for the preservation of fruit; I, x, 3). The pomegranate illustrates the relationship between macrocosm and microcosm: 'Pues el artificio de una hermosa granada ¿cuánto nos declara la hermosura y artificio del Criador?' (Then the artifice of a beautiful pomegranate, does it not demonstrate the beauty and artifice of the Creator?). Among the notable elements of the fruit is that 'mas dentro della están repartidos y asentados los granos por tal orden, que ningun lugar, por pequeño que sea, queda desocupado y vacío' (further inside of it, the seeds are distributed and arranged with such order that no place, no matter how small, remains unoccupied and empty; *Obras del v. p. m. fray Luis de Granada*, in *Biblioteca de Autores Españoles*, VI, 208).

23 As Baxter Hathaway notes, 'The man of the Renaissance believed in astrology – in an actual causal relation between the macrocosm and the microcosm and in the influence of stellar bodies on our lives' (*The Age of Criticism*, p. 402).

24 For a study of the idea of order in the age of Shakespeare, Donne, and Milton, see E.M.W. Tillyard's *The Elizabethan World Picture*, pp. 9–17 and *passim*. The Greek *Corpus hermeticum*, translated for the first time into Latin by Marsilio Ficino in 1463, is also infused with these ideas, as is the Latin *Asclepius*, for which see the translation of Brian P. Copenhaver, *Hermetica*, p. 91, among others.

25 'Almo celeste raggio, / de la cui santa luce / s'adorna il cielo e si ristora il mondo, / il cui certo viaggio / sì belle cose adduce, / che il viver di qua giù si fa giocondo, / perchè sendo ritondo, / infinito ed eterno, / il dì dopo la sera, e dopo primavera / mena la state, e poi l'autunno e il verno / onde la terra e il mare / s'empie di cose preziose e rare; / menaci un giorno fuore, / che non sia tanto carco, / come son questi, di soverchi affani' (vv. 596–611). My source is *La tragedia classica dalle origini al Maffei*, pp. 66–7.

26 '[C]hè l'avvenir ne la virtù divina / è posto, il cui non cognito costume / fa 'l nostro antiveder privo di lume' (vv. 2090–2).

27 '[C]osì 'l fil de' mortali / Dalle celeste sfere, / Onde legato pende, / Si tronca 'n mille modi' (pp. 176–7). I am reminded of Lucian's dialogue *Charon* in which Hermes points out the Fates spinning the threads of life. The threads seem cobwebs, from which, like puppets, hang the citizens of earth. See *Lucian*, II, 431.

28 I refer to *Le tragedie di M. Gio. Battista Giraldi Cinthio, nobile ferrarese ...*, pp. 100–2. The editor supplies a period after each ten-line stanza, instead of

a semicolon, and also neglects to mark off the first line of the sixth stanza. All future page numbers in the text referring to *Orbecche* are from this source.

29 'Et al moto del primo / Ciascun de gli altri il suo camino regge, / Nè mai da l'ordin certo alcun si parte, / Pur per un picciol pelo, / Dal più sublime cerchio infino a l'imo. / Onde con sì bel studio, e con tant'arte / Del Sol la vaga luce, / Chiede a la notte, e 'l dì doppò n'adduce' (p. 100). Could the text be emended by substituting 'cede' (yields) for 'chiede' (calls) or is this merely a *lectio facilior*? Cf. the use of the verb *cedere* in note 34.

30 'Perciò con tanta fè succede al verno / La bella Primavera, / E l'Autunno a l'Estate, / E l'honor, che dal gel levato gli era, / Rihanno i campi e frondi, e frutti et herbe' (pp. 101–2).

31 'Ben è vana, e fugace / questa felicità nostra mortale, / ch'un ombra è de l'eterna, / ... / Dunque a quella immortale, / ch'è là dov'è il signor che 'l ciel governa, / chiunque il ver discerna, / del veloce pensier spiegar dee l'ale, / e lasciar questa frale / qui godere a gli sciocchi / cui le cose terrene appannan gli occhi' (p. 215).

32 My source is *Teatro italiano antico*, vol. 4, pp. 42–3.

33 'Sta col cor nubiloso, e 'l ciglio grave; / E 'l sol de' suoi begli occhi / In pianto si distilla.' I quote from the text found in *Teatro italiano o sia scelta di tragedie per uso della scena*, vol. 1, p. 320.

34 'Ma non sempre sotterra / Stan Febo, o sua sorella: / Cedono le pruine, e 'l pigro gelo / A più graditi fiori: / Dopo gli ardenti soli / S'orna Pomona il crine / De' più graditi frutti' (ibid, p. 320).

35 Dolce's *Marianna* has both a detached Terentian prologue, delivered by 'La Tragedia,' and an integrated Grecian one, spoken by 'Plutone.' In the first prologue, Dolce asserts that he will *not* follow Aristotle in all things because, though the philosopher left rules, he himself was no poet. Nevertheless, with a reference to appropriate characters, Tragedy says she brings grief and death 'O di Tiranni, o di Re giusti, oppressi / Da nimica Fortuna, o di Reine; / Che di passar nel volgo non mi cale' (either of tyrants or of just kings or queens, weighed down by enemy fortune, for I do not care to walk among the common crowd; *Teatro italiano antico*, vol. 5, p. 198). Future page references in the text are to this edition.

36 For a study of this motif, see Gustavo Costa's *La leggenda dei secoli d'oro nella letteratura italiana*.

37 'Prima senno, valor, bontà, e fortezza / Alzava l'uomo a la regale altezza. / Or forza, e crudeltate, / Tradimenti, rapine, arti et inganni / (O te misera etate) / Pongon più d'un sopra gli aurati scanni' (Earlier, wisdom, valour, goodness, and fortitude lifted man to regal heights. Now, strength and

cruelty, treason, theft, craftiness, and deceit [O, you wretched age] place more than one on golden thrones; pp. 297–8).

38 P.R. Horne, in his fine study *The Tragedies of Giambattista Cinthio Giraldi*, makes the claim, clearly mistaken, that Dolce's *Marianna* is one of the small number of sixteenth-century tragedies that imitated Giraldi's happy ending (p. 16 n2). Horne's point is that few people imitated Giraldi's *fin lieto*, a claim that is only strengthened by removing the *Marianna* from the list of those few plays that do end happily.

39 It is not true, as Francesco Flamini claims, that 'il poligrafo veneziano mette in iscena personaggi che non sentono nè si commuovono, ma solo ragionano o predicano retoricamente' (the Venetian poligrafo places on the stage characters who do not feel or are touched, but who only reason and preach rhetorically; *Il Cinquecento*, p. 453). Flamini criticizes Dolce for not saying why Herod repents, yet to provide such a detailed exposition would, in my opinion, decrease the tragic tone with which the play (excluding the last brief chorus) so effectively closes. In response to the critic's statements that 'Il Canello in questa tragedia scoprì molte belle e buone cose: ad esempio, in Erode un embrione d'Otello, in Marianne un primo profilo di Desdemona. Il nostro sguardo è molto meno acuto' (Canello discovered many beautiful and good things in this tragedy; for example, in Herod an embryo of Othello, in Marianne a first profile of Desdemona. Our gaze is much less sharp), one can only agree with Flamini's last comment on his own short-sightedness. That others, like Canello, attempt to elevate the play by seeing in it embryonic forms of a later greater poet is understandable, but also to be regretted. The play stands on its own, not only for the 'psicologia netta-mente delineata dei due protagonisti Marianne ed Erode' (psychology clearly delineated of the two protagonists Marianne and Herod; Umberto Renda and Piero Operti, *Dizionario storico della letteratura italiana*, p. 401), but also for the excellently handled minor characters, especially the counsellor and the tyrant's captain.

5: From Imitation to Emulation

1 In his *Discorsi ... intorno al comporre de i romanzi, delle comedie, e delle tragedie, e di altre maniere di poesie*, p. 225, Giambattista Giraldi Cinthio cites both works of Homer as examples of tragedies: 'le [tragedie] infelici sono piu simili alla Iliade, et le liete alla Odissea, si per lo argumento, come per la mescolanza delle persone, che parue c'Homero in quiste due compositioni ci uolesse cosi dare l'essempio dell'una et dell'altra Tragedia: ... onde si vede quanto si si-ano ingannati coloro c'hanno detto che la Iliade ci da la forma della Trage-

dia, et l'Odissea quella della Comedia, dandoci insieme amendue l'essempio della Tragedia: quella della Tragedia del fine infelice: questa di quella di fin felice' (the tragedies with sad endings are closer to the *Iliad* and the tragedies with happy endings to the *Odyssey*, both as regards the subject-matter and the mixing of characters, for it seems that, in these two compositions, Homer wanted to give us an example of both types of tragedies. From this, one sees how much those people have deceived themselves who said that the *Iliad* gives us the form of tragedy, and the *Odyssey* that of comedy, since both give us an example of tragedy – the *Iliad* of tragedy with an unhappy ending, and the *Odyssey* of that with a happy ending; cited by Louise George Clubb, *Giambattista Della Porta. Dramatist*, pp. 88–9).

2 Without referring to Aristotle, Giambattista Giraldi makes the same point in the prologue to his tragedy *Didone*, where he comments on epic, first Homer and then Virgil, as the source of tragic subjects and on the moral aim of poetry: 'Cercaro tutti que' Poeti antichi, / Che degni fur di sì honorato nome, / Di porci innanzi una ben vera imago / De la vita miglior, co' lor Poemi, / Tal fù il Greco maggior', Onde poi gli altri / Tolser, come da fonte alti soggetti, / Questi l'ira cantò del forte Achille, / Con lunghi versi, e i vari error d'Ulisse, / Onde poi gli altri, che mostrare in fatto / Volsero quel, ch'egli narrato havea, / Trasser' vari argomenti di Tragedie, / E l'esposero in scena, à gli occhi altrui, / Per purgar l'humane alme col terrore, / E, con compassion de gli altrui casi, / Da la vana ridurle à miglior vita. / Soccesse al Greco il Mantoan divino, / Per cui bocca parlò Febo, e le Muse. / ... / Dunque, com'altri già tolse ad Homero / Varij argomenti di Tragedie antiche, / Fra molti, c'hor potuti havria il Poeta / Nostro tor da Vergilio, ha tolto questo / Soggetto, onde composta ha la Tragedia, / Di c'hoggi devete esser spettatori' (All those ancient poets who were worthy of the honoured name tried, with their poems, to place before us a truly good image of the better life. Such did the greatest Greek, from whom afterwards, the others took, as from a fount, lofty subjects. This one sang the anger of strong Achilles, in lengthy verses, and the various wanderings of Ulysses, whence, afterwards, others, who wanted to show in fact what he had narrated, took various subjects for tragedies and presented them on stage to the eyes of others, in order to purge human souls with terror, and, out of compassion for the misfortunes of others, lead them back from a vain to a better life. The divine Mantuan followed the Greek, through whose mouth Phoebus and the Muses spoke. Well then, as others took from Homer various subjects for ancient tragedies, our poet, from the many subjects that he could have taken from Virgil, took this one, whence he has composed the tragedy of which today you must be spectators). See the *Didone* in *Le tragedie di M. Gio. Battista*

Giraldi Cinthio, nobile ferrarese, pp. 7–8. (Each of the nine tragedies in this volume is paginated separately.)

3 As Robert Elson Turner notes, 'C'est un sujet qui est ... bien caractéristique du XVIe siècle. Les premiers tragiques italiens et français avaient ben compris qu'Aristote recommandait que l'on allât chercher des intrigues chez Homère. Or, Virgile étant à leur avis 'le meilleur ouvrage d'Homère', ils voulurent dramatiser des épisodes de l'Enéide, où ils ne trovèrent que le quatrième livre à leur goût' (This is a subject that is ... very characteristic of the sixteenth century. The first Italian and French tragedians clearly understood that Aristotle recommended seeking one's plots in Homer. Now, since Virgil, in their opinion, was 'the better work of Homer,' they wanted to dramatize episodes from the *Aeneid*, where they found the fourth book to their liking; *Didon dans la tragédie de la Renaissance italienne et française*, p. 7).

For the development and later evolution of the Dido story, I refer the reader to the many classical encyclopedias and to works such as those by Maria Rosa Lida de Malkeil, *Dido en la literatura española. Su retrato y defensa*, and Eberhard Leube, *Fortuna in Karthago; Die Aeneas–Dido–Mythe Vergils in den romanischen Literaturen vom 14. bis zum 16. Jahrhundert*. For a recent analysis of Dido's suffering and abandonment as a model for women poets of the Italian Renaissance, see Patricia Phillippy, ' "*Altera Dido*": The Model of Ovid's *Heroides* in the Poems of Gaspara Stampa and Veronica Franco,' pp. 1–18, and for a study that deals more broadly with the theme of abandonment, Lawrence Lipking, *Abandoned Women and Poetic Tradition*.

4 For the date of Giraldi's *Didone*, see P.R. Horne, *The Tragedies of Giambattista Cinthio Giraldi*, pp. 17 and 24. For an edition of the *Lettera sulla 'Didone,'* see *Il teatro italiano: La tragedia del Cinquecento*, ed. Marco Ariani, vol. 2, pp. 956–67, or the *Trattati di poetica e retorica del Cinquecento*, ed. Bernard Weinberg, vol. 1, pp. 471–86.

5 For a comparative study of all three plays, in addition to Etienne Jodelle's *Didon se sacrifiant* (1558–60), see Robert Turner's *Didon dans la tragédie de la Renaissance italienne et française*. Turner attempts to prove through a comparison of similar verses that Dolce *probably* had access to the plays of both Alessandro Pazzi and Giraldi. Regarding their comparative success, Turner notes that 'si nous excluons l'*Obecche* [*sic*], il est certain que les tragédies du Dolce furent mieux connues au XVIe siècle que celles du Giraldi' (If we exclude the *Orbecche*, the tragedies of Dolce were certainly better known in the sixteenth century than those of Giraldi; p. 51). Corinne Lucas focuses on the depiction of Aeneas in all three plays, with the goal of analysing each author's attitude towards the myths of antiquity, and finds a noticeable

evolution in little more than twenty years ('*Didon. Trois réécritures tragiques du livre IV de l'Eneide dans le théâtre italien du XVIe siècle*').

6 The author himself, of course, favours the perceptions of the male. As he comments, 'coniugium vocat; hoc praetexit nomine culpam' (she calls it marriage and with that name veils her sin; *Aeneid* IV, 172). All quotations from the *Aeneid*, including translations, come from vol. 1 of the Loeb Library edition of Virgil, with an English translation of H. Rushton Fairclough.

7 As regards the popularity of the *Aeneid*, Corinne Lucas notes that 67 editions of his works appeared between the *editio princeps* of 1469 and 1523, for which she cites Giuliano Mambelli, *Gli annali delle edizioni virgiliane* (Florence: Olschki, 1954). L. Febvre, in turn, has counted 161 editions in the fifteenth century, and 263 in Latin in the sixteenth, with 72 in Italian, 27 in French, and 5 in German (*L'Apparition du livre* [Paris: Albin Michel, 1971], pp. 372, 379). In the period dating from 1470 to 1599, Craig Kallendorf counts 124 Venetian editions of Virgil, with another 7 appearing in Treviso, Verona, and Vicenza (*A Bibliography of Venetian Editions of Virgil, 1470–1599*).

8 Of Pazzi's work, Federico Doglio says 'è testimonianza della sua personalità di studioso attento a ripensamenti fedeli ma incapace di autentica invenzione; la tragedia resta nei limiti di un dotto ricalco, i suoi personaggi vivono nell'eco virgiliana che li sovrasta e non riescono ad acquistare vita propria e rinnovata' (it is a testament to his personality as a scholar intent on faithful rethinkings but incapable of authentic invention. The tragedy remains in the limits of a learned tracing; its characters live in the Virgilian echo that hangs over them, and do not succeed in gaining a renewed life of their own; *Il teatro tragico italiano: Storia e testi del teatro tragico in Italia*, p. xxxix).

9 See *Le tragedie metriche di Alessandro Pazzi de' Medici*, ed. Angelo Solerti, pp. 6 and 30. All quotations from Pazzi's *Dido in Cartagine* are taken from this edition, although I have modernized the spelling of *u* to *v*.

10 For an extended analysis of the metres of Greek tragedy, see A.M. Dale, *The Lyric Metres of Greek Drama*.

11 In his preface, he writes: 'Quanto alli versi che ho usato in epse, maxime quelli che sono in loco degli antiqui tragici conosco manifestamente, che offenderanno nelle prima giunta il lectore, parendo non solo nuovi et inusitati (come certo sono) ma ancora aspri, et forse inepti' (As for the verses that I have used in this, especially those replacing the ancient tragic [metres], I clearly recognize that they will initially offend the reader, seeming not only new and unusual (as they certainly are) but also harsh, and perhaps inept; p. 49). Later readers criticized not only the verse, but also the language of Pazzi's plays. For Benedetto Varchi, 'oltre la misura de' versi di dodici

sillabe, e ancora tredici, che a pochissimi piaceva, vi notammo infino in quel tempo molti errori d'intorno alla lingua' (beyond the measure of the verses of twelve, and even thirteen, syllables, which pleased very few, we noted even at that time many errors as regards language; *Lezioni*, p. 681, cited in *Le tragedie metriche di Alessandro Pazzi de' Medici*, ed. Angelo Solerti, p. 23).

While Pazzi might have preferred to have used prose – 'havendo visto per experientia che li spectacoli che si recitano hoggi composti in quella specie di versi tanto sonori, sono manco grato, che quelli, che si recitano composti in prosa' (having seen by experience that the spectacles recited today, in that sort of sonorous verse, are less pleasing than those recited in prose; *Le tragedie*, p. 50) – he felt that the solemnity of tragedy required verse.

12 For Pazzi's life, see Corinne Lucas, '*Didon*. Trois réécritures tragiques du livre IV de l'Eneide dans le théâtre italien du XVIe siècle,' pp. 560–1, n11.

13 For the problem of creative interpretation and imitation in the context of Renaissance translation of the classical tragedians, see Carmelo Musumarra, *La poesia tragica italiana nel Rinascimento*, ch. 3, 'Imitatori e traduttori: Alamanni, Martelli, Rucellai' (pp. 67–91), as well as his comments in ch. 1, 'La poetica del Rinascimento e la tragedia' (pp. 21–5).

14 Greek theatre usually consisted of the following parts: a *prologos*, invented by Thespis and defined by Aristotle as anything that takes place before the chorus appears; the *parodos*, or the appearance of the chorus; the first *episode*, with dialogue in iambic trimetre; the first *stasimon*, or choral interlude in varied Doric and Aeolic lyric metres, usually accompanied by music; followed by up to four or five other *episodes* and *stasimons*, until the *exodos*, when all exit. Turner points out that in Pazzi's play we actually have five acts, with the following divisions: Act I, 338 verses; Act II, 337; Act III, 337; Act IV, 316; and Act V, 439.

15 As the shade of Sychaeus puts it, Dido will die within the span of two days: 'la cui vita tronca / da te stessa finir vedo avanti il sole / due volte all'orizzonte salito torni' (whose life, cut off by you yourself, I see end before the sun returns two times above the horizon; pp. 59–60).

16 The Dantesque commentator, Guido da Pisa, flourished in the first half of the fourteenth century. Chapter 2 of his *Fiore d'Italia*, written sometime after 1337, was dedicated to 'I fatti d'Enea' and was so popular that it circulated independently. Ravisius Textor (Jean Tixier de Ravisi) was a French humanist. Born in Saint-Saulge (Nivernais) around 1480, he was a professor of rhetoric in Navarre, and in 1520 became rector of the University of Paris. Noted for his works on Latin language, he died in 1524. Niccolò Perotti (or Perotto), born in Fano in 1429, became archbishop of Siponto in 1458 and died at Sassoferrato on 14 December 1480.

17 Or, as Corinne Lucas puts it in '*Didon*. Trois réécritures tragiques du livre IV de l'*Eneide* dans le théâtre italien du XVIe siècle' (p. 563n), 'L'invention du héros Iarbas pourrait donc bien révéler que l'intrigue entre Didon et Enée manque de substance dramatique' (the invention of the hero Iarbas could thus well reveal that the intrigue between Dido and Aeneas lacks dramatic substance). She goes on to call Iarbas the true hero of the play, from a structural point of view, and adds that he also represents 'un modèle culturel chevaleresque propre à son temps: l'amoureux sincère doublé du chevalier au coeur généreux' (a chivalric cultural model appropriate to his time: the sincere lover doubled with the knight of generous heart; pp. 564–5). All the positive elements (justice, valour, and grandeur of soul) and the moral of the play, she says, are expressed through him (p. 564).

18 For a brief discussion of Seneca's influence on cinquecento tragedy, see E. Paratore, 'L'influenza della letteratura latina da Ovidio ad Apuleio nell'età del Manierismo e del Barocco,' in particular pp. 290ff., in addition to the sources cited above in note 1 to chapter 4.

19 After saying she fears heaven, whose fury towards her the dream has foreshown, Dido laments her betrayal of her dead husband: 'a te miser Sicheo rompendo la fede / sprezando l'honorata mia fama antiqua. / Onde hor misera, et in odio sono a me stessa / et benchè i Re inimici in me coniu- rati / non tema, pur mi preme la conscientia, / la vita mia colpevole, che dia lor causa / per me poco honorata di tanta guerra' (breaking my faith to you, wretched Sychaeus, scorning my ancient honoured fame. Whence now I am wretched and hate myself, and, though not fearing the enemy kings con- spired against me, still my conscience weighs on me and my guilty life, which gave them a cause to wage so much war to my dishonour; pp. 65–6).

20 Robert Turner finds Pazzi's translation of his various sources to be that of a schoolboy (*Didon dans la tragédie de la Renaissance italienne et française*, p. 18). Here he says, 'Et tout cela est rendu par notre dramaturge avec une fidélité pénible et de la façon la moins dramatique qu'on puisse imaginer' (And all this is rendered by our dramatist with a painful fidelity and in the least dramatic manner that one can imagine; p. 20). Pazzi translates all, some- times with 'un verbiage insupportable' (p. 20). Turner's conclusion is that Pazzi's work is 'une traduction de troisième ordre' (p. 22).

21 See, for example, the Chorus's description of the Trojans' preparations for departure, where the hectic activity is captured through an effective repetition of *chi*, reminiscent of Dante's description of the Arsenale in Venice or Poliziano's later depiction of the hunt in the *Stanze per la giostra*, although in Pazzi the verses ultimately lack the smooth flow of the better poets.

22 Turner refers to the scene between Jarba and Mercury as one that develops 'avec leur concours une intrigue originale' (*Didon dans la tragédie de la Renaissance italienne et française*, p. 22), but it is hardly worth praising, being on the whole rather pedestrian. The use of stichomythia is particularly banal (for which see pp. 87–8).

23 I might note in passing that, as in Virgil, Dido next has recourse to magic arts, a moment which brings to the page a series of traditional *adynata*: ' "costei vedrai, sorella, con le arti sue / fermar il corso a i fiumi, nel cel le stelle / indietro rivoltare, i nocturni spirti / constringer, sotto i piedi la terra commovere" ' ('You will see her, sister, stop the flow of rivers with her arts, turn back the stars in the sky, constrain nocturnal spirits, move the earth beneath her feet'; p. 99). The Virgilian *adynata* were perhaps the best known, having been imitated throughout the Middle Ages, when they were often used to manifest the reversal of the entire order of nature, developing in time into the motif of the world upside down. By the twelfth century, Virgil's *adynata* were supplemented by those of Ovid and the Roman satirists, for which see Ernst Robert Curtius, *European Literature and the Latin Middle Ages*, pp. 95–8. The topos has been studied by others, including Galen D. Row, 'The *Adynaton* as a Stylistic Device,' and Paolo Cherchi, 'Gli "Adynata" dei trovatori,' but much remains to be done as far its utilization in all genres of Renaissance literature.

24 Corinne Lucas, with reference to A. Pertusi, 'Il ritorno alle fonti del teatro greco classico: Euripide nell'Umanesimo e nel Rinascimento,' makes the point that in the early part of the sixteenth century Euripides tended to replace Seneca as the source of horror. She cites, in particular, the *Medea*, *The Trojan Women*, and *The Bacchae* ('*Didon*. Trois réécritures tragiques du livre IV de l'*Eneide* dans le théâtre italien du XVIe siècle,' p. 569n).

25 Giraldi writes, 'Quanto alla introduzione degli dèi che parlano nella trage-dia, io dico prima che, pigliando questo soggetto da Vergilio, ho tenuto quell'ordine in legarlo e nello scioglierlo ... ch'egli ha tenuto in menare a fine quella sua finta favola; né maggior numero de dèi né minore vi ho posto ch'egli posto vi abbia' (As for the introduction of gods who speak in the tragedy, I say first that, taking this subject from Virgil, I have kept that order in binding and releasing them that he kept in guiding to a conclusion his feigned story; nor have I place there a greater or a lesser number of gods than he did; *Lettera sulla Didone*, as cited in *La tragedia del Cinquecento*, ed. Marco Ariani, vol. 1, p. 958).

26 Let me cite the following as examples: In Act III, scene 4, Enea, after his encounter with Mercurio says, 'Egli è ben ver, che, prima ch'avenisse, / Fra me, e Didone quel, ch'è avenuto hoggi, / Io avrei volentieri haver veduto /

Quel che di me tu statuito havessi' (It is indeed true that before what happened to me and Dido today occurred, I would willingly have seen to that which you today have prescribed for me; p. 71); in Act III, scene 6, Dido's *Cameriera* laments what Aeneas is doing: 'Questo dì hà giunto à la Reina mia, / Con infelice sorte, il Re Troiano, / E da lui la sciorrà questo dì stesso' (This day has joined the Trojan king to my queen, with unhappy fate, and it will loosen her from him this same day; p. 80); in Act IV, scene 3, Dido laments that Aeneas hasn't kept his word for even one day, since he is abandoning her 'nulla curando fè, nè il Matrimonio, / Pur'hoggi cominciato, oime, fra noi' (not caring for faith, nor for the matrimony just begun today, alas, between us; p. 97); and finally, in Act V, scene 3, Anna refers again to 'tutte le cose avenute hoggi' (all the things that have happened today; p. 117).

27 Giraldi expresses the play's thematic contrasts and its moral scope as follows: 'Quivi Enea, conformandosi col fato, / *La ragion*, ch'occupata era dal *senso*, / Ripiglierà per guida, e ad ubidire / Si disporra al Signor, che regge il Cielo. / Ma sospinta Didon dal *van disio*, / Da desperation fia interna vinta. / Or piacciavi benigni Spettatori / Udir questo soccesso, che il Poeta / Ad utile comun conduce in scena, / *Così mai sempre a ben'amar v'induca, / Con ben felice fine, honesto amore*' (Here, Aeneas, conforming to his fate, will again take reason, which was occupied by feeling, as his guide, and he will prepare himself to obey the Lord, who rules the sky. But Dido, driven by vain desire, will be conquered by inner despair. Now may it please you, kind spectators, to listen to this happening, which the poet brings to the stage for the utility of all; Prologue, p. 8; emphasis mine). The moralization becomes yet more superficial when the poet's son Celso Giraldi writes his dedicatory letter for the *Didone* to Don Alessandro di Este. This is a play 'Ove Enea ci rappresenta uno prudentissimo heroe, Giove la parte superiore dell'anima humana, Mercurio la discorsiva et ragionevole, et Didone la parte inferiore et sensuale' (where Aeneas represents a very prudent hero, Jove the superior part of the human soul, Mercury the discursive and reasoning, and Dido the inferior and sensual part; pp. 4–5).

28 Federico Doglio finds one positive thing to say about the play, noting that, in relation to Pazzi, we have with Giraldi 'un esempio di riduzione dal piano mitico al livello umano dei personaggi' (an example of reduction from the mythic plane to the human level of the characters; *Il teatro tragico italiano*, p. xlvi). Nevertheless, he, too, considers the tragedy 'prolissa e mediocre.'

29 As brief examples, see the following verses from Anna's lament in Act V, scene 4: 'Oime dolore, oime dolore, oime' (p. 121), 'Oime, cara Sorella, oime' (p. 124), 'Oime cara Didon, Sorella cara, / ... / Oime, cara Didone, oime

Sorella' (p. 125), 'oime, Sorella cara' (p. 125), 'Ahi care figlie,' 'Ahi, bocca cara,' 'Ahi ch'è caduta; ahi lassa,' 'oime dolente,' 'oime misera, oime, / Ahi ...' (all from p. 126). And what are Dido's last two words when (in an original moment) she gains consciousness on stage just before dying? 'Oime, oime' (p. 125). Not content with this, Anna bends over her sister and asks, 'Ahi, bocca cara, / Bocca già di rubin via più vermiglia / Hor pallida via più, che non è il busso, / Manda a mia contentezza una parola / Almeno fuori ...' This reader (disturbed as well by the distasteful use of imagery in the middle of a speech of grief) was ready to shout, 'No, please, enough! No more words!' But of course Barce has to exclaim 'Oime meschina, / Oime meschina, oime' (p. 127). If the response seems unsympathetic, I might note that I have quoted fewer than half of the twenty-eight examples of 'oime' in this scene alone, not to mention similar words, most repeated several times, such as *doloroso, miser, infelice, crudele, tristo, affanni, lamento, pianto, lagrimare, dolente, dorreste, pietade, dolore, duolo, doglia, angoscie, sofferto male, doglian, miserabile, lagrimando, pena, morte, amaro, piangendo, meschina, miseramente,* and *lagrimevol.*

30 Turner criticizes these scenes for their static quality – 'J'ai dit que ces scènes n'avancent pas l'action. Elles sont d'ailleurs assez maladroites, elles ne sont qu'une suite de monlogues et de dialogues forcés mis ensemble sans aucune liaison'(I have said that these scenes do not at all advance the action. They are, moreover, quite clumsy; they are nothing but a succession of monologues and forced dialogues, put together without any connection; *Didon dans la tragédie de la Renaissance italienne et française,* pp. 40–1), without taking into account how they advance the characterization of the protagonists and touch on the poet's thematic concerns.

31 The motif is common in the Renaissance. Here, Turner (ibid) cites Aeneas Sylvius Piccolomini's *Epistole di due amanti* (Venice, 1526), p. 18, first published in 1444, and the *Roman de la rose* (1321–9). In the *Heroides*, Ovid first presents letters of fifteen abandoned women – Penelope, Phyllis, Briseis, Phaedra, Oenone, Hypsipyle, Dido, Hermione, Deianira, Ariadne, Canace, Medea, Laodamia, Hypermnestra, and Sappho – then six letters between the couples Paris and Helen, Leandro and Hero, and Acontius and Cydippe.

32 Touching on the concept of free will, Giraldi elaborates on the various levels of creation, moving up the ladder of being rung by rung: 'altri di sassi / Prende la forma, e stassi / Come insensata pietra, / Altri, come huom, che dorma, / In pianta si trasforma, / Altri, che più di questi pur penetra / A perfettion maggior, si face uguale / A mobile, e sensibile animale' (Some like the form of rocks and exist as senseless stone; others, like a sleeping man, transform themselves to plants. Some, who come closer to perfection

than these, make themselves the equal of a mobile and sensible animal;
p. 83). Each level is then analysed again, after which the poet moves on to
the higher levels of being, creatures of 'miglior'alma, e miglior mente'
(better soul and better mind; p. 84).

33 Turner, interestingly but rather blindly, refers only to what he calls the
biblical philosophy of this passage (*Didon dans la tragédie de la Renaissance
italienne et française*, p. 43).

34 As Giraldi says, earthly goods – power ('reggere alto stato, e havere impero,'
'sovra ogn'altro altiero / Sedere'), treasure ('copia di fin'oro,' 'gemme,'
'habitar dorati tetti'), pleasure ('far satia ogni voglia'), and fame ('Famoso
andar da l'Indo litto, al Moro') – are transient and come and go like leaves
on a tree (p. 33). With blind desire, we allow our minds to be darkened by
flattery and deceit, failing to understand the true purpose of earthly joy,
which is to provide mortals with a taste of celestial pleasure in this life so
that we can say 'How much will that pleasure be, if this is so much?' (p. 34).
Turner calls this speech an 'anachronisme' because of its Christian philosophy (*Didon dans la tragédie de la Renaissance italienne et française*, p. 39), but
many of the motifs are developed as well by the classical world.

35 In the chorus at the end of Act II of his *Didone*, where the same theme is
developed, Dolce writes: 'Ben si dimostra chiaro, / C'hore tranquille,
riposate, o lieto / Fra noi durano poco: / Che quella, ch'i mortai si prende a
giuoco, / Dal suo vaso distilla / Il dolce a stilla a stilla, / M'a guisa d'onde
suol versar l'amaro: / E'l cielo è sempre avaro / D'ogni gioia quà giu, d'ogni
diletto' (It is truly clear that tranquil, restful, or happy hours last a short time
among us, for she, who makes fun of mortals, spills sweetness from her jar
drop by drop, while she usually pours bitterness in waves. And heaven,
down here, is always stingy with joy or with delight; p. 14^r).

36 See, among others, Antonio Piromalli, *La cultura a Ferrara al tempo di Ludovico
Ariosto*, particularly Part II, chapter 2, 'La corte e la cultura mondana,'
pp. 73–83.

37 Horne quotes Aeneas's speech in Act IV, scene 1 ('me ne scoppia il core' [my
heart is bursting]), and might have cited as well the 'mi si schianta il core'
(my heart is breaking) of Act III, scene 4 (p. 74).

38 There are other reasons, of course, for his preferences, including considerations of audience. Even Alessandro Pazzi de' Medici comments on the desire
to please through happier works, contrasting his *Dido in Carthagine* to his
Iphigenia in Tauris. In his preface to both works, he writes: 'Tornando ad
Iphigenia in Tauris dico haver preso ad scrivere questa, essendomi parsa
non tanto più docta, più eloquente, più affectuosa o più sententiosa d'ogni
altra, quanto manco lacrymevole et funesta, et in la quale oltra ad un raro

exemplo d'amicitia di Pylade, et d'Oreste, sia il successo lieto. Onde ancora si possa trarre una profitevole et salutare consideratione, cioè, che sicome il syncero et sancto amore d'amicitia partorisce il più delle volte felici successi, parimenti il disordinato et illecito produca lacrymevole et misero exitio. Le quali cose all'hora non solo furno assai secondo l'animo mio, levatosi di fresco da quella crudelissima et acerbissima morte di Didone, ma anchora stimai che la S.ᵗᵃ V. leggendo l'una et l'altra si havesse in questa alquanto più a delectare' (Returning to *Iphigenia in Tauris*, I began writing this, not because it seemed to me to be more learned, more moving, or more sententious than any other, but because it was less tearful and mournful, and because, in addition to offering a rare example of the friendship between Pylades and Orestes, it had a happy ending. From this, one can draw a profitable and salutary consideration; namely, that just as the sincere and holy love of friendship gives birth most often to happy results, so disordered and illicit love produces a tearful and wretched outcome. These things, then, were not only favourable to my mind, just having left that most grievous and bitter death of Dido, but also I thought that your holiness, reading the one and then the other, might enjoy the latter somewhat more; *Tutte le opere*, pp. 48–9).

39 For the discourse on the differences between tragedy and comedy, see *La Medea*, in *Tragedie di M. Lodovico Dolce*, pp. 2ʳ–3ᵛ.

40 See the *Hecuba, tragedia di M. Lodovico Dolce*, in *Tragedie di M. Lodovico Dolce*, pp. 2ʳ–3ʳ.

41 The language here reminds me of that used by Perrottino in Book I of Pietro Bembo's *Asolani*, where the youth says that poets resort to fables, under the veil of which they hide truth, in this guise delighting the people with the novelty of their fictions while sometimes revealing the truth in order to guide them, little by little, to a better life. For a study of the poetic use of fables to hide truth, see my article 'Mythological Exempla in Bembo's *Asolani*: Didactic or Decorative?' I might also note that the idea of fable as the source of both comedy and tragedy reappears in the *Poetics* of Giulio Cesare Scaligero, published posthumously in 1561: 'Tragoediae vero et Comoediae genus unum commune, commune unum nomen, Fabula' (I, 1, ch. V), cited in Musumarra, *La poesia tragica italiana nel Rinascimento*, p. 33.

42 I quote from *Didone, tragedia di M. Lodovico Dolce. Nuovamente dal medesimo riveduta e ricorretta*, in *Tragedie di M. Lodovico Dolce*, here pp. 3ʳ–4ᵛ. Turner, incidentally, claims that Dolce's prologue, unlike Pazzi's (which recalls Euripides), does not resemble any other classical prologue (*Didon dans la tragédie de la Renaissance italienne et française*, p. 53).

43 See, as one example of the dream in pastoral, Sincero's dream in chapter 12

of the *Arcadia*, where he sees an orange tree (perhaps his beloved) cut down by the Parcae and awakens in fear. The *Arcadia*, edited by Dolce in 1556, also provides many examples of delightful scenes that give way to scenes of lament, as, for example, in chapter 5. The dream just before dawn is a common motif in the theatre of the sixteenth century. Dolce also employed it in Act I of his *Marianna*, where Marianna's brother Aristobol appears to her with a bloody neck and chest, having come from the underworld to warn her about Herod. There, the Nurse says God sometimes uses dreams to tell us things, but others are false.

The oneiric motif, found in Greek tragedy (see Euripides' *Iphigenia in Tauris*, vv. 42–55, and *Hecuba*, vv. 73–91, as two examples of many), originates for the Renaissance tragedians with Trissino's *Sofonisba* (1515), where Sofonisba, in the play's first episode, narrates a dream in which she was in 'una selva oscura,' surrounded by dogs and shepherds who had bound her husband, Siface. Erminia, a character of Trissino's own creation, tells her one should not believe dreams. In Rucellai's *Rosmunda* (1516), the protagonist relates how her father appeared to her from the underworld: 'Che piena avea di polvere e di sangue / La barba, i crini e le squarciate veste, / Ferito 'l viso, e trapassato il petto, / In mille parti lacerato e guasto' (He had his beard full of dust and blood, his hair and clothes torn, his face wounded, and his chest, [which was] pierced in thousand places, lacerated and torn; Act I, cited from *Teatro italiano antico*, vol. 1), and Sperone Speroni, in his *Canace* (1542), describes a dream of Dejopea, after which he has her comment that 'Le visioni e i sogni / Sono immagini ed ombre / Delle nostre alme umane / Eterne ed immortali' (visions and dreams are images and shadows of our eternal and immortal human souls; Act III, cited from *Teatro italiano antico*, vol. 4). Rather than discount the dream, we are told here that we often see the future in visions. As one further example, Pietro Aretino, in his *Orazia*, published in 1546, one year before Dolce's *Didone*, has Celia narrate a dream she had when awakening. Though her nurse goes on to say visions and dreams are all lies (and that this one was caused by Celia's diet!), the young woman relates a violent, prophetic dream in which fierce, destructive winds are effectively personified: 'ecco a l'incontro / tre rabbiosi apparir venti condensi / con volto orrido e nero, e con le chiome / dinanzi al fronte scompigliate ed aspre, / pregne di sdegno, di fortezza e d'ira, / da le cui bocche perigliose usciva / stridente orror di foribondo suono' (Behold the approach of three enraged storm winds with horrible, black faces, and with hair on their foreheads dishevelled and rough, full of disdain, strength, and anger, from whose dangerous mouths issued the strident horror of furious sound; Act I, cited from *La tragedia classica dalle Origini al Maffei*.

44 Marco Ariani sees a fixed typology (part of which is expressed through a contrastive structure) that can be found, he says, in all sixteenth-century Italian tragedies: 'il processo colpa/punizione,' 'il processo virtú/sublimazione,' and 'processi legati da una introspezione acutissima delle antitesi: Fortuna/virtú / Potere-virtú' (*Il teatro italiano: La tragedia del Cinquecento,* vol. 1, p. xiv).

45 Lucas finds the supreme value to be honesty (or decency), articulated through the motif of marriage ('*Didon*. Trois réécritures tragiques du livre IV de l'*Eneide* dans le théâtre italien du XVIe siècle,' pp. 595–6).

46 Turner, in his analysis of the play, claims that Dolce probably knew the tragedies of both Pazzi and Giraldi, but, while that may be true, Turner's comparisons are not always convincing. For example, he says Dolce imitated Pazzi in Act I and Giraldi in Act II (*Didon dans la tragédie de la Renaissance italienne et française,* p. 57). However, when Turner cites specific verses, the parallels may be coincidental, as when he compares Giraldi's 'Et ivi de l'amor lor colsero il frutto' (*Didone,* Act III, scene 1) to Dolce's 'Egli de l'amor mio raccolse il frutto' (*Didone,* Act I, scene 1). As Turner admits, the metaphor is common and might have derived from Ariosto, among others (see *Orlando furioso* XXI, 55). Turner might also have quoted another verse much earlier in Giraldi's play, when Juno tells Venus her plan for Dido and Aeneas: 'E coglieran del loro amore il frutto' (Act I, scene 1). And two years before Giraldi wrote his play, Dolce had used the expression in his comedy *Il ragazzo,* published in 1541, where, in Act II, scene 1, the Spagnuolo says 'la mia maladetta fortuna mi toglie di poter raccogliere il frutto dell'amore' (*Commedie del Cinquecento,* p. 227). In fact, other than certain general features that might derive from their common source, the closest parallel Turner can find between Dolce and Pazzi, for example, is the following: 'Anna sorella et madre, il cui troppo amore' (Pazzi) and 'Anna sorella mia, sorella et madre, / Ch'al infinito amor che tu mi porti' (Dolce). This Turner calls 'presque exactement pareils' (p. 55), but, if one cites the verses immediately following, the parallels disappear. Furthermore, Turner seems to have missed that Giraldi, too, has Dido refer to her sister as 'cara, come madre' (Act V, scene 3), attesting more to the commonality of the expression than to a direct influence. Whether or not Dolce knew either or both predecessors is to a large extent irrelevant since he develops his work according to his own tastes.

47 See, for two examples of many, the prologues to *Giocasta,* and *Ifigenia* (which in my copy of the 1560 edition of *Le tragedie di M. Lodovico Dolce* appears at the end of the play), where, in the first case, Venice is called 'honor non pur d'Italia sola, / Ma di quanto sostien la terra, e 'l mare; / Ove mai crudeltà

non hebbe albergo, / Ma pietade, honestà, giustitia, e pace' (honour not only of Italy alone, but of what the earth and sea sustain, where cruelty never dwelt, but mercy, honesty, justice, and peace; p. 4^v), and, in the second, 'Ornamento e sostegno, ma splendore / Sovra quanti fur mai d'Italia tutta' (ornament and support, a splendour above all that ever were in all of Italy; p. 51^r).

48 Turner, noting that the theme of this chorus derives from Sophocles' *Oedipus Rex* and *Oedipus Colonnus*, says it is Dolce's best (*Didon dans la tragédie de la Renaissance italienne et française*, p. 61).

49 In her grief, she compares herself to other deceived women: 'È senza ugual l'alta miseria mia. / Paris lasciò la sfortunata Enone, / E Demofonte Fille; / Tradì Theseo la figlia di Pasife. / Cosi ingrato Giason fu gia a Medea' (My great misery is without equal. Paris left unfortunate Oenone, and Demophoon Phyllis; Theseus betrayed the daughter of Pasiphae. Thus was ungrateful Jason to Medea; Act IV, scene 1, p. 27^v). Dolce has added Oenone to Giraldi's list of abandoned women.

50 Among the 'cose stupende' that the priestess can do are the following: 'Fermar il corso a i più correnti fiumi; / Così contra le leggi di natura / Tornar sovente ogni pianeta a dietro. / Fa l'alme gir fuor de' sepolchri errando, / E sotto a piedi suoi trema la terra; / E, quando vuol, le più robuste quercie / Scendono giù da monti in bassa valle' (Stop the course of the most rushing rivers; contrary to the laws of nature, reverse the motion of the planets. She makes souls go wandering outside their tombs, and beneath her feet the earth trembles. And, when she wishes, the most robust oaks descend from mountains to the low valley; p. 31^r).

51 For an enumeration of the parallels between Dolce's play and Virgil's epic, see J. Friedrich, *Die Didodramen des Dolce, Jodelle und Marlowe in ihrem Verhältnis zu einander und zu Vergil's Aeneis*, pp. 15–29.

52 Wine turning to blood, for example, can be found in Seneca's *Oedipus*, where Manto says 'libata Bacchi dona permutat cruor' ('Bacchus's gift poured out changes to blood'; Loeb Library edition, translated by Frank Justus Miller, v. 324).

53 Lucas, with a slightly different focus (Dolce, she says, is essentially interested in the theme of culpable love in the face of the social code), sees this as an example of the children being punished for the sins of their fathers (i.e., Dido's lack of fidelity to her husband after his death; '*Didon*. Trois réécritures tragiques du livre IV de l'Eneide dans le théâtre italien du XVIe siècle,' pp. 596–7).

54 The distinction between inter- and transtexuality is one made by Gérard Genette in his *Figures of Literary Discourse*, a collection of essays first pub-

lished in *Figures I* (1966), *Figures II* (1969), and *Figures III* (1972). I take the term 'genealogy' from Paolo Valesio, who uses it in reference both to chronological and spiritual continuity. See, for example, his study *Gabriele D'Annunzio: The Dark Flame*.

6: 'Non Mai Stanco di Giovare'

1 The translator 'si riservava di provare che le sue ragioni sull'esser stato Annibale maggiore di coloro che lo vinsero erano false' (reserves the right to show that the author's reasons for calling Hannibal greater than those who defeated him were false; cited in Angela Paladini, 'La tragedia secondo Lodovico Dolce,' p. 39).
2 Translated by Frances Yates in *The Art of Memory*, p. 95, citing Dolce's *Dialogo ... nel quale si ragiona del modo di accrescere, et conservar la memoria* (Venice: Gio. Battista et Marchio Sessa fratelli, 1586), p. 15^v. Another addition pointed out by Yates is Dolce's modernization of Romberch's memory instructions by way of examples taken from modern artists, whose pictures are useful as memory images (pp. 163–4). Dolce writes: 'If we have some familiarity with the art of painters we shall be more skilful in forming our memory images. If you wish to remember the fable of Europa you may use as your memory image Titian's painting: also for Adonis, or any other fabulous history, profane or sacred, choosing figures which delight and thereby excite the memory' (Yates, p. 164, translating Dolce, as cited, p. 86^r).
3 For a discussion of Dolce's poetics of translation, see Angela Paladini, ' "Ornamenti" e "Bellezze": La tragedia secondo Lodovico Dolce,' whence I cite the letter.
4 Cited in ibid, p. 39, and Salvatore Bongi, *Annali di Gabriel Giolito de' Ferrari da Trino di Monferrato, stampatore in Venzia*, vol. 2, p. 60.
5 For a discussion of the development of the dialogue form in Italy during the century preceding Dolce, see David Marsh, *The Quattrocento Dialogue*, particularly chapter 1, 'Cicero and the Humanist Dialogue,' pp. 1–23, and, for the cinquecento, P. Floriani, 'Il dialogo a corte.'
6 In contrast to the many who have criticized Dolce, Giuseppe Toffanin perhaps comes closer to the mark when he says that the work is 'il più significativo documento del suo preenciclopedismo ... uno dei primi tentativi di ridurre appunto la storia del mondo in pillole, distrutte le vecchie impalcature retoriche' (the most significant document of his pre-encyclopedism ... one of the first attempts to reduce the history of the world into capsules, destroying the old rhetorical structures; *Il Cinquecento*, p. 584). Having said this, however, he adds that the method itself is ingenuous.

Azelia Arici repeats Toffanin's judgment without acknowledgment, in true Dolcean fashion (*Grande dizionario enciclopedico*, p. 459). For the *Giornale* and the *Vita di Carlo Quinto*, see also Paul F. Grendler, 'Francesco Sansovino and Italian Popular History. 1560–1600.'

7 For a comment on the nature of title pages and how they change through the course of the sixteenth century, with reference more specifically to Giolito, see Amadeo Quondam, '"Mercanzia d'onore," "Mercanzia d'utile." Produzione libraria e lavoro intellettuale a Venezia nel Cinquecento.'

8 The use of the word 'paraphrasi' for Dolce's translation of Juvenal's sixth satire is significant, for the work, fifty-six pages in length, is not simply a translation. Rather, it consists of three intertwined elements: a free translation, an integrated commentary, and many original additions worthy of further study. For those interested in the relationships between men and women in the sixteenth century, such a study, I believe, would be richly rewarded.

9 Only at the conclusion of the translation of Catullus does one find a reference to Dolce, reading 'Il fine dell'Epithalamio tradotto per M.L. Dolce,' followed by 'In Venegia per Curtio nauo e Fratelli.'

10 The dedicatory letter, for example, has an ornamental initial (the letter *c* with a *capra* grazing inside its arc); each page has a running head; and each leaf an arabic numeral, for a total of thirty-four pages of text in italic print, followed by a page for seven 'Errori fatti nel stampare.'

11 Francesco Flamini calls it 'un plagio dell'opera d'ugual soggetto dello spagnuolo Giovan Lodovico Vives' in *Il Cinquecento. Storia letteraria d'Italia*, p. 382. As for plagiarism, many works of this time have a tendency to focus on what Bareggi calls 'zone franche' (free zones) and to favour ambiguous tones, making them difficult to define and catalogue (p. 53); 'il concetto stesso di opera originale prende qui contorni incerti e sfuggenti' (p. 54). While Dolce in some cases relied heavily on one source (thus the charge of plagiarism), he usually tried to change the material to make it his own.

12 The expression regarding the work's fame derives from Daniela Frigo, 'Dal caos all'ordine: sulla questione del "prender moglie" nella trattatistica del sedicesimo secolo,' p. 71. For an in-depth study of Dolce's dialogue, see Adriana Chemello, 'L'*Institution delle donne* di Lodovico Dolce ossia l'*insegnar virtù et honesti costumi alla Donna*,' as well as her study 'La donna, il modello, l'immaginario: Moderata Fonte e Lucrezia Marinella.' Her response to the accusations of plagiarism made against Dolce can be found on pp. 113 and 188n, respectively. Paul Grendler also briefly discusses the work in his *Schooling in Renaissance Italy, 1300–1600*, pp. 87–8.

13 Chemello traces various strands in the discourse dealing with women, noting that, as regards titles alone, in the early cinquecento works exalting the excellence and nobility of women predominate, whereas, in the second half of the century, one finds works purportedly in defence of women but characterized in reality by a misogynistic tone. Within each of these 'categories,' of course, numerous variations exist ('L'*Institution delle donne*,' pp. 109–11). For Giuseppe Zonta's older, though still useful, classification, see the 'Avvertenza Generale' to his edition of *Trattati del Cinquecento sulla donna*, p. 374, and for additional comments on two currents within the category of works dealing with marriage, see Frigo, 'Dal caos all'ordine,' pp. 61–2.

14 Given the interest in 'women' as author and subject in the Renaissance, perhaps a bibliographical note in chronological form is appropriate, with full indications to be found in this study's bibliography of secondary sources. In addition to the well-known histories of Italian literature where women are discussed (i.e., Quadrio 1741, Tiraboschi 1796, Fachini 1824, Foscarini 1864, Magliani 1885, Musatti 1891, Flamini 1901, Mocenigo 1906, Croce 1931, Toffanin 1929 and 1935, Bonora 1966), the older bibliographies (Ferri 1842), older studies (e.g., Marchesi 1895, Rodocanachi 1907, Lugli 1909, Portigliotti 1927 translated by Miall 1929, Blasi 1930, to be distinguished from her anthology of the same date), older anthologies (ranging from works published in the cinquecento itself, such as Lodovico Domenichi's *Rime diverse d'alcune nobilissime et virtuosissime donne* [1559], through the first attempt to offer a truly comprehensive anthology – the collection containing 248 different women poets published by Luisa Bergalli 1726, to Jolanda de Blasi's *Antologia* [1930], more than 550 pages in length), more recent anthologies (Costa-Zalessow 1982; *The Defiant Muse*, edited by Allen, Kittel, and Jewell 1986; *Scrittrici d'Italia*, edited by Forlani and Savini 1991), and the many studies on individual women too numerous to cite, the bibliography dealing with women in Italy in the cinquecento (and earlier) has expanded in recent years. The following are among the works most commonly cited: Kelso 1956, with an extensive bibliography on pp. 326–462; Nelson 1958; Fahy 1956;, Leone 1962; Jaquinta 1978; Zarri 1980, with studies by Guidi, Piéjus, and Fiorato; Labalme, ed. 1980; Bellucci 1981; Tomalin 1982; *Nel cerchio della luna* 1983, with studies by Borsetto, Chemello, Frigo, and Zancan; Daenens 1983; King and Rabil, Jr. 1983; *Rewriting the Renaissance*, edited by Ferguson, Quilligan, and Vickers 1986; and *Ambiguous Realities*, edited by Levin and Watson 1987.

15 On page Mi[r], the abbreviation for Fronimo changes, apparently by mistake, from *Fr.* to *Fra.*, as if a Francesca were speaking. The dropped marker on the last page of the preceding octavo, however, reads *Fr.*, and clearly the

speaker remains the same. There is no reference to the names of the other women listening to the *disputatio*.

16 In response to Marcello's claim of not being at fault for what he is going to say, the *reggente* Madonna Flaminia counters with the astute observation that 'ci havete un poco di colpa ... poi che sete andato trovando i libri, che dicono mal di noi' (You have a bit of the blame here, since you went around finding books that speak ill of us), and of course he responds that he did so only to prepare himself better for their defence (Ii^r). Christopher Cairns thinks that the book referred to by Marcello has an Erasmian source – the *suasoria* and *dissuasoria* letter types that argue against and for marriage in Erasmus's *De conscribendis epistolis*, published in Venice in 1526 by Zoppino (and earlier elsewhere). See Cairns, *Pietro Aretino and the Republic of Venice*, pp. 131–4.

17 Along with the more obvious elements that reappear in the Italian tradition (which runs through works such as Speroni's *Della cura famigliare*, Alessandro Piccolomini's *Institution morale*, and Ercole Tasso's *Dell'ammogliarsi*), I think of other details such as Dolce's description of the effort that goes into achievement and the acquisition of knowledge – 'La vittoria, la scientia, e tutte le virtudi sono dolci, e pretiose: e queste anche sicco recano fatiche, sudori, ferite, vigilie, caldi, freddi, fame, sete, et infiniti altri disaggi' (Victory, science, and all the virtues are sweet and precious, but these also bring with them toil, sweat, wounds, sleepless nights, heat, cold, hunger, thirst, and an infinite number of other discomforts), a motif that shows up, to cite merely one example that comes immediately to mind, in works as disparate as the *Quijote*, where Cervantes writes: 'Alcanzar alguno o ser eminente en letras le cuesta tiempo, vigilias, hambre, desnudez, vaguidos de cabeza, indigestiones de estómago, y otras cosas a éstas adherentes' (To accomplish anything or to be eminent in letters costs you time, sleepless nights, hunger, nakedness, stomach indigestion, dizzy spells, and other things that accompany them; Part 1, ch. 38).

18 See Chemello, 'L'*Institution delle donne* di Lodovico Dolce,' pp. 113–16, and in particular the bibliography on imitation, p. 114 n18.

19 Cf., in addition to Erasmus's *De conscribendis epistolis*, the near-contemporary work of Giovanni Della Casa, the *Quaestio lepidissima an uxor sit ducenda*, where he writes that 'eam vero inire societatem, quam nostris quidem legibus unam mortem fas sit dirimere, maximae ac periculosissimae deliberationis non esse inficiari quis potest?' (in fact, who can deny that the decision to undertake a bond that according to our laws only death can break is not of the greatest importance and danger?): *Prose di Giovanni Della Casa*, ed. Arnaldo di Benedetto, p. 54.

20 'Dopo lo havere governato la sua republica, dopo le opere date à negotij de gl'amici, dopo havere ben disposto le cose de la famiglia, stanco di mente, e di corpo se ne torna à casa: come si parte il giorno: ò che consolatione: gli viene incontro la moglie coi rimbrotti, mal'agevole, e tutta crucciosa: Vassene à letto, per riposo de l'afflitte membra, e de gl'affaticati spiriti[;] ella il siegue di fatto, e con acuti stimuli pungendo lo muove qualche lite: sveglia nuove contese: intanto che si dà bando à'l sonno' (After having governed his republic, after the work given to negotiations among friends, after having arranged family matters well, tired in mind and in body, he returns home just as day is ending. Oh, what consolation! His wife, difficult and troublesome, accosts him with scoldings. He goes to bed in order to rest his afflicted limbs and tired spirits. She follows right after him, and, pricking him with sharp spurs, causes a fight and awakens new quarrels, until sleep is chased away; p. Ii^v).

21 One example of the latter technique is Marcello's description of how a wife corrupts those around her, so that she may satisfy her sexual needs: 'Hor sù, sial marito un'Hercole, un'Hettore, uno Achille temuti da tutti: Hor sù, che la moglie sia posta in una prigione, in una rocca, in una torre sotto mille chiavi: gl'adulteri si appiccheranno l'ali di Dedalo, e volarannovi la sù' (Come on, even if the husband is a Hercules, a Hector, an Achilles, feared by all; come on, even if the wife is placed in a prison, in a fortress, in a tower under a thousand keys, adulteries will put on the wings of Daedalus and fly up there; p. Iii^v). And even if she is enclosed where air cannot enter, a wife will find a means of committing adultery in her mind!

22 This response would support Cairns's contention that Dolce was influenced by Erasmus's *De conscribendis epistolis*, where letters for and against marriage are included (*Pietro Aretino and the Republic of Venice*, pp. 137–9).

23 Fronimo is careful to specify that we cannot all be 'virgins' if we want life to continue. Had he said 'wives' were essential for the continuation of the species, he would have fallen into an error in logic. Della Casa, in his contemporary treatise on whether or not to take a wife, says such a statement (on the necessity of wives for the propagation of the species) might seem a common conclusion, but is in fact false. If marriage was prohibited by law, the ability to procreate would not thereby be taken away or lessened ('Neque enim, si vel maxime vetitum interdictumque lege sit omninoque non liceat uxorem habere, continuo gignendi procreandique facultas sublata sit ac ne omnino quidem comminuta': *Prose di Giovanni Della Casa*, p. 56).

24 Earlier treatises, such as the *De re uxoria* (1415–16) of Francesco Barbaro, translated into Italian in 1538, but apparently not used by Dolce, tend to

justify sexual relations between spouses only for purposes of reproduction and, in particular, to provide sons for the future governance of the state. For a discussion and partial translation of Barbaro's treatise, see Benjamin G. Kohl, 'Introduction' (pp. 179–88) and 'Francesco Barbaro, *On Wifely Duties*' (pp. 189–228), in *The Earthly Republic: Italian Humanists on Government and Society*, edited by Kohl and Ronald G. Witt, with Elizabeth B. Welles.

25 In her enlightening analysis of works concerned with the comportment of women, Chemello notes that the celebratory formula of woman's 'excellence and nobility' is increasingly used in the cinquecento for didactic purposes – that is, as an example of what a woman 'must be.' Castiglione's *donna di palazzo*, by extension, becomes a model that is insistently repeated and transferred to other social and cultural situations of women of the time, with only partial retouchings of the portrait. On the one hand, we find women described as 'animali imperfettissimi e di poca o niuna dignità a rispetto degli omini' (most imperfect creatures and with little or no dignity compared with men) and, on the other, as beings not at all inferior to men as regards their virtue and dignity, with the comment that there are few men of valour who do not love women (where the use of what are in effect double negatives is interesting). See 'L'*Institution delle donne* di Lodovico Dolce,' pp. 105–6, 108. The quotation from B. Castiglione can be found in *Il libro del Cortegiano*, ed. E. Bonora (Milan: Mursia, 1972), p. 198.

Chemello's assertion, which applies to the development throughout the century, while accurate on the whole and recognizable in Dolce, does not fully describe what he does in this earliest of his dialogues on women, a work unexamined by Chemello. Here, the model is recognized as excessively demanding. Even Dolce's description of female beauty, as we will see, departs from the lofty Neoplatonic tones of his predecessors in this area, since he first provides a quite detailed depiction of the features that constitute physical beauty, although here, too, one finds ultimately an exaltation of the beauty of the soul.

26 Over a century earlier, in the first book of his *De re uxoria*, Francesco Barbaro had stressed that nobles should choose their wives only from women coming from the ruling class.

27 This is the response of Piccardo when Aretino mentions Cato's *sentenza*: 'Disse egli, che se la generatione humana potesse perpetuare, et mantenersi qua giù senza il bisogno delle femine; i Dei verrebono ad habitar con noi' (He said that, if human generation could be perpetuated and maintained down here without the use of women, the gods would come to live with us; 8^r).

28 For a more pleasant use of these rhetorical figures, particularly allegorized myths, see my study 'Mythological Exempla in Bembo's *Asolani*: Didactic or Decorative.'

29 'Quale credete voi, che fosse la Laura del Petrarcha, celebrata da lui con tanta bella copia di versi? Io per me credo, ch'ella sia stata men, che honesta. Et quando il Petrarcha haveva da lei le liete notti, correva a gli inchiostri; et spiegando le lodi di lei nel campo di molte carte, ne scriveva quelle tante meraviglie, che si leggono' (What do you think Petrarch's Laura was, celebrated by him in so many beautiful verses? As far as I'm concerned, I believe she was less than honest. And whenever Petrarch spent happy nights with her, he ran to his ink and, unfolding her praises in many pages, wrote all those marvels that one reads about her; p. 17^r).

30 All citations are from the 1575 edition of the *Dialogo di M. Lodovico Dolce, nel quale si ragiona del modo di accrescere, et conservar la memoria*. C. Ossola discusses this dialogue briefly in his 'Rassegna di testi e studi tra Manierismo e Barocco,' p. 446, and Frances Yates, at greater length in her book *The Art of Memory*.

31 Of the three Latin sources for the art of memory, Quintilian gives the clearest exposition of the art as a mnemotechnic. The complete text of his *Institutio oratoria* had been discovered by Poggio Bracciolini in 1416 and had its *edito princeps* in Rome in 1470. Unlike the *Ad Herennium*, around which many rules had grown up throughout the Middle Ages, the *Institutio oratoria* allowed for a lay approach to the art of memory. One of the first to take advantage of this was Peter of Ravenna, whose *Phoenix, sive artificiosa memoria* was first published in Venice in 1491, with many editions thereafter. His work became the most universally known of all the memory books, in part because of his own self-promotion. Petrarch was often cited by the writers of memory books, largely because of his *Rerum memorandarum libri*, probably written around 1343 to 1345, and based on the definitions in Cicero's *De inventione* of Prudence, Justice, Fortitude, and Temperance. The section on Prudence deals with her three parts *memoria, intelligentia,* and *Providentia*, commonly used by teachers of artificial memory. See Yates, *The Art of Memory*, pp. 101–4, 112–14, and, for Thomas Aquinas, pp. 70–6.

32 For an intriguing example, see pp. 53^r–56^r in the text I employ for all citations: *Dialogo di M. Lodovico Dolce, nel quale si ragiona del modo di accrescere, et conservar la Memoria* (1575). Dolce says the illustrations were made by Giacomo Publicio, a reference to the alphabet of 'objects' published in Jacobus Publicius's *Oratoriae artis epitome* (Venice, 1482), a work on rhetoric with the *Ars memorativa* treatise appearing as an appendix. Publicius's illustrations were also used by Romberch.

33 Even the brutes have memory, he adds, citing contemporary and ancient
examples (e.g., Ulysses's dog, who recognized him after twenty years; p. 6^v).
This and other examples are narrated, including one lengthy story, after
which Fabritio says, 'Parmi anco di haver veduto questo esempio in Quinti-
liano, ma seguita' (I think I've also seen this example in Quintilian, but
continue; p. 7^r).

34 For Camillo Leonardi, see Carla De Bellis, 'Astri, gemme e arti medico-
magiche nello *Speculum Lapidum* di Camillo Leonardi,' and the works cited
therein. De Bellis notes that the *Speculum* had a notably fortunate publication
record, appearing first in Venice in 1502, and then reappearing in Venice,
per Melchiorem Sessam et Petrum de Ravanis, in 1516; in Augusta [Turin],
apud Henricum Sileceum, in 1533; in Paris in 1610, along with the *Sym-*
pathia septem Metallorum ac septem selectorum lapidum ad planetas of Petrus
Arlensis de Scudalupis; in Hamburg in 1717, where a third text was added
to the other two, the *Magia astrologica* of Pietro Costanzo Albini. The most
interesting date in the *Speculum*'s history, however, is, she claims, Dolce's
translation of 1565, presented to the public as his own (p. 69). She also
points to the updating of the title, where Dolce moves away from the
medieval preference for the *Speculum* and towards the *Trattato*, a title
(specifically *Trattato delle gemme*) under which the work is also known. An
English translation of Leonardi was published in London in 1750 as *The*
Mirror of Stones.

35 All citations derive from the following first editions: *Speculum lapidum*
clarissimi artium et medicine doctoris Camilli Leonardi pisaurensis ... [Colophon:
Impressus Venetiis per Ioannem Baptistam Sessa anno domini. M.D.II. Die
Primo Decembris] and *Libri Tre di M. Lodovico Dolce; ne i quali si tratta delle*
diverse sorti delle Gemme, che produce la Natura, Della Qualità, grandezza,
bellezza, et virtù loro. In Venetia, Appresso Gio. Battista, Marchio Sessa, et
Fratelli, 1565.

36 For a study of the lapidary tradition from antiquity to the end of the Middle
Ages, see my article 'The Lapidary of *L'Intelligenza*: Its Literary Background.'
In Dolce's list, those that can be identified with some certainty include:
Pedanius Dioscorides, a first-century A.D. Greek physician, author of the
Materia medica, the standard work on substances used in medicine, including
gems, which are covered in the fifth book; Aristotle, most likely his *Meteoro-*
logica; Hermes (or Mercurius) Trismegistus, ancient pseudo-Egyptian sage,
purported author of the works in the *Corpus hermiticum*, rediscovered in the
fifteenth century and translated into Latin by Ficino; Evax, a mythical
Arabian king, for which see the discussion on Damigeron in my article cited
above; Luka ben Serapion or Ioannes Serapion, both Arabs; Avicenna

(980–1037), a Persian philosopher and physician who wrote in Arabic;
Giovanni Mesue (whose name is mistakenly divided by a comma); Solomon,
the name given to a Hebrew text, also ascribed to Chael; Physiologus; Pliny;
Solinus; Albertus Magnus; Vincent de Beauvais; the Lapidary, perhaps the
Alphabetical Lapidary based on Damigeron and Isidore; Helimantus;
Isidore of Seville; Arnaldus Saxo; Juba II of Numidia, cited as a source by
Pliny; Dionysius the Alexandrian, probably not Dionysius Periegetes, whose
Description of the World, a geographical poem of the first century A.D., was
popular in the Middle Ages, but a later Dionysius, whose name, however, is
often connected with Socrates; Thetel Rabanus (the form of the name given
in Camillo Leonardi), actually two figures, Thetel, perhaps the Judaic
philosopher Cethel, who wrote a work translated into Latin as *De sculpturis
lapidum*, and Rabanus Maurus, author of the *De universo*, which describes the
gods graphically with etymological, physical, and euhemeristic commentaries; Bartolomeo de Ripa Romea; Bishop Marbodus; the Hortolanus; the
Book of All Things; Cornucopia; the Kyranides; and the Book of the Nature
of Things, a title too common to identify with accuracy, but possibly one of
the following: the *De rerum natura* of Lucretius, the *De naturis rerum* of
Alexander Neckham (1157–1217), the *De natura rerum* of Thomas Cantimpra-
tensis (1201–1270).

37 Even though jewels are commonly prized, as our most noble poet says, by
foolish and avaricious folk, because of the gain derived from them, nevertheless they ought to be esteemed by every noble and singular mind for
their beauty and power.

38 Camillo Leonardi's interest in medical matters can be seen in the comparison of this *virtù minerale* to the generative power of sperm, defined as
'soverchio nudrimento, che discende a i vasi spermatici, e da essi vasi si
infonde nello stesso sperma virtù generativa ... La quale virtù non opera per
modo di essenza, ma (per così dire) d'inherenza ...' (excessive nourishment,
which descends to the spermatic vessels, and from these vessels it infuses a
generative power into the sperm itself. This power does not function by
means of the essence but, so to speak, by means of what it adheres to; pp.
7^v–8^r). The idea, itself, however, derives from Albert the Great, although the
language is at times of alchemical and hermetic origin. The underlying
principle is the universal correspondence between *cosmos* (here exemplified
in the precious stones) and the microcosm (the human organism). For the
importance of analogy in the hermetic texts dealing with alchemy, see
Wayne Shumaker, *The Occult Sciences in the Renaissance. A Study in Intellectual Patterns*, ch. 4, especially pp. 193–7.

39 The following table shows how many colours are cited for each letter of the alphabet, the total being 228:

A 35	B 1	C 36	E 20	F 13
I 8	L 6	M 2	N 32	0 5
P 10	R 20	S 7	V 33	

Where possible, Dolce translates Leonardi's Latin into the appropriate shade in Italian, so that we have colours such as 'candido tramezato di colori crocei,' for the alabaster. The alphabet begins with 'Argentino – Andomantino' and concludes with 'Verde con macchie Serpentine – Porfido' (pp. 24^r, 28^r).

40 For the alphabet of stones in chapter 6, where 282 appear, Dolce follows Leonardi, translating and occasionally clarifying along the lines of 'Adamante, cioè Diamante' for the original *Adamas*. As regards the numbers of stones for each letter, we have the following in Camillo Leonardi:

A 29	B 9	C 47	D 7	E 19	F 5
G 15	H 6	I 11	K 6	L 21	M 14
N 5	O 16	P 16	Q 2	R 3	S 26
T 9	V 7	X 1	Y 3	Z 5	

Dolce's list varies slightly from the original. He adds one of the *I* stones to the *H* list, and, while he has fourteen stones beginning with *M*, one of them (the *Magnete*) is translated as 'Calamita,' revealing, if nothing else had, the Latin origin of his source. He also has only fifteen gems beginning with *O*, ten for *T*, and six for *V*.

41 Here, as elsewhere, Dolce follows Leonardi so closely that he repeats the ellipses for material missing in the original, a feature that also makes one wonder whether Leonardi's text is truly a compilation from diverse sources, as he claims, or is simply a copy of someone else's work. I raise the issue because the ellipses appear, among other places, even in Leonardi's chapter titles, where one would not expect them (e.g., chapter 4).

42 Dolce (or his typesetter) makes two of his few mistakes in translation in chapters 5 and 6. The title for chapter 5 reads 'Come nelle pietre si dica, che v'habbia virtù utili e come particolari' (p. 71^v), where 'utili' should have been 'universali,' and, in chapter 6, where Leonardi (and thus Dolce!) mentions one of his own gems, a *Diaspro*, we learn that it depicts the figure of an armed man who has the head of a chicken; bears a shield in his *left*

hand and a whip in his *left* hand; and, for thighs, legs, and feet, has two snakes. The original, of course, reads: 'In sinistra tenens clipeum; In dextra vero flagellum' (C. L., leaf LII; Dolce, p. 73ʳ).

43 Mario Pozzi briefly traces the fortune of Dolce's treatise in his study 'L'''ut pictura poësis'' in un dialogo di L. Dolce,' first published in the *Giornale storico della letteratura italiana* 144 (1967): 234–60, and now appearing in his *Lingua e cultura del Cinquecento*. This article is important for what it has to say about Dolce's originality (against those who claim the ideas derive from Pietro Aretino, Dolce's main interlocutor). A year later, Mark W. Roskill's bilingual translation appeared, with an appendix that sums up 'the subsequent history and influence of the Dialogue.' See *Dolce's 'Aretino' and Venetian Art Theory of the Cinquecento*, pp. 63–73 (and, for the relationship between Dolce and Aretino, pp. 32–5). The dialogue itself is also available in *Trattati d'arte del Cinquecento fra Manierismo e Controriforma*, edited with commentary by P. Barocchi, who criticizes Dolce rather harshly for the work's depiction of Michelangelo. In contrast, see the praise heaped on the work's theoretical aspect by Lionello Venturi in his *Storia della critica d'arte*, pp. 111–15. Among the sources not mentioned by either Pozzi or Roskill, see also Anthony Blunt, *Artistic Theory in Italy, 1450–1600*, pp. 83–4.

44 Blunt, for example, writes: 'The attack [on Michelangelo] ... was launched by Aretino and carried on in his name by his friend, Lodovico Dolce. It was inspired by purely personal motives and was in no way connected with the serious and religious criticisms of the *Last Judgement*, though later Gilio da Fabriano seems to have borrowed arguments from Dolce's work. The story of Aretino's relations with Michelangelo has been told at length by various writers [e.g., by Gauthiez in *L'Arétin* (Paris, 1895)], and need only be summarized here. Aretino, who greatly admired Michelangelo, did everything to gain the latter's good graces. But his flattering letters, in which he begged for a drawing, received no reply, and his attempt to dictate to the artist how he should paint the *Last Judgement* was met with insulting evasion. For ten years Aretino persisted, but in 1545 his patience gave way, and he wrote to Michelangelo that letter on the *Last Judgement* which is now famous as an example of insincere prudishness. From a man of Aretino's character it seems strange to hear passionate horror at the indecencies of the *Last Judgement*, but they pour out with far more violence than from Gilio or any seriously minded priest. Dolce's dialogue, *L'Aretino*, which was published in 1557, repeats all Aretino's arguments with the same intensity, and, since the authors were close friends, there is no doubt that they were working in collaboration' (*Artistic Theory in Italy*, p. 123). For a discussion of the problematical nature of Aretino's letter, see Roskill, *Dolce's 'Aretino,'* pp. 27–9,

and for the relationship between Aretino and Michelangelo, S. Ortolani's article 'Pietro Aretino e Michelangelo.'

45 See, for one example of many, the praise of 'the divine Michelangelo' cited in Dolce's *Trattato delle gemme*, pp. 67ᵛ–68ʳ, a work published two years after *L'Aretino*, in 1565.

46 See Roskill, *Dolce's 'Aretino,'* pp. 17–18, for a discussion of the individual's *giudizio naturale*, and Pozzi, 'L'"ut pictura poësis,"' pp. 1–4, for the relationship between artists and writers in the sixteenth century.

47 Mario Pozzi briefly discusses this work in a note to his study 'L'"ut pictura poësis,"' referring to 'la sciattezza e la pedanteria di questo scritto dolciano' and adding that it would be impossible to reevaluate the work's content (p. 21). If one concentrates on colour solely from the point of view of an artist – that is, from the point of view of someone interested only in its physical properties – perhaps Pozzi's statement is true, but the work, as we will see, is filled with other fascinating details, elements referred to by Pozzi simply as 'altre cose assai astrúse.'

48 All quotations derive from the *Dialogo di M. Lodovico Dolce, nel quale si ragiona delle qualità, diversità, e proprietà de i colori*, published in facsimile by Arnaldo Forni (Bologna, 1985).

49 Born in Cosenza in 1482, Antonio Telesio (or Tilesius) was an erudite philologist, uncle and tutor of the more famous Bernardino Telesio (1509–1588). Of noble family, Antonio received a brilliant education under Taddeo Acciarini, and eventually became professor of Greek and Latin in the college of nobles in Milan (around 1518). He left the city as a result of the French invasion of 1524, travelling to Rome, where he was protected by Cardinal Giberti. He taught Latin poetry in the *ginnasio romano* until the city was sacked in 1527, at which time he fled for Venice. He appears to have taught in Padua, where Dolce might have made his acquaintance. Antonio Telesio's treatise *De coloribus* was published in Venice in 1528, and his complete works were published in Naples in 1762. Pierre Larousse, *Grand Dictionnaire universel du XIXᵉ siècle* (Paris, 1866–79, rpt. Geneva and Paris: Slatkine, 1982), vol. 14, s.v. 'Telesio.'

50 I refer to the edition of 1528: *Antonii Thylesii Cosentini Libellus de coloribus, ubi multa leguntur praeter aliorum opinionem* (In fine: Impressum Venetiis opera Bernardini Vitalis Veneti Mense Iunio M.D.XXVIII).

51 Editions appeared in 1547, 1551, 1558, 1559, and 1564. Among his other works, Morato (Mantua *ca* 1495–Ferrara 1547/1548) published *Rimario di tutte le cadentie di Dante e Petrarca* (1528), the first Italian rhyming dictionary. His daughter, Olimpia Morata (Ferrara 1526–Heidelberg 1555) was also a renowned humanist, having learned Greek and Latin as a child. Like her

father, who left Ferrara from around 1528 to 1538 for Venice and other cities, she was attracted by reform ideas.

52 In Dolce, chess is criticized as one of the 'vani giuochi' (useless games; p. 47^r). Cornelio (Dolce's spokesman) does not want to deny the individual the right to 'qualche ricreatione e ristoro' (some recreation and restoration), but holds that one should seek pastimes that are more virtuous, such as 'ragionamenti dilettevoli' (agreeable discussions). Ultimately, games like chess are 'rincrescevoli, e dannosi' (regrettable and damaging; p. 47^v).

53 Telesio wrote: 'nam Chara græce, ira quoque dicitur latine. & ex eodem, ut puto, horrore Charybdis nominata est, & Charon. de quo cum inquit Virgilius, Stant circum lumina flammæ. Cæsium uoluit Senem illum horribilem, ac dirum significare' (for *Chara* in Greek is called *ira* in Latin. And from this same [use of the term for] dread, I believe, Charybdis and Charon took their names. Because of this, Virgil says that he [Charon] has flames around his eyes. He wanted blue-grey to signify that dreadful and dire old man; b^r, abbreviations expanded). Where Dolce employs Telesio, he translates word for word, as seen in the repetition of the authorial 'ut puto' as 'stimo.'

54 Charon's boat comes up for discussion a second time under the colour 'ferrugineo' (chapter 6 in Telesio; p. 13^v in Dolce). I regret to note that, when writing *Charon and the Crossing* (see, in particular, p. 80 for Virgil, and pp. 131–2 for Dante), I was unaware of either Telesio's or Dolce's references to the colour of Charon's eyes or that of his boat. I might have been less eager to accept W. McLeod's explanation of the adjectives *caeruleus* and *ferrugineus* as an example of 'elegant variation' and 'vivid particularization,' imitating Homer's apparent contradictions. The sordid colour of Charon's clothes is also discussed by both Telesio (in his epilogue) and Dolce (pp. 17^{r-v}), with Virgil being cited as the source.

55 Responding to Mario's citation of a Petrarchan *terzina* from the *Trionfi* ('Perseo era quivi: e volli saper, come / Andromeda gli piacque in Ethiopia / Giovane bruna, i begli occhi, e le chiome' [Perseus was here and I wanted to know how Andromeda pleased him in Ethiopia, a dark young woman with beautiful eyes and hair]), Cornelio responds as follows: 'Hai da sapere, che'l Petrarca in questo luogo prende il bruno per il nero, o per quello, che troppo si accosta al nero: il qual colore in un capo humano, che dee esser bianco, non è lodato. Oltre a cio dannava insieme con la negrezza del corpo il Petrarca i capelli neri, lodando egli sempre i biondi; e volendo significare, che Andromeda essendo ella nata in Ethiopia era dal capo al piede tutta nera' (You should know that Petrarch in this passage uses 'brown' for 'black,' or for that which is too close to black. This colour on a human head, which ought to be white, is not praised. Moreover, along with the blackness

of the body, Petrarch condemned black hair, praising always blonde. He wanted to signify that Andromeda, being born in Ethiopia, was completely black from head to toe; p. 12^r).

56 Dolce's comments derive from Morato, who writes, in part: 'Il Petrarcha dicendo che la sua speme era giunta al verde nel Sonetto. Già fiammeggiava l'amorosa stella, a questo hebbe riguardo, dimostrandosi esser fuor d'ogni speranza, & esser già pervenute a niente le cose che sperava, ben che ignoranti esponghino in contrario, che era venuto al lauro, liquali non di corona di lauro, ma di ortica degni sono, di qui è nato il dir commune de volgari, liquali volendo accennare alcuno essere caduto nelle miserie estreme, & vltima perditione, dicono quello essere al verde, perchè quando la candela è consumata fin là, niente più le resta in che possi ardere, & render luce' (Petrarch, in writing that his hope had reached the green in his sonnet, 'Already the amorous star was flaming,' considered this, showing himself to be beyond any hope and to have already come to naught the things that he hoped for, even though the ignorant state the contrary, that he had come to the laurel, demonstrating that they are worthy, not of a crown of laurel, but of nettles. From this comes the commonplace of the crowd, who, wanting to point out that someone has fallen into extreme poverty and ultimate ruin, say that he is at the green, because, when the candle is consumed to the end, nothing remains to burn and give off light; p. A 5^v). I quote from the edition published in Brixiæ [Brescia] apud Damianum Turlinum, 1564, a text lacking accents and much condensed. I have modernized the orthography of *v* to *u*.

57 I derive the terminology from the illustration of a crossbow in Reginald Bragonier, Jr, and David Fisher, eds., *What's What: A Visual Glossary of the Physical World*, p. 456.

58 Cornelio does criticize Italians for wearing clothes that come from France, Spain, and Germany, with Mario adding that one should dress 'secondo il costume della città, in cui si è nato' (according to the custom of the city where one was born; p. 37^v).

59 The process is one in which digression follows upon digression, as can be seen in the discussion of snakes, which continues with references to other authors. The discussion of snakes, for example, not only alludes to 'malignità' as used in the *imprese* of Ariosto, but also to prudence. The reason, in part, is that the snake hides all winter and then renews itself by casting off its skin, which in turn alludes to the immortality of the soul. Virgil, we learn, mentioned this in a simile in the *Aeneid* and was later felicitously imitated by Ariosto. The Egyptians used the snake to denote the year, depicting it with its tail in its mouth, signifying the fact that, in turning, the year returns, and will always do so, a concept that brings to the page a passage from Sannaz-

zaro: 'E'l Sol fuggendo ancor da mane a sera / Ne mena i giorni, e'l viver nostro inseme, / Et ei ritorna pur, come prim'era' (And the sun, still fleeing from morn to night, brings us the days, along with our life, and he returns again, just as he was – a motif analysed in chapter 4 of this study, as it appears in the tragic poets), which in turn is seen as an imitation of those verses of Catullus that read: 'Soles fugere et redire possunt: / Nobis cum semel occidit brevis lux, / Nox est perpetua una dormienda' (The sun sets and rises each day. When our brief light dies once and for all, night follows and an endless sleep; p. 50^v). By the time we reach the end of the discourse, the subject has nothing to do with snakes.

60 Three examples follow: 'Aglio amore sporco, e puzzolente' (garlic, a dirty, stinking love), 'Anello, dar la fede a cui si manda' (ring, a pledge of faith to whom sent), 'Artichiocchi, aiutati meglio che poi' (artichokes, help yourself the best you can; Morato, *Il significato de mazzoli*, p. D 2^v).

Conclusion

1 Charles Speroni, *Wit and Wisdom of the Italian Renaissance*, pp. 223–4. Speroni cites two sources for Lodovico Domenichi: *Facetie, motti et burle di diversi signori et persone private* (Venice: F.B. Bonfadino, 1609) and *Facezie*, a cura di Giovanni Fabris (Rome: Formiggini, 1923).

2 It should be unnecessary to mention again the many achievements of the man, ranging from his youthful contributions to literary criticism, including the first translation into the vernacular of Horace's *Ars poetica* (1535), a work that ushered in the age of criticism in Italy, to his late pre-encyclopedic efforts that demonstrate an interest in all aspects of the world around us.

3 In addition to those works mentioned in other chapters, I might cite Giuseppe Betussi, who refers to him as 'gentile e veramente dolce' in his dialogue on love, *Il Raverta*. See Giuseppe Zonta's edition of *Trattati d'amore del Cinquecento*, p. 57.

4 Found in the 1545 and 1547 editions of Dolce's comedy *Il capitano*, published in Venice by Giolito, this work has been seen by some as an antecedent of G.B. Marino's *Adone*. See, for example, Giuseppe Bianchini's article in the *Giornale storico della letteratura italiana* 29, 568–70, as well as Antonio Belloni, *Il poema epico e mitologico* (Milan: Vallardi, [1912]), p. 361, who includes Dolce along with Giovanni Turcagnota and Girolamo Parabosco as 'precedenti del Marino.' In studying the work, one might also pay attention to what Dolce has to say elsewhere about Titian's painting *Venere e Adone*, beginning with Cicogna's reference to one of his letters to Alessandro Contarini ('Memoria intorno la vita e gli scritti di Messer Lodovico Dolce,' p. 101).

5 Anne Reynolds quotes a brief selection from one of Dolce's *Capitoli in lode dello sputo* in her study 'Galileo Galilei's Poem "Against Wearing the Toga,,"' p. 335, and Paolo Cherchi quotes part of Dolce's *Capitolo in lode del naso* in his article entitled 'L'encomio paradossale nel Manierismo,' p. 375. Along with various other *capitoli* (for which see the primary bibliography), Dolce also wrote a *satira* addressed to Ercole Bentivoglio, in which, as the title says, 'Loda meritevolmente le Satire del Bentivoglio, ed esaltando le operazioni virtuose, riprende gli uomini di oggidì, che amano solamente il vizio' (he praises deservingly the satires of Ercole Bentivoglio, and, exalting virtuous deeds, reproves the men of today, who only love vice). For this work, see *Satire di Antonio Vinciguerra, Lodovico Ariosto, Ercole Bentivoglio, Luigi Alamanni, Lodovico Dolce.*

6 For manuscript collections containing poems of Dolce, see Kristeller's *Iter italicum.* Cicogna provides a long list of *Rime varie*, with sources (pp. 161–7).

7 For a discussion of the Dream of Parnassus as a literary theme for the generation of writers contemporary with Aretino, see Cairns, *Pietro Aretino and the Republic of Venice*, pp. 231–49, and, for Dolce in particular, pp. 233–40.

8 See the primary bibliography under *Sorti.*

9 Giuseppe Toffanin mentions Dolce's praiseworthy work in this area, in a paragraph devoted primarily to other authors active in this genre. See *Il Cinquecento*, pp. 584–5. For a recent study of *imprese*, see Mauda Bregoli-Russo, *L'impresa come ritratto del Rinascimento.*

10 The Newberry Library in Chicago has two editions of the *Vita* of Charles V, both with the same title page (published in Venice by Giolito in 1561), catalogued as 'distinctly different.' One may be Dolce's translation of Anatholius Desbarres, although the first edition is usually listed as being published in 1567. Alfonso Ulloa, who translated Dolce's expositions on Ariosto into Spanish (published by Giolito in 1553), also published a *Vita* of Charles V with the rival Valgrisi press in 1562 (the University of Wisconsin library lists a 1560 edition) and a *Vita* of Ferdinando I in 1565. One wonders if Dolce borrowed from Ulloa. Giusto Fontanini, in *Della eloquenza italiana ... libri tre novellamente ristampati*, p. 603, says that Dolce praised Ulloa as a translator from Spanish to Italian. Bongi, however, seems not to think so, since he quotes from Dolce's 'Avviso ai lettori' the author's assertion that he writes without partiality, having been born and raised in Italy and thus 'libero dal sospetto della affettione,' perhaps an arrow at the Spaniard Ulloa (*Annali*, vol. 1, pp. 134–6).

Bibliography

I. The Works of Lodovico Dolce

The entries in Part I of this bibliography are divided into three categories: (1) Original Works and *Rifacimenti*, (2) Translations, and (3) Editions. A few works, most notably of theatre, appear under sections 1 and 2, since the distinction between adaptation and translation is often confused, in the Renaissance itself and later. What Dolce calls an adaptation, some modern critics would call a free translation (or, as some would have it, applying modern standards, a 'bad' translation).

Consistency has been a consideration throughout this bibliography, particularly as regards the spelling of publishers' names and the place of origin. In the latter case, the modern English form of the city has been used in place of the varied Italian forms (e.g., Venice for 'In Venetia,' 'Venetia,' 'Venetiis, 'In Vinegia,' 'Vinegia,' 'Venezia'). References to the press of Gabriel Giolito de' Ferrari, with all its variants, have been abbreviated to Gabriel Giolito. In Italian titles, nothing has been capitalized except the first word, proper names, centuries (e.g., *Il Cinquecento*), terms for cultural periods (e.g., *Rinascimento* and *Barocco*), and, where capitalized in the original source, the honorific *M*, for *Messer*. For ease of reading, archaic *u* (= *v*) and *V* (= *U*) have been transcribed according to modern standards and accents have been added where needed.

Finally, following Salvatore Bongi's divisions, I should note that, for the Giolito press, not always cited in full by all sources, the publisher can be specified according to the following chronological indications: (1) 1536–1540: Giovanni the older in association with his son Gabriel; (2) 1541–1550 in part: Gabriel by himself; (3) 1550 in part–1556 in part: Gabriel along with his brothers, none of whom, however, had a visible hand in the business; (4) 1556 in part–1578 in part: Gabriel, alone for the second time; (5) 1578 in part–1590: Giovanni the younger and Giovan Paolo, sons and heirs of Gabriel; and (6) 1591–1606: Giovan Paolo with the orphaned children of Giovanni.

1. Original Works and Rifacimenti

Achille et Enea = *L'Achille et l'Enea di Messer Lodovico Dolce. Dove egli tessendo l'historia della Iliade d'Homero à quella dell'Eneide di Vergilio, ambedue l'ha divinamente ridotte in ottava rima. Con argomenti, et allegorie per ogni canto: et due tavole: l'una delle sentenze; l'altra de i nomi, & delle cose più notabili. Al potentissimo, et invittissimo Filippo d'Austria re catholico.* Venice: Gabriel Giolito, 1570.

Amore = *L'Amore di Florio e Biancofiore.* Venice: M. Bernardino de Vitali Veneziano, 1532.

Apologia contra i detrattori dell'Autore. In *Orlando furioso di Messer Ludovico Ariosto nobile ferrarese con la giunta, novissimamente stampato e corretto. Con una apologia di M. Lodovico Dolcio contra i detrattori dell'autore, et un modo brevissimo di trovar le cose aggiunte. E tavola di tutto quello ch'è contenuto nel libro. Aggiuntovi una breve expositione de i luoghi difficili. Se vendono in Turino da Jacobino Dulci ditto Cunni.* Turin: Martino Cravoto & Francesco Robi de Saviliano, 1536. [Contains dedication of Dolce to his cousin M. Gasparo Spinelli, Gran Cancelliere del Regno di Cipri]

Capitano = *Il capitano; comedia di M. Lodovico Dolce, recitata in Mantova all'eccellentiss. signor duca. Con alcune stanze del medesimo nella favola d'Adone ...* Venice: Gabriel Giolito, 1545. See also *Comedie.*

Capitoli = *Capitoli del s. Pietro Aretino, di messer Lodovico Dolce, di m. Francesco Sansovino e di altri acutissimi ingegni.* Venice: C. Navò e fratelli, 1540. [Includes 'Del naso,' 'Della speranza,' 'In lode dello sputo,' 'D'un ragazzo,' 'Della poesia,' 'A. Mons. Grimaldi' (on Dolce's life), 'A M. Daniel Buonriccio']

Comedie di M. Lodovico Dolce, cioè, Il ragazzo, Il capitano, Il marito, La Fabritia, Il ruffiano. Venice: Gabriel Giolito, 1560.

Dell'arte di honestamente amare. Manuscript lost.

Dialogo della milizia marittima. 1548 manuscript. Siena, Biblioteca Comunale, K II 42, s. XVI. *Lod. Dolce, della milizia marittima,* a dialogue to the Duke of Florence (1548). [Kristeller cites L. Ilari, *La biblioteca pubblica di Siena disposta secondo le materie,* 7 vols. (Siena, 1844–8), vol. 3, p. 166, and the Biblioteca Apostolica Vaticana, Fondo Reginense Latino 2030, Lod. Dolce (Crist. Canale), *Milizia marittima* (dialogue) (Montfaucon, n. 570, p. 27)]

Dialogo della pittura di M. Lodovico Dolce, intitolato l'Aretino. Nel quale si ragiona della dignità di essa pittura, e di tutte le parti necessarie, che a perfetto pittore si acconvengono: con esempi di pittori antichi, & moderni: e nel fine si fa mentione delle virtù e delle opere del divin Titiano. Venice: Gabriel Giolito, 1557.

Dialogo di M. Lodovico Dolce della institution delle donne, secondo li tre stati, che cadono nella vita humana ... Venice: Gabriel Giolito, 1545; reissued 'Da lui medesimo nuovamente ricorretto, et ampliato,' 1547; '3ª impressione riveduto, e di più utili cose ampliato,' 1553; '4ª impressione,' 1559; '... & con la tavola delle cose più degne di memoria,' 1560. Also published as *De gli ammaestramenti pregiatissimi, che appartengono alla educatione, & honorevole a virtuosa vita virginale, maritale, e vedovile, libri tre; ne' quali con leggiadra, e dolce maniera concatenati si veggono sentenze scelte, documenti singolari, ricordi prudentissimi, avvisi, regole utilissime, & precetti lodevoli* ... In Agnolo Firenzuola. *Le bellezze, le lodi, gli amori & i costumi delle donne.* Venice: Presso Barezzo Barezzi, 1622.

Dialogo di M. Lodovico Dolce, nel quale si ragiona delle qualità, diversità, e proprietà de i colori. Venice: Gio. Battista, Marchio Sessa et fratelli, 1565.

Dialogo di M. Lodovico Dolce, nel quale si ragiona del modo di accrescere, et conservar la memoria. Venice: Gio. Battista et Marchio Sessa fratelli, 1552; Venice: Per gli Heredi di Marchiò Sessa, 1575. [Based on the *Congestorium artificiose memorie* of Johann Host von Romberch (fl. 1485–1533)]

Dialogo in cui si parla di che qualità si dee tor moglie, e del modo che vi si ha a tenere. Venice: Curzio Navò e fratelli, 1538. [See Dolce's translation of Juvenal]

Dialogo piacevole di Messer Lodovico Dolce, nelquale Messer Pietro Aretino parla in difesa d'i male aventurati mariti. [Venice], C. Navò, 1542. [In fine: Per Curtio Troiano d'i Navò]

Didone, tragedia di M. Lodovico Dolce. Venice: In casa de' figliuoli di Aldo, 1547. *Nuovamente dal medesimo riveduta e ricorretta.* Venice: Gabriel Giolito, 1560. [See also *Tragedie*]

Discorso in materia di rettorica. 1563. [See Cicero under 'Translations']

Eleganze, con un discorso sopra a mutamenti e diversi ornamenti dell'Ariosto. Venice: Gio. Battista et Marchio Sessa et fratelli, 1564.

Enea = L'Enea di M. Lodovico Dolce; tratto dall'Eneide di Vergilio, all'illustrissimo et eccellentissimo signor Don Francesco de Medici principe di Fiorenza e di Siena. Venice: Giovanni Varisco e compagnia, 1568.

Espositione di tutti i vocaboli et luoghi difficili, che nel libro [Il furioso] si trovano. Raccolte da M. Lodovico Dolce. Venice: Gabriel Giolito, 1542. Translated into Spanish ('Exposición de todos los lugares difficultosos') by Alfonso de Ulloa in his translation of Ariosto (Venice: Gabriel Giolito, 1553) and by Hieronimo de Urrea (Lyon: Bastano di Bartholomeo Honorati, 1556).

Fabritia, comedia di M. Lodovico Dolce. Venice: Aldi filii, 1549; *Di nuovo ricoretta e ristampata.* Venice: Gabriel Giolito, 1560. [See also *Comedie*]

Favola d'Adone. 1545; 1547. [See also *Il capitano*]

Giocasta, tragedia di M. Lodovico Dolce. Venice: I figliuoli di Aldo, 1549. [See also under 'Translations']

Giornale delle historie del mondo, delle cose degne di memoria di giorno in giorno occorse dal principio del mondo sino a suoi tempi, di M. Lodovico Dolce. Riveduto, corretto, &

ampliato da Guglielmo Rinaldi. Venice: Al Segno della Salamandra [D. Zenaro], 1572.

Hecuba = La Hecuba, tragedia di M. Lodovico Dolce, tratta da Euripide. Venice: Gabriel Giolito, 1543. [See also *Tragedie* and under 'Translations']

Imprese = Di Battista Pittoni pittore vicentino ... Imprese di diversi prencipi, duchi, signori e d'altri personaggi et huomini letterati et illustri. Con privilegio di Venetia per anni XV. Con alcune stanze del Dolce, che dichiarano i motti di esse imprese. Venice: n.p., 1562; Venice: I Valegii, 1566. [Dolce's verses are printed on separate pages within ornamental woodcut borders]

Lettere. Della nuova scielta di lettere di diversi nobiliss. huomini ... con un discorso ... di M. Bernardino Pino, Venice: Gabriel Giolito, 1554. [See II, 218, for a letter of Dolce's]

Marianna, tragedia di M. Lodovico Dolce, recitata in Vinegia nel palazzo dell'eccellentiss. s. duca di Ferrara, con alcune rime e versi del detto ... Venice: Gabriel Giolito, 1565.

Marito = Il marito, comedia di M. Lodovico Dolce. Venice: Gabriel Giolito, 1545. [See also *Comedie*]

Modi affigurati e voci scelte et eleganti della volgar lingua, con un discorso sopra a mutamenti e diversi ornamenti dell'Ariosto, di M. Lodovico Dolce. Venice: Gio. Battista et Marchio Sessa et fratelli, 1554.

Origine della satira, Discorso sopra le satire [di Orazio], Discorso sopra le epistole, e Discorso sopra la poetica. 1559. [See Horace under 'Translations']

Osservationi = Osservationi nella volgar lingua di M. Lodovico Dolce, divise in quattro libri. Venice: Gabriel Giolito, 1550.

Palmerino = Il Palmerino di M. Lodovico Dolce. Venice: Gio. Battista Sessa et fratelli, 1561. [*Rifacimento*]

Prefazione all'Amadigi di Bernardo Tasso. 1560. [See 'Prefazione antica di Lodovico Dolce,' p. iii. In *L'Amadigi di M. Bernardo Tasso, colle vita dell'autore e varie illustrazioni dell'opera ...,* vol. 3. Bergamo: P. Lancellotti, 1755]

Primaleone, figliuolo di Palmerino, di M. Lodovico Dolce. Venice: G.B. et M. Sessa et fratelli, 1562. [*Rifacimento*]

Prime imprese = Le prime imprese del conte Orlando di M. Lodovico Dolce. Da lui composte in ottava rima, et nuovamente stampate. Con argomenti et allegorie per ogni canto. Et una tavola de' nomi & delle cose più notabili. All'illustriss. et eccellentiss. signor Francesco Maria della Rovere prencipe d'Urbino. Venice: Gabriel Golito, 1572. Translated into Spanish as: *El Nascimiento y primeras empresas del conde Orlando, traduzidas por Pero López Henríquez de Calatayud.* Valladolid: Diego F. de Cordova y Oviedo, n.d. [1595?].

Ragazzo = Il ragazzo, comedia di M. Lodovico Dolce. Venice: Curtio de Navò et Fratelli, al Leone, 1541.

Rime. Various scattered *Rime* in Italian and Latin.

Ruffiano. Il roffiano. Comedia di Lodovico Dolce tratta dal Rudente. Venice: Gabriel Giolito, 1551.

Sacripante = Cinque primi canti di Sacripante, di messer Lodovico Dolcio. Venice: Francesco Bindoni et Mapheo Pasini, 1535 [Published against the poet's wishes]; *Il primo libro di Sacripante di messer Lodovico Dolce.* Venice: Francesco Bindoni et Mapheo Pasini, 1536; *Dieci canti di Sacripante.* Venice: N. Zoppino, 1537.

'Satira di M. Lodovico Dolce, al signor Ercole Bentivoglio.' In *Satire di Antonio Vinciguerra, Lodovico Ariosto, Ercole Bentivoglio, Luigi Alamanni, Lodovico Dolce.* London, T. Masi e compagni, 1786.

Sogno = Il sogno di Parnaso con alcune altre rime d'amore. Venice: B. de Vitali Venetiano, 1532.

Somma della filosofia d'Aristotele, e prima della dialettica. Raccolta da M. Lodovico Dolce. Venice: Gio. Battista et Marchò Sessa et fratelli, 1565. [3 parts in 1 volume, with an internal title for part 3: *La somma di tutta la natural philosophia di Aristotele*]

Sonetti spirituali. In *Rime di diversi. Libro secondo.* Venice: Gabriel Giolito, 1547. [18 sonnets]

Sorti = Le sorti di Francesco Marcolini da Forli, intitolate giardino di pensieri. Venice: F. Marcolino, 1540. [Dolce composed explanatory verses in *terza rima* to accompany this work on fortune-telling by cards]

Stanze composte nella vittoria africana nuovamente avuta dal sacratissimo imperatore Carlo V. Rome, 1535; Genoa: G.A. Bellon, 1535.

Thyeste, tragedia di M. Lodovico Dolce, tratta da Seneca. Venice: Gabriel Giolito, 1543. [See also *Tragedie*]

Tragedie di M. Lodovico Dolce, cape, Giocasta, Didone, Thieste, Medea, Ifigenia, Hecuba, di nuovo ricorrette e ristampate. Venice: Gabriel Giolito, 1560.

Trattato delle gemme = Libri tre di M. Lodovico Dolce, ne i quali si tratta delle diverse sorti delle gemme, che produce la natura, della qualità, grandezza, bellezza, & virtù loro ... Venice: Gio. Battista, Marchio Sessa et fratelli, 1565. [Translation of Camillo Leonardi's *Speculum lapidum*]

Troiane = Le troiane, tragedia di M. Lodovico Dolce, recitata in Venezia l'anno MDLXVI. Venice: Gabriel Giolito, 1567 [Includes 'sonetti del Dolce'; see also *Tragedie*]

Vita del Boccaccio. 1552. [See Giovanni Boccaccio, *Il Decamerone* ... *alla sua vera lettione ridotto da M. Lodovico Dolce,* under 'Editions']

Vita dell' invittiss. e gloriosiss. imperador Carlo Quinto, discritta da M. Lodovico Dolce. Con la tavola nel fine. Venice: Gabriel Giolito, 1561 [96 pp.] and 1561 [168 pp. for the text of the life, followed by other material; dedicated by Dolce to Emanuele Filiberto, Duca di Savoia]. *Vita di Carlo Quinto imp. descritta da M. Lodovico Dolce.* Venice: Gabriel Giolito, 1567. [186 pp. for the text of the life, followed in many copies by the *Immortalità dell'* ... *imperator Carlo Quinto; dedicatagli in lingua latina dal signor Anatholio Desbarres, e nuovamente tradotta nella volgar lingua da M.*

Lodovico Dolce. Venice: Gabriel Giolito, 1567 (315 pp.)] [Charles V, Holy Roman Emperor, 1500–1558. According to Bongi, Giolito issued three different editions in 1561, plus the fourth in 1567. See also Desbarres and Mexia]

Vita di Cicerone. 1562. [See Cicero, under 'Translations']

Vita di Dante. 1555. [See Dante Alighieri, under 'Editions']

Vita di Ferdinando, primo imperadore di questo nome, discritta da M. Lodovico Dolce, nella quale sotto brevità sono comprese l'historie dall'anno M.D.III al M.D.LXIIII. Venice: Gabriel Giolito, 1566.

Vita di Giammatteo Bembo. Manuscript lost.

Vita di Giuseppe, discritta in ottava rima, da M. Lodovico Dolce. Venice: Gabriel Giolito, 1551 [in three cantos]. Venice: Gabriel Giolito, 1561. [Joseph the Patriarch]

Vita di Ovidio. 1568. [See Ovid, *Le trasformationi*, under 'Translations']

Possibly from a draft of Dolce: *Discorso universale di M. Agostino Ferentilli. Nel quale discorrendosi per le sei età, et le quattro monarchie, si raccontano tutte l'historie, & l'origine di tutti gl'imperij, regni & nationi, cominciando dal principio del mondo fino all'anno MDLXIX. Nel fine del quale si mostra con diligente calcolo de' tempi, quanto habbia da durare il presente secolo, seguitando in ciò l'opinione di Elia Rabino, & di Lattantio Firmiano. Aggiuntovi la creatione del mondo, descritta da Filone Hebreo, & tradotta dal medesimo Ferentilli.* Venice: Gabriel Giolito, 1570. [Bongi notes that the Venetian Senate, on 29 November 1561, granted a fifteen-year privilege to Giolito for the publication of a work to be written by Lodovico Dolce, under this title. Promised on the frontispiece of Mexia's *Vite degli imperatori* in 1561, the work never appeared during Dolce's lifetime. Ferentilli, who inherited Dolce's projects from Giolito and who had been working on several of them during the last year or so of Dolce's life, very possibly received a draft of this work or an outline that he then made his own (2: 310–11)]

2. Translations

Achilles Tatius. *Amorosi ragionamenti. Dialogo, nel quale si racconta un compassionevole amore di due amanti, tradotto per M. Lodovico Dolce dai fragmenti d'un antico scrittor greco.* Venice: Gabriel Giolito, 1546. [*Gli amori di Leucippe e Cletofonte*, Books V–VIII of Achilles Tatius's *Erotica*, translated from the Latin of Luigi Annibale della Croce, *Narrationis amatoriae fragmentum* (Presso il Griffio di Lione, 1544), which contains the same four books]

Acominatus, Nicetas. *Historia de gl'imperatori greci, descritta da Niceta Coniate, gran secretario, & giudice di Belo, il quale comincia dall'imperio di Giovanni Conneno, dove lascia il Zonara, & segue fino alla presa di Costantinopoli, che fu l'anno M.CCCC.LIII. alla quale s'è aggiunta l'historia di Niceforo Gregora, che seguendo il Niceta per l'istesso *ordine de gl'imperatori greci: dall'imperio di Teodoro Lascaro primo, viene fino alla morte di Andronico Paleologo il giovane. Amendue tradotte da M. Lodovico Dolce, & riscontrate co' testi greci, & migliorate da M. Agostino Ferentilli. E questa è la seconda (e terza) parte dell'historie de gli imperatori greci.* Venice: Gabriel Giolito, 1569.

Appian of Alexandria. *Historie delle guerre esterne de romani di Appiano Alessandrino. Prima parte. Tradotta da Messer Alessandro Braccio secretario fiorentino, e di nuovo impressa, & con somma diligenza da M. Lodovico Dolce corretta. Con nuova tavola aggiunta non più stampata.* Venice: Gabriel Giolito, 1554.

– *Historia delle guerre civili de' romani di Appiano Alessandrino. Seconda parte.* [Ibid], 1559.

– *Tre libri di Appiano, cioè della guerra illirica, della Spagnuola: e della guerra che fece Annibale in Italia, non più veduti, e da M. Lodovico Dolce tradotti, con la lor tavola.* Venice: Gabriel Giolito, 1559.

Catullus, Gaius Valerius. *Lo Epithalamio di Ca-Catullo* [sic] *nelle nozze di Peleo & di Theti.* [See Juvenal]

Ceriola, Furio. *Il concilio, overo consiglio, et i consiglieri del prencipe, di Furio Ceriola, tradotto di Spagnuolo in volgare da Lodovico Dolce.* Venice: Gabriel Giolito, 1560.

Cicero. *Il dialogo dell'oratore di Cicerone, tradotto per M. Lodovico Dolce.* Venice: Gabriel Giolito, 1547. [trans. of *De Oratore*] *Brevi annotationi ne i tre libri del dialogo dell'oratore di Cicerone.* Venice: Gabriel Giolito, 1555. *Le orationi di M. T. Cicerone, tradotte da Lodovico Dolce con la vita dell'autore, con un breve discorso in materia di rhetorica ...* Venice: Gabriel Giolito, 1562.

Desbarres, Anatholius. *Immortalità dell'invittissimo et gloriosiss. imperator Carlo Quinto; dedicatagli in lingua latina dal signor Anatholio Desbarres, e nuovamente* [sic] *tradotta nella volgar lingua da M. Lodovico Dolce.* Venice: Gabriel Giolito, 1566. [Some copies of this work were added to the end of Dolce's *Vita di Carlo Quinto.* See also Mexia]

Euripides. *Giocasta, tragedia.* Venice: i figliuoli d'Aldo, 1549. [*Phoenissae*]

– *La Hecuba; tragedia di M. Lodovico Dolce, tratta da Euripide ...* Venice: Gabriel Giolito, 1543.

– *Ifigenia, tragedia di M. Lodovico Dolce.* Venice: Gabriel Giolito, 1551.

– *La Medea, tragedia di M. Lodovico Dolce.* Venice: Gabriel Giolito, 1557. [See also under 'Original Works and *Rifacimenti*' s.v. '*Tragedie*']

Galen. *Oratione di Galeno, nella quale si essortano i giovani alla cognitione delle arti. Tradotta per M. Lodovico Dolce.* Venice: Gabriel Giolito, 1548. [*Oratio suasoria ad artes*]

Gregoras, Niceforo. *Historie di Constantinopoli ...* Venice: Gabriel Giolito, 1570. [See also Acominatus, in *Historia de gl'imperatori greci, descritta da Niceta Coniate*]

Guilleo, Guglielmo. *Discorso di Guglielmo Guilleo Alemanno sopra i fatti di Annibale. Nel quale dimostrandosi lui essere stato nel valor delle arme superiore a tutti gli altri capitani, si descrive generalmente l'ufficio di perfetto capitano, tradotto per il Dolce.* Venice: Gabriel Giolito, 1551. [Translated, with amplifications, from a Latin original]

Homer. *L'Ulisse di M. Lodovico Dolce, da lui tratto dall'Odissea d'Homero et ridotto in ottava rima, nel quale si raccontano tutti gli errori, & le fatiche d'Ulisse dalla partita sua di Troia, fino al ritorno alla patria per lo spatio di venti anni. Con argomenti et allegorie a ciascun canto, così dell'historie, come delle favole, et con due tavole: una delle sententie, et l'altra delle cose più notabili.* Venice: Gabriel Giolito, 1573. [Includes Dolce's translation of the *Batracomiomachia* in octaves, under the title *Battaglia dei topi e delle rane cavata da Homero.* Regarding the translation of the *Odyssey,* Bongi says it is 'tanto larga da non vedercisi più quasi niente dell'originale omerico' (so expanded that one is able to see almost nothing of the Homeric original) (2: 335)]

Horace. *I dilettevoli sermoni, altrimenti satire, e le morali epistole di Horatio, illustre poeta lirico, insieme con la poetica. Ridotte da M. Lodovico Dolce dal poema latino in versi sciolti volgari. Con la vita di Horatio. Origine della satira. Discorso sopra le epistole. Discorso sopra la poetica.* Venice: Gabriel Giolito, 1559.

– *La poetica d'Horatio; tradotta per Messer Lodovico Dolce. Dialogo contra i poeti del Bernia.* [Venice?: F. Bindoni & M. Pasini?], 1535. [Includes Francesco Berni, *Dialogo contra i poeti*]

Juvenal. *Paraphrasi nella sesta satira di Giuvenale, nella quale si ragiona delle miserie de gli huomini maritati. Dialogo in cui si parla di che qualità si dee tor moglie, & del modo, che vi si ha a tenere. Lo Epithalamio di Ca-Catullo* [sic] *nelle nozze di Peleo & di Theti.* Venice: Curtio Navò e fratelli, 1538. [Dedication signed Lodovico Dolce. At end: 'Il fine dell'epithalamio tradotto per M. Lodovico Dolce.' Juvenal translated in prose, Catullus in free verse. Listed as 1530 in Marino Parenti, *Prime edizioni italiane* (Florence: Sansoni, 1961), p. 204]

Mexia, Pedro. *Le vite di tutti gl' imperadori romani da Giulio Cesare insino a Massimiliano tratte per M. Lodovico Dolce dal libro spagnuolo del nobile cavaliere Pietro Messia, con alcune utili cose in diversi luoghi aggiunte. Con una tavola copiosissima de' fatti più notabili in esse vite contenuti.* Venice: Gabriel Giolito, 1558; *Aggiuntavi la vita dell'invitissimo Carlo Quinto imperatore, discritta dal medesimo M. Lodovico Dolce: e di più nel fine un breve discorso di tutte l'età e principati del mondo. Con due tavole copiosissime; l'una de fatti notabili, che in esse vite, et l'altra di quelli, che nella vita di Carlo Quinto si contengono.* 1561.

Mohammed II, Sultan of the Turks. *Lettere del gran Mahumeto imperadore de' turchi: scritte a diversi re, prencipi, signori, e republiche, con le risposte loro; ridotte nella volgar lingua da M. Lodovico Dolce. Insieme con le lettere di Falaride Tiranno degli agrigentini.* Venice: Gabriel Giolito, 1562. [Author: Laudivio, Zacchia, de Vezzano, fl. 1473. Mehmet II, the Great, Sultan of the Turks, *ca.* 1430–1481. Includes: Phalaris. *Lettere di Falaride*. Dedication dated: V. di Novembre, MDLXII. Purportedly a translation of letters of Mehmet II, Sultan of Turkey, actually written by Laudivio. Cf. F.C.H. Babinger. *Laudivius Zacchia Erdichter der Epistolae magni Turci*. 1960] ['Lettere di Falaride, tiranno de gli agrigentini': pp. 56–189]

Ovid. *Il primo libro delle trasformationi d'Ovidio da M. Lodovico Dolce … tradotto*. Venice: F. Bindone et M. Pasini, 1539. Complete edition: *All'invitiss. e gloriosiss. imp. Carlo Quinto. Le trasformationi di M. Lodovico Dolce*. Venice: Gabriel Giolito, 1553. [Facsimile editon published in New York and London by Garland Publishing, 1979, with introductory notes by Stephen Orgel. For a discussion of the early publication of fragments of this translation and its history, see Savatore Bongi, vol. 1, pp. 396–401]

Philostratus the Elder. *La vita del gran philosopho Apollonio Tianeo, composta da Philostrato scrittor greco, et tradotta nella lingua volgare da M. Lodovico Dolce*. Venice: Gabriel Giolito, 1549 [In fine: 1550].

Pliny the Younger (Plinius Cæcilius Secundus), Francesco Petrarca, Pico della Mirandola, Ermolao Barbaro, Girolamo Donati, Angelo Poliziano, Marsilio Ficino, Paolo Cortese, etc. *Epistole di G. Plinio, di M. Franc. Petrarca, del s. Pico della Mirandola et d'altri eccellentiss. huomini. Tradotte per M. Lodovico Dolce*. Venice: Gabriel Giolito, 1548. [Contains 52 letters of Pliny]

Rufinus, Sextus. *La dignità de' consoli e de gl'imperadori, e i fatti de' romani, e dell'accrescimento dell'imperio, ridotti in compendio da Sesto Ruffo, e similmente da Cassiodoro, e da M. Lodovico Dolce tradotti & ampliati*. Venice: Gabriel Giolito, 1560. [Sextus Rufus, *Breviarium historiae populi Romani*]

Sabellico, Marco Antonio Coccio. *Le historie vinitiane di Marco Antonio Sabellico, divise in tre deche, con tre libri della quarta deca. Novamente da messer Lodovico Dolce in volgare tradotte*. N.p.: Curtio Trojano di Navo, 1544 [dedication of Dolce, 10 April 1543]. [Translation of 1544 published under Lodovico Dolce's name but disclaimed by him. Cf. Melzi, *Dizionario di opere anonime*, I, 328]

Seneca. *Le tragedie di Seneca tradotte da M. Lodovico Dolce*. Venice: Gio. Battista et Marchion Sessa, 1560. [Includes *Thyeste, Troade, Medea* (not to be confused with that drawn from Euripides), *Hercole Furioso, Tebaide, Hippolito, Edippo, Agamennone, Ottavia, Ercole Etheo*. This volume is not to be confused with *Tragedie di M. Lodovico Dolce, cape, Giocasta, Didone, Thieste, Medea, Ifigenia, Hecuba, di nuovo ricorrette e ristampate*. Venice: Gabriel Giolito, 1560] The following were also published separately: *Thyeste. Tragedia di M. Lodovico Dolce, tratta da Seneca …* Venice: Gabriel Giolito, 1543; *Troade*. Venice: Gabriel Giolito, 1547.

Ulstio, Antonio. *Stadio del cursore christiano, il quale sotto al lieve peso di Christo s'indirizza alla Meta; cioè al segno e termine della vita eterna. Composto dal venerabil padre F. Antonio Ulstio, canonico dell'ordine di Santo Agostino. Et nuovamente tradotto di latino in volgare dal s. Lodovico Dolce*. Venice: Gabriel Giolito, 1568.

Virgil. *L'Enea di M. Lodovico Dolce, tratta dall'Eneide di Vergilio, all'illustrissimo et eccellentissimo signor Don Francesco de Medici principe di Fiorenze & di Siena.* Venice: Giovanni Varisco & compagni, 1568. [Published a few days after Dolce's death; different from *L'Achille et l'Enea*]

Zonaras, Joannes. *Historie di Giovanni Zonara monaco diligentissimo scrittore greco dal cominciamento del mondo insino all'imperatore Alessio Conneno: diviso in tre libri, tradotte nella volgar lingua da Lodovico Dolce; con una tavola delle cose, che in esse si contengono, separatamente per ciascuna parte.* Venice: Gabriel Giolito, 1564. [Translation of *Historia rerum in Oriente gestarum ab exordio mundi et orbe condito ad nostra haec usque tempora*]

3. Editions

Ariosto, Lodovico. *La Lena.* N.d., but soon after 1530. Reprint; Venice: Gabriel Giolito, 1551.

– *Il negromante: comedia di m. Lodovico Ariosto, tratta dalo esemplare di man propria dell'autore.* N.d., but soon after 1530. Reprint; Venice: Gabriel Giolito, 1551.

– *Orlando furioso.* 1535. *Orlando furioso. Con una apologia di L. Dolce.* Venice: A. de Torti, 1539; *Orlando furioso ... novissimamente alla sua integrità ridotto ornato di varie figure... . Aggiuntovi per ciascun canto alcune allegorie et nel fine una brieve espositione et tavola di tutto quello, che nell'opera si contiene.* Venice: Gabriel Giolito, 1542. [With *Cinque canti*]

– *Orlando furioso ... Con gli argomenti in ottava rima di m. Lodovico Dolce, & con le allegorie, & l'annotationi a ciascun canto di Thomaso Porcacchi ...* Venice: D. & G. Battista Guerra, 1570. [Valvasori, 1566 ed. has 'Annotazioni' of Dolce]

– *Rime di M. Lodovico Ariosto. Satire del medesimo con i suoi argomenti di nuovo rivedute & emendate, per M. Lodovico Dolce.* Venice: Gabriel Giolito, 1557.

– *I suppositi.* Venice: Gabriel Giolito, 1551.

Bembo, Pietro. *Le prose di M. Pietro Bembo, nelle quali si ragiona della volgar lingua, scritte al cardinale de' Medici, che poi fu creato a sommo pontefice, & detto papa Clemente VII. Divise in tre libri, et reviste con somma diligenza da M. Lodovico Dolce. Con la tavola.* Venice: Gabriel Giolito, 1556.

Boccaccio, Giovanni. *L'amorosa Fiammetta di M. Giovanni Boccaccio, nuovamente per M. Lodovico Dolce da ogni errore emendata et dal medesimo aggiontovi una nuova tavola delle cose degne di memoria.* Venice: Gabriel Giolito, 1542.

– *Il Corbaccio; altrimenti liberinto d'amore.* Venice: Gabriel Giolito, 1541.

– *Il Decamerone ... alla sua vera lettione ridotto da M. Lodovico Dolce.* Venice: Bindoni e Pasini, 1541; *Il Decamerone di M. Giovanni Boccaccio di nuovo emendato secondo gli antichi esemplari, per giudicio et diligenza di più autori, con la diversità di molti testi posta per ordine in margine, & nel fine con gli epiteti dell'autore; espositione de proverbi et luoghi difficili, che nell'opera si contengono, con tavole & altre cose notabili & molto utili alli studiosi della lingua volgare.* Venice: Gabriel Giolito, 1546 [joint edition of Dolce and Francesco Sansovino]; *Con tutte quelle allegorie, annotationi, e tavole, che nelle altre nostre impressioni si contengono; e di più ornato di molte figure. Aggiuntovi separatamente un'indice copiosissimo d'i vocaboli e delle materie composto da messer Lodovico Dolce.* Venice: Gabriel Giolito, 1552.

Camillo Delminio, Giulio. *Annotationi sopra le rime del Petrarca. Tavola di Lodovico Dolce de i concetti ...* Venice: Gabriel Giolito, 1557.

– *Di M. Giulio Camillo tutte le opere, cioè: discorso in materia del suo theatro. Lettera del rivolgimento dell'huomo a dio. La idea. Due trattati, l'uno delle materie, l'altro della imitatione. Due orationi. Rime del detto. (Pubblicato da Lodovico Dolce).* Venice: Gabriel Giolito, 1552.

Castiglione, Baldessar. *Il libro del cortegiano, del conte Baldessar Castiglione, nuovamente con diligenza corretto e revisto per il Dolce, secondo l'esemplare del proprio autore.* Venice: G. Giolito, 1552.

Cicero. *Opere morali di Marco Tullio Cicerone: cioè tre libri de gli uffici, due dialoghi; l'uno dell'amicitia, e l'altro della vecchiezza, sei paradossi secondo l'openione de gli stoici. Tradotti da M. Federico Vendramino nobile vinitiano. Alle quali opere s'è aggiunto il sogno di Scipione. Nuovamente riveduti e corretti da M. Lodovico Dolce, con le postille, & con due tavole; una de' capitoli, & l'altra delle cose notabili.* Venice: Gabriel Giolito, 1563.

Colonna, Vittoria. *Le rime della signora Vittoria Colonna.* Venice: Gabriel Giolito, 1552; *Con l'aggiunta delle rime spirituali. Di nuovo ricorrette, per M. Lodovico Dolce.* Venice: Gabriel Giolito, 1559.

Dante Alighieri. *La divina commedia di Dante, di nuovo alla sua vera lezione ridotta con lo aiuto di molti antichissimi esemplari. Con argomenti, et allegorie per ciascun canto, & apostille nel margine. Et indice copiosissimo di tutti i vocaboli più importanti usati dal poeta, con la sposition loro.* [Col ritratto di Dante, e con figure in legno] Venice: Gabriel Giolito, 1555. [Using 'un esemplare frascritto dal proprio scritto di mano del figliuolo di Dante.' First edition to add the adjective 'divine' to the title]

Delfino, Domenico. *Sommario di tutte le scienze, del magnifico Domenico Delfino, nobile vinitiano, dal quale si possono imparare molte cose appartenenti al vivere humano, & alla cognition di dio. Con la tavola, & le postille delle cose più notabili.* Venice: Gabriel Giolito, 1565. [Issued after the death of Domenico Delfino, supposed translator of Alfonso de la Torre's *Vision deleytable dela philosophia et delas otras sciencias.* Dedication of Lodovico Dolce]

Equicola, Mario. *Libro di natura d'amore di Mario Equicola. Di nuovo con somma diligenza ristampato e corretto da M. Lodovico Dolce. Con una tavola delle cose più notabili che nell'opera si contengono.* Venice: Gabriel Giolito, 1554.

Erizzo, Sebastiano. *Esposizione di M. Sebastiano Erizzo nelle tre canzoni di M. Francesco Petrarca, chiamate le tre sorelle. Nuovamente mandata in luce da M. Lodovico Dolce.* Venice: Arrivabene, 1561.

- *Le sei giornate di M. Sebastiano Erizzo, mandate in luce da M. Lodovico Dolce.* Venice: Giovan Varisco, e compagni, 1567.

Lampridio, Benedetto. *Benedicti Lampridii, necnon Jo. Bap. Amalthei carmina.* Venice: Gabriel Giolito, 1550.

Lettere di diversi eccellentiss. huomini, raccolte da diversi libri; tra lequali se ne leggono molte, non più stampate. Con gli argomenti per ciascuna delle materie, di che elle trattano, e nel fine annotationi e tavole delle cose più notabili, a utile de gli studiosi. Venice: Gabriel Giolito, 1554. [Dedication signed Lodovico Dolce. An edition dated 1559 contains several different letters]

Molino, Antonio, detto Burchiella. *I fatti e le prodezze di Manoli Blessi Strathioto.* Venice: Gabriel Giolito, 1561. [Dedicatory epistle of Dolce]

Orologi, Giuseppe [G. Dondi dall'Orologio]. *Vita dell'illustrissimo signor Camillo Orsino. discritta da Gioseppe Horologgi, nella quale si vengono brevemente a narrare tutte le guerre successe dalla venuta di Carlo VIII, re di Francia in Italia, fin'all'anno MDLIX. Con due tavole; l'una delle cose più generali; et l'altra delle cose più notabili.* Venice: Gabriel Giolito, 1565. [Dedicatory epistle of Dolce]

Pascale, Lodovico, et al. *Ludovici Pascalis, Iulii Camilli, Molsae, et aliorum illustrium poetarum carmina, ... per L. Dulcium ... in lucem ædita.* Venice: Giolito, 1551.

Petrarca, Francesco. *Il Petrarca, corretto da M. Lodovico Dolce, et alla sua integrità ridotto.* [Edition of the *Canzoniere* using the autograph manuscript in the library of Pietro Bembo, now Vaticano Lat. 3195; includes the *Trionfi*] Venice: Gabriel Giolito, 1547. ['Trionfi di M. Francesco Petrarca corretti da messer Lodovico Dolce' has special title page]

Poliziano, Angelo. *Rime.* 1552.

- *Stanze per la giostra.* 1560.

Rime. Delle rime scelte di diversi autori, di nuovo corrette, e ristampate. Il secondo volume. Venice: i Gioliti, 1587.

- *Il primo volume delle rime scelte da diversi autori.* Venice: Gabriel Giolito, 1563.

- *Il primo (secondo) volume delle rime scelte di diversi autori, di nuovo corrette e ristampate,* 2 vols. Venice: Gabriel Giolito, 1564. [Changed in manuscript hand to 1565]

- *Rime di diversi illustri signori napoletani, e d'altri nobiliss. intelletti nuovamente raccolte, et non più stampate. Terzo libro.* Venice: Gabriel Giolito, 1552; *Rime di diversi illustri signori napoletani, e d'altri nobiliss. ingegni. Nuovamente raccolte, et con nuova additione ristampate. Libro quinto.* Venice: Gabriel Giolito, 1552 [For an explanation of the 'Terzo' and 'Quinto' for essentially the same volume, see Bongi, vol. 1, pp. 357, 365]. *Libro settimo.* Venice: Gabriel Giolito, 1556.

– *Rime diverse di molti eccellentiss. autori, nuovamente raccolte.* Venice: Gabriel Giolito, 1545–60 (in 9 vols., vol. 5 edited by Dolce); 1548–86 (vols. 5 and 7, edited by Dolce). *Rime di diversi eccellenti autori raccolte dai libri da noi altre volte impressi, tra le quali se ne leggono molto non più vedute.* Venice: Gabriel Giolito, 1553.

Sannazzaro, Jacopo. *Arcadia del Sannazaro, di nuovo ristampata, et ritornata alla sua vera lettione da M. Lodovico Dolce.* Venice: Gabriel Giolito, 1553.

– *Le rime del Sannazaro, nuovamente corrette et reviste per il Dolce.* Venice: Gabriel Giolito, 1552.

Solinus. *Solino delle cose maravigliose del mondo, tradotto dall'illustriss. s. Gio. Vincenzo Belprato conte di Anversa.* Venice: Gabriel Giolito, 1557. [Anversa = Aversa, near Naples. Contains dedication of Dolce]

Stanzas (poems in *ottava rima*). *Prima parte delle stanze di diversi illustri poeti. Raccolte da M. Lodovico Dolce, à commodità, & utile de gli studiosi della lingua thoscana.* Venice: Gabriel Giolito, 1553.

– *Prima (seconda) parte delle stanze di diversi illustri poeti ... nuovamente ristampate & con diligentia reviste, & corrette,* 2 vols. Venice: Gabriel Giolito, 1572, 1575.

– *Stanze di diversi illustri poeti, nuovamente raccolte da M. Lodovico Dolce a comodo & utile de gli studiosi della lingua thoscana.* Venice: Gabriel Giolito, 1553.

– *La seconda parte delle stanze di diversi autori.* Ed. Antonio Terminio. Venice: Gabriel Giolito, 1564.

Tasso, Bernardo. *L'Amadigi del s. Bernardo Tasso.* Venice: Gabriel Giolito, 1560.

– *I tre libri de gli amori di M. Bernardo Tasso. A iquali nuovamente dal Proprio autore s'è aggiunto il quarto libro, per adietro non più stampato.* Venice: Gabriel Giolito, 1555.

Terminio, Antonio. *Antonii Termini contursini lucani. Iunii Albini Terminii senioris, Molsae, Bernardini Rotae, equitis Neapolitani, et aliorum illustrium poetarum carmina.* Venice: Gabriel Giolito, 1554.

II. Other Works Consulted

Allen, Beverly, Muriel Kittel, and Keala Jane Jewell, eds. *The Defiant Muse: Italian Feminist Poems from the Middle Ages to the Present. A Bilingual Anthology.* New York: Feminist Press at the City University of New York, 1986.

Altieri Biagi, M.L. 'Appunti sulla lingua della commedia del '500.' In *Il teatro classico italiano nel '500,* pp. 253–300. Atti del Convegno dell'Accademia Nazionale dei Lincei, no. 138. Rome: Accademia nazionale dei Lincei, 1971.

Apollonio, Mario. *Storia del teatro italiano,* 4 vols. Florence: Sansoni, 1939–45. 3 vols. Florence: Sansoni, 1954.

Aretino, Pietro. *Lettere.* Introduzione, scelta e commento di Paolo Procaccioli, 2 vols. Milan: Biblioteca Universale Rizzoli, 1991.

– *Lettere. Libro primo*. Edited by Francesco Erspamer. Parma: Ugo Guanda Editore, 1955.

– *Lettere. Il primo e il secondo libro*. Edited by Francesco Flora. With notes by Alessandro del Vita. In *Tutte le opere di Pietro Aretino*. Verona: Arnoldo Mondadori Editore, 1960.

– *Lettere scritte al signor Pietro Aretino, da molti signori, comunità, donne di valore, poeti, & altri eccellentissimi spiriti. Divise in due libri*. Venice: Francesco Marcolini, 1551. [In fine: 1552]

– *Lettere scritte a Pietro Aretino*. Vol. 1, part 1, edited by Teodorico Landoni. Vol. 1, part 2 and vol. 2, parts 1 and 2, edited by Giuliano Vanzolini. Scelta di curiosità letterarie inedite o rare dal secolo XIII al XIX, dispensa 132. Bologna: Gaetano Romagnoli, 1873, 1875. Reprint; Bologna: Commissione per i testi di lingua, 1968.

– *The Marescalco (Il marescalco)*. Translated, with Introduction and Notes, by Leonard G. Sbrocchi and J. Douglas Campbell. Carleton Plays in Translation. Published for the Carleton University Centre for Renaissance Studies and Research. Ottawa, ON: Dovehouse, 1986.

– *Orazia*. In *La tragedia classica dalle origini al Maffei*. Ed. Giammaria Gasparini. Turin: UTET, 1963.

– *Il primo (-sesto) libro delle lettere*. Paris: n.p., 1609.

– *Ragionamento delle corti*. Venezia: Marcolini, 1538.

– *The Letters of Pietro Aretino*. Translated by Thomas Caldecot Chubb. Hamden, CT: Archon, 1967.

Ariani, Marco. 'L'*Orbecche* di G. B. Giraldi e la poetica dell'orrore.' *La rassegna della letteratura italiana* 75 (1971), 432–50.

– *Tra classicismo e manierismo: Il teatro tragico del Cinquecento*. Florence: Olschki 1974.

– ed. *Il teatro italiano*. Vol. 2: *La tragedia del Cinquecento*. Turin: Einaudi, 1977.

Ariosto, Lodovico. *Orlando furioso*. In *Opere*. Ed. Giuliano Innamorati. Bologna: Zanichelli, 1967.

Armato, Rosario P. 'The Play Is the Thing: A Study of Giraldi's *Orbecche* and Its Senecan Antecedents.' In *Studies in Language, Literature, and Culture of the Middle Ages and Later*, ed. E. Bagby Atwood and Archibald A. Hill, pp. 57–83. Austin: University of Texas Press, 1969.

Bacchelli, Franco. 'Il "Palmerin de Olivia" nel rifacimento di Lodovico Dolce.' In *Studi sul 'Palmerin de Olivia,'* vol. 3, pp. 159–76. Pubblicazioni dell'Istituto di Letteratura Spagnola e Ispano-americana dell'Università di Pisa, vols. 11–13. Pisa, 1966.

Baillet, Adriano. *Iugemens des savans sur les principaux ouvrages des auteurs*. Amsterdam: Aux depens de la compagnie, 1725.

Baratto, Mario. ' "Pavano" e "Latino": *La piovana* e il problema dell'imitazione.' In Ruzante. *La piovana*, ed. Ludovico Zorzi, pp. v–xxvii. Turin: Einaudi, 1990.

Barbaro, Francesco. *De re uxoria*. Ed. Attilio Gnesotto. In *Atti e memorie della regia accademia di scienze, lettere ed arti di Padova*, n.s. 32 (1915), 6–105.

– *Francisci Barbari Patricii Veneti ... De re uxoria libri duo.* Antwerp: Apud Martinum Caesarem, [1535?].

– 'On Wifely Duties.' In *The Earthly Republic: Italian Humanists on Government and Society*, ed. Benjamin G. Kohl and Ronald G. Witt, with Elizabeth Welles, pp. 179–228. Philadelphia: University of Pennsylvania Press, 1978.

– *Prudentissimi et gravi documenti circa la elettion della moglie dello eccellente & dottissimo M. Francesco Barbaro, gentilhuomo venitiano al molto magnifico M. Lorenzo de Medici, cittadin florentino, nuovamente dal latino tradotti per M. Alberto Lollio, ferrarese.* Ferrara: Gabriel Giolito, 1548.

Barberino, Andrea da. *L'Aspramonte*. Ed. Marco Boni. Bologna: Per i tipi dell'Antiquaria Palmaverde, 1951.

Bareggi, Claudia Di Filippo. *Il mestiere di scrivere: Lavoro intellettuale e mercato librario a Venezia nel Cinquecento*. Rome: Bulzoni, 1988.

Barocchi, P., ed. *Trattati d'arte del Cinquecento fra Manierismo e Controriforma*, vol. 1, pp. 141–206. Bari: Laterza, 1960.

Battaglia, Roberto. 'Note sul dissolversi della forma rinascimentale. Dall'Ariosto al Tasso.' *Cultura Neolatina* 2 (1942), 174–90.

Beer, Marina. *Romanzi di cavalleria. Il 'furioso' e il romanzo italiano del primo cinquecento*. Rome: Bulzoni, 1987.

Bello, Francesco. *Libro d'arme e d'amore nomato Mambriano*. Ed. Giuseppe Rua. Turin: UTET, 1951.

Bellucci, N. 'Lettere di molte valorose donne ... e di alcune pettegolette, ovvero: Di un libro di lettere di Ortensio Lando.' In *Le 'carte messagiere.' Retorica e modelli di comunicazione epistolare: per un indice dei libri di lettere del Cinquecento*, ed. Amadeo Quondam, pp. 255–76. Rome: Bulzoni, 1981.

Beolco, Angelo, detto Ruzzante. In Ruzante, *La piovana. Testo originale a fronte*. Ed. Ludovico Zorzi. Introduzione di Mario Baratto. Turin: Einaudi, 1990.

Bertana, Emilio. *Storia dei generi letterari italiani: La tragedia*. Milan: Vallardi, 1905.

Betussi, Giuseppe. *Il Raverta. Dialogo nel quale si ragiona d'amore e degli effetti suoi.* 1544. In *Trattati d'amore del Cinquecento*, ed. Giuseppe Zonta. 1912. Reprint; Bari: Laterza, 1975.

Bilancini, Pietro. *G.B. Giraldi e la tragedia italiana nel secolo XVI: Studio critico.* Aquila: Vecchioni, 1890.

Blasi, Jolanda de, ed. *Antologia delle scrittrici italiane dalle origini al 1800.* Florence: Nemi, 1930.

– *Le scrittrici italiane dalle origini al 1800.* Florence: Nemi, 1930.

Blunt, Anthony. *Artistic Theory in Italy, 1450–1600*. Oxford: Clarendon Press, 1940.

Boccaccio, Giovanni. *Rime*. In *Opere minori in volgare*, vol. 4, ed. Mario Marti. Milan: Rizzoli, 1972.

– *Teseida*. In *Opere minori in volgare*, vol. 2, ed. Mario Marti. Milan: Rizzoli, 1970.

Boccalini, Traiano. *Ragguaglio* V. In *De' ragguagli di Parnaso ... centuria prima (-seconda)*. Venice: Giovanni Guerigli, 1617, 1624.

Boiardo, Matteo Maria. *Orlando innamorato, sonetti e canzoni di Matteo Maria Boiardo*, vol. 2, ed. Aldo Scaglione. Turin: UTET, 1951.

Bongi, Salvatore. *Annali di Gabriel Giolito de' Ferrari da Trino di Monferrato, stampatore in Venezia*, 2 vols. Rome: Presso i Principali Librai, 1890–5.

Bonora, Ettore. *Il Cinquecento*. Milan: Storia letteraria Garzanti, 1955.

– *Critica e letteratura nel Cinquecento*. Turin: Giappichelli, 1964.

– 'Le donne poetesse.' In *Storia della letteratura italiana. Il Cinquecento*, vol. 4, ed. Emilio Cecchi and Natalino Sapegno, pp. 241–68. Milan: Garzanti, 1966.

– 'La Tragedia.' In *Storia della letteratura italiana: Il Cinquecento*, ed. Emilio Cecchi and Natalino Sapegno, pp. 321–39. 1966. Reprint; Milan: Garzanti, 1976.

Borlenghi, Aldo. 'Regolarità ed originalità della commedia del Cinquecento.' In *Studi di letteratura italiana dal Trecento al Cinquecento*, pp. 122–230. Milan and Varesel: Cisalpino, 1959.

Borsellino, Nino. 'Il teatro del Cinquecento.' In *Letteratura italiana Laterza*, pp. 9–72. Bari: Laterza, 1973.

Borsellino, Nino, and Marcello Aurigemma, eds. *Il Cinquecento: Dal Rinascimento alla Controriforma*. La letteratura italiana. Storia e testi, vol. 4, part 1. Bari: Laterza, 1973.

Borsetto, Luciana. 'Narciso ed Eco. Figura e scrittura nella lirica femminile del Cinquecento: esemplificazioni ed appunti.' In *Nel cerchio della luna: Figure di donna in alcuni testi del XVI secolo*, ed. Marina Zancan, pp. 171–234. Venice: Marsilio Editori, 1983.

– 'Riscrivere l'historia, riscrivere lo stile: il poema di Virgilio nelle "riduzioni" cinquecentesche di Lodovico Dolce.' In *Scritture di scritture. Testi, generi, modelli nel Rinascimento*, ed. Giancarlo Mazzacurati and Michel Plaisance, pp. 405–37. Rome: Bulzoni, 1987.

Bragonier, Jr., Reginald, and David Fisher. *What's What: A Visual Glossary of the Physical World*. New York: Ballantine, 1981.

Branca, Vittorio. 'Le raccolte di rime e le collezioni di classici.' In *Notizie introduttive e sussidi bibliografici*. Problemi ed orientamenti critici di lingua e di letteratura italiana, vol. 1, pp. 143–67. Milan: Marzorati, 1948.

Bregoli-Russo, Mauda. *L'impresa come ritratto del Rinascimento*. Naples: Loffredo, 1990.

Cabrol, Fernand. *Dictionnaire d'archéologie chrétienne et de liturgie*. Paris: Letouzey et Ane, 1928.

Cairns, Christopher. *Pietro Aretino and the Republic of Venice: Researches on Aretino and his Circle in Venice, 1527–1556*. Florence: Olschki, 1985.

Carmina Burana, cantiones profanae. Ed. Carl Orff. Original text with introduction by Judith Lynn Sebesta and a new translation by Jeffrey M. Duban. Bolchazy: Carducci, 1985.

Casini, Tommaso, ed. *La vita nuova di Dante Alighieri*. Florence: Sansoni, rpt. 1964.

Chemello, Adriana. 'La donna, il modello, l'immaginario: Moderata Fonte e Lucrezia Marinella.' In *Nel cerchio della luna: Figure di donna in alcuni testi del XVI secolo*, ed. Marina Zancan, pp. 95–170. Venice: Marsilio Editori, 1983.

– 'L'*Institution delle donne* di Lodovico Dolce ossia l'*insegnar virtù et honesti costumi alla donna*.' In *Trattati scientifici nel Veneto fra il XV e XVI secolo*, pp. 103–34. Introduzione di Ezio Riondato. Vicenza: Pozzi, 1985.

Cherchi, Paolo. 'Gli "Adynata" dei trovatori.' *Modern Philology* 68/3 (1971), 223–41.

– 'L'encomio paradossale nel Manierismo.' *Forum Italicum* 9 (1975), 368–84.

Cian, V. 'Varietà letterarie del Rinascimento. II. Una polemica dantesca nel secolo XVI: il Bembo, il Dolce ed il Gelli.' In *Raccolta di studi critici dedicati ad Alessandro D'Ancona*. Florence: G. Barbera, 1901.

Cicogna, Emmanuel Antonio. 'Memoria intorno la vita e gli scritti di Messer Lodovico Dolce letterato veneziano del secolo XVI.' In *Memorie dell'I. R. Istituto veneto di scienze, lettere e arti* 11 (1863–4), 93–200.

Clubb, Louise George. *Giambattista Della Porta. Dramatist*. Princeton, NJ: Princeton University Press, 1965.

– *Italian Drama in Shakespeare's Time*. New Haven, CT: Yale University Press, 1989.

– *Italian Plays (1500–1700) in the Folger Library*. Florence: Olschki, 1968.

Clubb, Louise George, and William G. Clubb. 'Building a Lyric Canon: Gabriel Giolito and the Rival Anthologists, 1545–1590.' *Italica* 68/3 (1991), 332–44.

Commedie del Cinquecento. Ed. A. Borlenghi. 2 vols. with an appendix of prologues. Milan: Classici Rizzoli, 1959.

Commedie del Cinquecento. Ed. N. Borsellino. 2 vols. Milan: Feltrinelli, 1962, 1967.

Commedie del Cinquecento. Ed. Maria Luisa Doglio. Bari: Laterza, 1975.

Componimenti poetici delle più illustri rimatrici d'ogni secolo. Ed. Luisa Bergalli. Venice: Antonio Mora, 1726.

Copenhaver, Brian P. *Hermetica. The Greek* Corpus Hermeticum *and the Latin* Asclepius *in a New English Translation, with Notes and Introduction*. Cambridge: Cambridge University Press, 1992.

Costa, Gustavo. *La leggenda dei secoli d'oro nella letteratura italiana*. Bari: Laterza, 1972.

Costa-Zalessow, Natalia. *Scrittrici italiane dal XIII al XX secolo. Testi e critica.* Ravenna: Longo, 1982.

Crescimbeni, Gio. Maria. *Istoria della volgar poesia.* Rome: Per il Chracas, 1698; 3d edition, Venice: Lorenzo Basegio, 1731.

Croce, Benedetto. 'Gli "Amadigi" e i "Palmerini." ' In *Poeti e scrittori del pieno e del tardo Rinascimento,* vol. 1, pp. 310–25. 1945. Reprint; Bari: Laterza, 1958.

– 'La "commedia" del Cinquecento.' In *Poesia popolare e poesia d'arte,* pp. 237–304. Bari: Laterza, 1933.

– 'Donne letterate nel Seicento.' In *Nuovi saggi sulla letteratura italiana del Seicento,* pp. 154–71. Bari: Laterza, 1931.

– *Poeti e scrittori del pieno e del tardo Rinascimento,* 3 vols. Bari: Laterza, 1945–52.

– 'La Tragedia.' In *Poesia popolare e poesia d'arte,* pp. 305–40. Bari: Laterza, 1933.

Curtius, Ernst Robert. *European Literature and the Latin Middle Ages.* 1948. Translated by Willard R. Trask. 1953. Reprint; New York: Harper & Row, 1963.

Daenens, F. 'Superiore perché inferiore: il paradosso della superiorità della donna in alcuni trattati italiani del Cinquecento.' In *Trasgressione tragica e norma domestica. Esemplari di tipologie femminili dalla letteratura europea,* ed. V. Gentili, pp. 11–50. Rome: Edizioni di Storia e Letteratura, 1983.

Dale, A.M. *The Lyric Metres of Greek Drama.* 2d ed. Cambridge: Cambridge University Press, 1968.

Dal Pra, Antonietta. *L'influenza di Euripide nel teatro tragico italiano dei secoli XVI, XVII e XVIII.* Messina: Industrie grafiche meridionali, n.d.

Damerini, Gino. 'Il sodalizio artistico di Lodovico Dolce con Antonio Molino detto il Burchiella per la Marianna e le Troiane.' *Dramma: mensile dello spettacolo* 41/342 (Rome, 1965), 37–44.

D'Amico, Silvio. *Storia del teatro drammatico,* 4 vols. 1937. 4th ed. Milan: Garzanti, 1958.

D'Ancona, A. *Origini del teatro italiano,* vol. 2. 2d ed. Turin: Loescher, 1891.

Dante Alighieri. *La commedia secondo l'antica vulgata.* Ed. Giorgio Petrocchi. Florence: Società Dantesca, 1966.

Daremberg, Charles, and Edmond Saglio. *Dictionnaire des antiquités grècques et romaines d'après les textes et les monuments,* 5 vols. in 9. Paris: Hachette, 1887–1919.

De Amicis, Vincenzo. *L'imitazione latina nella commedia italiana nel XVI secolo.* Florence: Sansoni, 1897.

De Bellis, Carla. 'Astri, gemme e arti medico-magiche nello *Speculum lapidum* di Camillo Leonardi.' In *Il mago, il cosmo, il teatro degli astri. Saggi sulla letteratura esoterica del Rinascimento,* pp. 67–113. Rome: Bulzoni, 1985.

Della Casa, Giovanni. *Quaestio lepidissima an uxor sit ducenda.* In *Prose di Giovanni Della Casa e altri trattatisti cinquecenteschi del comportamento,* ed. Arnaldo di Benedetto, pp. 53–139. Turin: UTET, 1991.

– *Se s'abbia da prender moglie (Quaestio lepidissima, an uxor sit ducenda)*. Translated by Ugo Enrico Paoli. Florence: Le Monnier, 1946.

Della nuova scielta di lettere di diversi huomini et eccellenti ingegni, 2 vols. in 1. Venice: n.p., 1582.

Der Kleine Pauly, vol. 2. Stuttgart: Druckenmüller, 1967.

Dionisotti, Carlo. 'La guerra d'Oriente nella letteratura veneziana del Cinquecento.' In *Geografia e storia della letteratura italiana*. Turin: Einaudi, 1967.

Doglio, Federico. *Il teatro tragico italiano: Storia e testi del teatro tragico in Italia*. Bologna: Guanda, 1960.

Domenichi, Lodovico. *Facetie et motti arguti di alcuni eccellentissimi ingegni et nobilissimi signori*. 1548; *Della scelta de motti, burle, facetie di diversi signori, et d'altre persone private. Libri sei. Raccolto [!] da M. Lodovico Domenichi, & da lui ultimamente riformate. Con l'aggiunta del settimo libro raccolto da diuerse persone* ... Florence: Figliuoli di L. Torrentino, & C. Pettinari Compagno, 1566; *Facetie, motti et burle di diuersi signori et persone priuate / raccolte per M. Lodouico Domenichi & da lui di nuouo del settimo libro ampliate; con una nuoua aggiunta di motti raccolti da M. Tomaso Porcacchi & con un discorso intorno ad essi, con ogni diligentia ricorrette et ristampate. Di nuouo reuista in Roma & ripurgata da' luoghi infetti*. Fano: Pietro Farri, 1593.

– *Rime diverse d'alcune nobilissime et virtuosissime donne*. Lucca: Busdrago, 1559.

Doni, Anton Francesco. 'Mondo Risibile.' *I mondi*. In *Opere di Pietro Aretino e di Anton Francesco Doni*. Ed. Carlo Cordié. In *Folengo-Aretino-Doni*, vol. 2, pp. 927–34. Milan and Naples: Riccardo Ricciardi Editore, 1976.

– *Zucca*. Venice: Polo, 1589.

Erspamer, Francesco, ed. *Pietro Aretino. Lettere. Libro primo*. Parma: Ugo Guanda Editore, 1955.

Fachini, G. Canonici. *Prospetto biografico delle donne italiane rinomate in letteratura dal secolo XIV fino a' giorni nostri*. Venice: Alvisopoli, 1824.

Fahy, Conor. 'Three Early Renaissance Treatises on Women.' *Italian Studies* 11 (1956), 30–55.

Ferguson, Margret W., Maureen Quilligan, and Nancy J. Vickers, eds. *Rewriting the Renaissance: The Discourse of Sexual Difference in Early Modern Europe*. Chicago: University of Chicago Press, 1986.

Ferrario, Giulio. *Storia ed analisi degli antichi romanzi di cavalleria e dei poemi romanzeschi d'Italia con dissertazioni sull'origine, sugl'istituti, sulle ceremonie de' cavalieri, sulle corti d'amore, sui tornei, sulle giostre ed armature de' paladini, sull'invenzione e sull'uso degli stemmi*, 4 vols. Milan: Tipografia dell'autore, 1828–9.

Ferri, L. *Biblioteca femminile italiana*. Padua: Crescini, 1842.

Ferrini, Luige Boni. 'Il ragazzo di Ludovico Dolce: Rilettura.' *Italianistica. Rivista di letteratura italiana* 17/3 (1988): 471–9.

Finlay, Robert. *Politics in Renaissance Venice*. New Brunswick, NJ: Rutgers University Press, 1980.

Flamini, Francesco. *Il Cinquecento*. Milan: Vallardi, 1901, 1903.

Floriani, P. 'Il dialogo e la corte.' In *I gentiluomini letterati. Studi sul dibattito culturale nel primo Cinquecento*, pp. 33–49. Naples: Liguori, 1981.

Fòffano, Francesco. *Il poema cavalleresco*. Storia dei generi letterari italiani. Milan: Vallardi, n.d.; preface, 1904.

Folena, G. 'Presentazione.' In L. Vanossi, M. Milani, M. Tonello, D. Battaglia, P. Spezzani, *Lingua e strutture del teatro italiano del Rinascimento: Machiavelli, Ruzzante, Aretino, Guarini, Commedia dell'arte*, pp. i–xix. Padua: Liviana Editrice, 1970.

Fontanini, Giusto. *Della eloquenza italiana ... libri tre novellamente ristampati*. Venice: Cristoforo Zane, 1737.

Forlani, Alma, and Marta Savini, eds. *Scrittrici d'Italia: Le voci femminili più rappresentative della nostra letteratura raccolte in una straordinaria antologia di prose e di versi: dalle eroine e dalle sante dei primi secoli fino alle donne dei giorni nostri*. Rome: Newton Compton, 1991.

Foscarini, Marco. *Della letteratura veneziana ed altri saggi scritti intorno ad essa*. Venice: Gattei, 1854.

– *La letteratura veneziana e le sue donne passate e presenti*. Venice: Tip. Commercio, 1864.

Friedrich, J. *Die Didodramen des Dolce, Jodelle und Marlowe in ihrem Verhältnis zu einander und zu Vergil's Aeneis*. Kempfen: Köselschen, 1888.

Frigo, Daniela. 'Dal caos all'ordine: Sulla questione del "prender moglie" nella trattatistica del sedicesimo secolo.' In *Nel cerchio della luna: Figure di donna in alcuni testi del XVI secolo*, ed. Marina Zancan, pp. 57–93. Venice: Marsilio Editori, 1983.

Frye, Northrop. *Anatomy of Criticism: Four Essays*. 1957. Reprint; Princeton, NJ: Princeton University Press, 1971.

Gamba, Bartolommeo. *Serie dei testi di lingua e di altre opere importanti nella italiana letteratura, scritte dal secolo XIV al XIX*, 4th ed. 'Riveduta, emendata e notabilmente accresciuta.' Venice: Co' tipi del Gondoliere, 1839.

Garin, Eugenio. *L'educazione in Europa, 1400–1600*, 3d ed. Bari: Laterza, 1976.

Garzoni, Tommaso. *Opere*. Ed. Paolo Cherchi. Naples: Casa Editrice Fulvio Rossi, 1972.

– *La piazza universale di tutte le professioni del mondo ... 1585*. Venice: Michiel Miloco, 1665; Venice: Meietti, 1601.

Genette, Gérard. *Figures of Literary Discourse*. Translated by Alan Sheridan. Introduction by Marie-Rose Logan. New York: Columbia University Press, 1982.

Gerardo, Paolo. *Novo libro di lettere scritte da i più rari auttori della lingua volgare italiana*. Venice: Comin da Trino, 1544.

Ghilini, Gerolamo. *Teatro d'huomini letterati aperto dall'abbate Gerolamo Ghilini, academico incognito.* Venice: Per li Guerigli, 1647.

Ginguiné, Pierre-Luis. *Histoire littéraire d'Italie.* 1810. Reprint in 14 volumes; Paris: Michaud, 1824.

Ginzburg, Carlo. 'Morelli, Freud and Sherlock Holmes. Clues and Scientific Method.' *History Workshop. A Journal of Socialist Historians* 9 (Spring 1980), 5–36.

Giraldi Cinthio, Giambattista. *Didone.* In *Le tragedie di M. Gio. Battista Giraldi Cinthio, nobile ferrarese* ... Venice: Giulio Cesare Cagnacini, 1583.

– *Discorsi ... intorno al comporre de i romanzi, delle comedie, e delle tragedie, e di altre maniere di poesie.* Venice: Gabriel Giolito, 1554.

– *Hecatommithi, overo cento novelle.* Venetia: D. Imberti, 1593.

– *Lettera sulla 'Didone.'* In *La tragedia del Cinquecento*, vol 2, pp. 956–67, ed. Marco Ariani. Turin: Einaudi, 1977.

– *Orbecche.* In *Le tragedie di M. Gio. Battista Giraldi Cinthio.* Venice: Giulio Cesare Cagnacini, 1583.

Goldoni, Carlo. *Mémoires de Monsieur Goldoni pour servir à l'histoire de sa vie et à celle de son théâtre.* In *Opere con appendice del teatro comico nel Settecento*, ed. Filippo Zampieri. Milan and Naples: Riccardo Ricciardi Editore, 1964.

Granada, Fray Luis de. *Introducción del símbolo de la fe.* In *Biblioteca de autores españoles.* Vol. 6: *Obras del v.p.m. fray Luis de Granada.* Madrid: Real Academia Español, 1944.

Grande dizionario enciclopedico, vol. 6. Turin: UTET, 1968.

Grendler, Paul F. *Critics of the Italian World, 1530–1560: Anton Francesco Doni, Nicolò Franco & Ortensio Lando.* Madison: University of Wisconsin Press, 1969.

– 'Francesco Sansovino and Italian Popular History. 1560–1600.' In *Studies in the Renaissance* 16 (1969), 139–80. Reprinted in *Culture and Censorship in Late Renaissance Italy and France*, ch. 1. London: Variorum Reprints, 1981.

– *Schooling in Renaissance Italy. Literacy and Learning, 1300–1600.* Baltimore and London: Johns Hopkins University Press, 1989.

– *The Roman Inquisition and the Venetian Press, 1540–1605.* Princeton, NJ: Princeton University Press, 1977.

Grendler, Paul F., and Marcella Grendler. 'The Survival of Erasmus in Italy.' In *Erasmus in English* 8 (1976), 2–22. Reprinted in *Culture and Censorship in Late Renaissance Italy and France*, ch. 11. London: Variorum Reprints, 1981.

Guazzo, Stefano. *Lettere del signor Stefano Guazzo ... ordinate sotto i capi seguenti. Di raguagli, di lode, di raccommandatione, di essortatione, di ringratiamenti, di congratulatione, di scusa, di consolatione, di complimenti misti. Aggiuntovi in questa nostra seconda editione molte lettere dell'stesso autore* ... Venice: Barezzo Barezzi, 1592.

Guerrieri-Crocetti, Camillo. *G.B. Giraldi ed il pensiero critico del secolo XVI.* Milan and Rome: Albrighi e Segati, 1932.

Hathaway, Baxter. *The Age of Criticism: The Late Renaissance In Italy*. Ithaca, NY: Cornell University Press, 1962.

Herrick, Marvin T. *Comic Theory in the Sixteenth Century*. 1949. Reprint; Urbana: University of Illinois, 1964.

– *Italian Comedy in the Renaissance*. 1960. Urbana: University of Illinois, 1966.

– *Italian Tragedy of the Renaissance*. Urbana: University of Illinois Press, 1965.

Hillebrand, Karl. *Études historiques et littéraires*. Vol. 1: *Études italiennes*. Paris: Franck, 1868.

Hirdt, Willi. *Studien zum Epischen Prolog: Der Eingang in der Erzählenden Verdichtung Italiens*. Munich: Wilhelm Fink, 1975.

Horne, P.R. *The Tragedies of Giambattista Cinthio Giraldi*. Oxford: Oxford University Press, 1962.

Il teatro classico italiano nel '500. Atti del Convegno dell'Accademia nazionale dei Lincei, no. 138. Rome: Accademia nazionale dei Lincei, 1971.

Images de la femme dans la littérature italienne de la Renaissance: Préjugés misogynes et aspirations nouvelles. Castiglione, Piccolomini, Bandello. Études réunies par André Rochon. Paris: Centre de Recherche sur la Renaissance Italienne, 1980.

Jacquot, Jean. *Les tragédies de Sénèque et le théâtre de la Renaissance*. Paris: Editions du Centre Nationale de la Recherche Scientifique, 1964.

Jaquinta, A. 'Tentativi di autocoscienza in un gruppo del Cinquecento.' In *La presenza dell'uomo nel femminismo*, pp. 45–78. Milan: Scritti di rivolta femminile, 1978.

Javitch, Daniel. *Proclaiming a Classic: The Canonization of* Orlando Furioso. Princeton, NJ: Princeton University Press, 1991.

– 'The Influence of the *Orlando furioso* on Ovid's *Metamorphoses* in Italian.' *Journal of Medieval and Renaissance Studies* 11/1 (1981), 1–21.

Jocasta: A tragedie written in Greke by Euripides; translated and digested into acte by George Gascoygne and Francis Kinwelmarshe of Grayes Inne, and there by them presented, 1566 (half-title, pp. [71]–164). In George Gascoigne, *A hundreth sundrie flowres bounde up in one small poesie* ... London: Imprinted for Richard Smith, 1573.

Kallendorf, Craig. *A Bibliography of Venetian Editions of Virgil, 1470–1599*. Florence: Olschki, 1991.

Kelso, Ruth. *Doctrine for the Lady of the Renaissance*. Urbana: University of Illinois Press, 1956.

King, Margaret L., and Albert Rabil, Jr, eds. *Her Immaculate Hand. Selected Works By and About the Women Humanists of Quattrocento Italy*. Binghamton, NY: Medieval & Renaissance Texts and Studies, 1983.

Kretzschmar, Rudolf Wilhelm. *Lodovico Dolce: ein Beitrag zur Geschichte der italienischen Padogogik im 16. Jahrhundert*. Leipzig: Konig & Freter, 1886.

Kristeller, Paul Oskar. *Iter italicum.* London: Warburg Institute; and Leiden: E.J. Brill, 1963.

- *Renaissance Thought and Its Sources.* Ed. Michael Mooney. New York: Columbia University Press, 1979.

Labalme, Patricia H., ed. *Beyond Their Sex: Learned Women of the European Past.* New York and London: New York University Press, 1980, 1984.

Larivaille, Paul. *Lettere di, a, su Pietro Aretino nel fondo Bongi dell'Archivio di Stato di Lucca.* Nanterre: Prepublications du Centre de Recherche de Langue et Littérature Italiennes de l'Université de Paris X – Nanterre, 1980.

Larivey, Pierre de. *Les laquais.* In *Les six premières comedies facecieuses de Pierre de Larivey Champenois a l'imitation des anciens grecs, latins et modernes italiens.* In *Ancien théâtre français ou collection des ouvrages dramatiques les plus remarquables depuis les mystères jusqu'a Corneille publié avec des notes et éclaircissements par M. Viollet Le Duc*, vol. 5. Paris: P. Jannet, 1860. [The first edition of these comedies was published in Paris by Abel l'Angelier in 1579]

Lettere di diversi eccellentissimi signori. Libro primo. Venice: Trajano, 1542.

Leo, Ulrich. *Angelica ed i 'migliori plettri.' Appunti allo stile della Controriforma.* Krefeld: Scherpe-Verlag, 1953.

Leonardi, Camillo. *Speculum lapidum clarissimi artium et medicine doctoris Camilli Leonardi pisaurensis* ... [Venice, 1502]; Colophon: Impressus Venetiis per Ioannem Baptistam Sessa anno Dñi. M.D.II. Die Primo Decembris.

Leone, G. 'Per lo studio della letteratura femminile del Cinquecento.' In *Convivium* 2 (1962), 293–300.

Leube, Eberhard. *Fortuna in Karthago; Die Aeneas–Dido–Mythe Vergils in den romanischen Literaturen vom 14. bis zum 16. Jahrhundert.* Heidelberg: C. Winter, 1969.

Levin, Carole, and Jeanne Watson, eds. *Ambiguous Realities: Women in the Middle Ages and Renaissance.* Detroit: Wayne State University Press, 1987.

Lida de Malkiel, Maria Rosa. *Dido en la literatura española. Su retrato y defensa.* London: Tamesis, 1974.

Limentani, A. 'Struttura e storia dell'ottava rima.' *Lettere italiane* 13 (1961), 20–77.

Lipking, Lawrence. *Abandoned Women and Poetic Tradition.* Chicago: University of Chicago Press, 1988.

Lucas, Corinne. 'Didon. Trois réécritures tragiques du livre IV de l'*Eneide* dans le théâtre italien du XVIe siècle.' In *Scritture di scritture. Testi, generi, modelli nel rinascimento*, ed. Giancarlo Mazzacurati and Michel Plaisance, pp. 557–604. Rome: Bulzoni, 1987.

Lucas, D.W. *The Greek Tragic Poets.* 1958. 2d ed. Aberdeen: Cohen & West, 1959.

Lucian. Trans. by A.M. Harmon. Loeb Library; Cambridge, MA: Harvard University Press; and London: William Heinemann, 1963.

Lugli, Vittorio. *I trattatisti della famiglia nel Quattrocento*. Bologna: Formiggini, 1909.

Machiavelli, Niccolò. *Capitolo*. 'Dell'Occasione.' In *Tutte le opere di Niccolò Machiavelli*, vol 2. Ed. Francesco Flora and Carlo Cordié. Verona: Mondadori, 1950.

– *Il principe e Discorsi sopra la prima deca di Tito Livio*. Ed. Sergio Bertelli. 1960. Milan: Feltrinelli, 1968.

Magliani, Eduardo. *Storia letteraria delle donne italiane*. Naples: Morano, 1885.

Mango, Achille. *La commedia in lingua nel Cinquecento: Bibliografia critica*. Milan: Lerici Editore, 1966.

Marchesi, G.B. 'Le polemiche sul sesso femminile ne' secoli XVI e XVII.' *Giornale storico della letteratura italiana* 74–75 (1895), 362–9.

Mariani, G. *Il Morgante e i cantari trecenteschi*. Florence: Le Monnier, 1953.

Marsh, David. *The Quattrocento Dialogue: Classical Tradition and Humanist Innovation*. Cambridge, MA, and London: Harvard University Press, 1980.

Martinengo, Fortunato. In *Lettere di diversi*, vol. 1. Mantua: Ruffinello, 1547.

Medici, Lorenzo de'. *Tutte le opere: Scritti spirituali*. Ed. Gigi Cavalli. Milan: Rizzoli–BUR, 1958.

Melczer, William. 'Toward the Dignification of the Vulgar Tongues: Humanistic Translations into Italian and Spanish in the Renaissance.' *Canadian Review of Comparative Literature* 8/2 (1981), 256–71.

Milano, A. Angelo. *Le tragedie di G.B. Giraldi*. Cagliari: Tip. Commerciale, 1901.

Mocenigo, F.N. 'Donne veneziane fino al secolo XVIII.' In *Memorie veneziane*, pp. 441–82. Venice: Pellizzato, 1906.

Monaci, Ernesto. *Crestomazia italiana dei primi secoli: con prospetto grammaticale e glossario*. Nuova edizione rivista e aumentata per cura di Felice Arese. Rome and Naples: Società editrice D. Alighieri, 1955.

Morato, Fulvio Pellegrino. *Del significato de colori e de mazzoli*. Brixiæ [Brescia], apud Damianum Turlinum, 1564.

Muratori, Lodovico Antonio. *Della perfetta poesia italiana*. Modena: Bartolommeo Saliani, 1706.

Musatti, E. *La donna in Venezia*. Padua: Draghi, 1891.

Musumarra, Carmelo. *La poesia tragica italiana nel Rinascimento*. Florence: Olschki, 1972.

Nelson, John Charles. *Renaissance Theory of Love: The Context of Giordano Bruno's Eroici Furori*. New York: Columbia University Press, 1958.

Neri, Ferdinando. *La tragedia italiana del Cinquecento*. Florence: Tipografia Galletti e Cocci, 1904.

Novellino (Il) ossia Libro di bel parlare gentile, I fatti di Enea di Guido da Pisa, Il governo della famiglia di Agnolo Pandolfini. Milan: Edoardo Sonzogno, 1877.

Orologi, Giuseppe. *L'Inganno: dialogo di M. Gioseppe Horologgi*. Venice: Gabriel Giolito, 1562.

Ortolani, S. 'Le origini della critica d'arte a Venezia.' *L'Arte* 26 (1923), 1–17.

– 'Pietro Aretino e Michelangelo.' *L'Arte* 25 (1922), 15–26.

Ossola, Carlo. 'Rassegna di testi e studi tra Manierismo e Barocco.' *Lettere italiane* 27/4 (1975), 437–72.

Ovid. *Heroides and Amores*. Trans. by Grant Showerman, 2d ed. Revised by G.P. Goold. Cambridge, MA: Harvard University Press, 1977.

Padoan, Giorgio. *La commedia rinascimentale veneta (1433–1565)*. Vicenza: Neri Pozza, 1982.

– *Momenti del Rinascimento veneto*. Padua: Editrice Antenore, 1978.

– 'Su un noto "plagio" plautino-ruzantesco di Lodovico Dolce. Hommage a Andre Rochon.' In *Culture et société en Italie du Moyen Age a la Renaissance*, pp. 285–91. Paris: Université de la Sorbonne Nouvelle, 1985.

Paladini, Angela. '"Ornamenti" e "Bellezze": La tragedia secondo Lodovico Dolce.' In *Scritti in onore di Giovanni Macchia*, vol. 2, pp. 35–45. Milan: Arnoldo Mondadori, 1983.

Paratore, E. 'L'influenza della letteratura latina da Ovidio ad Apuleio nell'età del Manierismo e del Barocco.' In *Manierismo, Barocco, Rococò*, pp. 286–301. Rome: Accademia nazionale dei Lincei, 1962.

– 'Nuove prospettive dell'influsso del teatro classico nel '500.' In *Il teatro classico italiano nel '500*, pp. 9–95. Rome: Accademia nazionale dei Lincei, 1971.

Pauly, August Friedrich von, and Georg Wissowa. *Paulys Realencyclopädie der classischen Altertumswissenschaft*, vol. 9. Stuttgart: Metzlersche, 1903.

Pazzi de' Medici, Alessandro. *Dido in Cartagine*. In *Le tragedie metriche di Alessandro Pazzi de' Medici*, ed. Angelo Solerti. Bologna: Commissione per i testi di lingua, 1969.

Pazzini, Adalberto. *Le pietre preziose nella storia della medicina e nella leggenda*. Rome: Casa editrice mediterranea, 1939.

Pertusi, Agostino. 'Il ritorno alle fonti del teatro greco classico: Euripide nell'Umanesimo e nel Rinascimento.' In *Venezia e l'Oriente fra tardo medioevo e rinascimento*, ed. Agostino Pertusi, pp. 205–24. Florence: Sansoni, 1966.

Phillippy, Patricia. '"*Altera Dido*": The Model of Ovid's *Heroides* in the Poems of Gaspara Stampa and Veronica Franco.' *Italica* 69/1 (1992), 1–18.

Pino, Bernardino. *Della nuova scielta di lettere di diversi nobilissimi huomini, et eccellentissimi ingegni ... con un discorso della commodita dello scrivere di M. Bernardino Pino*, 4 vols. Venice: Aldus, 1574.

Piromalli, Antonio. *La cultura a Ferrara al tempo di Ludovico Ariosto*. Rome: Bulzoni, 1975.

Plautus. *Three Comedies: Miles Gloriosus, Pseudolus, Rudens*. Trans. with an introduction by Peter L. Smith. Ithaca and London: Cornell University Press, 1991.

Poliziano, Angelo. *Stanze per la giostra.* In *Le stanze, l'Orfeo e le rime di messer Angelo Ambrogini Poliziano.* Ed. Giosuè Carducci. Florence: Barbera, 1863.

Portigliotti, Giuseppe. *Donne del rinascimento.* Milan: Treves, 1927.

– *Some Fascinating Women of the Renaissance.* Trans. by Bernard Miall. London: Allen & Unwin, 1929.

Pozzi, Mario. 'L'"ut pictura poësis" in un dialogo di L. Dolce.' In *Lingua e cultura del Cinquecento. Dolce, Aretino, Machiavelli, Guiciardini, Sarpi, Borghini,* pp. 1–22. Padua: Liviana Editrice, 1975.

– ed. *Trattatisti del Cinquecento.* Milan and Naples: Riccardo Ricciardi Editore, 1978.

Pullini, G. 'Teatralità di alcune commedie del Cinquecento.' In *Lettere italiane* 7 (1955), 68–97.

Quadrio, Francesco Saverio. *Della storia e ragione d'ogni poesia.* 1741. Milan: Agnelli, 1752.

Quondam, Amedeo. '"Mercanzia d'onore," "Mercanzia d'utile." Produzione libraria e lavoro intellettuale a Venezia nel Cinquecento.' In *Libri, editori e pubblico nell'europa moderna. Guida storica e critica,* ed. Armando Petrucci, pp. 53–104. Rome and Bari: Laterza, 1977.

– 'Nascita della grammatica. Appunti per una descrizione analitica.' *Quaderni storici* 13 (1978), 555–92.

Rabac-Čondrić, Gloria. 'La realtà sociale nel teatro rinascimentale.' In *Il Rinascimento: Aspetti e problemi attuali,* pp. 589–601. Atti del X Congresso dell'Associazione Internazionale per gli Studi di Lingua e Letteratura Italiana, Belgrade, 17–21 April 1979. Ed. Vittore Branca, Claudio Griggio, Marco e Elisanna Pecoraro, Gilberto Pizzammiglio, and Eros Sequi. Florence: Olschki, 1982.

Radcliff-Umstead, Douglas. *The Birth of Modern Comedy in Renaissance Italy.* Chicago and London: University of Chicago Press, 1969.

Reali di Francia. Ed. Giuseppe Vandelli and Giovanni Gambarin. Bari: Laterza, 1947. [Attributed to Andrea da Barberino]

Renda, Umberto, and Piero Operti. *Dizionario storico della letteratura italiana,* 4th ed. Ed. Vittorio Turri. Turin: Paravia, 1959.

Reynolds, Anne. 'Galileo Galilei's Poem "Against Wearing the Toga."' *Italica* 59/4 (1982), 330–41.

Rodocanachi, E. *La femme italienne à l'époque de la Renaissance.* Paris: Hachette, 1907.

Romei, G. 'Dolce, Lodovico.' *Dizionario biografico degli italiani,* vol. 40, pp. 399–405. Rome: Istituto della Enciclopedia Italiana, 1991.

Ronconi, A. 'Prologhi "plautini" e prologhi "terenziani" nella commedia italiana del '500.' In *Il teatro classico italiano del '500.* Atti del Convegno dell'Accademia nazionale dei Lincei, no. 138, pp. 197–214. Rome: Accademia nazionale dei Lincei 1971.

Roscher, Wilhelm H. *Ausführliches Lexikon der griechischen und römischen Mythologie.* Leipzig: Teubner, 1884–1937.

Roskill, Mark W. *Dolce's 'Aretino' and Venetian Art Theory of the Cinquecento.* New York: Published for the College Art Association of America by New York University Press, 1968.

Row, Galen D. 'The *Adynaton* as a Stylistic Device.' *American Journal of Philology* 86/344 (1965), 387–96.

Rucellai, Giovanni. *Rosmunda.* In *Teatro italiano antico*, vol. 1. Milan: Dalla Società Tipografica de' Classici Italiani, 1809.

Ruscelli, Girolamo. *Delle comedie elette nuovamente raccolte insieme, con le correttioni, et annotationi di Girolamo Ruscelli.* Venice: Plinio Pietrasanta, 1554.

– *Tre discorsi a M. Lodovico Dolce.* Venice: Plinio Pietrasanta, 1553.

Salza, Abd-El-Kader. *Delle commedie di Lodovico Dolce.* Melfi [Potenza]: Antonio Liccione, 1899.

Sanesi, Ireneo. *La commedia.* 1911, 2 vols. Reprint; Milan: Vallardi, 1954.

Sannazaro, Iacopo. *Arcadia.* In *Opere di Iacopo Sannazaro.* Ed. Enrico Carrara. 1952. Turin: UTET, 1970.

Sansovino, Francesco. *Venezia città nobilissima et singolare, descritta in XIII. libri.* Venice: Iacomo Sansovino, 1581.

Segre, Cesare, and Mario Marti, eds. *La prosa del Duecento.* Letteratura italiana. Storia e testi, vol. 3. Milan and Naples: Riccardo Ricciardi Editore, 1959.

Seneca. *Tragedies.* Trans. by Frank Justus Miller. Loeb Library; Cambridge, MA.: Harvard University Press, and London: William Heinemann, 1968.

Seznec. Jean. *The Survival of the Pagan Gods: The Mythological Tradition and Its Place in Renaissance Humanism and Art.* Trans. from the French by Barbara F. Sessions. New York: Pantheon, 1953.

Shumaker, Wayne. *The Occult Sciences in the Renaissance. A Study in Intellectual Patterns.* Berkeley: University of California Press, 1972.

Soldati, B. *Il collegio Mamertino e le origini del teatro gesuitico: con l'aggiunta di notizie inedite sulla drammatica conventuale messinese nei secoli XVI, XVII, XVIII e con pubblicazione della Giuditta del P. Tuccio.* Turin: Loescher, 1908.

Soren, David, Aïcha Ben Abed Ben Khader, and Hédi Slim. *Carthage: Uncovering the Mysteries and Splendors of Ancient Tunisia.* New York: Simon & Schuster, 1990.

Speroni, Sperone. *Canace.* In *Teatro italiano antico*, vol. 4. Milan: Dalla Società Tipografica de' Classici Italiani, 1809.

Speroni, Charles. *Wit and Wisdom of the Italian Renaissance.* Berkeley and Los Angeles: University of California Press, 1964.

Spingarn, Joel Elias. *A History of Literary Criticism in the Renaissance.* New York: Macmillan, 1899.

Symonds, John Addington. *Renaissance in Italy*. Vol. 4: *Italian Literature*. Parts 1 and 2. 1881. Reprint; London: John Murray, 1921.

Tannen, Deborah. *You Just Don't Understand: Women and Men in Conversation*. New York: Ballantine, 1990.

Tasso, Torquato. *Rinaldo*. In *Opere di Torquato Tasso*, vol. 2. Ed. B.T. Sozzi. Turin: UTET, 1956.

Teatro italiano antico, vols. 1–5. Milan: Dalla Società Tipografica de' Classici Italiani, 1809.

Teatro italiano o sia scelta di tragedie per uso della scena, vol. 1. Verona: Jacopo Vallarsi, 1723.

Telesio, Antonio. *Antonii Thylesii cosentini Libellus de coloribus. Ubi multa leguntur praeter aliorum opinionem*. Venice: Bernardini Vitalis, 1528.

Terpening, Ronnie H. 'Between Ariosto and Tasso: Lodovico Dolce and the Chivalric Romance.' *Italian Quarterly* 27/103 (1986), 21–37.

– 'Between Lord and Lady: The Tyrant's Captain in Rucellai's *Rosmunda* and Dolce's *Marianna*.' *Forum Italicum* 15/2–3 (1981), 153–70.

– *Charon and the Crossing: Ancient, Medieval, and Renaissance Transformations of a Myth*. Lewisburg, PA: Bucknell University Press, 1985.

– 'The Lapidary of *L'Intelligenza*: Its Literary Background. *Neophilologus* 60/1 (1976), 75–88.

– 'Lodovico Dolce and the Chivalric Romance.' In *Studies in the Italian Renaissance: Essays in Memory of Arnolfo B. Ferruolo*, ed. Nicolas J. Perella, Gian Paolo Biasin, and Albert N. Mancini, pp. 167–79. Naples: Società Editrice Napoletana, 1985.

– 'Mythological Exempla in Bembo's *Asolani*: Didactic or Decorative?' *Forum Italicum* 8/3 (1974), 331–43.

– 'Topoi tragici del '500: La figura del capitano nella *Rosmunda* del Rucellai e nella *Marianna* del Dolce.' In *Il Rinascimento: Aspetti e problemi attuali*, ed. Vittore Branca, Claudio Griggio, Marco e Elisanna Pecoraro, Gilberto Pizzammiglio, and Eros Sequi, pp. 651–65. Atti del X Congresso dell'Associazione Internazionale per gli Studi di Lingua e Letteratura Italiana, Belgrade, 17–21 April 1979. Florence: Olschki, 1982.

Terracina, Laura. *Discorso sopra il principio di tutti i canti d'Orlando furioso*. Venice: Gabriel Giolito, 1551.

– *Quarte rime*. Venice: Valvassori, 1550.

Tillyard, E.M.W. *The Elizabethan World Picture*. New York: Vintage, n.d.

Tiraboschi, Girolamo. *Storia della letteratura italiana*. 9 vols. in 16. Vol. 7, Parts II and III. Venice: n.p., 1796.

Toffanin, Giuseppe. *Il Cinquecento. Storia letteraria d'Italia*. 1927. 7th ed. Milan: Vallardi, 1965.

– 'Le donne poetesse e Michelangelo.' In *Il Cinquecento. Storia letteraria d'Italia*, pp. 354–67. Milan: Vallardi, 1929.

– *Le più belle pagine di V. Colonna, G. Stampa, I. di Morra, V. Gambara*. Milan: Treves, 1935.

Tomalin, Margaret. *The Fortunes of the Warrior Heroine in Italian Literature: An Index of Emancipation*. Ravenna: Longo, 1982.

Tonelli, Luigi. *Il teatro italiano dalle origini ai giorni nostri*. Milan: Modernissima, 1924.

Torelli, Pomponio. *Merope*. In *Teatro italiano o sia scelta di tragedie per uso della scena*, vol. 1. Verona: Jacopo Vallarsi, 1723.

La tragedia classica dalle origini al Maffei. Ed. Giammaria Gasparini. Turin: UTET, 1963.

Le tragedie metriche di Alessandro Pazzi de' Medici. Ed. Angelo Solerti. Bologna: Commissione per i testi di lingua, 1969.

Trattati di poetica e retorica del Cinquecento, vol. 1. Ed. Bernard Weinberg. Bari: Laterza, 1970.

Trissino, Gian Giorgio. *Sofonisba*. In *La Tragedia classica dalle origini al Maffei*, ed. Giammaria Gasparini. Turin: UTET, 1963.

Turner, Robert Elson. *Didon dans la tragédie de la Renaissance italienne et française*. Paris: Fouillot, 1926.

Valesio, Paolo. *Gabriele D'Annunzio: The Dark Flame*. Trans. by Marilyn Migiel. New Haven and London: Yale University Press, 1992.

Varchi, Benedetto. *Lezioni*. Florence: F. Giunti, 1590.

– *L'Hercolano, dialogo ... nel qual si ragiona generalmente delle lingue, & in particolare della toscana, e della fiorentina ...* Forence: F. Giunti e fratelli, 1570.

Venturi, Lionello. *Storia della critica d'arte*. Turin: Einaudi, 1964.

Vickers, Brian. *Towards Greek Tragedy: Drama, Myth, Society*. London: Longman, 1973.

Virgil. *Aeneid*. In *Eclogues, Georgics, Aeneid I–VI*. With an English Translation by H. Rushton Fairclough. Rev. ed. Loeb Library; Cambridge, MA: Harvard University Press, and London: William Heinemann, 1974.

Vivaldi, V. *La Gerusalemme liberata studiata nelle sue fonti (azione principale del poema)*. Trani: Vecchi, 1901.

Weinberg, Bernard. *A History of Literary Criticism in the Renaissance*, 2 vols. Chicago and London: University of Chicago Press, 1961; Midway rpt. 1974.

– ed. *Trattati di poetica e retorica del Cinquecento*, vol. 1. Bari: Laterza, 1970.

Wright, Thomas, ed. *Popular Treatises on Science Written During the Middle Ages, in Anglo-Saxon, Anglo-Norman, and English*. London: Taylor, 1841.

Yates, Frances. *The Art of Memory*. London: Routledge & Kegan Paul, 1966.

Zancan, Marina, ed. *Nel cerchio della luna: Figure di donna in alcuni testi del XVI secolo*. Venice: Marsilio Editori, 1983.

Zannini, Andrea. *Burocrazia e burocrati a Venezia in età moderna: I cittadini originari (sec. XVI–XVIII)*. Venice: Istituto Veneto di Scienze, Lettere ed Arti, 1993.

Zarri, G. 'Le sante vive. Per una tipologia della santità femminile nel primo Cinquecento.' In *Annali dell'Istituto Storico Italo-Germanico in Trento* 6 (1980), 371–445.

Zonta, Giuseppe, ed. 'Avvertenza generale.' *Trattati del Cinquecento sulla donna*, pp. 373–93. Bari: Laterza, 1913.

– ed. *Trattati d'amore del Cinquecento*. 1912. Reprint edited by Mario Pozzi. Bari: Laterza, 1975.

Index